New for 1991!

LET'S GO:
NEW YORK CITY

is the best book for anyone traveling on a budget. Here's why:

No other guidebook has as many budget listings.

In and around New York City we found dozens of hotels and hostels for less than $36 a night. We tell you how to get there the cheapest way, whether by bus, plane, or thumb, and where to get an inexpensive and satisfying meal once you've arrived. There are hundreds of money-saving tips for everyone plus lots of information on student discounts.

LET'S GO researchers have to make it on their own.

Our Harvard-Radcliffe researchers travel on budgets as tight as your own—no expense accounts, no free hotel rooms.

LET'S GO is completely revised every year.

We don't just update the prices, we go back to the places. If a charming café has become an overpriced tourist trap, we'll replace the listing with a new and better one.

No other budget guidebook includes all this:

Coverage of both the city and daytrips out of the city; directions, addresses, phone numbers, and hours to get you in and around; in-depth information on culture, history, and inhabitants; tips on work, study, sights, nightlife, and special splurges; detailed city maps; and much, much, more.

LET'S GO is for anyone who wants to see New York City on a budget.

Books by the Harvard Student Agencies, Inc.

Let's Go: London
Let's Go: New York City

Let's Go: Europe
Let's Go: Britain and Ireland
Let's Go: France
Let's Go: Greece
Let's Go: Italy
Let's Go: Spain, Portugal, and Morocco
Let's Go: Israel and Egypt

Let's Go: USA
Let's Go: California and Hawaii
Let's Go: The Pacific Northwest, Western Canada, and Alaska
Let's Go: Mexico

LET'S GO:

The Budget Guide to

NEW YORK CITY

1991

Jenny Lyn Bader
Editor

Maggie S. Tucker
Assistant Editor

Written by Harvard Student Agencies, Inc.

ST. MARTIN'S PRESS
New York

Helping Let's Go

If you have suggestions or corrections, or just want to share your discoveries, drop us a line. We read every piece of correspondence, whether a 10-page letter, a postcard, or, as in one case, a collage. All suggestions are passed along to our researcher/writers. Please note that mail received after June 1, 1991 will probably be too late for the 1992 book, but will be retained for the following edition. Address mail to: *Let's Go: New York City;* Harvard Student Agencies, Inc.; Thayer Hall-B; Harvard University; Cambridge, MA 02138; USA.

In addition to the invaluable travel advice our readers share with us, many are kind enough to offer their services as researchers or editors. Unfortunately, the charter of Harvard Student Agencies, Inc. enables us to employ only currently enrolled Harvard students.

Editor	Jenny Lyn Bader
Assistant Editor	Maggie S. Tucker
Publishing Manager	Ravi Desai
Managing Editors	Jessica V.V. Avery
	Michael Scott Krivan
	Alexandra M. Tyler
Production/Communication Coordinator	C.W. Cowell
Researcher/Writers	
Manhattan, Brooklyn	Darren Aronofsky
Manhattan, Bronx, Staten Island	Vladimir Perlovich
Manhattan, Queens, Long Island	Jacob Press
New Haven, CT	Kelly A.E. Mason
Atlantic City and Princeton, NJ	Joshua W. Shenk
Sales Group Manager	Robert D. Frost
Sales Group Representatives	Christine J. Hahn
	Cristina D. Toro-Hernandez
	David R. Tunnell
President	David A. Kopp
C.E.O.	Michele Ponti
Legal Counsel	Posternak, Blankstein, and Lund

New York is not all bricks and steel. There are hearts there too, and if they do not break, then they at least know how to leap.

—H.L. Mencken

ACKNOWLEDGMENTS

Some summers ago in a midtown office, I met two tourists from Washington state who had three hours to spend in New York and wanted to know the quickest route to the Empire State Building. When I told them to take the express subway, they looked terrified, so I escorted them to the station, flashbulbs popping. "New Yorkers," they said with amazement as we parted, "aren't supposed to be nice."

Well maybe we aren't. I'm not all the time. But while I'm in a fleeting good mood, I'd like to dedicate this book to those travelers, whose names I never learned, and to anyone who arrives in New York expecting a rude welcome from the intimidating city, the impolite natives, and the unhelpful travel guides. I hope this book will pleasantly surprise them and will even surprise those visitors and dwellers who thought they knew their way around.

Creating this guide from scratch would not have been possible without an extraordinary staff. Mike Krivan has been a careful, caring managing editor; he managed copyright complications and copybatches wisely, managing above all to stay in good spirits all summer long. Maggie Tucker braved towing crises and assorted tragedies to emerge as the Rolls Royce of assistant editors: brilliant, poised, and even the speediest in the northeast. My researchers brought humor and insight to Manhattan. Darren Aronofsky combined his love of Brooklyn and his familiarity with the whole city, discovered clubs where no one has dared to go before, and sent in witty, streetsmart prose. Vladimir Perlovich, who could find a metaphor in a sewer, spoke seven languages in his heroic odyssey through New York. Jacob Press made this book his life's work; he demystified Long Island for the layperson, conquered Queens, and lingered lovingly in Manhattan, mailing in graceful writing all the while. Josh Shenk and Kelly Mason took care of daytrips to those other nearby states.

I am grateful to the other *Let's Go* editors for brightening up the office and failing to agree on reductive slogans. Andrew Kaplan countered sarcasm with glee. Ian MacGregor and Jenny Schuessler made foreign language dictionaries unnecessary. Kevin Young had one-liners ready for every occasion, no matter how bureaucratic. Ghita Schwartz maintained a serene presence through the best of times and the worst of times. Jessica Avery saw the comedy in things. Jamie Rosen spent hours seeking the perfect punchline in between thesaurus thefts. Jody Dushay turned grammatical issues into stimulating debates and made the fantasy of homemade bagels a daily reality.

I am indebted to Elliot Thomson for providing chassidic tales of manners on cue, to Robbie Kellman for cutting through miles of red tape, to Linda Rottenberg for doing justice to New Haven. Aleen Keshishian made an even better secretary than Melanie Griffith in *Working Girl*. Camille Landau meted out advice with Corsican élan. Jessica Goldberg provided postcards and hospitality. Bob Baxter pitched in with last-minute typing. I'd like to thank Manson for cooking, Dil and Andrew for braving the traffic, Pam for typing in Newyorkese. Joe Hayashi fruitlessly trekked to Medford to stave off an impending computer anxiety attack. David, Michele, and April proved supportive as well as administrative.

And thanks to the folks at home who put up with the houseguests, the busy signals, the canceled reservations; to St. Martin, the patron saint of publishing and the originator of the *Let's Go* city guides; and to everyone who made my years in New York as idyllic as possible—for them, I remember and return.

—Jenny Lyn

Thanks to WHB, JMB, SJN, and everyone else who kept me sane this summer. Thanks especially to Caraway, for chocolate cake, sympathy, and a sofa; and to my mother, who was right from the very beginning.

—MST

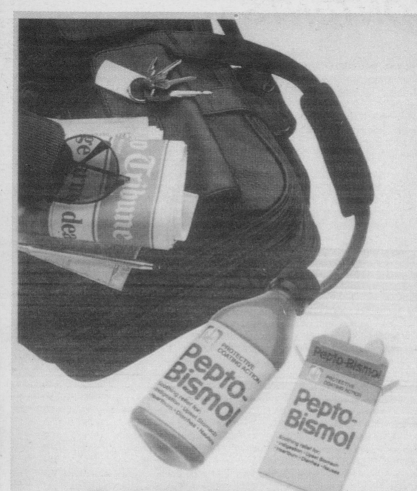

CARRY-ON RELIEF.

CONTENTS

LIST OF MAPS

About Let's Go

In 1960, Harvard Student Agencies, a three-year-old nonprofit corporation established to provide employment opportunities to Harvard and Radcliffe students, was doing a booming business selling charter flights to Europe. One of the extras HSA offered passengers on these flights was a 20-page mimeographed pamphlet entitled *1960 European Guide,* a collection of tips on continental travel compiled by the staff at HSA. The following year, students traveling to Europe researched the first full-fledged edition of *Let's Go: Europe,* a pocket-sized book with a smattering of tips on budget accommodations, irreverent write-ups of sights, and a decidedly youthful slant. The first editions proclaimed themselves to be the companions of the "adventurous and often impecunious student."

Throughout the 60s, the series reflected its era: a section of the 1968 *Let's Go: Europe* was entitled "Street Singing in Europe on No Dollars a Day;" the 1969 guide to America led off with a feature on drug-ridden Haight-Ashbury. During the 70s, *Let's Go* gradually became a large-scale operation, adding regional European guides and expanding coverage into North Africa and Asia. In 1981, *Let's Go: USA* returned after an eight-year hiatus, and in the next year HSA joined forces with its current publisher, St. Martin's Press. Now in its 31st year, *Let's Go* publishes 13 titles covering more than 40 countries.

Each spring, over 150 Harvard-Radcliffe students compete for some 70 positions as *Let's Go* researcher/writers. Those hired possess a rare combination of budget travel sense, writing ability, stamina, and courage. Each researcher/writer travels on a shoestring budget for seven weeks, researching seven days per week, and overcoming countless obstacles in the quest for better bargains.

Back in a basement in Harvard Yard, an editorial staff of 25, a management team of five, and countless typists and proofreaders—all students—spend four months poring over more than 50,000 pages of manuscript as they push the copy through 12 stages of intensive editing. In September the efforts of summer are converted from computer diskettes to nine-track tapes and delivered to Com Com in Allentown, Pennsylvania, where their computerized typesetting equipment turns them into books in record time. And even before the books hit the stands, next year's editions are well underway.

A Note to our Readers

The information for this book is gathered by Harvard Student Agencies' researchers during the late spring and summer months. Each listing is derived from the assigned researcher's opinion based on his or her visit at a particular time. The opinions are expressed in a candid and forthright manner. Other travelers might disagree. Those traveling at a different time may have a different experience since prices, dates, hours, and conditions are always subject to change. You are urged to check beforehand to avoid inconvenience and surprises. Travel always involves a certain degree of risk, especially in low cost areas. When traveling, especially on a budget, you should always take particular care to ensure your safety.

LET'S GO: NEW YORK CITY

This rural America thing. It's a joke.
—Edward I. Koch, former mayor of New York City

New York City is not quite attached to the U.S. mainland either geographically or otherwise, and some Americans probably wouldn't mind if New York seceded from the union or sank into the sea. The insomniacal metropolis moves faster and lights up brighter than most of the planet and has never aspired to anything remotely rugged. While America revels in the open plain, nine million New Yorkers think vertically. At Halloween, trick-or-treaters descend upon the buildings with the greatest number of elevators. The New York wealthy flaunt their status with tall apartments—duplexes, brownstones, penthouses. And developers partition the sky.

Like Ed Koch, New York has a *chutzpah* at once offensive and endearing. New Yorkers have been known to spend years rooting for losing baseball teams, weeks creating street art that will be cleaned off instantly by bureaucrats or rain, and months rehearsing shows that close in a day.

While the Big Apple seems too full of itself to fit into the American pie, in some ways it dreams the American dream to its wildest. No one takes the first amendment more seriously than the self-appointed prophets that stand on street corners with megaphones, and no one takes the Fifth as well as the smart aleck willing to sell you the Brooklyn Bridge. From flea market to stock market, free enterprise has flourished here since the town's first and most notorious transaction; even Lewis and Clark didn't beat the extraordinary Manhattan Purchase. Peter Minuit shelled out 24 bucks for the slender island back in 1626, and the likes of Horatio Alger have been honing the art of the deal ever since. New York has traded in old-world charm for highrise vitality and has bartered backyards for hip bars. The concrete archipelago rejected a future of federal administration in George Washington's day and yielded the state government to Albany, but naturally assumed the crown of global politics as the seat of the United Nations.

Gotham remembers a history obscured by layers of construction. The buildings of a once-fashionable neighborhood have become dilapidated tenements on the Lower East Side. Young artists spray their canvasses in the one-time industrial complexes of SoHo. An old Native American trail winding its way through an ordered street grid has turned into a stretch of marquees and swank called Broadway.

Even those urban sophisticates who laugh at the "rural America thing" engage in a provincialism of their own. When too far removed—from the smell of rain drying on the pavement and the murmur of streaming traffic, from all-night delicatessens or sarcastic hot dog vendors—they grow nostalgic, as if on the verge of clicking their heels and announcing, "There's no place like home."

Life and Times

History

The present in New York is so powerful that the past is lost
—John Chapman (letter, 1909)

1

During the 1940s, legendary New York Parks Commissioner Robert Moses made a development proposal that required tearing down Castle Clinton. A public outcry mounted in defense of the old fort, a regal structure built in preparation for the War of 1812. Several court battles later, Congress finally declared Castle Clinton a national monument. The movement for the preservation of historical sites has gained momentum since then, but physical reminders of New York's history remain few and far between. Other cities maintain a stronger sense of the past: in Paris, you can still stroll the stately boulevards where Napoleon marched triumphantly; in Delft, you can duck down narrow cobblestone streets right out of Vermeer. New York will have none of it. This city inhabits the present.

New York has one good reason to lack a sense of history: like any U.S. urban center, it is brand new compared to the timeworn cities of Europe. Algonquin tribes had lived on Manhattan island for centuries, and the woolly snuffalupagus had roamed it for millenia before that, but the first European explorer only "discovered" New York Bay in 1524. And the town of Nieuw Amsterdam was not established until 1624, when a tiny group of Dutch and Walloon families took up residence on the southern tip of the island. But the city is not much younger than Boston or Philadelphia, both of which teem with historical atmosphere. The difference lies in New York's powerful impulse to change—its relentless urge to tear down, pave over, and build up.

Incessant change has driven the city from its earliest days as a colony, yanked back and forth between the warring Dutch and British. The possessive imperial powers changed the colony's name three times between 1664 and 1674—from New Netherland to New York to New Orange and then back to New York. In the end, the Treaty of Westminster settled the colony with the British. They in turn replaced the Dutch-appointed burgomasters with a mayor of their own and installed Richard Nicolls in place of the Dutch colonial governor Peter "peg-leg" Stuyvesant, who had already made himself unpopular for his despotic management methods and persecution of religious dissenters. Recurring Yellow Fever epidemics forced the townspeople to flee to less populated parts of the island (such as the future site of Greenwich Village) to avoid contagion. So the settlement shifted and spread northwards.

New York soon fell under the rule of autocratic British governors viewed by many residents as power-abusing twits. Popular resentment brewed, and in 1689 enterprising merchant Jacob Leister—inspired by news of the Glorious Revolution in England and of Bostonians' overthrow of their colonial governor—grasped control of New York's government and instituted a more representative system. But nice guys don't last; in 1691 the British retook New York and executed Leister for treason. The Evil Empire was back—in 1741, the colonial government claimed to have uncovered a slave plot to burn the city and tortured and killed about 30 African Americans in response.

The Stamp Act of 1765 enraged the colonial public. New York rose up against British rule, and in 1775, the Sons of Liberty forced Governor William Tryon and his flunkies out of town. George Washington's Continental Army defended New York through most of 1776, posing heroically along the way, but after losing the battle of Long Island, Washington gave up his stance and the city. The British occupied the latter until the end of the war; coincidentally, two mysterious fires occurred during this time, destroying much of the settlement.

In 1789, the first U.S. Congress met in New York's City Hall and didn't have to look very far while choosing a capital for the infant nation. One year later, the North and South made one of their classic sibling rivalry compromises. Hamilton persuaded everyone that the federal government should assume state debts, and in exchange accepted Jefferson's plan to move the capital to a malarial swamp on the banks of the Potomac. New York still remained a state capital, but in 1797 ungainly Albany took even that distinction from poor New York.

While New York slipped away as a political locus, it endured as a financial center. Commerce thrived, thanks to a well-situated port. In 1784, treasury-meister Alexander Hamilton founded his Bank of New York, and the city became a national fiscal leader. In 1792, the New York Stock Exchange began with a few men trading stocks in the shade of a buttonwood tree on Wall St., and the area evolved into the financial heart of the city and then of the nation. By the turn of the 19th century, New York had developed into the largest city in the U.S. With the opening of the Erie Canal in 1825, New York became the Atlantic gateway to the Great Lakes region and the nation's undisputed commercial capital.

More of a city meant more city planning: in 1811, the municipal government adopted the easily navigable street grid in existence today. Though it destroyed much of the old Dutch settlement, the great fire of 1835 cleared the way for new buildings, zoning laws, and sewers. The modern city began to take shape. The first electric lights turned on in 1882, the first skyscraper (the Flatiron Building) shot up in 1902, and the first subway took off in 1904. In 1897, a charter brought all five boroughs together to form Greater New York.

Meanwhile, the gears of the Tammany Hall Democratic political machine had begun to churn. Founded as a patriotic society soon after the revolution, Tammany took the name of a Native American confederation, engaged in pseudo-tribal rituals, became a defender of the Jeffersonian faith, and soon reigned supreme in both city and state politics. The working class resented the "aristocrats" who controlled Tammany. Soon the Democratic party split into factions with unlikely names, as the Locofocos revolted and a decade later the Barnburners and the Hunkers maintained a raging rivalry. Class tensions heated up and came to a boil by the Civil War, when the federal government conscripted into the Union army everyone unable to pay a $300 fee. The draft set off furious rioting; nearly 1000 people were killed in the chaos. Tammany's voting base was strengthened by the influx of European immigrants grateful enough for the help Tammany provided them to overlook the more glaring instances of graft and election fraud. Political corruption reached an all-time low under the administration of the notorious William M. "Boss" Tweed. Despite sporadic efforts at reform, no one until Fiorello LaGuardia (mayor 1933-45) succeeded in cleaning up the city's act.

1927 ushered in celebration, as city residents threw more than 1500 tons of ticker tape and confetti into the air upon the triumphant return of pilot Charles Lindbergh. But the party was over in 1929 when the stock market crashed on Black Monday (Oct. 29), touching off the Great Depression. And some of the public welfare problems that became a serious consideration to the metropolitan government at that time would resurface after World War II, when the city had to contend with widening gaps in public transportation, education, and housing. During the 60s, these problems were joined by racial unrest and a rapidly rising crime rate.

New York needed more funds for public services, but corporations and middle class residents were beginning to head for the suburbs, taking the city's tax base with them. The state made up some of the difference in funding, but the financial crunch worsened—by 1975 the city was nearing bankruptcy. About to default on city notes, the city asked the federal government for support and was rebuffed (the *Daily News* headline the next day read "Ford to New York: Drop Dead"). But New York wasn't quite ready to die or even to fade away, and budget wizard Felix Rohatyn trimmed the city's costs down to size. A massive "I Love New York" public relations campaign was mounted. And between the leaner budget and all the fat little red hearts on bumper stickers, something must have worked. Corporations stopped leaving, international investors were persuaded that they, too, loved NY, and tourism provided an ever-increasing source of revenue. Although currently New York ranks second in the world only to the original Amsterdam in tons of cargo processed per year, its present success lies not in licorice bales and scrap metal but in the less tangible stuff of high finance. Billions of dollars pass through the city every day now, and real estate values have skyrocketed, making New York worth a little more now in European terms than it was in 1626, when Peter Minuit bought it for $24 and got more change than he bargained for.

Politics

On March 22, 1989, the U.S. Supreme Court declared the New York City government illegal. The court abolished the archaic Board of Estimate, overturning a state court decision, thrilling Manhattan and very much annoying Staten Island in the process. This musty old voting panel included the mayor, comptroller, Council president, and borough presidents; inexplicably, each borough president had one vote, although borough populations range from Brooklyn's 2.2 million to Staten Island's 350,000.

Mild havoc broke loose. The people of New York voted in a new charter. Soon a newly formed 35-member City Council started to throw its weight around, its finance division started allocating the city's $28 billion annual budget, and local representation became fairer. Today the mayor interacts directly with the city council, without the Board of Estimate in the way, and each borough can initiate zoning, propose legislation, and coerce contract renewal hearings on its own.

In 1989, New York also replaced moderate, abrasive, and colorful Ed Koch with methodical liberal David Dinkins. Dinkins goes everywhere with a well-prepared speech, perhaps careful not to revisit the outspoken Koch's penchant for gaffes. Vibrant Ruth Messinger presides over Manhattan.

What best characterizes city politics is not the reform charter of '89 but the fact that the Board of Estimate controlled the city for so many years. The unfair state of affairs prevailed since no one wanted to rock the bureaucratic boat. In an interview in 1990, former Mayor John Lindsay, who guided New York through the turbulent late 60s, said of the city government, "Mediocrity abounds." Lindsay also remarked that running New York in the 90s couldn't be done in the same old way, given the suspension of federal funding and the advent of the homelessness and AIDS crises. As the issues swell out of proportion, stagnation has even more detrimental effects. Yet while mediocrity and stasis infect the governance of Gotham, the ruling body of New York has enough personality—and personalities—to keep politics perpetually pugnacious, somewhat legal, and never dull.

Ethnic New York

> To Europe she was America, to America she was the
> gateway of the earth. But to tell the story of New York
> would be to write a social history of the world.
> —H.G. Wells

In 1643, Jesuit missionary Isaac Jogues wrote a description of a lively New Amsterdam fort. Among the 500 people living in this 17th-century melting pot community were artisans, soldiers, trappers, sailors, and slaves—and they spoke 18 languages among them.

New Yorkers have always claimed a wide range of national origins. The first black settlement grew around today's SoHo beginning in 1644, and by the time of the American Revolution the city had a black population of 20,000. From 1840 to 1860, the Germans and Irish were coming, and in 1855 European-born persons constituted nearly half of New York's population.

After the Civil War, a massive wave of immigration began to roll that would crest around the turn of the century. Europeans left famine, religious persecution, and political unrest in their native lands for the perils of seasickness and the brimming promise of America. The majority of these immigrants settled in distinct neighborhoods, which more often than not consisted of crowded tenements in areas like Hell's Kitchen near the Hudson River in Midtown. The Germans and the Irish continued to come, and starting in 1890 they were joined by the Italians, Russians, Poles, and Greeks. Immigrants worked long hours for miniscule wages in unsafe conditions; only the tragic Triangle Shirtwaist Fire of 1911, which killed 146 women factory workers, brought about enough public protest to force stricter regulations on working conditions. Meanwhile, Tammany-based "ward bosses" stepped in to take care of the confused new arrivals, helping them find jobs and housing and even providing them with emergency funds in cases of illness or accident; all the immigrants needed to produce in return were their votes. The U.S. Congress restricted immigration from Europe in the 1920s, and the Great Depression of the 30s brought it to a virtual halt.

Today New York has more Italians than Rome, more Irish than Dublin, and more Jews than Jerusalem. Immigrants from Asia and the Caribbean now flock to the city where Ellis Island has already become a museum. Today, the melting pot simmers with 9 million people, speaking 80 languages among them. New York continues to take the just-add-water approach to those who care to navigate to its shores: while it takes years or lifetimes to blend into other cities, newcomers become New Yorkers almost instantly.

Architecture

A hundred times have I thought New York is a catastrophe and fifty times: It is a beautiful catastrophe.
—Le Corbusier

The Early Years and the European Influence

In 1965, the owner of Grand Central Station proposed the construction of an office building that would obliterate the extraordinary façade of the station's main concourse. The newly formed Landmarks Preservation Commission wouldn't hear of it. Penn Central sued. In 1978, the case went to the Supreme Court, which ruled the commission's act unconstitutional. And what of the right to property? The justices suggested in their opinion that Penn Central could make a buck or two by selling air rights, which it did for $2.2 million to Philip Morris across the street. Ever since this landmark case, the Landmarks Preservation Commission has been doing its damnedest to designate what shouldn't be torn down, and developers have been seeking air rights and loopholes to explode city building into the sky.

In 1979, the Landmarks Preservation Commission conducted the first large-scale archeological dig in Manhattan on the current site of a 30-story office building; they uncovered the foundation walls of Lovelace's Tavern, used by Dutch settlers as a temporary City Hall in 1698. After arriving, the enterprising Dutch had gone straight to work, digging a network of canals and constructing Manhattan's first dock at the foot of what is now Broad St.

The great fire of 1835 destroyed most of the Dutch settlement. Little remains. The Dyckman House, the only 18th-century farmhouse intact in Manhattan, stands at 204th St. and Broadway. Pre-revolutionary St. Paul's Chapel still stands between Broadway and Church St. Its designer, Thomas McBean, studied under James Gibbs, the London architect who followed in Christopher Wren's classical footsteps.

The English succeeded the Dutch and started building Georgian structures with red-brick simplicity and clear lines; at 54 Pearl St. stands the reconstructed Fraunces Tavern, the 20th century's idea of what an 18th-century hall might have looked like. The British used the Vechte-Cortelyou House as a fort during the Revolutionary War. Now called the Old Stone House, this 1699 Dutch home has been restored and stands near Fifth Ave. and 3rd St. in Brooklyn.

Having rid themselves of the British, New Yorkers created the federalist look to go with federalist politics, but the influence of Anglo-architecture remained. Designer Pierre L'enfant, Washington D.C.'s main planner, injected Roman allusions into the Georgian mold, while Robert Adam trimmed Georgiana with bold reliefs and precise classical detail. Federalists built City Hall. Federal houses still line Charlton St. and Northern Vandam St.; houses combining the federal and Georgian styles comprise Shermerhorn Row on S. Fulton St.

The 19th century saw a booming Greek Revival, exemplified by the Federal Hall National Memorial. Neo-Grecian cornices and foliage began to sprout on buildings.

Cast iron laurel wreaths were all the rage, and architects began setting buildings back behind deep front yards or gardens. Greek Revival dominates Washington Square North and crops up on Lafayette St. and on W. 20th St. If you see a house with uneven bricks it probably predates the 1830s, when machines started making bricks. Grey granite St. Peter's, built in 1838, was the first Greek Revival Catholic Church in New York. Around 1850, cast iron and Italianate palazzo bloomed. Snooty clubs took to the palazzo style with a vengeance. McKim, Mead & White, the most prolific architectural firm ever, busied themselves by bringing the Renaissance back into city planning.

The Birth of the Skyscraper and an American Aesthetic

The 1870s witnessed the first skyscrapers with elevators. Building codes soon allowed them to grow. In 1897, Frank Lloyd Wright's teacher, Louis Sullivan of the Chicago School, designed the amazing art nouveau Bayard-Condict Building at 65 Bleecker St. In 1913, Cass Gilbert gilded the 55-story Woolworth Building with Gothic flourishes, piling terracotta salamanders onto antique "W"s. To create the U.S. Custom House, Gilbert dressed a steel skeleton up in Beaux-Arts finery. Named after the Ecole des Beaux-Arts in Paris, this style, which borrows from the idioms of French Second Empire design, can be recognized by its lavishly textured doubly sloped roof. A team of designers used the Beaux-Arts approach for the Grand Central Terminal. Art deco, officially codified as a stylistic movement at the 1925 International Exposition in Paris and associated with the giddiness of high society in the 20s, gave New York a facelift in the 30s. Its curvaceous quirks appear in the most unexpected of places, so keep your head up. Those addicted to ornament should contact the **Art Deco Society** at 385-2744 immediately for help or information.

But not all New York monoliths look the same. The urban landscape that shot up at the turn of the century, vast and variegated, does have some quirks and even some personality. Learn to read between the skylines and you'll be able to distinguish and date just about every tower. Since 1919, New York has been instituting zoning laws that can help you approximate an architectural era better than Carbon 14.

Does the building have a ziggurat on top? Does it look so much like a wedding cake that you could eat it? Zoning restrictions of the late 1940s stipulated that tall buildings had to be set back at the summit. New York's first curtain of pure glass was the 1950 U.N. Secretariat Building, which inspired Lever House, a 24-story glass tower designed by Gordon Bunshaft. Then in 1958 Mies Van der Rohe and Philip Johnson created the Seagram Building, a glass tower set behind a plaza on Park Avenue. Crowds soon gathered to mingle, sunbathe, and picnic, to the surprise of planners and builders. The planning commission decided that a star had been born and began offering financial incentives to every builder who offset a highrise with public open space. In the decade to come, architects stuck empty plazas next to their towering office complexes. In fact, some of them looked a little too empty to the picky planning commission, which in 1975 changed the rules to stipulate that every plaza should provide public seating. By the late 70s, the plazas moved indoors and the designers moved on to high-tech atriums, complete with cafés and vegetation.

Architects grew so busy planting trees in lobbies that they seemed not to notice the forest of edifices piling up on East Midtown. From 1977-81, builders negotiated with the planning commission and a few wangled permission to mount larger buildings on smaller sites—resulting in a series of massive monoliths trimmed with skylights and foliage. Do you see a building that looks like it went on a diet? It probably dates from 1981 or 1982. In the early 80s, some weight-conscious developers realized that they could get office space, bypass zoning regulations, and even receive a bonus from the commission, if they started to put up "sliver" buildings. Comprised largely of elevators and stairs and disturbingly anorexic-looking to boot, the newcomers did not make many friends. In fact, everyone hated them, and still does.

In 1983, those tired of living in the shadow of shafts altered zoning policy so that structural planning would revolve more around the sun.

Builders have finally come to terms with the overcrowding problem in East Midtown and expanded their horizons somewhat. New residential complexes have been rising on the Upper East Side above 95th St.; new office complexes promise to clean out some of the sleaze of West Midtown in the 40s and 50s. Some developers have even begun building in Queens. And with the restructuring of the city government in 1989, citizens have a greater say about development projects in their community. New York's postmodern architecture has put on a human face as concerns about overcrowding and environmental issues affect the decisions of the planning commission that perpetuates the beautiful catastrophe.

Media

New York City is the red light district of media whores. ABC, CBS, NBC, two major wire services, umpteen leading magazines, and more newspapers than anywhere else in the world have taken up residence here, to the delight of raving publicity-mongers, roving inquiring minds, and bored couch potatoes everywhere.

New York draws on an illustrious history of news coverage. The city's first newspaper, the *Gazette,* appeared in 1725. Ten years later, John Peter Zenger, editor of the *New-York Weekly Journal,* was charged with libel for satirizing public officials. (Among other offenses, he portrayed the city recorder as "a large spaniel . . . that has lately strayed from his kennel with his mouth full of fulsome panegyrics.") The governor threw Zenger into jail and burned copies of his paper in public. But in a landmark decision, the court acquitted him, setting a precedent for the eventual creation of freedom of the press.

The city soon became the crux of the nation's rapidly developing network of print media. It was from here that Horace Greeley's *Tribune* became the first paper to be nationally distributed—and from here that Greeley issued his famous exhortation to go west, young man. In the 1830s and 40s the proliferation of papers up and down Nassau Street led it to be dubbed "Newspaper Row."

Today New York reads well over 100 different newspapers, and many reflect the diversity of its urban landscape; weekly ethnic papers cater to the black, Hispanic, Irish, Japanese, Chinese, Indian, Korean, and Greek communities. Candidates for local public office frequently court voters in these communities by seeking photo ops and endorsements from their papers. Meanwhile, candidates for national office seek the prestigious endorsement of the *New York Times.* The *Times'* liberal-minded editorial board tends to back Democrats, but in the spectrum of city papers its tone emerges as a moderate one. The *Times* maintains more conservative news policies than the outrageous tabloid dailies and takes more conservative political and aesthetic stands than the artsy *Village Voice,* but veers to the left of the staunch *Wall Street Journal,* that well-crafted daily of the business world. The *Journal,* as the high finance cognoscenti call it, gives a quick world news summary on page one for breakfasting brokers flipping to the market pages who don't have time to consume more depth of coverage. With its pen-and-ink drawings in lieu of photographs, its clever and sometimes subtle editorials, and its cool analyses of the changing price of gold, the condescending *Journal* commands respectability.

Neither of New York's main tabloid dailies, the *New York Post* and the *Daily News,* have built their reputations on respectability. The *News* has slightly better taste—it doesn't use red ink, and it has less of an appetite for reporting gruesome murders. *Post* headlines, often printed in unwieldy lettering 3 inches high, can have a nasty ring. One notorious *Post* headline read, "Headless Body Found in Topless Bar." Both of these papers indulge in comics, advice columns, and gossip pages. The *Post* has a great sports section, and both have conservative editorial policies, excellent metropolitan coverage, and fine astrologers. New York *Newsday* also offers thorough local coverage. After more than 40 years as a successful Long Island paper—with a youngish staff, some entertaining columnists, and a special Sunday section just for the kids—*Newsday* recently decided to make the jump to city tabloid and is unfortunately now trying to compete with the worst of its peers.

If you do want to read about headless bodies, the *New York Times* will not satisfy you. The distinguished elder statesman of the city papers, the *Times* maintains an air of sober respectability in its coverage. Its Op Ed page provides a nationally respected forum for policy debate. Praise from its Book Review section can immortalize living authors and bring dead ones back to life. And its Sunday crossword puzzles enliven brunches across the nation. Recently, the *Times* has increased its regional coverage, expanding "National Editions" geared toward audiences other than New Yorkers.Real estate brokers, theatre directors, and some diehard readers even clamor to buy the Sunday *Times* around midnight on Saturday.

The *Village Voice* would never dream of finding another audience; it has forged its niche here. Printed on the same kind of paper as the conservative *Post* and *Daily News,* it shares nothing else in common with them. Don't search here for syndicated advice columnists, baseball stats, or the bikini-clad woman du jour. Hardly a primary source for straight news information, the *Voice* stages lively political debates and prints quirky reflections on New York life and some good investigative city reporting along with the city's most intriguing set of personal ads. On the other end of town, the Upper East Side's *New York Observer* prints articles and commentary on city political life on dapper pink paper.

Magazines rise and fall constantly in New York, but a few have managed to endure. The somewhat rarefied *New Yorker* publishes new fiction and poetry by old standbys and the occasional fledgling discovery. Even its ads contain considered prose. Its world-famous cover by Steinberg, showing the rest of the world in terms of the city's perspective, reflects not only the vision of the typical New Yorker but of the Newyorkcentric literary scene. *The New Yorker* also carries the most thorough listings and reviews of films and events—and the finest cartoons—in the tri-state area. *New York* magazine also prints extensive listings but focuses on lifestyle and entertainment. Its final pages can prove very entertaining, with a death-defying British crossword puzzle, a monthly word game contest, and a slew of personal ads ranging from the whiny to the outrageous.

Condé Nast's glossy empire thrives here, producing page-turning magazines for women, countered by a breed of magazines for men such as *Esquire* and *Men's Life. Spy* magazine, famous for irreverent sobriquets like "garden gnome" or "three-toed barbarian" for Donald Trump, may have gotten a lot of mileage out of its implicit belief that readers will peruse even the tiniest of type as long as it is lovably trenchant. *Spy* has certainly made a bundle on its Separated at Birth series (pairing, say, Leona Helmsley with the Joker), publishing spin-off books on this theme. *Spy* succeeds in the medium of meta-media (newspapers or magazines about other newspapers or magazines) where New York's short-lived *7 Days* failed, as it takes vicious jabs at the professional and personal sides of other journals, occasionally infuriating those in the know and invariably baffling laypeople.

Laypeople can also feel baffled by the entertainment newspapers. The magazines listed above, along with the *Observer,* contain good entertainment sections. *Variety* is a trade journal, written for people in the business, and reveals the gritty underworkings of show biz. *Show Business* and *Backstage* advertise cattle calls, agents, and resume photographers for struggling performers.

To buy foreign language newspapers and magazines, go to the Times Square stand (142 W. 42nd St.), which stays open all night. Other 24-hr. newsstands include: Sixth Ave. and 8th St., Second Ave. and St. Mark's Place, Third Ave. and 35th St., Port Authority Bus Terminal (Eighth Ave. and 41st St.), Seventh Ave. and 43rd St., Second Ave. and 50th St., Third Ave. and 53rd St., Third Ave. and 59th St., Broadway and 72nd St., Broadway and 79th St., First Ave. and 79th St.

Graffiti

Some New York artists have descended underground into a world of crime, gang warfare, and big billowing letters. The art of graffiti is based around the artist's tag. A tag is a penname that the artist uses to gain fame by placing it anywhere and everywhere he or she can. Talent presents itself in the way the artist creates and relates the characters in the tag. In fact, graffiti can be considered a complex system of calligraphy. Ed Koch's war on graffiti destroyed many famous works and helped to destroy the artists' major canvas—the train. Now art fans must look above ground to see the present trends. Some of the more proficient writers to look for include: CHINO, SEEN, ZEPHYR, and SANE (who tagged the Brooklyn Bridge).

Literary New York

> Hemingway described literary New York as a bottle
> full of tapeworms trying to feed on each other.
> —*John Updike*

You go to a party. You have a couple of drinks. You go home. You see the sun rising. You try to finish the chapter you wrote yesterday. You throw it out. You realize that the best way to make a buck in New York is to write a novel in the second person. You call your agent. You wonder if anyone has thought of this before. You pour yourself a gin and tonic and watch the dawn emerge.

You sign a contract for your book though you haven't written a word. You realize that New York, the publishing capital of the U.S. since 1850, may be a great place to get published but is a lousy place to write. Maybe you should go on a promotion tour and get out of town. The city's first literary figure did. Washington Irving stayed there just long enough to make himself famous by penning those satirical essays on New York society, "from the beginning of the world to the end of the Dutch dynasty" and quickly took off for Europe. Edith Wharton got out of town too, you know she did the right thing.

You know that some of America's finest early writers found New York downright inhospitable. Those ridiculous critics dismissed Edgar Allen Poe as a hack. Poe rented a house in the rural Bronx, thinking that the cleaner air would be good for his ailing wife. But the rent turned out to be such a financial burden that Poe's mother-in-law had to scour nearby fields for edible roots to feed the family. You know you shouldn't take the critics seriously. Herman Melville got pretty discouraged with the critics and their indifference to *Moby-Dick,* took a job in a New York customs house for four bucks a day, and died unrecognized and unappreciated. Poor guy. The *Times* called him Henry in his obituary.

You imagine Walt Whitman wandered into the city to work on this magazine called the *Aurora* and then stuck around to write poems in homage to "Manahatta" and the Brooklyn Bridge. You wander out onto the street alone, thinking about all the solitary writers who ever wrote nifty stream-of-consciousness prose. Of course 20th-century lonely writers started clubbing it. In 1919, at the Algonquin Hotel, the wits of the Round Table began meeting for weekly lunches—writers like Robert Benchley, Dorothy Parker, Alexander Woollcott, and Franklin P. Adams. Adams reported the table's one-liners every week in his column in *New York World.*

And it strikes you that one of America's first novelists ever, James Fenimore Cooper, was a New Yorker. He and a group of his friends formed the city's first literary club ("The Bread and Cheese") in a back room in a bookstore on New St. They created an obscure but edible system of admissions—bread meant a vote for a new member, and cheese a vote against. Your stomach yawns.

You've always liked Greenwich Village. You know a lot of writers have, from patrician to bohemian to middle class. During the 19th century, salons gathered at the homes of Evert Duyckinck and Anne Charlotte Lynch. Henry James was born in Washington Square. Edith Wharton belonged to a more fashionable and less intellectual society described in *Age of Innocence.* Right off the square, Mark Twain lived at 21 Fifth Ave. for a time. You can't. Yet.

At the turn of the century, the Village began sowing its bohemian oats, as Italian immigrants moved into the neighborhood, joined by young and poor artists and writers. Willa Cather, John Reed, and Theodore Dreiser numbered among the Village's many literary souls. In the 20s, critics and poets moved in—Marianne Moore, Hart Crane, e.e. cummings, and Edna St. Vincent Millay, plus major league novelists like John Dos Passos and Thomas Wolfe. But when the 20s stopped roaring, the Village did too. And lively young writers like you can no longer afford to live there.

You've been walking for hours now. You start thinking about writing farther uptown where you could still afford to pay the rent, maybe in Harlem. The Harlem Renaissance sparked the beginnings of black American literature back in the 1920s. Early lights like Countee Cullen and Langston Hughes began a tradition that Ralph Ellison and James Baldwin would later carry on.

You realize the city has fostered a distinctive literature of its own: in the first half of this century, some streetsmart writers portrayed the immigrant poor, including Jacob Riis in *How the Other Half Lives,* Stephen Crane in *Maggie: A Girl of the Streets,* and Henry Roth in *Call It Sleep.* E.B. White and John Cheever captured a more privileged city lifestyle, the lifestyle you hope to effect.

Today more writers lunch with their agents than schmooze at the Algonquin. Merchandising has gotten increasingly important, as shown by the ingenuity of Tama Janowitz, who made a big splash with the first book promotion video, made to advertise *Slaves of New York.*

You trade your bolo tie for a crusty hot bagel. You realize that New York's literary tradition springs from its primacy as a marketplace of words rather than any great intellectual angst. You decide to make a video.

Etiquette

There's an old yarn, buried somewhere in the yellow pages of the Talmud, about a man who comes to New York City with a beautiful place setting—all silver, the finest silver West of Eden. He heads to the Lower East Side—so the story goes—and coughs up a few pennies for a knish (as he is very hungry). He sits on a bench, spreads a napkin over his lap, pulls out his fork and knife, and begins to eat, when some fellows on the block start scoffing, "Manners. This man has no manners." "Don't you know," they ask, "that it's rude not to eat a knish with your hands?" A fracas ensues, the tourist fends off his assailants with his silverware, and the knish topples to the ground. The moral of the story: a knife is a valuable implement to have in New York, but you have to know when and when not to use it.

Debutantes and dilettantes, don't be put off by New York's elusive etiquette. New Yorkers have an undying reputation for rudeness. In truth, they're not impolite as a matter of course, although (except for certain refugees from Nashville), most of them have not been studying etiquette books either. Chivalry is not dead, it simply arrives in new disguises. Subway etiquette, for example, is a widely unappreciated but subtle art. New Yorkers who give up subway seats for the elderly, the handicapped, and the shopping-bag-ridden, throw dimes into an underground musician's guitar case, or go to great lengths not to crush anyone in rush hour throngs are practicing their own special code of manners. When crushed into train cars like sardines, they are very polite sardines.

New Yorkers may not hold doors open for others, but they do hold elevator doors. They do not greet everyone they see with a friendly smile, but some do save up a little warmth for the familiar faces in their building or neighborhood; many know their local grocer, or stationer, or dry cleaner. You won't make friends with the person sitting next to you on the bus, but many a cabdriver can chat engagingly for eons of gridlock. Most preciously, New Yorkers have great respect for privacy and intimacy; don't bother standing on your head on the street. You won't get the attention you deserve.

When in New York, do as New Yorkers do. Dress according to the neighborhood you're visiting. Don't wear the red leather minidress if you're bound for Wall St. and leave the tux at home on the way to the south Bronx. When choosing shoes, go for comfort. You need only peer through a few shop windows on Madison Avenue to know that even the most expensive shoes in New York can be exceedingly ugly. No one looks at your feet anyway (except on subways). People rarely wear sandals in New York except during the summer months. Women should avoid wearing extremely short skirts or shorts; in seedy parts of town they will receive a barrage of whistles and in marbled boutiques they will shiver from the air conditioning.

When deciding what to wear for a night out, remember that most clubs, moviehouses, and theatres air condition their little velvet hearts out. Dance clubs can get very hot: you may want to wear a jacket or sweater, something you can take off. Dress for the theatre leans toward the casual. You shouldn't wear your denim shorts to a Broadway show, though tornish jeans might be just the thing for a 50-seat avant-garde playhouse. Not even Broadway houses require a jacket and tie or a semi-formal dress (except on certain opening nights). Some people dress slightly up for the big musicals, and everyone turns out in their finest silks and suits for the Metropolitan Opera, newcomers and subscribers alike. If you want to know what's in style at the top, just check out a French fashion magazine from a year ago.

Service is never included on a New York tab, and sales tax is 8.25%, a doubly convenient state of affairs: you always have to tip in case you were wondering, and the tip will come to about twice the tax. Tip hairdressers 10%, and bellhops at least $1 per bag. Cab drivers and waiters expect 15%. Knish peddlers don't, but you never know.

Safety

> At the centre of the first cross-roads, I saw a splendid
> and erect individual, flashing forth authority, gaity,
> and utter smartness in the gloom. Impossible not to
> believe that he was the owner of all the adjacent
> ground, disguised as a cavalry officer on foot.
> "What is that archduke?" I inquired.
> "He's just a cop."
> I knew then that I was in a great city.
> —Arnold Bennett, Those United States, 1912

When people say they hail from New York, the interested or impressed response is invariably followed by the question, "Get mugged often?"

Incidents do happen, even to most seasoned natives, even in the most fashionable districts. The FBI reports that 93,337 robberies took place in the city during 1989, making the NYC rate for muggings and street robberies the worst in the country. But some—nay, many—New Yorkers have never been cheated, swindled, or held up at gunpoint. This state of affairs has a little to do with luck, and a lot to do with street wisdom.

With some coaching, out-of-towners can learn to be streetwise. Above all, bear in mind that petty criminals seek naïve, hapless victims, which often translates into tourists. Make every effort not to be taken for one. Even people who have lived in New York all their lives can be perceived as tourists if they err on the side of conspicuous innocence. While in other cities, natives can tell themselves from tourists by accents or dress, in New York, looking different will never give anyone away—everyone does. Behavior is what gives you away. In a recent interview, a savvy city cop told reporters, "They go for the gawkers"—which means that smalltime crooks scam on the unwary, the wide-eyed, or the merely spaced-out. Leave the three cameras at home and don't put the one you did bring on public display around your neck. Use street maps discreetly and don't fold them out in all their glory if you can help it. Take your *Let's Go* guide with you by all means, but don't read it in a loud whisper to yourself in the middle of traffic. If you get lost and have to ask for directions, direct your queries to a traffic cop or store keeper, or choose your denizen carefully. If you feel like you're being followed, duck into a store or a restaurant. Some East Side shops near school districts have yellow and black signs that say "safe haven" in their windows. Learn to recognize them; they mean that shop managers have agreed to let people—especially students—loiter in their stores for long periods of time, or to help them call the police if they feel unsafe.

Safety on Foot

Even your guidebooks and flashbulbs won't scream out "rob me" as much as the way you move. The city is fast-paced. Moving at an average rate of 300 feet per minute, the New Yorker walks briskly; the tourist wanders blithely. Don't fall into a skyscraper trance and gaze at tall buildings for extended periods of time. Occasionally, a tourist will walk into a lamppost doing just that. Even when you don't know where you are, walk as if you do. Maintain at all times the fiction that you know where you are going.

Rip-off artists seek not only the unwary but the rich. Hide any wealth at all costs. Conceal your fancy watch, necklace, or bracelet under your clothing if you feel that you've entered a dubious neighborhood. Chain-snatching is a particular hazard in the subway. Turn the huge diamond on your ring around on your finger so jewelry-swipers can only see the band. Never count money in public—take the time to put it away in the safety of the store, restaurant, or cab—and don't wave large bills around. If you wear a handbag, keep a firm grip on it and wear the strap diagonally if possible. If you keep the bag and the strap on one side, not only can it be pulled off easily, but some clever thief with scissors may cut the strap so adeptly that you won't even notice. Most street criminals don't aspire to challenging work and are daunted by the gymnastics involved in cutting off a diagonally draped handbag when a straight one dangles simply in front of them.

Tourists get preyed upon most severely by thieves because they carry around more money than the rest of the world. If you must carry a lot of cash, take some precautions. If an unambitious mugger asks for a twenty, don't let that extra hundred be seen. Tuck your wallet into a concealed money belt or discreet pocket and keep an extra 10 bucks or so in an obvious pocket. If a mugger happens to hold a knife to your neck and ask for all you've got, you hand over the contents of the latter. The odd New Yorker has even been known to invest in a cheap extra wallet, designated especially for "mugging money". And don't be left fundless by the successful pickpocket who scours all pockets; keep an extra bill or two for emergencies in an even more unlikely place, such as your shoe or sock. Some recent sneaker and shoe models come equipped with special money compartments; use them if you've got them.

Con artists love tourists too. Don't get caught off guard by their sidewalk routines. One spills ketchup on you while another picks your pocket. Or while one plays a slow hand of three-card monte, another, the front, pretends to lose tons of money ineptly at what seems an easy game. Yet another watches for the cops. If you make the mistake of playing, you'll soon find that the cards have sped up and that you're out 60 bucks. Don't succumb to the tempting gambling opportunities on the street. Don't be distracted by spilt ketchup. And don't believe anyone who tells you a fishy sob story that can be rectified only through your financial assistance; one gullible tourist shelled out $50 to someone who claimed to have a family and a car with no gas and no way of getting back home, only to be told the exact same story by the same person six months later. Don't believe anyone who tells you they just found a huge pile of unmarked bills or valuable coins, and they need your advice about what to do with it. The cash will inevitably be fake and the lucky finder will only try to extort something more genuine from you in the course of this saga. Don't believe anyone who crashes into you with a bottle of wine and asks you, as it splinters on the sidewalk, how you could have broken such a precious, expensive item. Some people on the street do beg for a living, but many just want to sell you a bridge. Don't buy it.

Be aware of your surroundings. Although it's as possible to have your pocket picked on Fifth in full daylight as it is in the Bowery at midnight, some neighborhoods are shiftier than others. And districts can change character drastically in the course of a single block. Watch out, for example, as the haughty Upper East Side becomes the lower stretches of Harlem as the streets hit triple digits. Don't go on a midnight stroll by yourself at whim; do trust in the safety in numbers concept. It works. Especially at night, avoid poverty-stricken or drug-ridden areas like Harlem, the South Bronx, Washington Heights, Fort Greene, Bedford-Stuyvesant, and Alphabet City—the segment of lower east Manhattan where numbered avenues ominously become lettered. After dark, veer away from silent neighborhoods with looming warehouses, or graffiti-infested, neglected buildings. West Midtown and the lower-middle East Side, both well-populated commercial centers during the day, can be foreboding at night.

Central Park, land of the frisbee and the Good Humor truck by day, also changes mood soon after sunset. Those looking for the mugging experience will assuredly find it here. They'll especially find it if they're not looking. Many people forget that the park grows dangerous at night, and police officers have been known to escort such waifs out with a squad car trailing behind them. A few years ago, a criminal set fire to a homeless couple in the park, shocking the city and bringing home the simple fact that the meadows of Central Park can transform into sinister territories at night. If you find yourself penniless, busless, and on the wrong side of the park, walk around it by Central Park South rather than north of it or through it. If you're uptown, walk through the 85th St. transverse by the police station. Avoid the woodsy deserted areas far from the main path. You may not want to hang out by the West Side docks along the Hudson River at night, an area full of some of New York's trendiest clubs and bars that cater mostly to gay men. The gay bar life in this neighborhood is a tad rougher than it is in the Village. Further inland, stay out of the Times Square and Penn Station area, a region ridden with prostitutes and problems.

After dark, stay in residential areas as much as possible, particularly ones manned by doormen. Stay out of creepy alleyways and dimly lit, twisty streets like those in the curvy Lower East Side. Stay on the main thoroughfares; walk on avenues rather than streets, and when you have to cross over, walk down one of the wide two-way streets if you can. Fifth and Park are the least dangerous avenues in the evening on the East Side, Central Park West and Broadway the safest on the West.

Safety in Vehicles

Car drivers won't have to deal with walking around in dangerous neighborhoods as frequently, but they will have to take precautions to keep that car. Crooks gravitate to cars with out-of-state plates, heavily laden roofs, and good radios. Most car thieves in New York actually make their living stealing only radios; hence the many "NO RADIO" or "RADIO ALREADY STOLEN" signs adorning car windows everywhere. If your tape deck or radio can be removed, hide it in the trunk or take it with you. If you must leave it there, conceal it under junk or put your own sign in the window. Some New Yorkers (with high-tech security systems that prevent outsiders from driving away with their cars) have gotten so frustrated by the epidemic radio theft that they opt to leave their car doors unlocked so that crooks can take the radio without smashing the windows. To avoid all forms of car theft, park your vehicle in a lot or a garage, or at least in a well-lit or well-traveled area. Don't leave obviously visible baggage or gems lying around. If you have to leave suitcases in the car, make sure they're not bursting out of a trunk tied down with rope for all to see. Even if baggage is neatly hidden away, savvy thieves can tell if a car is heavily loaded by the way it is settled on its tires. It is extremely dangerous to sleep in a car or van parked on the city street, and even the most budget-minded of travelers should not consider it an option.

If you didn't bring the car, it's gotten late, and you're far from your bed, opt for a bus over the subway. Since the driver is in plain view, buses see little violence. On weekends, it's fairly safe to take the subway into the evening, even for solo travelers, since most major lines are quite crowded then. If an empty subway station gives you the creeps, stand near the token counter or be on the lookout for the Guardian Angels, self-appointed crime-fighters clad in red berets who have made the subway system safer in recent years. If waiting for a bus makes you nervous and you feel you're about to turn into a pumpkin, treat yourself to a taxi. Calling a cab and taking it door-to-door may be the safest mode of travel in New York.

But don't assume that taxi equals safety. Unlicensed taxi dispatchers can try to fool you. If you walk out of a train from Grand Central or Penn Station, some person may claim to be a porter, carry your bags, hail you a cab, and then ask for a commission or share of the fare. If so, don't fall for it—give directions to the driver as fast as you can and drive off in style. Many a clueless tourist has been taken by this baggage-carrying scam, New York's version of the great train robbery. Official dispatchers do not receive any part of the cab fare for their services. Doormen who spend a long time finding you a taxi may be tipped, a couple of dollars at most; porters who carry enormous amounts of luggage may be tipped for that service. Cab fares can only be paid at the end of the ride.

But watch those cab fares. New York taxis must drop off individuals and charge a bulk fare at the end; any driver who tries to charge you per person by location has no business doing so. Unless you find yourself stranded and desperate, take a yellow cab with a meter and a medallion on the hood. Avoid cabs with no fare meters, illegal "gypsy cabs," which come in any color but yellow. In a legitimate cab, you can find the driver's name posted over the glove compartment, and when you get out you can request a receipt that lists a phone number to call about complaints or lost articles. State your destination with authority, and suggest the quickest route if you know it. If you hesitate or sound unsure about where you are going, the driver knows that you can be taken out of your way without noticing. Some hacks will take tortuous routes and when confronted will try to excuse themselves by saying things like, "It's to avoid the toll" or "I thought there would be horse-and-buggy traffic in the park." They can charge you more if they drive you around in circles; don't let them.

Above all, avoid public bathrooms (such as those in parks and subway or train stations). They are usually as far from safe as they are from clean, and no sane New Yorker would even consider going into one. Instead, try the big department stores, the better hotels, or any restaurant, bar, or café without a sign on the door saying "restrooms for patrons only."

Planning Your Trip

Millions of penniless immigrants disembarked at Ellis Island with visions of streets paved with gold, and quickly learned to survive in New York. You can too.

Use your address book as a supplementary travel guide; staying with friends, enemies, and remote acquaintances reduces the cost of living. The off-season helps too: in May and September, the weather improves, the hordes of tourists thin out, and prices descend. Facilities and sights don't close in the off-season—the city is a year-round attraction.

Travel offices, tourist information centers, chambers of commerce, and special interest organizations conspire to barrage you with an impressive amount of free information; it's best to write with specific requests. (See Practical Information for addresses.) Travel agents can advise you on the cheapest transportation options, but don't rely exclusively on their information. Do some calling on your own, scan newspaper travel sections, or consult your local bulletin boards.

Documents

Carry at least two forms of identification, one of which should be a photo ID. Banks, in particular, will want to see more than one form of identification whenever you cash a traveler's check. Before you leave, photocopy both sides of your important documents, such as ID and credit cards, and leave them with someone you can contact easily. Students should bring proof of their status. (Don't expect, though, the extensive student discounts on museum admission, entertainment, transportation, and accommodations available in Europe.) A current university ID card will generally suffice for U.S. students. Foreign students may want to purchase an **International Student Identification Card (ISIC),** available through several sources (see Information for Foreign Visitors below).

Money

Most city establishments accept **traveler's checks** but some cynical New York types treat them as dubious and require the same kind of ID (driver's license, major credit card) that they do for personal checks. A "no checks" sign usually only refers to personal checks. All banks issue traveler's checks, some at face value, others with a 1-2% commission. Members of the **American Automobile Association (AAA)** can avoid paying a commission by purchasing traveler's checks at any AAA office (see Transportation below). You can call your favorite company for information; some companies also have theft or loss hotline numbers. American Express (800-221-7282), Bank of America (800-227-3460; hotline 800-368-7878), Barclay's (800-221-2426; hotline 800-227-6811), Citicorp (800-645-6556; hotline 800-523-1199), MasterCard (800-223-9920), Thomas Cook (800-223-7373), and Visa (800-227-6811). Most of these companies will cash and refund checks through banks and other institutions throughout the U.S. Keep at least one record of your check numbers separate from the checks to facilitate replacement if they get lost or stolen. Some stores will not accept checks in denominations larger than $20.

With a major **credit card** you can rent cars, make reservations, and obtain cash advances at most banks. Don't plan on relying exclusively on plastic money, as budget places don't trust it. And note that many stores set a minimum limit of $15 or more for charges. Local **American Express** offices will cash personal checks (including foreign checks) in any 21-day period up to $1000 ($5000 with a gold card); they pay in cash and traveler's checks depending on the office's money supply. They also cancel stolen credit cards, arrange for temporary ID, help change airline, hotel, and car rental reservations, and send mailgrams or international cables. American Express offices in the U.S. will act as a mail service if you contact them in writing beforehand and request that they hold your mail (see Keeping in Touch below). American Express also operates machines at major airports through which you can purchase traveler's checks with your card. For more information, write to American Express Card Division, 770 Broadway, New York, NY 10003 (800-528-4800). Most places also take **Mastercard** and **Visa.** Visa in particular now offers many of the same travel services as American Express. Check with local banks about these services, or write to Visa, P.O. Box 5111, 1400 Union Turnpike, New Hyde Park, NY 11042 (800-227-6811).

Credit cards are also compatible with the latest form of plastic financing—**electronic banking.** At least two banking networks offer 24-hr. service at automated tellers (operated by bank cards) in major cities across the country. The **Cirrus** network (800-424-7787) includes BayBanks in New England, New York Cash Exchange, First Interstate in the West, and Manufacturers Hanover in New York, among others; the **Plus** network (800-843-7587) includes Bank of America in the West, Chase Manhattan in New York, Continental in Chicago, and First City Bank of Dallas. If you'll be staying in New York for your whole vacation, a bank card may be better than traveler's checks. Most banks impose a limit (usually $500) on the amount you can withdraw in any one day. Visa and Mastercard sometimes also work with these machines. Check with local banks about these and competing services.

If you run out of money on the road, you can have more mailed to you in the form of a **certified check,** redeemable at any bank. Money can also be wired directly from bank to bank for about $6. Or use a postal money order; you can purchase them with cash at any U.S. post office for a fee of up to $1 per order, and can be cashed at another office upon display of two IDs (one with photo). Keep a receipt: orders are refundable if lost. A generous relative inside the U.S. can wire money

Don't forget to write.

If your American Express® Travelers Cheques are lost or stolen, we can hand-deliver a refund virtually anywhere you travel. Just give us a call. You'll find it's a lot less embarrassing than calling home.

AMERICAN EXPRESS **Travelers Cheques**

to you in minutes via **Western Union** (800-325-4176), which charges a wiring fee based on the amount wired and the method of payment; call for information. You need a Mastercard or Visa to wire by phone.

The prices quoted throughout *Let's Go: New York City* are the amounts before **sales tax** has been added. Sales tax in New York state is 8.25%, depending on the item. Hotels have begun to charge a special tax of 5% on rooms costing over $100 per night, on top of sales tax.

Packing

Don't schlep. Pack light, especially if New York is just a stop on a longer trip for you, or if you'll be moving around the area a lot. But if you're planning to stay in one place for a long time, you might want to bring more clothes along. You might also prefer a suitcase or duffel bag to a backpack.

Remember to take good footwear and rainwear. Bring an umbrella. You may want to take an outfit for going out in the evening—some restaurants, theatres, and events require or at least seem to demand an upscale outfit. Clothing should be comfortable and should require minimal care. Laundromats do their thing throughout the city, but if you don't want to spend your valuable vacation time planted in front of a Maytag, consider doing laundry by hand. Pack a plastic clothesline that can be hung up in your room; your clothes can dry while you enjoy the local sights.

Travelers are sometimes separated from their luggage, temporarily or permanently. Always keep valuable items (traveler's checks, tickets, credit cards) and identification on your person. Stow a change of clothes, medication, and any other irreplaceable items in a carry-on bag.

Serious camera equipment costs a lot, breaks easily, and weighs a ton. If you only want snapshots, bring a pocket camera or a small automatic 35mm camera. Buy film at supermarkets or drugstores since tourist shops often charge ridiculous prices. Steer clear of film (even of well-known name brands) manufactured in underdeveloped nations, which can be of dubious quality. Have your film hand-checked at airport X-ray machines. Prices for camera equipment in New York City are the lowest in the country. (See Shopping.)

Keeping in Touch

You haven't called, you haven't written.
I'm lost, I'm cold, I'm all frostbitten.
My heart's a phone now, I am smitten.
—Martha Scharfstein, "AT&T Blues," Poems of a New York Winter

If you plan to rely on the phone, a calling card offered by AT&T or one of its various competitors, or a Visa, Mastercard, or American Express card, can save money over calling collect. If you want to send a **telegram**, call **Western Union** (800-325-6000). A 25-word message sent from New York to Los Angeles cost $35, including delivery. Even cheaper, post offices offer **mailgrams**, which can be sent to any General Delivery location.

Depending on how neurotic your family is, consider making arrangements for the folks back home to get in touch with you. Post offices are either closed or open only a half-day on Saturdays, and are closed on Sundays and holidays as well. Plan your mailstops for mid-week. Once a letter arrives it will be held for about a week, but may be held longer if it has an arrival date marked clearly on the front of the envelope. If you've reserved accommodations in advance, you can usually have mail sent to their addresses, with your arrival date marked on the envelope. For emergencies, leave phone numbers where you can be reached.

American Express does not automatically offer a Poste Restante service as it does in Europe, but the offices in New York City will act as a mail service for cardholders if you contact them in writing in advance. They will hold mail for one month, for-

ward upon request, and accept telegrams. For a complete list of offices and instructions on how to use the service, get the "Directory of Travel Service Offices" at any office or call 800-528-4800.

Health and Insurance

If you know that you will require medication while you travel, obtain a full supply before you leave and carry medicine prescriptions with you. If you wear glasses or contact lenses, carry either an extra pair or a copy of your prescription.

Travelers with chronic medical conditions should wear a **Medic Alert identification tag.** In addition to indicating the nature of the condition, the tag provides the number of Medic Alert's 24-hr. hotline, through which attending personnel can obtain information about the member's medical history. Lifetime membership, including a stainless steel bracelet or necklace, costs $25; write to Medic Alert Foundation International, P.O. Box 1009, Turlock, CA 95381 (800-432-5378).

Before you leave, find out what your health insurance covers. Always have proof of insurance and policy numbers with you. If you're a student, you may be covered by your family's policy. If you have insurance through your school, find out if the policy includes summer travel. For only $11 per month, the **Council on International Educational Exchange (CIEE)** (212-661-1414) offers a **Trip-Safe Plan** that provides $2000 of medical coverage within the U.S.

A compact **first-aid kit** should suffice for minor health problems. Bring aspirin. Other basic items include band-aids, elastic bandage, scissors, tweezers, a Swiss army knife, burn ointment, a thermometer, antiseptic, and motion sickness tablets. Backpackers and bicyclists especially should pack a first-aid kit.

If you get sick while traveling and require emergency treatment, call the police or other emergency facilities for assistance (dial 911 or 0). See our Practical Information listings, consult a telephone book for the numbers of help lines, or go directly to the emergency room of the local hospital. In general, health facilities in the U.S. are excellent, and correspondingly expensive. If the situation does not require immediate attention, look for low-cost or free clinics (e.g. public health clinics, crisis centers, or women's health centers). Hotlines can refer you to clinics where you can receive treatment without proof of insurance. Low-cost medical and dental clinics at universities and colleges may help as well.

Accommodations

Speaking of New York . . . he said that it was impossible to have a picturesque address there.
—Logan Pearsall Smith, quoting Henry James

Hotels and Motels

In accommodation listings throughout this guide, "single" refers to one bed, which often sleeps two people; "double" means two beds. You should verify how many people the room accommodates, whether there is a fee for extra people, and whether cots are available.

Expect to pay at least $20-30 for a single in a cheap hotel. Most hotels and motels require a key deposit when you register. You will be told in advance if the bathroom is communal. Check-in usually takes place between 11am and 1pm, check-out probably before 11am. You may be able to store your gear for the day even after vacating your room and returning the key, but most proprietors will not take responsibility for the safety of your belongings.

Let's Go: New York City determines the best budget hotels or motels and ranks them in order of the best value, based on price, safety, and location. Ask the hotel owner if you can see a room before you pay for it.

5,300 hostels in 68 countries on 6 continents.

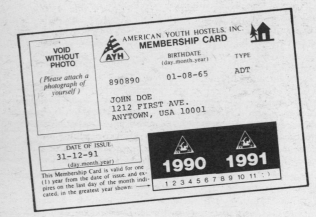

You can reserve most hotel and motel rooms in advance. Motels tend to fill up by evening, so try not to wait until nightfall to look for a room. You may receive some tips from employees at the bus or train station. If the situation looks hopeless, call Travelers Aid or the police (*not* the emergency telephone number) for assistance.

Hostels

Open to everyone, regardless of age, hostels offer the least expensive ($4-12) indoor lodgings. To stay in certain hostels, you must be a paid member of **American Youth Hostels, Inc. (AYH)**. A one-year membership costs $25 for those 18 to 54, $10 for seniors and those under 18, and $30 for families. AYH maintains 230 U.S. hostels; their branch in New York City is of superior grade, with much space and many amenities. Friendly, well-run, dorm-style lodgings, AYH hostels are the best places to meet other budget travelers. **International Youth Hostel Federation (IYHF)** memberships are honored at all AYH hostels. The indispensable *AYH Handbook* (free with membership) includes a list of U.S. hostels, complete with their specific requirements and services. For more information write to American Youth Hostels, Inc., P.O. Box 37613, Washington, DC 20013-7613 (202-783-6161). The maximum length of stay at a hostel is usually three nights. Make reservations four to six weeks in advance.

YMCAs and YWCAs

Don't overlook the **Young Men's Christian Association (YMCA).** Not all YMCAs offer overnight accommodations, but those that do often have rates comparable to city hotels. Singles aaverage $28, doubles average $41; rooms include use of a library, pool, and other facilities. Advance reservations are recommended; a $3 reservation fee is waived for reservations made at least two months in advance.

Some YMCAs accept women and families in addition to men. You may have to share a room with another sleeper and use a communal bath or shower. They charge a refundable key deposit of about $5. Economy packages (2-8 days, $40-270) that include lodging, breakfast, dinners, and excursions are available. The YMCA of Greater New York offers an **International Program,** accommodation centers for students and young adults. For information and reservations, write or call **The Y's Way,** 356 W. 34th St., New York, NY 10001 (212-760-5856).

The **Young Women's Christian Association (YWCA)** also provides inexpensive housing and recreational facilities. Most YWCAs accommodate only women. Generally, facilities must be shared with others on the same floor. Nonmembers are required to pay a small membership fee in addition to the overnight fee. Information on YWCAs with residence facilities across the country is available for $3 from the Order Department, Young Women's Christian Association of the USA, 726 Broadway, New York, NY 10003 (212-614-2700).

Dormitories

Some colleges and universities open their residence halls to conferences and travelers, especially during the summer. You may have to share a bath, but rates are often low and facilities are usually clean and well-maintained. If you hope to stay at a school, contact its housing office before your vacation.

Alternative Accommodations

As an alternative to the lodging described above, contact **Servas,** an international cooperative system of hosts and travelers throughout the U.S. This non-profit organization matches travelers with hosts who provide accommodations for two to three days. You have to provide two letters of reference and arrange for an interview at least one month before your trip. Participation in the program costs $45 per year, but no money is exchanged between travelers and hosts. Contact the U.S. Servas

Committee, 11 John St. #706, New York, NY 10038 (212-267-0252). If you belong to a church or synagogue, you may be able to line up similar contacts across the country.

If a night under the stars doesn't seem appealing, but you can't spare the cost of a night's lodgings, call the local Travelers Aid (see Safety and Security above) for information on places to stay in an emergency. The local crisis center hotline may have a list of persons or organizations who will provide some sort of space for the evening.

Average Monthly Temperatures

> *"Oh dear, I'm so hot and thirsty—and what a hideous place New York is!" She looked despairingly up and down the dreary thoroughfare. "Other cities put on their best clothes in summer, but New York seems to sit in its shirt-sleeves."*
> —Edith Wharton, The House of Mirth

City summers have been getting hotter, but in general New York weather stays mild. In cold weather, gusts of wind swirl near the rivers and Central Park, but pretty much come to a halt at the unperturbed edifices of Midtown. Umbrellas are nice to have, though sometimes you'll find enough construction and canopies to keep you dry all the way home.

January	32°
February	33°
March	41°
April	53°
May	62°
June	71°
July	77°
August	75°
September	68°
October	58°
November	47°
December	36°

Additional Information for Foreign Visitors

> *When I arrived for the first time at New York, by that part of the Atlantic Ocean which is called the East River, I was surprised to perceive along the shore, at some distance from the city, a number of little palaces of white marble, several of which were of classic architecture. When I went the next day to inspect more closely one which had particularly attracted my notice, I found that its walls were of whitewashed brick, and its columns of painted wood. All the edifices that I had admired the night before were of the same kind.*
> —Alexis de Tocqueville, Democracy in America, 1840

AARON®
Driveaway • Truckaway Co., Inc.

Orientation to the United States

The continental U.S. is enormous by European standards (3100 by 1800 mi., 5000 by 2900km), and some parts of it are largely uninhabited. The regions of the United States are often as culturally distinct as two nations; a Texan might feel as much a foreigner in New England as a Tahitian would.

Useful Organizations

When you begin planning your trip, you might contact the **United States Travel and Tourism Administration** (branches located in Australia, the U.K., Belgium, France, Canada, W. Germany, Japan, and Mexico), which runneth over with free literature. Contact the branch in your country or write to the U.S. Travel and Tourism Administration, Department of Commerce, 14th and Constitution Ave. NW, Washington, DC 20230 (202-377-4003 or 202-377-3811). You may also want to write to the tourist offices of the states or cities you'll be visiting. (See *Let's Go: USA.*) The more specific your inquiry, the better your chances of getting the information you need. Visit local tourist information centers when you arrive.

The **Council on International Educational Exchange (CIEE)** has offices overseas that sell travel literature, hostel cards, and charter airline tickets. They keep busy issuing the ISIC (see Documents below) and putting out the *Student Travel Catalog* ($1 postage) and a publication about where visitors can stay, appropriately entitled *Where to Stay USA* ($10.95). Write to CIEE at 205 E. 42nd St., New York, NY 10017 (800-223-7402 charter flights only; 212-661-1450 for Council Travel; or 212-661-1414), or contact their other offices in Paris, Tokyo, Madrid, or Germany. In Canada, write to **Travel CUTS (Canadian University Travel Services Limited),** 171 College St., Toronto, Ont. M5T 1P7 (416-979-2406). In the U.K., write to **London Student Travel,** 52 Grosvenor Gardens, London, WC1 (tel. (071) 730 3402). In Australia, contact **SSA/STA,** 220 Faraday St., Carlton, Melbourne, Victoria 3053 (tel. (03) 347 6911).

The **International Student Travel Confederation (ISTC),** to which CIEE belongs, is a godsend for European students. It arranges charter flights and discount airfares, provides travel insurance, issues ISICs in a new and improved plastic form, and sponsors the Student Air Travel Association for European students. Write for their Student Travel Guide at ISTC, Weinbergstrasse 31, CH-8006 Zurich, Switzerland (tel. (411) 262 29 96).

STA Travel, based in the U.K., wields over 100 offices worldwide that can help arrange discounted overseas flights. In the U.S., call 800-777-0112 or write to 7202 Melrose Ave., Los Angeles, CA 90046. Abroad, write to them at 74 and 86 Old Brompton Rd., London SW7 3LQ, England, or call (071) 937 9971 for flights to North America.

If you wish to stay in a American home during your vacation, many organizations can flock to your aid. The **Experiment in International Living** coordinates homestay programs for enthusiastic international visitors wishing to join an U.S. family for an extended period of time. Visitors of all ages live with host families long enough to receive a full dose of American culture. For the address in your country, write to the U.S. Headquarters, Black Mountain Rd., Brattleboro, VT 05301 (800-451-4465). The **Institute of International Education (IIE)** (see Study below) publishes a "Homestay Information Sheet" listing many homestay programs. Write to them at 809 United Nations Plaza, New York, NY 10017 (212-883-8200). See Accommodations for information on **Servas,** an international travel organization that does the same thing, only different.

Documents and Formalities

In addition to a **passport,** almost all visitors to the U.S. must have a visitor's **visa** and proof of plans to leave the U.S. For stays of only a few days, Canadian citizens bearing proof of citizenship do not need a visa or passport. Mexican citizens with an I-186 form can enter through a U.S. border station, then obtain an I-94 form 25 mi. in from the border. Other travelers have to apply for visas at a U.S. consulate. International visitors usually obtain a B-1 or B-2 (non-immigrant traveling for pleasure) visa valid for a maximum of six months. The citizens of eight countries—the U.K., Japan, Italy, W. Germany, France, the Netherlands, Sweden, and Switzerland—do not need visas to enter the U.S.; however, they must meet certain criteria, such as being in possession of a ticket to leave the U.S. within 90 days and flying on one of a specified group of air carriers. For more information, contact a U.S. consulate near you.

If you lose your passport once in the U.S., first cry and then replace it through the embassy of your country. If you lose your visa or your I-94 form (the arrival/departure certificate attached to your visa upon arrival), replace it at the nearest **U.S. Immigration and Naturalization Service** office. You can procure a list of offices from the INS, Central Office Information Operations Unit, #5044, 425 I St. NW, Washington, DC 20536 (202-633-1900). This information does not necessarily apply for work or study in the U.S. (see Work and Study below). To extend your length of stay in the U.S., you must acquire separate INS forms. An application for an extension must be filed well before your original departure date; plan ahead.

Foreign students should obtain an **International Student Identification Card (ISIC)** as proof of student status. Obtain the ISIC at local travel agencies, from the International Student Travel Confederation, from CIEE, or from **Let's Go Travel Services,** Thayer Hall-B, Harvard University, Cambridge, MA 02138 (617-495-9649 or 800-5-LETS-GO). Let's Go Travel also sells American Youth Hostel memberships. The ISIC and the AYH card are available by mail.

If your home country signed the Geneva Road Traffic Convention back in 1949, you can legally drive in the U.S. for one year from the date of your arrival, provided that you drive a U.S. registered car with proper insurance. An **international driver's**

license is useful only to enable policemen to understand your license; it has no effect on your legal status. If your country is not a signatory of the Convention, it is illegal for you to drive in the U.S. without obtaining a U.S. license, even if you have an international license. Consult the resident sages at your national automobile association before you leave. Keep in mind that the usual minimum age for car rental and auto transport services is 21; recently a number of New York rental agencies were charged with violating state business codes by setting minimums as high as 25.

Customs

All travelers lug into the U.S. 200 cigarettes, $100 worth of gifts, and all personal belongings duty-free. Travelers 21 and over may also drag along up to one liter of alcohol duty-free. You may bring in any amount of currency without a charge, but if you carry over $10,000, you'll have to fill out a dreary report form. Carry prescription drugs in clearly labeled containers, accompanied by a doctor's statement or prescription. Customs officials will often inquire about the amount of money you are carrying and ask your planned departure date to ensure that you will be able to support yourself while in the U.S. For more information, or for the trusty pamphlet *Know Before You Go,* contact the nearest U.S. Embassy or write to the **U.S. Customs Service,** 1301 Constitution Ave. NW, Washington, DC 20229 (202-566-8195). Remember to check customs regulations in your country so that you will know what you may take with you on your return trip.

Currency and Exchange

> *In Boston they ask, How much does he know? In New*
> *York, How much is he worth?*
> —*Mark Twain*

U.S. currency uses a decimal system based on the **dollar ($).** Paper money ("bills") comes in six denominations, all the same size, shape, and dull green color. The bills now issued are $1, $5, $10, $20, $50, and $100. You may occasionally see fun denominations of $2 and $500 which are no longer printed, but are still acceptable as currency. Some restaurants and stores may be squeamish about accepting bills larger than $50. The dollar is divided into 100 cents ($\cent$). Pick your favorite notation for values of less than a dollar: 35 cents can be represented as 35$\cent$ or $0.35. U.S. currency uses six coins. The penny (1$\cent$), nickel (5$\cent$), dime (10$\cent$), and quarter (25$\cent$) are the most common. Half-dollar (50$\cent$) and one-dollar coins are rarely seen and make nice gifts.

Convert your currency infrequently and in large amounts to minimize exorbitant exchange fees. Try to buy traveler's checks in U.S. dollars so that you won't have to exchange them. Personal checks can be difficult to cash in the U.S. Most banks require that you have an account with them before they will cash a personal check, and opening an account can be a time-consuming affair.

Sending Money

Sending money overseas is a bewildering, expensive process. If you think you'll need money sent during your stay in the U.S., visit your bank before you leave to get a list of its correspondent American banks. Or you can arrange in advance for your bank to send money from your account to certain correspondent banks on specific dates.

Cabling money is the fastest method of transport; it usually takes 48 hours to get to a major city or a bit longer to a more remote location. You pay cabling costs plus the commission charged by your home bank; rates vary according to the amount cabled. **Western Union** (800-325-4176 or 800-325-6000) offers a safe method for wiring money usually within two working days. Their U.S. offices can receive money from Germany and England, but not from France. A cheaper but slower method of sending money is by **bank draft** (international money order). You pay a commission (around $15-20) on the draft, plus the cost of registered air mail. An **American Express** office at home can cable you up to $10,000; it costs $35 to cable $500, and as the amount cabled grows larger, the fee follows in its wake. Non-cardholders may also use this service for no extra charge. For some unknown reason, it costs less to send money from Europe to the U.S. than from the U.S. to Europe. Money takes from one to three days to reach the U.S. One problem with the American Express Moneygram (800-543-4080) is that foreigners can only cable to the U.S. from France, England, and Germany—the rest of Europe and Australia only have receiving stations. Whichever method you choose, make sure that you and the sender know the exact name and address of the bank or office to which the money is being sent.

Finally, if you're stranded in the U.S. with no recourse or friends, a consulate will wire home for you and deduct the cost from the money you receive. Consulates are often less than gracious about performing this service, however.

Mail and Telephones

Individual branches of the **United States Post Office** usually open weekdays from 8am to 5pm and Saturday from 8am to noon. They all shut down vehemently on national holidays. A postcard mailed within the U.S. (including Alaska and Hawaii) or to Mexico costs 15¢; a letter costs 25¢. Postcards mailed overseas cost 36¢, letters 45¢; aerograms are available at the post office for 36¢. Mail within the country takes between one day and one week to arrive; to northern Europe and South America, a week to 10 days; to southern Europe, North Africa, and the Middle East, two to three weeks. Large city post offices offer **International Express Mail** service in case you need to mail something to a major European city in 40 to 72 hours.

The U.S. is divided into postal zones, each with a five-digit **ZIP code** particular to a region, city, or part of a city. Some addresses have nine-digit ZIP codes, used primarily for business mailings to speed up delivery.

The telephone system, once controlled by Bell, is no longer a monopoly. **AT&T** is the leading company and competes with other long-distance phone companies such as **MCI** and **Sprint**. Telephone numbers in the U.S. consist of a three-digit area code, a three-digit exchange, and a four-digit number, usually written as (212) 123-4567. Normally only the last seven digits are used in a **local call**. **Non-local calls** within the area code from which you are dialing require a "1" dialed before the last seven digits. **Long-distance calls** require a "1," the area code, and then the seven-digit number. Canada and the greater part of Mexico share the same area code system. The area code "800" indicates a toll-free number, usually for a business. A "1" must be dialed before the "800." For information on specific toll-free numbers, call 1-800-555-1212. Be careful—the age of information technology has recently given birth to the "900" number. Its area code is deceptively similar to the toll-free code, but "900" calls are staggeringly expensive. Average charges range from $2-5 for the first minute, with a smaller charge for each additional minute. You can have phone sex, make donations to political candidates, or hear about Teenage Mutant Ninja Turtles, but it'll cost you.

The New York telephone directory contains most of the information you will need about telephone usage, including area codes for the U.S., many foreign country codes, and rates. To obtain local phone numbers or area codes of other cities, call directory assistance (411 within your area code or 1-(area code)-555-1212). From any phone you can reach the **operator** by dialing "0." The operator will help you with rates and other information and give assistance in an emergency. Directory assistance and the operator can be reached without payment from any pay phone.

Pay phones hang out on street corners (usually every two blocks on avenues) and in public areas. Be wary of private, more expensive pay phones—the rate they charge per call will be printed on the phone. Put your coins (10-25¢ for a local call) into the slot and listen for a dial tone before dialing; if there is no answer or if you get a busy signal, you will get your money back after hanging up. To make a long-distance direct call, deposit the coins and dial; an operator will tell you the cost of the first three minutes. The operator will cut in after your time is up and tell you to deposit more money. Long-distance rates usually take a nose-dive after 5pm on weekdays and plummet even further between 11pm and 8am and on weekends.

If you don't carry around barrels of change, you may want to make a **collect call** (i.e. charge the call to the recipient). First dial "0" and then the area code and number you wish to reach. An operator will cut in and ask to help you. Tell her or him that you wish to place a collect call from Elisa Loti or whatever your name happens to be. You might opt for a **person-to-person** call, which costs more than collect but cuts right to the heart of things. To call person-to-person, you must also give the recipient's name to the operator, but you will only be charged if the person you want to speak with happens to be there. (Another party may accept collect charges.) In some areas, particularly rural ones, you may have to tell the operator what number you wish to reach, and he or she will put the call through for you.

You can place **international calls** from any telephone. To call direct, dial the international access code (011), the country code, the city code, and the local number. Country codes may be listed with a zero in front (e.g. 044), but when using 011, drop the zero (e.g. 011-44). In some areas you will have to give the operator the number and she or he will place the call. To find out the cheapest time to call various countries in Europe or the Middle East, call the operator (dial "0"). The cheapest time to call Australia and Japan is between 3am and 2pm, New Zealand 11pm and 10am.

Cabling may be the only way to contact someone quickly overseas. A short message usually flits to its destination by the following day. For most overseas telegrams, Western Union charges $7, plus 40-60¢ per word, including name and address. Exact charges depend on the length of the message and its destination. Call Western Union (800-325-6000) to check rates for specific countries.

Holidays

Some listings in *Let's Go: New York City* refer to holidays that may be unfamiliar to foreign travelers. **Martin Luther King Jr.'s Birthday** is celebrated on the third Monday in January, **Presidents' Day** on the third Monday in February. **Memorial Day,** falling on the last Monday of May, honors all U.S. citizens who have died in wars and signals the unofficial start of summer. Halfway through summer, **Independence Day** explodes on July 4. Americans celebrate their independence from England with barbecues and fireworks. Summer ends with another long weekend, **Labor Day,** on the first Monday of September, occasioning a flurry of back-to-school sales. **Columbus Day** comes on the second Monday in October. **Thanksgiving,** the fourth Thursday of November, celebrates the arrival of the Pilgrims' in New England in 1620. Thanksgiving unofficially marks the start of the holiday season that runs through **New Year's Day** (Jan. 1). All public agencies and offices and many businesses close on these holidays, as well as on several others scattered throughout the calendar.

Measurements

The British system of weights and measures is still in use in the U.S., despite half-hearted efforts to convert to the metric system. The following is a list of American units and their metric equivalents:

    1 inch = 25 millimeters
    1 foot = 0.30 meter
    1 yard = 0.91 meter
    1 mile = 1.61 kilometers

1 ounce = 25 grams
1 pound = 0.45 kilogram
1 quart(liquid) = 0.94 liter

12 inches equal 1 foot; 3 feet equal 1 yard; 5280 feet equal 1 mile. 16 ounces (weight) equal 1 pound (abbreviated as 1 lb.). 8 ounces (volume) equal 1 cup; 2 cups equal 1 pint; 2 pints equal 1 quart; and 4 quarts equal 1 gallon. Call *Let's Go* if you have any questions.

Electric outlets throughout the U.S. provide current at 117 volts, 60 cycles (Hertz). European voltage is usually 220; you might need a transformer in order to operate your non-U.S. appliances. This is an extremely important purchase for those with small appliances such as electric systems for disinfecting contact lenses. Transformers are sold to convert specific wattages (e.g. 0-50 watt transformers for razors and radios; larger watt transformers for hair dryers and other appliances). You might also need an adapter to change the shape of the plug; U.S. plugs usually have two rectangular prongs, but plugs for larger appliances often have a third prong.

The U.S. uses the Fahrenheit temperature scale rather than the Centigrade (Celsius) scale. To convert Fahrenheit to approximate Centigrade temperatures, subtract 32, then divide by 2. To convert them properly, subtract 32 then multiply by 9 and divide by 5. Or just remember that 32° is the freezing point of water, 212° its boiling point, normal human body temperature 98.6°, and room temperature around 70°.

Time

Americans tell time on the 12-hour, not 24-hour, clock. Hours after noon are post meridiem or pm (e.g. 2pm); hours before noon are ante meridiem or am (e.g. 2am). Noon is 12pm and midnight is 12am. (To avoid confusion, *Let's Go: New York City* uses only "noon" and "midnight.") The Continental U.S. divides into four time zones: Eastern, Central, Mountain, and Pacific. When it's noon Eastern time, it's 11am Central, 10am Mountain, 9am Pacific, and 7am central Alaskan and Hawaiian. Most areas of the country switch to daylight saving time (1 hr. ahead of standard) from mid-April to October. All of New York City follows Eastern Time.

Alcohol and Drugs

> *And then there's also ten thousand rumsellers there*
> *Oh! wonderful to think, I do declare!*
> *To accommodate the people of that city therein*
> *And to encourage them to commit all sorts of sin.*
> —William McGonagall, "Jottings of New York,"
> *1890*

You must 21 years old to purchase alcoholic beverages legally. Many places will want to see a photo ID (preferably a driver's license or other valid government-issued document) when ordering or buying alcohol. Possession of marijuana, cocaine, and most opiate derivatives (among many other chemicals) is punishable by stiff fines and/or imprisonment. Check with the U.S. Customs Service before your trip (see Customs above) about any questionable drugs.

Transportation

Getting to the U.S.

From Canada and Mexico

The U.S. and Canada share the world's longest undefended border, easily crossed by U.S. and Canadian citizens alike. Entering the U.S. from Mexico proves a bit more problematic. Mexican citizens may need a tourist visa for travel in the U.S.; contact the U.S. Embassy in Mexico City with questions. For Mexicans, as for Canadians, bargains on travel in the States may not come easy. Residents of the Americas may not be eligible for the discounts that airlines, bus, and train companies give to visitors from overseas.

Mexican and U.S. carriers offer many flights between the two countries. It may be cheaper to fly on a Mexican airline to one of the border towns and travel by train or bus from there. For more information regarding transportation to and from Mexico and the U.S. west coast, see *Let's Go: Mexico* or *Let's Go: California and Hawaii.*

Amtrak, Greyhound/Trailways, or one of their subsidiaries connects with all the Mexican border towns. Most buses and trains do no more than cross the Mexico/U.S. border, but you can make connections at San Diego, CA; Nogales, AZ; and El Paso, Eagle Pass, Laredo, or Brownsville, TX. To drive in the U.S. (see Transportation above) you need both a license and insurance; contact your local auto club or the American Automobile Association (800-336-4357) for details.

From Europe

Prices and market conditions fluctuate significantly from one week to the next. Begin looking for a flight as soon as you think you might be traveling to the U.S.

Be flexible. Direct, regularly scheduled flights often soar out of any budget traveler's range. Consider leaving from a travel hub; certain cities—such as London, Paris, Amsterdam, and Athens—offer competitively priced flights. The money you save on a flight out of Paris, for example, might exceed the cost of getting to the airport. London is the major travel hub for transatlantic budget flights. And New York City proves a consistently cheap travel target.

A **charter flight** usually proffers the most economical option. You must choose your departure and return dates when you book, and you will lose some or all of your money if you change or cancel your ticket. Charter companies also reserve the right to change the dates of your flight or the cost of the ticket, or even to cancel your flight within 48 hours of departure. Check with a travel agent about a charter company's reliability and reputation. The most common problem with charters is delays. Get your ticket in advance, and arrive at the airport well before departure time to ensure a seat. The relatively low cost of a charter flight will usually entail fewer creature comforts.

If you decide to take a non-charter flight, you'll be purchasing greater reliability and flexibility. Major airlines offer reduced fare options. The advantage of flying **standby** is flexibility, since you can come and go as you please. Standby flights, however, have become difficult to snag. Confer with a favorite travel agent about availability. **TWA, British Airways,** and **Pan Am** offer standby service from London to most major U.S. cities. Most airlines allow you to purchase an open ticket in advance that, depending on seat availability, will be confirmed the day of departure. Seat availability is known only on the day of the flight, though some airlines will issue tarot card predictions. The worst crunch leaving Europe is from mid-June to early July, while August is uniformly tight for returning flights; at no time can you count on getting a seat right away.

Always reliable, STA Travel arranges charter flights; call 800-777-0112 for information or call the London office ((071) 937 9971) for North American travel (see Information for Foreign Visitors above). You might also try contacting the CIEE, which has two charter services—**Council Charter** (800-223-7402) and **Council Travel** (212-661-1450; discounts for students and teachers only). Some reliable charter companies include: **DER Tours** (800-937-1234 or the London office at (071) 408 0111), **Tourlite** (800-272-7600), **Travac** (800-872-8800), **Unitravel** (800-325-2222), and **Canadian Holidays** (800-237-0314 or 800-426-7000). Many of these organizations have offices throughout Europe; call the toll-free number and ask for the number of your local office.

Yet another reduced fare option, the **Advanced Purchase Excursion Fare (APEX)**, provides you with confirmed reservations and allows you to arrive and depart from different cities. APEX requires a minimum stay of seven to 14 days and a maximum stay of 60 to 90 days. You must purchase your ticket 21 days in advance and pay a $50-100 penalty if you change it. For summer travel, book APEX fares early; by June you may have difficulty getting the departure date you want.

Smaller airlines often undercut major carriers by offering bargain fares on regularly scheduled flights. Competition for seats on these smaller carriers during peak season is fierce; book early. Some discount transatlantic airlines include **Icelandair** (800-223-5500; New York to Luxembourg) and **Virgin Atlantic Airways** (800-862-8621; Newark, NJ to London).

From Asia and Australia

Unfortunately, Asian and Australian travelers have few inexpensive options for air travel to the U.S. and must make do with the APEX. There is about a $100 difference between peak and off-season flights between the U.S. and Japan. U.S. carriers offer cheaper flights than **Japan Airlines** does. Seasonal fares from and to Australia are a bit more complicated; call around to see what airlines offer the best deal. A difference of a few days can save you a good deal of money. The following airlines fly between Australia and the U.S.: **Qantas, Air New Zealand, United, Continental, UTA French Airlines,** and **Canadian Pacific Airlines.** Prices are roughly equivalent among the six, although the cities they serve vary. One compensation for the exorbitant fares is that transpacific flights often allow a stop over in Honolulu, Hawaii.

Getting Around the U.S.

In the 50s, President Dwight D. Eisenhower envisioned an **interstate system,** a national network of highways designed primarily to aid the military in defending U.S. soil against foreign invasion. Eisenhower's asphalt dream has gradually been realized, although Toyotas far outnumber tanks on the federally funded roads. Even-numbered roads run east-west and odd run north-south. If the interstate has a three digit number, it is a branch of another interstate (i.e., I-285 is a branch of I-85). An even digit in the hundreds place means the branch will eventually return to the main interstate; an odd digit means it won't. North-south routes begin on the West Coast with I-5 and end with I-95 on the East Coast. I-10 stretches across the entire southern border, from Los Angeles along the coast of the Gulf of Mexico to Jacksonville, FL. The northernmost east-west route is I-94. The national speed limit of 55 miles per hour (88km per hour) has been raised to 65 mph in some areas. The main routes through most towns are **U.S. highways,** often locally referred to by non-numerical names. **State highways** are usually less heavily traveled and may lead travelers to down-home farming communities. Of course U.S. and state highway numbers don't follow any particular numbering pattern.

Airline, bus, and train companies offer discounts to foreign visitors within the U.S. **Greyhound/Trailways** offers an **International Ameripass** for foreign students and faculty members. They primarily peddle in foreign countries, but you can purchase 'em for a slightly higher price in New York, Los Angeles, San Francisco, or Miami. You part with $125 for a 7-day pass ($135 in the U.S.), $199 for a 15-day pass ($214 in the U.S.), and $279 for a 30-day pass ($299 in the U.S.). To come and get it, you need a valid passport and proof of eligibility; the pass cannot be extended. Those without school affiliation must pay $189 for seven days, $249 for 15 days, and $349 for 30 days, with optional extensions of $10 per day. Call Greyhound at 800-237-8211 for information or to request their *Visit USA Vacation Guide,* which details services for foreigners.

Amtrak's **USA Rail Pass,** similar to the Eurailpass, entitles foreigners to unlimited travel anywhere in the U.S. A 45-day pass costs $295. Purchase a Regional Rail Pass instead to travel around a particular area. Each pass serves a single region, including Eastern ($179), Western ($229), Far Western ($179), and Florida ($59). USA Rail Passes for children (ages 2-11) are half-fare. With a valid passport, purchase the USA Rail Pass outside the country or in New York, Boston, Miami, Los Angeles, or San Francisco. Check with travel agents or Amtrak representatives in Europe. Or call Amtrack in the U.S. of A. at 800-872-7245. Use your proverbial marbles when buying passes; they're a rip-off unless you make an impressive number of stops. Remember that many U.S. cities are not accessible by train.

Many major U.S. airlines offer special **Visit USA** air passes and fares to foreign travelers. Purchase passes outside the U.S., paying one price for a certain number of "flight coupons" good for one flight segment on an airline's domestic system within a given time period; cross-country trips may require two segments. Most airline passes can be purchased only by those living outside the Western Hemisphere, though a few crop up for Canadians, Mexicans, and residents of Latin America if they purchase a pass from a travel agent located at least 100 mi. from the U.S. border. Those who do buy "Visit USA" fares instantly enter a maze of restrictions and guidelines.

Work

There is some electric influence in the air and sun here which we don't experience on our side of the globe. Under this sun people can't sit still people can't ruminate over their dinners dawdle in their studies and be lazy and tranquil—they must keep moving, rush from

*one activity to another, jump out of sleep and to their
business, have lean eager faces—I want to dash into
the street now.*

—*W. M. Thackeray, 1855*

Working in the U.S. with only a B-2 visa is grounds for deportation. Before a work visa can be issued, you must present the U.S. Consulate in your country with a letter from a U.S. employer stating that you have a job offer and a permanent address. The letter must mention you by name and briefly outline the job, its salary, and its employment period. Alternatively, a U.S. employer can obtain an H visa for you (hopefully an H-2, which means that they've scoured the U.S. without finding anyone as qualified as thou art). For more specific visa information, write the Consumer Information Center, Department 455W, Pueblo, CO 81009 (719-948-3334). Send 50¢ for a brochure on visas for foreigners.

Student travel organizations like CIEE and its fun-loving affiliates often assist students in securing work visas. Some have work-exchange programs. Some hire individuals who speak English fluently to act as leaders for tour groups. The **Association for International Practical Training (AIPT)** is the bubble umbrella organization for the **International Association for the Exchange of Students for Technology Experience.** AIPT offers on-the-job training in the U.S. to foreign students in agriculture, engineering, architecture, computer science, mathematics, and the sciences. Apply by December 10 for summer placement, six months in advance for other placement. Contact AIPT at 10 Corporate Center, Suite 250, Columbia, MD 21044 (301-997-2200). The government agency in your own country that handles educational exchanges and visits to other countries can provide local contacts for suitable organizations.

If you're studying in the U.S., you can take any on-campus job once you have applied for a social security number. Check with your student employment office for job listings and requirements for work clearance. The government has recently begun a strict campaign to prohibit businesses from hiring employees without an H-visa; don't expect leniency. Before being hired, all job applicants must obtain an I-9 validation by showing a work permit or proof of U.S. citizenship.

Study

Foreigners with a burning desire to study in the U.S. must apply for either an **F-1 visa** (for exchange students) or a **J-1 visa** (for full-time students enrolled in a degree-granting program). To obtain a J-1, fill out a mystifying IAP 66 eligibility form, issued by the program in which you will enroll. Neither the F-1 nor J-1 visa specifies any expiration date; both remain valid for the "duration of stay," which includes the length of your particular program and an abortive grace period thereafter. To extend a student visa, fill out an I-538 form. Requests to extend a visa must be submitted 15 to 60 days before the initial departure date. Many foreign schools—and most U.S. colleges—have offices that give advice and information on study in the U.S.

Admission offices at almost all U.S. institutions accept applications directly from international students. If English is not your first language, you'll probably have to pass the **Test of English as a Foreign Language and Test of Spoken English (TOEFL/TSE),** administered in many countries. For more information, contact the TOEFL/TSE Application Office, P.O. Box 6155, Princeton, NJ 08541 (609-921-9000).

One excellent information source is the user-friendly **Institute of International Education (IIE),** which administers zillions of educational exchange programs in the U.S. and abroad. IIE also prints *Fields of Study at U.S. Colleges,* a handbook detailing courses of study. *Study in U.S. Colleges and Universities. A Selected Bibliography* brims with information relating to your field and to U.S. education in general. If you plan a summer visit, take a look at *Summer Learning Options USA:*

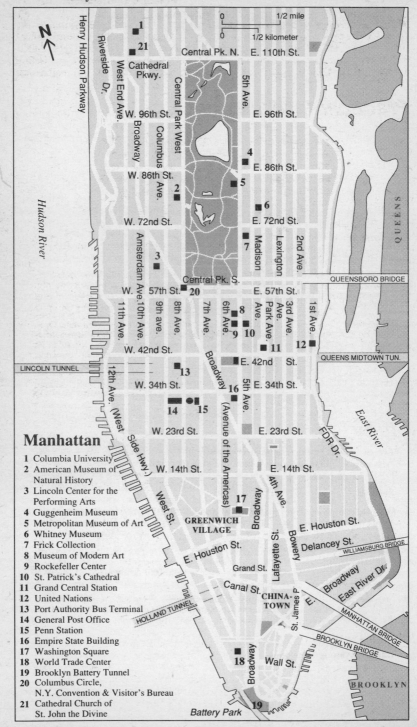

N

Henry Hudson Parkway

Riverside Dr.

West End Ave.

Hudson River

Broadway

W. 96th St.

Cathedral
Pkwy.

Central Park West

Columbus
Ave.

W. 86th St.

W. 72nd St.

Amsterdam Ave.

10th Ave.

9th ave.

8th Ave.

7th Ave.

Central Pk. S.

W. 57th St.

W. 42nd St.

Broadway

W. 34th St.

West St.

11th Ave.

12th Ave. (West Side Hwy.)

1/2 mile
0

1/2 kilometer
0

Central Pk. N.   E. 110th St.

5th Ave.

E. 96th St.

E. 86th St.

E. 72nd St.

Madison

Lexington

2nd Ave.

QUEENSBORO BRIDGE

E. 57th St.

3rd Ave.

Park Ave.

1st Ave.

E. 42nd   St.

QUEENS MIDTOWN TUN.

E. 34th St.

5th Ave. (Avenue of the Americas)

E. 23rd St.

W. 23rd St.

W. 14th St.

E. 14th St.

GREENWICH
VILLAGE

Broadway

4th Ave.

E. Houston St.

E. Houston St.

Lafayette St.

Bowery

Delancey St.

WILLIAMSBURG BRIDGE

Grand St.

Canal St.

CHINA-
TOWN

St. James P.

E.

Broadway

East River Dr.

MANHATTAN BRIDGE

BROOKLYN BRIDGE

QUEENS

East River

FDR Dr.

LINCOLN TUNNEL

HOLLAND TUNNEL

Battery Park

Broadway

Wall St.

BROOKLYN

Manhattan

1 Columbia University
2 American Museum of
   Natural History
3 Lincoln Center for the
   Performing Arts
4 Guggenheim Museum
5 Metropolitan Museum of Art
6 Whitney Museum
7 Frick Collection
8 Museum of Modern Art
9 Rockefeller Center
10 St. Patrick's Cathedral
11 Grand Central Station
12 United Nations
13 Port Authority Bus Terminal
14 General Post Office
15 Penn Station
16 Empire State Building
17 Washington Square
18 World Trade Center
19 Brooklyn Battery Tunnel
20 Columbus Circle,
   N.Y. Convention & Visitor's Bureau
21 Cathedral Church of
   St. John the Divine

1
21

2

3

4

5

6

7

20

8

9

10

11

12

13

16

14

15

17

18

19

A Guide for Foreign Nationals. English Language and Orientation Programs in the United States raves about language and cultural programs. To obtain these publications, contact IIE, 809 United Nations Plaza, New York, NY 10017 (212-883-8200). They also pop up at local Fulbright Commission offices, private counseling agencies, or the U.S. International Commission Agency offices in U.S. embassies.

Practical Information

> *The Americans are justly very proud of it, and its residents passionately attached to it . . . a young New Yorker, who had been in Europe for more than a year, was in the same sleigh with me. "There goes the old city!" said he in his enthusiasm, as we entered Broadway; "I could almost jump out and hug a lamp-post!"*
> *—Alexander Mackay, The Western World, 1849*

Emergency: Call 911.

Police: 212-374-5000. Use this for inquiries that are not urgent. 24 hr.

Visitor Information: New York Convention and Visitors Bureau, 2 Columbus Circle (397-8222), 59th and Broadway. Subway: A, D, 1. Friendly multilingual staff will help you with directions, hotel listings, entertainment ideas, safety tips, and "insiders'" descriptions of New York's neighborhoods. Request 3 live-saving maps: *I Love New York Travel Guide* (a street map), the *MTA Manhattan Bus Map,* and the *MTA New York City Subway Map.* Try to show up in person; the phone lines tend to be busy, the maps and brochures worthwhile. Open Mon.-Fri. 9am-6pm, Sat.-Sun. and holidays 10am-6pm. Branch office at **Times Square Information Center,** 158 W. 42nd St., between Broadway and Seventh Ave. Subway: A, E, N, R, D, or F. Open Wed.-Fri. 9am-6pm, Sat.-Sun. 10am-6pm. Similar information available, but no telephone service. For Queens, contact **The Office of the Queens Borough President,** 120-155 Queens Blvd., Kew Gardens (520-3823), or the **Queens Chamber of Commerce,** 29-15 Queens Plaza North, Long Island City (784-7700). **Entertainment Information: Ticketron,** 399-4444. **Free Daily Events in the City,** 360-1333, 24 hours. **Jazz line,** 718-465-7500. **NYC Onstage,** 587-1111; updates on theatre, dance, music, children's entertainment, and other events. **Tkts.** 354-5800; at Broadway and 47th St., and at 2 World Trade Center. Half-price tickets for Broadway and Off-Broadway shows sold the day of the performance only.

Travelers Aid Society: at 158-160 W. 42nd St. (944-0013) between Broadway and Seventh Ave.; and at JFK International Airport (718-656-4870), in the International Arrivals Bldg. Subway to 42nd St. branch: A, E, N, R, D or F. 42nd St. branch specializes in crisis intervention services for stranded travelers or crime victims. JFK office offers general counseling and referral to travelers, as well as emergency assistance. 42nd St. branch open Mon.-Fri. 9am-5pm; JFK branch open Mon.-Fri. 10am-7pm.

Consulates: Australian, 636 Fifth Ave. (245-4000). **British,** 845 Third Ave. (752-8400). **Canadian,** 1251 Sixth Ave. (768-2400). **Danish,** 825 Third Ave. (223-4545). **Dutch,** 1 Rockefeller Plaza (246-1429).**Egyptian,** 1110 Second Ave. (759-7120). **Finnish,** 380 Madison Ave. (573-6007). **French,** 934 Fifth Ave. (983-5660). **German,** 460 Park Ave. (308-8700). **Indian,** 3 E. 64th St. (879-8700). **Israeli,** 800 Second Ave. (351-5200). **Italian,** 320 Park Ave. (737-9100). **Japanese,** 299 Park Ave. (371-8222). **Norwegian,** 825 Third Ave. (421-7333). **South African,** 326 E. 48th St. (371-7997). **Spanish,** 150 E. 58th St. (355-4090). **Swedish,** 885 Second Ave. (751-5900). **Swiss,** 665 Fifth Ave. (758-2560).

American Express: 150 E. 42nd St. (687-3700), between Lexington and Third Ave. Protean travel agency providing traveler's checks, financial services, and other assistance. Open Mon.-Fri. 9am-5pm. Call for other locations.

Airports: see Getting There below.

Trains: see Getting There below.

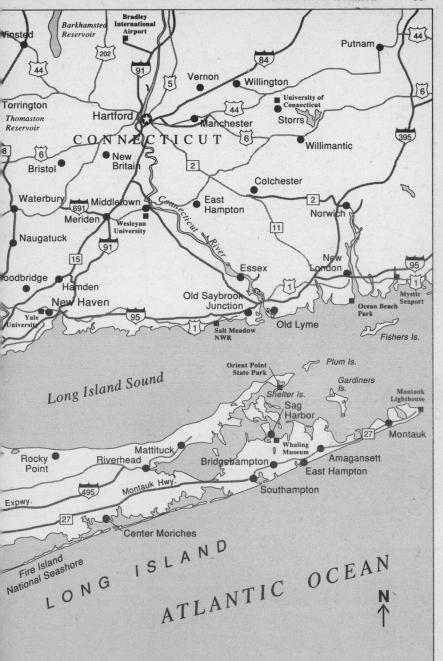

New York Metropolitan Area

Buses: see Getting There below.

Public Transit: see Getting Around below.

Taxis: Radio-dispatched taxis, Utog, 718-361-7270; and **Skyline,** 718-482-8686. These companies do not use meters; they charge a flat rate. To JFK, $35 with either company. **Taxi Commission,** 869-4513; general complaints and lost and found. Yellow cabs can be hailed on the street. See Getting Around below for more information.

Car Rental: All agencies have minimum age requirements and require deposits. Call in advance to reserve, especially near the weekend. **Discount Rent-a-Car,** 240 E. 92nd St. (410-2211), between Second and Third Ave.; offices also in Jackson Heights, Queens. Mon.-Thurs. $47 per day, 100 free miles, 20¢ each additional mile. Fri.-Sun. $162, 500 free miles, 20¢ each additional mile. Open Mon.-Fri. 8am-7pm, Sat. 9am-2pm. Must be 21 with major credit card. **Rent-a-Wreck:** in Manhattan, 202 W. 77th St. (721-0080 or 800-221-8282). Mon.-Fri. $50 per day, 100 free miles, 25¢ each additional mile. Sat.-Sun. two-day minimum of $120, 200 free miles, 25¢ each additional mile. Open Mon.-Fri. 7:30am-6:30pm, Sat. 8:30am-5:30pm, Sun. 8:30am-6:30pm. Must be 21 with major credit card. In Queens (718-784-3302), Mon.-Fri. $25 per day, 30 free miles, 22¢ each additional mile; $170 per week, 200 free miles, 22¢ each additional mile; for 14 days, $300; 400 free miles, 22¢ each additional mile. Open Mon.-Fri. 7:30am-5pm, Sat. 8am-noon. In Brooklyn (718-998-9100), $40 per day, 100 free miles, 12¢ each additional mile; $205 per week, 500 free miles, 12¢ each additional mile. Open Mon.-Fri. 8am-5pm, Sat.-Sun. 8am-noon. **Goldie's Leasing Corp.,** 47-11 11th St., Long Island City, Queens (718-392-5435 or 718-392-5339), across the Queensborough Bridge, south of Astoria. Mon.-Thurs. $37 per day, Fri.-Sun. $45 per day, 100 free miles, 20¢ each additional mile. Weekly $226, 700 free miles, 20¢ per additional mile. Open Mon.-Fri. 8am-6pm, Sat. 9am-5pm. Sunday drop-off possible. Must be 21 with a major credit card.

Auto Transport Companies: New York is the major departure point for auto transport agencies. Applications take about a week to process. Most agencies require more than one ID; some ask for references. **Dependable Car Services,** 1501 Broadway (840-6262). Must be 19; $50-150 deposit (depending on the model of car) returned upon delivery. **Transporters, Inc.,** 450 Seventh Ave., at 34th St. (594-2690). Must be 21 and deposit $150-300. **Auto Driveaway,** 264 W. 35th St. (967-2344), offers similar services and prices.

Bicycle Rentals: Whatever the time of day, city streets are always busy. But on weekends from May-Oct. and on weekdays from 10am-3pm, parts of Central Park close to cars, allowing bicycles to rule its roads. **Metro Bicycle,** 332 E. 14th St. (228-4344), between First and Second Ave., rents 3-speeds for $4 per hr., $20 per day, and 10-speeds for $6.50 per hr., $25 per day. Open daily 9:30am-6:30pm. $20 deposit or credit card required, as well as ID. Other locations throughout the city. **The Boathouse,** in Central Park, at the northeast corner of the Lake. Enter at 72nd St. and Fifth Ave. (861-4137). 3-speeds $6 per hr., $24 per day; 10-speeds $8 per hr., $32 per day. Open Mon.-Fri. 10am-7pm, Sat.-Sun. 9am-7pm. Last rental 6pm. I.D. and $20 deposit required.

New York Public Library: 11 W. 40th St. (930-0830), entrance at Fifth Ave. at 42nd St. Non-lending research library. Open Mon.-Wed. 10am-8:45pm, Thurs.-Sat. 10am-5:45pm. Over 80 branch locations. Two of the larger branches are the **Mid-Manhattan,** 455 Fifth Ave. at 40th St. (340-0934) and the **Donnell,** 20 W. 53rd St. (621-0618).

Help Lines: Crime Victim's Hotline, 577-7777; 24-hour counseling and referrals. **Sex Crimes Report Line,** New York Police Department, 267-7273; 24-hour help, counseling, and referrals.

Medical Care: Walk-in Clinic, 57 E. 34th St. (683-1010), between Park and Madison Ave. Open Mon.-Fri. 8am-6pm, Sat. 10am-2pm. Affiliated with Beth Israel Hospital. **24-hr. Pharmacy: Kaufman's Pharmacy,** 557 Lexington Ave. (755-2266), at 50th St. **24-hr. Emergency Doctor,** 718-745-5900. **The Eastern's Women's Center,** 40 E. 30th St. (686-6066), between Park and Madison. Gynecological exams and surgical procedures for women, by appointment only. **AIDS Information,** 807-6655, 10:30am-9pm.

Post Office: Central branch 380 W. 33rd St., (967-8585), at Eighth Ave. across from Madison Square Garden. To pick up general delivery mail, use the entrance at 390 Ninth Ave. Open Mon.-Sat. 10am-1pm. For information call 330-3099. **ZIP code:** 10001. 59 branches in Manhattan alone—to find the post office nearest you, call the main information number.

Area Code: 212 (Manhattan and the Bronx); **718** (Brooklyn, Queens, and Staten Island). No extra charge for calls between these area codes, but dial "1" first. Unless otherwise specified, all telephone numbers in this book have a 212 area code.

Getting Here

By Plane

Not only will you have to choose a carrier, but an airport as well. Three airports service the New York Metropolitan Region. The largest, John F. Kennedy Airport (JFK) (718-656-4520), 12 miles from Midtown in southern Queens, handles most international flights. JFK boasts the greatest number of flights, but intra-airport travel is time-consuming. LaGuardia Airport (718-656-4520), 6 miles from mid-town in northwestern Queens, is the smallest, offering domestic flights and air shut-tles (see below). Newark International Airport, 12 miles from Midtown in Newark, NJ, offers both domestic and international flights at budget fares not available at the other airports.

Many airlines offer budget flights, but the cut-rate market fluctuates under the strain of constant price wars. In general, it is cheapest to fly between Monday after-noon and Thursday morning, and stay over one Saturday night. Booking at least 14 days in advance often qualifies you for a cheaper seat, subject to availability. Standby travel makes a good alternative if all the budget flights are booked. Scan the *New York Times,* especially the Sunday "Travel" section, for the latest deals, or consult a travel agent with complete computer access to all airlines. Travel agents won't always direct you to the dirt-cheap flights because commissions are low; you may have to call the airlines yourself.

The excellent *Airport Flight Guide,* put out by the Port Authority, has compre-hensive flight schedules, airport maps, and data on airport parking and other serv-ices. It is available free by mail (Airport Flight Guide, One World Trade Center 65N, New York 10048).

Continental Airlines: 800-525-0280. Reduced fares with advance purchase.

Pan Am: 800-221-1111. Lots of international flights. The **Pan Am Air Shuttle** flies between New York and Boston or Washington every hour on the ½ hour. Mon.-Fri. 6:30am-9:30pm, Sat. 7:30am-8:30pm, Sun. 8:30am-8:30pm. The fare is $65 for those 24 and under (fare avail-able Mon.-Fri. 10:30am-2:30pm, Sat. all day, and Sun. until 6:30pm). No reservations neces-sary; just show up ½ hr. prior to departure at the elusive Marine Air Terminal at LaGuardia. Call first; shuttles are often cancelled due to inclement weather.

Trump Shuttle: 800-247-8786. Similar to the Pan Am Air Shuttle, but leaves every hour on the hour daily, 7am-10pm. For those 24 and under, $59 on weekdays between 10am-2pm and 7-10pm, $49 all day Sat., and $49 Sun. 9am-3pm, then $59 until the end of the day. Leaves from LaGuardia; no reservations necessary.

U.S. Air: 800-428-4322. Budget flights all over New York State and the Northeast. Also runs **U.S. Air Express,** a collection of independent operators who fly small planes connecting with U.S. Air flights. Cheap fares and special deals to many U.S. port cities.

To and From the Airports

Travel between each of the airports and New York City without a car of your own becomes simpler as cost increases; you pay in time or money. The cheapest way in dollars is public transportation. This option usually involves changing mid-route from a bus to a subway or train, but service is frequent. Moving up the price scale, private bus companies will charge slightly more, but will take you directly from the airport to one of three destinations: Grand Central Station (42nd St. and Park Ave.), the Port Authority Bus Terminal (41st St. and Eighth Ave.) or the World Trade Center (1 West St.). Private companies run frequently and according to a set schedule (see below). If you want to set your own destination and schedule, however, and if you're willing to pay, you can take one of New York's infamous yellow cabs. From JFK or Newark, cabs cost at least $30; from LaGuardia at least $17. The trip costs less in light traffic. **Utog** (718-361-7270) and **Skyline** (718-482-8686) are taxi companies that charge a flat $35 for travel to JFK. For the most up-to-date information on reaching the airports, call AirRide, the Port Authority's airport travel hotline, at 800-247-7433. Some services peter out or vanish entirely between midnight and 6am. Finally, if you make lodging reservations ahead of time,

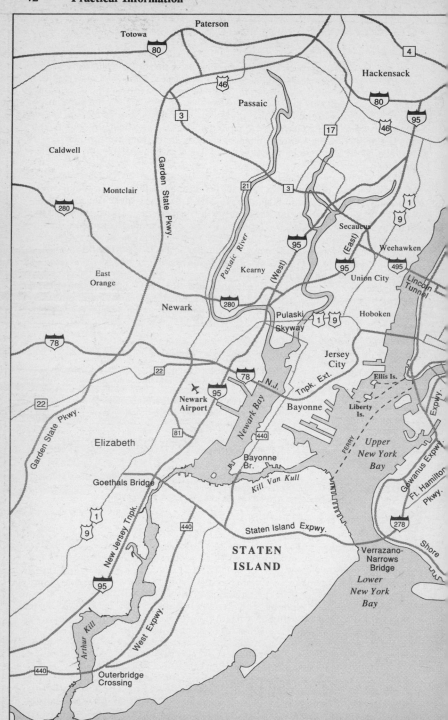

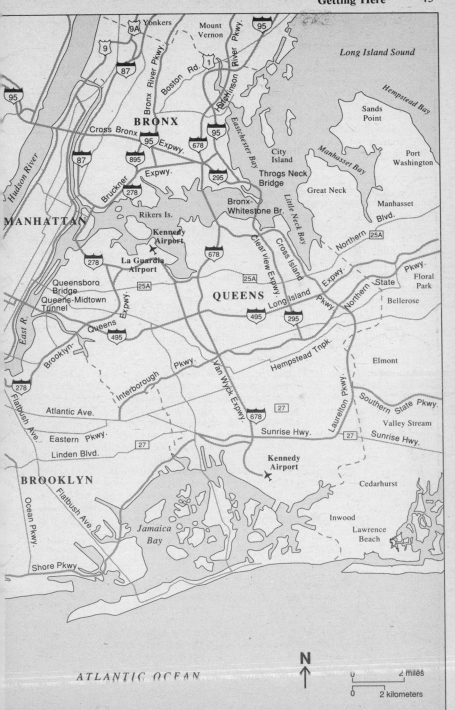

Long Island Sound

Yonkers

Mount Vernon

9A

9

87

95

BRONX

Cross Bronx Expwy.

95

678

895

Bruckner Expwy.

87

278

Rikers Is.

MANHATTAN

Kennedy Airport

278

La Guardia Airport

Queensboro Bridge
Queens-Midtown Tunnel

Queens Expwy.

East R.

Brooklyn-

278

Flatbush Ave.

Atlantic Ave.

Eastern Pkwy.

Linden Blvd.

BROOKLYN

Ocean Pkwy.

Flatbush Ave.

Shore Pkwy

Boston Rd.

1

Hudson River

Bronx River Pkwy.

Hutchinson River Pkwy.

Eastchester Bay

95

295

City Island

Throgs Neck Bridge

Bronx-Whitestone Br.

Little Neck Bay

Clearview Expwy.

Cross Island

678

QUEENS

25A

25A

Interborough Pkwy.

Van Wyck Expwy.

495

495

Long Island

Northern

Hempstead Tnpk.

678

27

27

Sunrise Hwy.

Kennedy Airport

Jamaica Bay

Sands Point

Hempstead Bay

Manhasset Bay

Great Neck

Manhasset Blvd.

Port Washington

Northern State Pkwy.

Floral Park

Bellerose

Expwy.

495

295

Elmont

Laurelton Pkwy.

Southern State Pkwy.

Valley Stream

27

Sunrise Hwy.

Cedarhurst

Inwood

Lawrence Beach

N

ATLANTIC OCEAN

0   2 miles

0   2 kilometers

be sure to ask about limousine services—some Ys and hostels offer door-to-door transportation from the airports for reasonable fares. Rush hour traffic (7:30-9:30am and 4:30-7pm) is always heavy; at other times conditions vary. Get directions from your rental agent.

Public transportation can easily whisk you to midtown Manhattan. You can catch a **JFK Express Shuttle Bus** (718-330-1234) from any airport terminal to the **Howard Beach-JFK subway station,** where you can take the **IND** to the city: the IND stops at 57th St. and Ave. of the Americas; 50th St. and Rockefeller Center; 42nd St. and Ave. of the Americas; 34th St. and Ave. of the Americas; Washington Square; the World Trade Center; Broadway and Nassau St.; and Borough Hall in Brooklyn. Allow at least one hour travel time. The service costs $6.50. Or you can take one of the city buses (the Q10, Q9, or Q3; fare $1.15) from the airport into Queens. The Q10 connects with the E, F, R, and A subway lines and Q3 and Q9 connect with the F and R lines, all of which will take you into Manhattan. Ask the bus driver where to get off, and make sure you know which subway line you want. Allow 90 min. travel time. The total cost for this trip will be only $2.30, but it also requires some degree of caution. Some of the areas serviced by these buses are unsafe. Those willing to pay more can take the **Carey Bus Service** (718-632-0500), a private line that runs between JFK and Grand Central Station and the Port Authority Terminal. Buses leave every 30 minutes from Kennedy during the day (1-1¼ hr., fare $9.50).

There are two ways to get into Manhattan from LaGuardia. If you have extra time and light luggage, take the MTA "Q 33" bus ($1.15 exact change or token) to the Eighth Ave. subway in Queens, and from there, take the E or F train into Manhattan ($1.15 token). You can catch the Q 33 from the lower level of the terminal. Allow at least 90 minutes travel time. The same word of caution applies here as with the Q buses above. The second option, the Carey Bus Service, makes four stops in the Midtown area, the first of which is Grand Central Station. (Every 20 min., 55 min., $7.50.)

The commute from Newark Airport, in New Jersey, takes about as long as from JFK or LaGuardia. **New Jersey Transit Authority (NJTA)** (201-460-8444) runs a fast, efficient bus (NJTA #300) between the airport and Port Authority every 15 minutes during the day ($7). For the same fare, the **Olympia Trails Coach** (212-964-6233) travels between either Grand Central or the World Trade Center and the airport. (6am-1am, every 20 min., 45 min.-1 hr. depending on traffic, $7.) **NJTA Bus #107** will take you to Midtown for $2.60 (exact change required), but don't try it unless you have little luggage and lots of time. The NJTA also runs an **Air Link bus** ($4) between the airport and Newark's Penn Station (*not* Manhattan's), and from there **PATH** trains ($1) run into Manhattan, stopping at the World Trade Center, Christopher St., Sixth Ave., 9th St., 14th St., 23rd St. and 33rd St. For PATH information 212-732-8920. From Manhattan, **Giraldo Limousine Service** (757-6840) will pick you up anywhere between 14th and 95th St. and take you to the airport of your choice for $11-16.

By Bus or Train

New York, that unnatural city where eveyone is an
exile, none more so than the American.
        —Charlotte Perkins Gilman

Getting in and out of New York can be done less expensively and more scenically by bus or train than by plane. **Port Authority,** 41st St. and Eighth Ave. (564-8484), is a tremendous modern facility with labyrinthine bus terminals. Port Authority has good information and security services, but is located in an extremely unsafe neighborhood. Be wary of pickpockets, and call a cab at night. Its bathrooms are dangerous at all times. The station is the hub of the Northeast bus network, and **Greyhound/Trailways** (971-6363 or 730-7460) is the titan here. On some routes, a 10% discount is offered to students with ID. Purchase your tickets at least 14 days in advance for substantially reduced fares. To: Boston ($29), Philadelphia ($17), Washington, DC ($30), and Montreal ($65).

Grand Central Station, 42nd St. and Park Ave., the grandiose transportation colossus of the metropolis, has more than 550 trains running daily on its two levels of tracks. It handles **Metro-North** (532-4900) commuter lines to Connecticut and New York suburbs, and **Amtrak** (800-872-7245 or 582-6875) lines to upstate New York and Canada. From the smaller **Penn Station**, 33rd St. and Eighth Ave., Amtrak serves most major cities in the U.S., especially those in the Northeast (to Washington, DC $59, Boston $45). Penn Station also handles the **Long Island Railroad (LIRR)** (718-454-5477, see Long Island) and **PATH** service to New Jersey (432-1272).

By Car

During rush hour, millions of commuters jam the roads; amidst the exhaust, see the American Dream at work . . . or trying to get there. Any time of day, be prepared to be terrorized by reckless cab drivers and determined jaywalkers. On the way into the city, you and your windshield may fall prey to opportunistic window "cleaners" who hang out at traffic lights; some people pay them a quarter to go away, others opt for a quick escape. Or who knows, you may actually wish to pay to have your windshield slimed.

The four major highways are: on the East Side, the **FDR Drive** (a.k.a. the Harlem River Drive and the East Side Highway) and the **Major Deegan;** on the West Side, the **Henry Hudson Parkway** (a.k.a. the West Side Highway, soon to be WestWay). From outside the city, I-95 leads to the Major Deegan, the FDR Drive, and the Henry Hudson. Go south on any of these roads, but be prepared for an amazing number of signs, intersecting roads and other cars separating you from your destination.

Once you are in Manhattan, traffic continues to be a problem, especially between 57th and 34th St. The even greater hassle of parking joins in to plague the weary. Would-be parallel parkers can rise to this challenge in one of three ways. **Parking lots** are the easiest but the most expensive. In midtown, where lots are the only option, expect to pay at least $25 per day and up to $15 for two hours. The cheapest parking lots are downtown—try the far west end of Houston St.—but make sure you feel comfortable with the area and the lot. Is it populated? Is the lot guarded? Is it lit? Which *Honeymooners* episode is being shown tonight? Municipal parking at 53rd St. and Eighth Ave. costs $1 per half-hour.

The second alternative is short-term parking. On the streets, **parking meters** cost 25¢ per 15 minutes, with a limit of one or two hours. Competition is ruthless for the third option, **free parking** at spots on the crosstown streets in residential areas, but competition is ruthless. Read the signs carefully; a space is usually legal only certain days of the week. The city has never been squeamish about towing, and recovering your car once it's towed will cost $100 or more. Break-ins and car theft are definite possibilities, particularly if you have a flashy radio. The wailing of a car alarm, a noise as familiar and ritualistic to city residents as the crowing of a rooster is to rural Americans, attracts little if any attention.

Hitchhiking is illegal in New York State and the laws tend to be strictly enforced within New York City. Offenders will usually be asked to move on. It's best to take the train or bus out of the metropolitan area; hitching in and around New York City is dangerous. If someone offers you a free ride, don't accept it.

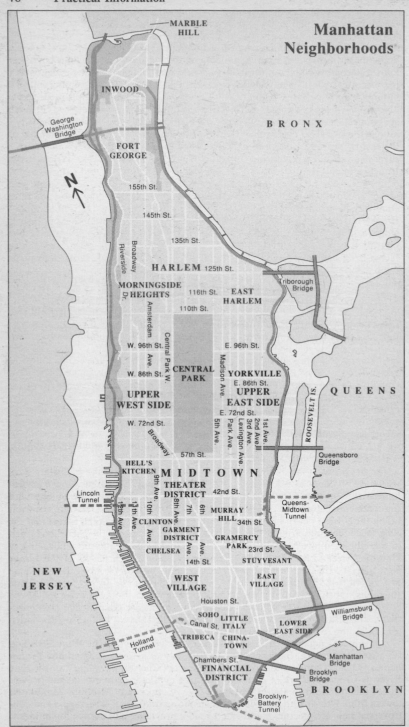

Manhattan Neighborhoods

MARBLE HILL

INWOOD

George Washington Bridge

FORT GEORGE

B R O N X

155th St.

145th St.

135th St.

Broadway
Riverside

HARLEM   125th St.

MORNINGSIDE HEIGHTS
Amsterdam Dr.

116th St.
110th St.

EAST HARLEM

Triborough Bridge

W. 96th St.
Central Park W.
E. 96th St.

CENTRAL PARK
Madison Ave.

YORKVILLE
E. 86th St.
UPPER EAST SIDE

W. 86th St.

UPPER WEST SIDE

E. 72nd St.

W. 72nd St.
5th Ave.
Park Ave.
Lexington Ave.
3rd Ave.
2nd Ave.
1st Ave.

ROOSEVELT IS.

Q U E E N S

Broadway

57th St.

HELL'S KITCHEN

MIDTOWN

THEATER DISTRICT

Queensboro Bridge

Lincoln Tunnel

9th Ave.
10th Ave.
11th Ave.
12th Ave.

42nd St.

8th Ave.
7th
6th

CLINTON

MURRAY HILL

Queens-Midtown Tunnel

GARMENT DISTRICT
34th St.

9th Ave.
8th Ave.

GRAMERCY PARK

CHELSEA
23rd St.

N E W
J E R S E Y

14th St.
STUYVESANT

WEST VILLAGE

EAST VILLAGE

Houston St.

SOHO   LITTLE ITALY
Canal St.

LOWER EAST SIDE

Williamsburg Bridge

Holland Tunnel

TRIBECA   CHINA-TOWN

Chambers St.
FINANCIAL DISTRICT

Manhattan Bridge

Brooklyn Bridge

Brooklyn-Battery Tunnel

B R O O K L Y N

Orientation

New York City is composed of five boroughs: Brooklyn, the Bronx, Queens, Staten Island, and Manhattan. But plenty of tourists and Manhattanites have been known to confuse Manhattan with New York. This Manhattancentric chauvinism has historical roots. The island's original inhabitants, the Algonquin, called it "Man-a-hat-ta" or "Heavenly Land." The British were the first to call the island "New York," and it was only in 1898 that the other four boroughs joined the city's government. No matter how often you hear Manhattan referred to as "The City," however, each of the other boroughs has a right to share in the name. Flanked on the east by the East River and on the west by the Hudson River, Manhattan is a sliver of an island, severed from the rest of New York by the narrow Harlem River. It measures only 13 mi. long and 2½ mi. wide. Fatter Queens and Brooklyn look onto their svelte neighbor from the other side of the East River, and pudgy, self-reliant Staten Island averts its eyes in the south. **Queens,** the city's largest and most ethnically diverse borough, is dotted with light industry, airports, and stadiums. **Brooklyn,** the city's most populous borough (with 2.24 million residents), is even older than Manhattan. Founded by the Dutch in 1600, the borough today cradles several charming residential neighborhoods along with a dangerous slum. **Staten Island** has remained a staunchly residential borough, similar to the suburban bed-room communities of outer Long Island. North of Manhattan nests the **Bronx,** the only borough connected by land to the rest of the U.S. Originally a Dutch estate owned by Jonas Bronck, an excursion to his family's farm was referred to as a visit to "the Broncks'." Today's Bronx encompasses both the lovely suburb of Riverdale and New York's most devastated area, the South Bronx.

Districts of Manhattan

> New York is a sucked orange.
> —Ralph Waldo Emerson

Glimpsed from the window of an approaching plane, New York City can seem a monolithic jungle of urbania. But up close, New York breaks down into manage-able neighborhoods, each with a history and personality of its own. As a result of city zoning ordinances, quirks of history, and random forces of urban evolution, boundaries between these neighborhoods can often be abrupt.

The city began at the southern tip of Manhattan, in the area around Battery Park where the first Dutch settlers made their homes. The nearby harbor, now a jazzed-up tourist attraction as the **South Street Seaport,** provided the growing city with the commercial opportunities that helped it succeed. Historic Manhattan, however, lies in the shadows of the imposing financial buildings around **Wall Street** and the civic office buildings around **City Hall.** A little farther north, neighborhoods rich in the ethnic culture brought by late 19th-century immigrants rub elbows below Houston Street—**Little Italy, Chinatown,** and the southern blocks of the **Lower East Side.** To the west lies the newly fashionable **TriBeCa** (Triangle Below Canal St.). **SoHo** (for "South of Houston"), a former warehouse district west of Little Italy, has transformed into a pocket of gleaming art studios and galleries. Above SoHo huddles **Greenwich Village,** once a center of intense political and artistic ac-tivity, still a literal village of lower buildings, jumbled streets, and neon glitz curled up nearby the towering financial district.

A few blocks north of Greenwich Village, stretching across the West teens and twenties, lies **Chelsea,** the late artist Andy Warhol's favorite hangout and former home of Dylan Thomas and Arthur Miller. East of Chelsea, presiding over the East River, is **Gramercy Park,** a pastoral collection of Victorian mansions and brown-stones immortalized in Edith Wharton's *Age of Innocence.* **Midtown Manhattan** towers from 34th to 59th St., where awe-inspiring traditional skyscrapers and con-troversial new architecture stand side by side, providing office space for millions.

Here department stores outfit New York, and the nearby **Theatre District** entertains the world—or tries to.

North of Midtown, **Central Park** slices Manhattan into East and West. On the **Upper West Side,** the gracious museums and residences of Central Park West neighbor the chic boutiques and sidewalk cafés of Columbus Ave. On the **Upper East Side,** the galleries and museums scattered among the elegant apartments of Fifth and Park Ave. create an even more rarefied atmosphere.

Above 97th St., the Upper East Side's opulence ends with a whimper where commuter trains emerge from the tunnel and the *barrio* begins. Above 110th St. on the Upper West Side sits majestic **Columbia University** (founded as King's College in 1754), an urban member of the Ivy League. The communities of **Harlem, East Harlem,** and **Morningside Heights** produced the Harlem Renaissance of black artists and writers in the 1920s and the revolutionary Black Power movement of the 1960s. Although torn by crime, **Washington Heights,** just north of St. Nicholas Park, is nevertheless somewhat safer and more attractive than much of Harlem, and is home to Fort Tryon Park, the Met's Medieval Cloisters, and a quiet community of Old World immigrants. Still farther north, the island ends in a rural patch of wooded land where caves once inhabited by the Algonquin remain.

Manhattan's Street Plan

> *The city of right angles and tough, damaged people.*
> —Pete Hamill

Most of Manhattan's street plan was the result of an organized expansion scheme adopted in 1811, and the major part of the city grew in straight lines and at right angles. Above 14th St., the streets form a grid that a novice can quickly master. In the older areas of Lower Manhattan, though, the streets are named rather than numbered. Here, the orderly grid of the northern section dissolves into a charming but confusing tangle of old, narrow streets. Bring a map: even long-time neighborhood residents may have trouble directing you to an address.

Above Washington Square, avenues run north-south and streets run east-west. Avenue numbers increase from east to west, and street numbers increase from south to north. Traffic flows east on most even-numbered streets and west on most odd-numbered ones. And two way traffic flows on the wider streets—Canal, Houston, 14th, 23rd, 34th, 42nd, 57th, 72nd, 79th, 86th, 96th, 110th, 116th, 125th, 145th, and 155th. Four transverses cross Central Park: 65/66th St., 79/81th St., 85/86th and 96/97th St. Most avenues are one-way. Tenth, Amsterdam, Hudson, Eighth, Avenue of the Americas, Madison, Fourth, Third, and First Avenues are northbound. Ninth, Columbus, Broadway below 59th Street, Seventh, Fifth, Lexington, and Second Avenues are southbound. Some avenues allow two-way traffic: York, Park, Central Park West, Broadway above 59th Street, West End, and Riverside Drive.

New York's east/west division refers to an address's location in relation to the two borders of Central Park—**Fifth Avenue** along the east side and **Central Park West** along the west. Below 59th St. where the park ends, the West Side begins at Fifth Ave. Looking for an adjective to describe where you are relative to something else? Uptown is anywhere north of you, downtown is south, and crosstown means to the east or the west. Want to use a noun? Uptown (above 59th St.) is the area north of Midtown. Downtown (below 34th St.) is the area south of Midtown.

Now for the discrepancies in the system. You may still hear the **Avenue of the Americas** referred to by its original name, **Sixth Avenue.** Also, Lexington, Park, and Madison Ave. lie *between* Third and Fifth Ave. On the Lower East Side, there are several avenues east of First Avenue that are lettered rather than numbered: Avenues A, B, C, and D. Finally, above 59th St. on the West Side, Eighth Avenue becomes Central Park West, Ninth Avenue becomes Columbus Avenue, Tenth Avenue becomes Amsterdam Avenue, and Eleventh Avenue becomes West End Avenue. **Broadway,** which follows an old Algonquin trail, ignores the rectangular pattern and cuts diagonally across the island, veering west of Fifth Ave. above 23rd St. and east of Fifth Ave. below 23rd St.

Tracking down an address in Manhattan is easy. When given the street number of an address (e.g. #250 E. 52nd St.), find the avenue closest to the address by thinking of Fifth Ave. as point zero on the given street. Address numbers increase as you move east or west of Fifth Ave., in stages of 100. On the East Side, address numbers are 1 at Fifth Ave., 100 at Park Ave., 200 at Third Ave., 300 at Second Ave., 400 at First Ave., 500 at York Ave. (uptown) or Avenue A (in the Village). On the West Side, address numbers are 1 at Fifth Ave., 100 at the Avenue of the Americas (Sixth Ave.), 200 at Seventh Ave., 300 at Eighth Ave., 400 at Ninth Ave., 500 at Tenth Ave., and 600 at Eleventh Ave. In general, numbers increase from south to north along the avenues, but you should always ask for a cross street when you are getting an avenue address. Or you can figure it out for yourself using the following simple formula: Take the address number, cancel its last digit, divide by two, and add or subtract the key number from the following list:

First Avenue: Add 3.

Second Avenue: Add 3.

Third Avenue: Add 10.

Fourth Avenue: Add 8.

Fifth Avenue: Up to 200, add 13; 200-400, add 16; 400-600, add 18; 600-775, add 20; 775-1286, eliminate the last digit, do not divide by two, subtract 18; 1286-1500, add 45; above 2000, add 24.

Sixth Avenue: Subtract 12.

Seventh Avenue: Below 110th St., add 12; above 110th St., add 20.

Eighth Avenue: Add 10.

Ninth Avenue: Add 13.

Tenth Avenue: Add 14.

Amsterdam Avenue: Add 60.

Broadway: Subtract 30.

Central Park West: Divide number by 10 and add 60.

Columbus Avenue: Add 60.

Lexington Avenue: Add 22.

Madison Avenue: Add 26.

Park Avenue: Add 35.

West End Avenue: Add 60.

Riverside Drive: Divide number by 10 and add 72.

Getting Around

> I have two faults to find with [New York]. In the first
> place, there is nothing to see; and in the second place,
> there is no mode of getting about to see anything.
> —Anthony Trollope, North America, 1862.

To be equipped for the New York City navigation experience, you will need more than an understanding of the logic underlying its streets. You will need to know how to use the public transportation system. Get a free subway map from station

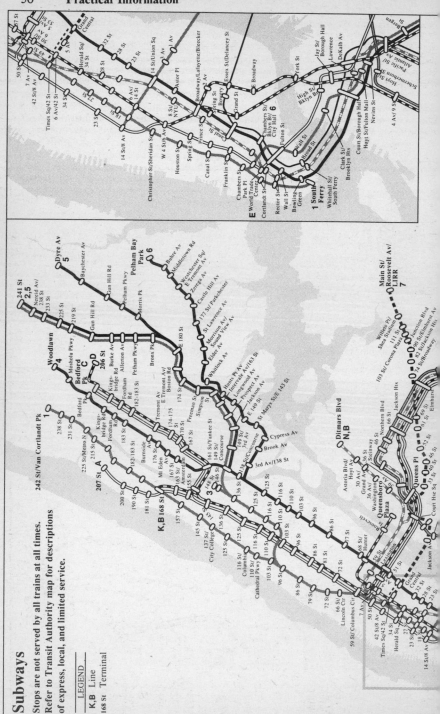

Subways

Stops are not served by all trains at all times.
Refer to Transit Authority map for descriptions
of express, local, and limited service.

LEGEND

K,B Line

168 St Terminal

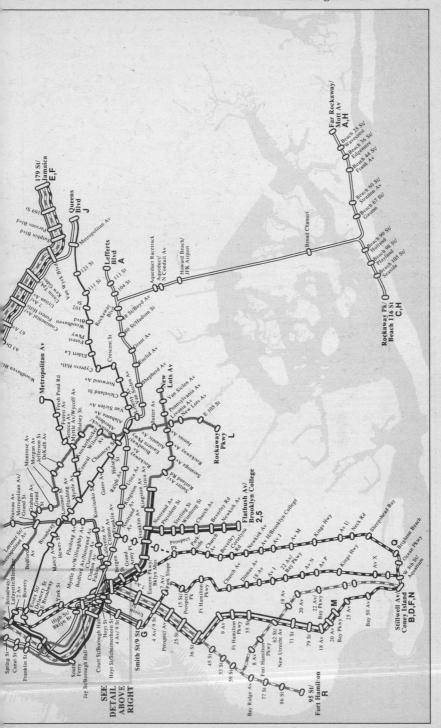

token booths or the visitors bureau, which also has a free street map (see Practical Information above). Ask at the visitors bureau first, since token booth operators are usually less cooperative. For a more detailed program of interborough travel, find a Manhattan Yellow Pages, which contains detailed subway, PATH, and bus maps. For other bus or subway maps, send a self-addressed, stamped envelope about a month before you need the information to **NYC Transit Authority,** 370 Jay St. Brooklyn 11201. In the city, round-the-clock staff at the **Transit Authority Information Bureau** (718-330-1234) dispense subway and bus information.

Subways and Buses

> *New York has total depth in every area.*
> —*John Lindsay, quoted in Vogue*

The fare for Metropolitan Transit Authority (MTA) subways and buses is a hefty $1.15, so groups of four or more may find cabs cheaper for short rides. More often than not, however, the MTA provides the best way to get around New York City. Most buses are equipped with access ramps, but steep stairs make subway transit more difficult for the disabled. Call the Transit Authority Information Bureau (718-330-1234) for specific information on public transportation. Queens is served in addition by five private bus lines: **Metropolitan Suburban Bus Authority** (222-1000), **Green Bus Lines** (995-4700), **Jamaica Buses, Inc.** (526-0800), **Queens Surface Corp.** (445-3100), **Triboro Coach Corp.** (335-1000), and **Bus Systems, Inc.** (297-1700).

The **subway** is by far the quickest means of transportation in Manhattan, but mainly useful for traveling north-south rather than east-west—there are only two crosstown shuttle trains (42nd and 14th St.). Crosstown buses are much more common (see below). In upper Manhattan and in Queens, Brooklyn, and the Bronx, the subways become "El" trains (for "elevated") and ride above street level to the far reaches of the city.

The New York subway system has 461 stations with 25 free transfer points where subway lines intersect. It can be extremely confusing, even with subway route map in hand. Token clerks can tell you how to get anywhere, but can be impatient and uncooperative during rush hour. Don't lose your cool, but if you're not gaining any ground turn to a transit police officer for advice. "Express" trains stop only at pre-selected busy stations; "locals" stop everywhere. Be sure to check the letter or number and the destination of each train, since trains with different destinations often use the same track. When in doubt, ask a friendly passenger or the conductor, who usually sits near the middle of the train. Even once you're on the train, pay attention to the often garbled announcements—trains occasionally change mid-route from local to express.

The stations are slowly being rehabilitated, but some are still dirty and filled with the stench of stale urine and vintage filth. A major subway clean-up campaign, including new spray paint-resistant shiny cars, has erased much of the crude graffiti and made the atmosphere more aesthetically pleasing. However, the modernization also wiped out truly creative underground art, remnants of which can still be viewed on the few old cars that remain in service.

But it will take more than paint-resistant cars to erase subway crime. In crowded stations (most notably those around 42nd St.), pickpockets find plenty of work; in stations that are deserted, violent crimes are more possible. Always watch yourself and your belongings, and try to stay in lit areas near a transit cop or token clerk. Some stations have clearly marked "off-hours" waiting areas that are under observation and significantly safer. At any time and at any place, don't stand too close to the platform edge (people have been pushed) and keep to well-lit areas when waiting for a train. Boarding the train, make sure to pick a car with a number of other passengers on it.

The subways run 24 hours, but at all costs avoid using them between 11pm and 7am, especially above E. 96th St. and W. 120th St. Also try to avoid rush-hour crowds, where you'll be fortunate to find air, let alone seating—on an average morning, more commuters take the E and the F than use the entire rapid transit system of Chicago (which has the nation's second largest system—guess which is first). If you must travel at rush hour (7:30-9:30am and 5-6:30pm on every train in every direction.), the local train is usually less crowded than the express. Buy a bunch of tokens at once: you'll not only avoid a long line, but you'll be able to use all the entrances to a station (some lack token clerks).

The subway network integrates once-separate systems known as the **IRT, IND,** and **BMT** lines. The names of these lines are still in use, and their routes remain color-coded on subway maps. Certain routes also have common, unofficial names based on where they travel, such as the "7th Ave. Line" or "Broadway" for the #1, 2, or 3; the "Lexington Line" for the #4, 5, or 6; and the "Flushing Line" for the #7. The official names are numbers and letters, but for clarity's sake, many listings in this chapter employ the alternative designations.

Because **buses** sit in traffic, during the day they often take twice as long as subways, but they are also twice as safe, are usually cleaner, and always have windows. They'll also get you closer to your destination, since they stop every 2 blocks or so and run crosstown (east-west), as well as uptown and downtown (north-south). The MTA transfer system provides north-south travelers with a slip good for a free ride east-west, or vice-versa. Just ask the driver for a transfer when you pay. Make sure you ring when you want to get off. Bus stops are indicated by a yellow-painted curb, but you're better off looking for the blue sign post announcing the bus number or for a glass-walled shelter displaying a map of the bus's route and a schedule (usually unreliable) of arrival times. Either exact change or a subway token is required; dollar bills are not accepted.

Taxis

With drivers cruising at warp speed along near-deserted avenues or dodging through bumper-to-bumper traffic with a micron or two to spare, cab rides can give you ulcers. And even if your stomach survives the ride, your budget may not. Still, it's likely that you'll have to take a taxi once in a while, in the interest of convenience or safety. Rides are expensive: The meter starts at $1.15 and clicks 15¢ for each additional ninth of a mile; passengers pay all tolls and, in about half of the cabs, a 50¢ surcharge after 8pm. Finally, cabbies expect tips of around 15%, and won't hesitate to let you know when they're displeased. Before you leave the cab, ask for a receipt, which will have the taxi's identification number. This number is necessary to trace lost articles or to make a complaint to the Taxi Commission (869-4513). Some drivers may try to take advantage of visitors. Remember, the fare on the meter is the basic charge for the ride, not charge per person. You might also want to glance at a street map before embarking, so you'll have some clue if you're being given a personalized New York tour rather than just delivered to your destination.

Use only yellow cabs—they're licensed by the state of New York and are safe to ride. Only the plump Checker Marathon cabs take five passengers. If you're desperate and can't find anything on the street, or if you like to plan ahead, commandeer a radio-dispatched cab (see Practical Information above). Use common sense to make rides cheaper—catch a cab going your direction and get off at a nearby street corner.

To hail a cab, stand on the curb and raise your arm. Yelling worked for Dustin Hoffman in *Tootsie,* but will attract more critical glances from real-life New Yorkers than if you too were in drag. A free cab will have the "On Call" light on its roof illuminated and the "Off-Duty" signs around it unlit. Taxis make themselves more scarce during rush hour and on rainy days.

Walking, Running, and Biking

Walking is the cheapest, the most entertaining, and often the fastest way to get around town. During rush hours the sidewalks are packed with suited and sneak-

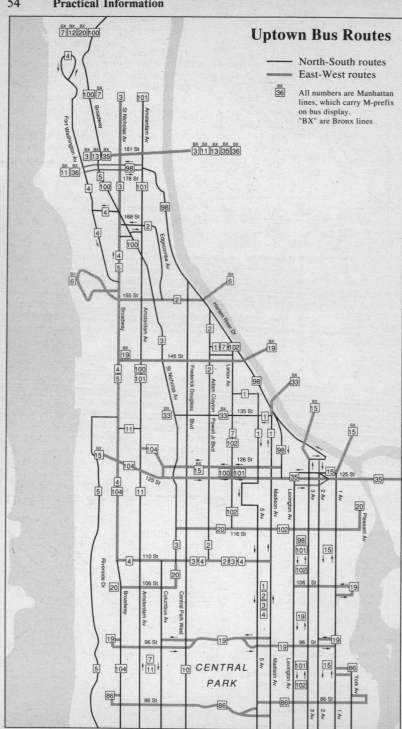

Uptown Bus Routes

—— North-South routes
—— East-West routes

All numbers are Manhattan lines, which carry M-prefix on bus display. "BX" are Bronx lines.

Downtown Bus Routes

—— North-South routes

≈≈≈ East-West routes

$\begin{array}{c}B\\15\end{array}$ All numbers are Manhattan lines, which carry M-prefix on bus display.
"Q" are Queens lines;
"B" are Brooklyn lines

ered commuters. In between rush hours, the sidewalks are still full of street life. Twenty street blocks (north-south) make up a mile; the distance east-west from one avenue to the next is about triple that from block to block. For scenic strolls and educational excursions, try a walking tour of Manhattan (see Guided Tours below).

If you plan on running along the street, be prepared to dodge pedestrians and to break your stride at intersections. Women can expect cat calls and stares. The alternative to the sidewalk are paths in Central Park—most are pavement, but there is a 1.57 mile cinder loop that circles the Reservoir (between 84th and 96th St.). Joggers pack the path from 6-9am and 5-7pm on weekdays and all day on weekends. For information on running clubs, call **American Youth Hostels** (431-7100) or the **New York Roadrunner's Club** (860-4455).

Weekday biking in commuter traffic poses a mortal challenge even for veteran natives. But on weekends, when the traffic thins, cyclists who use helmets and caution can tour the Big Apple on two wheels. From May-Oct., the park (except the lower loop) is closed to traffic on weekdays from 10am-3pm, and from Fri. 7pm-Mon. 6am. Otherwise, Sunday mornings are best. For a challenging and aesthetic traffic-free course, try circumnavigating the 3.5-mile path within Central Park. If you must leave your bike unattended anywhere in Manhattan, use a strong lock. Theft artists specialize in snipping weaker chain locks. If you want to see your bike again, invest in a **Kryptonite K-5** lock ($28.50). Don't leave any removable parts unlocked, as they may be quickly stripped from your bike.

Those who can't bring their bikes can rent from **Metro Bicycle** (throughout Manhattan; call 228-4344) and the **Boathouse,** in Central Park (861-4137), both rent bicycles. (See Practical Information above.)

For the adventurous and skillful, roller skates are available at **Peck and Goodie Skates,** 917 Eighth Ave. (246-6123), between 54th and 55th St. Whiz past your favorite New York sights for $10 per 2 hr., $15 per 4 hr., or $20 per day. $100 deposit or credit card required. (Open Mon.-Tues., Thurs., Sat.-Sun. 10am-6pm, Wed. and Fri. 10am-8pm.)

Accommodations

If you know someone who knows someone who once heard of someone who lives in New York—get that person's phone number. The cost of living in New York is high. Don't expect to fall into a hotel—if you do, odds are it will be a pit. Rates in real full-service hotels hover at around $125 a night. Anything below $50 a night is reasonable. Think about your priorities and select accordingly. People traveling alone may want to pay more to stay in a safer neighborhood. The young and the outgoing may prefer a budget-style place crowded with students. Privacy lovers will not.

Cheap, safe YMCAs and hostels manage to preserve the homeyness and camaraderie of travelers that more commercial establishments lack. These places advise you to reserve in advance—even once you get to New York, you should call to make sure there are rooms available before trekking anyplace with large bags. Cheap hotels pack in hapless innocents and ingenues around the Penn Station and Times Square areas of midtown. Avoid these sleazy, honky-tonk spots. The neighborhoods have no redeeming qualities, and the hotel rooms often rent to the less ingenuous by the hour. Another high concentration of budget hotels can be found in lower midtown, on the East Side, the area just below the Empire State building. These spots, around Park Avenue South in the 20s, vary widely in quality, as the neighborhood changes drastically from block to block. You may encounter some unpleasantness or a good deal.

Never leave anything of value in your room. Most places have safes or lockers available, some for an extra fee. And never, ever sleep outdoors, anywhere in Manhattan. The city has a hard enough time protecting its vast homeless population—tourists would simply not stand a chance.

Student Accommodations

Student accommodations can run as cheap as $10 per night, but don't expect luxury or intimacy. You can pay a little more for a room with fewer occupants and more conveniences. University housing, though mostly reserved for affiliated students, becomes a viable option in the summer. Always try to call or write to a hotel or hostel ahead of time.

Chelsea Center Hostel, 511 W. 20th St. (243-4922) at Tenth Ave. Attractive bunks in a large common room, with kitchen and bath. Gregarious, multilingual staff will bend over backwards for guests. Closed 11am-4pm. Dorm-style beds $19 per day, including breakfast and tea at any hour. Write or phone 2 weeks in advance and confirm 1-2 days before arriving. In peak season (June-Aug.) they'll only hold your reservation until 7:30pm. If they're booked, they'll try to find you another place to stay.

International Student Center, 38 W. 88th St. (787-7706). Subway: Seventh Ave. IND to 86th St. Close to Central Park and Columbus Ave. Open only to foreigners, preferably students; you must show a foreign passport to be admitted. Single-sex bunk rooms, no frills, in a somewhat tired brownstone on a cheerful, tree-lined St. 7-day max. stay. Open daily 8am-11pm. Call after 10:30am on day of arrival. A bargain. $10. Closed June-last week in July.

YMCA—West Side, 5 W. 63rd St. (787-4400). Subway: 59th St./Columbus Circle. Dilapidated but clean rooms in a handsome Gothic building, with free access to 2 pools, indoor track, racquet courts, and Nautilus equipment. Shower on every floor. Check out noon; check in until 11pm unless you have a reservation. Singles $29, with bath $44. Doubles $46, with bath $52. Newly renovated singles with color TV and cable $38, with bath $53. A/C $3.25 extra. Student discount 10%.

New York International AYH-Hostel, 891 Amsterdam Ave. (932-2300) at 103rd St. Located in a landmark building designed by Richard Morris Hunt. The largest hostel in the U.S., with 90 dorm-style rooms and 480 beds. Spiffy new soft carpets, blondewood bunks, spotless bathrooms. Members' kitchens and dining rooms, coin-operated laundry machines, in-room storage space, communal lounges, and a large outdoor garden. Open 24 hr. Check in any time, check out 11am. No curfew. $20, nonmembers $23. Doubles $30 per person. Family room $60. Bed sheet rental $3. Towels $2.

Fashion Institute of Technology, 210 W. 27th St. (760-7885). Subway: Seventh Ave. IRT to 28th St. Decent neighborhood, but adjacent to a bad one; exercise caution at night. Office open Mon.-Fri. 8am-7pm. Summer housing in standard dorm doubles (communal bath) from second week of June to July 31. Application required; approval can take a week. $122 per person per week, 1-week min. stay. Double occupancy suites with kitchen and a bath, $640 per person per month, 1-month min. stay. Reservations necessary for suites; full payment in advance.

Mid-City Hostel, 608 Eighth Ave. (704-0562) between 39th and 40th St., on the 4th floor. A 175-year-old building with skylights, brick walls, and old wooden beams. Friendly owner aims to attract long-time backpackers fed up with the barracks. Lockout 12:30-6pm. Curfew Sun.-Thurs. midnight, Fri.-Sat. 1am. Only 25 beds. Dorm-style beds $15 per night, including breakfast of fruit salad.

Central Park Hostel, 72 W. 106th St. (366-5930), near Central Park West. New and anxious. Room for 50; keys given. American breakfast included. $17.

CIEE New York Student Center (YMCA), William Sloane House, 356 W. 34th St. (760-5850). Subway: A, C, or E to 34th St./Penn Station. Standard YMCA fare. A hulking place. Tiny, parsimonious but tidy rooms. Serves as a hotel for regular travelers and as a hostel for students with ID. Laundry facilities, recreation room, and oodles of helpful student travel advice. Open 24 hr. Check out at noon. In summer, book 2-3 weeks in advance. Singles $32, with bath $46. Doubles with bath $60. Twins $47.50. Hostel rates $15 per person, in a 2-person room. Key deposit $5. TV $1.50 per day. Discount for IYHF/AYH members.

YMCA—McBurney, 206 W. 24th St. (741-9226). Subway: Seventh Ave. IRT to 23rd St. Men only. Should be co-ed by fall 1990. An all-night soup line stands wearily and dangerously across the street. But inside security is tight. Small singles $26, large singles with TV $29-31. Doubles $44.

YMCA—Vanderbilt, 224 E. 47th St. (755-2410), between Second and Third. Subway: #6 to 51st St. One of the best places to stay in New York. 750 tiny rooms, all with A/C and some with balconies. Semi-dingy hallways; immaculate hall baths. Cosmopolitan guests fill the lobby. The front desk keeps close tabs on who is doing what, as does the 24-hr. security guard. Lockers, Nautilus equipment, pool, luggage storage for early arrivals, and safe deposit boxes. All rooms have desk, dresser, and color TV. It's popular; make reservations and guarantee them with a deposit. Visa, Mastercard, and money orders accepted; personal checks taken only for reservations. Check-in 1-6pm. Van service to airports: Jack's Airport Bus Service to JFK $9.50, to LaGuardia $8. Buses leave at 12:15 and 3:15pm. Sign up at the security desk and pay the driver. 25-day max. stay. $10 key deposit. Singles $36-47. Doubles $46-54. Triples $60-65. Quads $76-80. Rates lower off season.

Allerton House, 130 E. 57th St. (753-8841), between Park and Lexington. Subway: #6 to 59th St. Women only. A classy operation in a swanky district, 2 blocks from Bloomingdale's. Full of bridge players heading up to the Beverly Bridge Club on the 3rd floor. Many recently redecorated rooms. New leaded glass windows and clean, angular spaces. Singles $45, with connecting bath $50, with shower $60. Doubles $75. Weekly $175, with connecting bath $195, with shower or private bath $210. TVs $25 per week.

Whittier Hall, 1230 Amsterdam Ave. (678-3235). Columbia-affiliated, across the street from campus. All rooms have access to cooking facilities. Small singles $20. Doubles with A/C, bath, and kitchen $40. Reserve well in advance.

Martha Washington, 30 E. 30th St. (689-1900) near Madison. Subway: #6 to 28th St. Women only. A cold, institutional place in a business district. Neighborhood a little too deserted at night. Singles $35, with private lavatory $39, with private bath $54. Doubles $50, with private bath $69. Weekly: $133, with private lavatory $140, with private bath $168. Weekly (doubles): $91, with private bath $112, with private bath and kitchenette $119.

The Manhattan Hostel, 145 E. 23rd St. (979-8043). Subway: #6 to 23rd St. For international travelers only. Look under the decaying "Kenmore" marquee for the hostel sign. A 3rd-floor oasis created by a young Swiss couple for carriers of foreign passports. Clean hall baths. Complete kitchen facilities, a common room with free coffee, and the small scale of the place (only 32 rooms) enable travelers to meet each other in a family atmosphere. Airport service available. Entrance locked midnight-8am, but guests receive keys. Reservations a good idea. Singles or doubles $40. Extra mattress for a third person $12. Rooms with bunk beds $20 per person. Private bath $5 extra.

International Student Hospice, 154 E. 33rd St. (228-7470), between Lexington and Third. Subway: #6 to 33rd St. This inconspicuous converted brownstone bears a brass plaque saying "I.S.H." by the door. You must be buzzed in. Very small rooms with bunk beds bursting with crusty bric-a-brac, cracked porcelain tea cups, and clunky oak night tables. The ceilings are crumbling, the stairs are listing precariously, and close examination of the carpet could be a dismaying proposition. Only 20 beds, and proprietor Art Stabile keeps a close eye on all of them. Stabile maintains a selective policy in admitting guests and enforces a strict midnight curfew. The ISH, sponsored by a non-profit foundation, prefers but is not limited to Internationals or Students. Generous neighbors provide special dinners in the formal dining room on Thanksgiving and July 4. 2-4 person rooms. Hall bathrooms. Library, lounge, and enough dusty books to last a summer. $25 a night.

The Penthouse Hostel, 250 W. 43rd St. (391-4202), on the 24th floor. In the heart of the theatre district and uncomfortably close to Times Square, this refuge bills itself as the "world's highest hostel." Open 24 hr. No curfew. Check in any time, check out 11am. Passport requested. Eight beds per room. $15.

International House, 500 Riverside Drive (316-8436), at 123rd St. near Columbia University. Subway: #1 to 125th St. and Broadway. Minimum age 18; students preferred. Exercise caution at all times; this is a dangerous neighborhood. Available 2 weeks in advance as transient summer housing. Ultramodern facilities: gymnasium, TV lounge, cafeteria, coin-op laundry, personal mailbox, 24-hr. security, pub. Office open daily 8am-5pm. Singles $25, doubles and guest rooms $55-65. Bath included. Write or call for reservations. Housing available from the 2nd week in May to the 3rd week in Aug.

Amandla House, 722 Saint Nicholas Ave. (926-7030) at 146th St. Subway: #1 train to 145th St. and Broadway. Located in Sugar Hill, just yards away from the Harlem Dance Theater, the Schomburg Center, and the houses where Duke Ellington and James Baldwin grew up. One block west, brownstones line safe Convent St. 25-person occupancy with 4-6 people per room in standard bunkbeds. Exceptionally helpful staff. Facilities include kitchens, TV, stereo, and instant book library salvaged from Doubleday. Check in 9-11am. No curfew. $12; includes a bagel and coffee breakfast. No min. or max. stay.

YWCA—Brooklyn, 30 Third Ave. (718-875-1190), near Atlantic Ave. in Brooklyn. Subway: Atlantic Ave./Pacific St. Women only. An octagenarian building still in good shape. Plain rooms with access to kitchen facilities. Rough neighborhood draws residents of varying respectability. Singles $68-90 per week. Application necessary—guests must be 18-55 and employed—but can be filed on the day of arrival.

YMCA, 138-46 Northern Blvd. (961-6880), in Flushing, Queens. Men only. Convenient to Flushing's central shopping district. The turrets on this old brick building fit the siege-like atmosphere, and the neighborhood takes a drastic turn for the worse once you cross Northern Blvd. Gym, Nautilus, paddleball, squash, 2 pools. $25 per person. Key deposit $20. Subway: #7 to Main St. About ½ hr. from Manhattan. Walk down to the end of Main St. and turn right onto Northern Blvd.

Hotels

Carlton Arms Hotel, 160 E. 25th St. at Third Ave. (679-0680). Subway: #6 to 23rd St. Photographs of people revealing their scars adorn the lobby in what has been nicknamed the "Artbreak Hotel." Stay inside a submarine and peer through windows at the lost city of Atlantis, travel to Renaissance Venice, or stow your clothes in a dresser suspended on an astroturf wall. Each room has been designed by a different avant-garde artist, not one of whom has left many motel pastels around. "I sought to create a resounding rhythm that echoed wall-to-wall, layer upon layer, to fuse our separate impressions into one existence," writes the artist of Room 5B. Hmm. Aggressive adornment doesn't completely obscure the age of these budget rooms, or their lack of air, but it goes a long way toward providing distractions. Strong sense of solidarity among the guests. The artist staff might be wearing pins saying "I'd Rather Be Sculpting," but they get the job done. Not the best of neighborhoods, but tolerable. Discounts for students and foreign tourists. Confirm reservations at least 10 days in advance. Singles $37, with private bath $44, with student/foreign discount $33). Doubles $49 (with discount $44), with private bath $56 (with discount $50). Triples $59 (with discount $44), with private bath $56 (with discount $50). Triples $59 (with discount $53), with private bath $68 (with discount $61). Anyone who pays for six nights at once gets the seventh free. Visa and Mastercard accepted for stays of 2 nights or more. Most major traveler's checks accepted.

Hotel Wolcott, 4 W. 31st St. (268-2900), just west of Fifth Ave. The budget traveler's New York fantasy. A robust renaissance-style mansion, its grand entrance complete with shield and winged cherubs. Greek warrior heads act as quasi-caryatids below the kind of balcony from which dictators and popes make speeches. Crystal chandeliers and wrought iron staircases. Singles $35. Doubles $40. Singles and doubles with bath $50. Triples with bath $60.

Herald Square Hotel, 19 W. 31st St. (279-4017 or 800-727-1888), just west of Fifth. Quartered in the original Beaux-Arts home of *Life* magazine, built in 1893. Above the entrance note the reading, winged cherub titled the "Winged Life" carved by Philip Martiny. The sculpture has been a frequent presence on the pages of early *Life* magazines. The work of some of America's most noted illustrators adorns the walls of the lobby, halls, and rooms. Immaculate rooms with color TV and A/C. Singles (one person only) $35, single/double (1 bed, 1 bathroom) $50. Larger singles with bath $60. Larger doubles (1 bed) with bath $65.

Hotel Roger Williams, 28 E. 31st St. (684-7500) at Madison in safe, pleasant Murray Hill area. Great value. Comfortable rooms all equipped with kitchenettes, 2-burner gas stoves, sink, refrigerator, full bath, and color cable TV. 24-hr. security. Singles $55. Doubles $60-65. Special deal for students: $20 per person (two to three to a room).

Hotel Remington, 129 W. 46th St. (221-2600), between Broadway and Sixth. Tidy, homey, recently remodeled rooms. Spotless bathrooms. All rooms with color TV and A/C; no bath. Singles or doubles $60. Triples $65. Reserve 1 week in advance.

Pickwick Arms Hotel, 230 E. 51st St. (355-0300), between Second and Third Ave. Subway: #6 to 51st St. A chandeliered, marbled lobby raises expectations but gives way to disappointing, dismal, and miniscule—albeit well-decorated—rooms. A clean place with unbeatable rates in a great neighborhood nonetheless. Roof garden, parking, and airport service available. Even with almost 400 rooms to fill, the Pickwick Arms gets very busy; make reservations. Call toll-free 800-PIC-KWIK (742-5945). Singles from $40. Doubles $80. Studios $90. $12 each additional person.

Portland Square Hotel, 132 W. 47th St. (382-0600). Since 1904, Portland has been a "theatre" hotel, accommodating Broadway casts and audiences. Also close to the emporiums of Fifth Ave. and "Restaurant Row" on 46th St. Neoclassical front. Run-of-the-mill rooms. Small one-person singles $35. Standard rooms with bath (one person) $50. Doubles $65, with 2 beds $75. Triples $80.

Washington Square Hotel, 103 Waverly Place (777-9515). Subway: Lexington Ave. IRT to Astor Pl. Fantastic location. Glitzy marble and brass lobby. TV, A/C, and programmed key security cards. Singles and doubles $80. Twins $90. Quads $100. Reserve 1 month in advance, and send deposit 3 weeks ahead.

Hotel Grand Union, 34 E. 32nd St. (683-5890), between Madison and Park. Subway: #6 to 33rd St. A real hotel, centrally located but reasonably priced. All rooms and bathrooms have recently been renovated and redecorated, with bright, pleasant results. TV, electronic phones, A/C. Major credit cards accepted. Singles $55-65. Doubles $65-90. Suites from $105.

Arlington Hotel, 18-20 W. 25th St. (645-3990), between Fifth and Sixth. Arlington prides itself on hospitality and courteous service. Clean with contemporary neutral decor. Rooms come equipped with phone, color TV, and A/C. Free transportation to Jacob Javits Convention Center during trade shows. Single/doubles $65. Twin triples $77. Triple/quads $83.

Penn Plaza Hotel, 215 W. 34th St., (947-5050), between Seventh and Eighth in the shadows of Penn Station. Pleasant if institutional rooms, newly renovated with A/C and cable TV. New furniture, and carpeting. Singles $58. Twins $68. $5 each additional person. Reserve 2 weeks in advance.

The Aberdeen, 17 W. 32nd St. (736-1600), between Broadway and Fifth. A new Korean community around the hotel offers good food and safety. Upscale lobby leads to pleasant rooms. Singles $70. Doubles $80. Triples $95. Quads $105.

Hotel Stanford, 43 W. 32nd St. (563-1480), between Broadway and Fifth. Come here if the previous listing is full. A bit nicer, with ritzier guests. Singles $80. Doubles $90. Twins $100. $15 each additional person.

Mansfield Hotel, 12 W. 44th St., (944-6050 or 800-255-5167), off 5th Ave. A dignified establishment housed in a turn-of-the-century building with a large, comfortable lobby and resplendent oak doors lining the hallways. Good for families or large groups. 200 rooms, all with TV and A/C. Parking, babysitters, and airport service available. Major credit cards honored. Deposit of one day's rent required. Singles with bath $65-70. Doubles with bath $75-80. Junior suites $85 for 2 people, $95 for 3, and $100 for 4. Large suite $120 for 5, $140 for six.

Senton Hotel, 39-41 W. 27th St. (684-5800), between Broadway and Sixth Ave. A mediocre neighborhood surrounds this newly renovated but slightly smelly place. No guests. Singles $40. Doubles $50. Suites $65.

Malibu Studios Hotel, 2688 Broadway (222-2954) at 103rd. Near Columbia, in an area undergoing gentrification. Tropical motif. Clean rooms with refrigerator and hot plate. Check in at noon. Check out at 10am. Singles $30-40. Doubles $22-30. TV $15 per week.

Bed and Breakfasts

Referral services can help you find private individuals who will rent out part or all of their apartment to you and provide a breakfast of their choosing. Although not your stereotypical bed and breakfasts—no sleepy New England village squares or big front porches—Manhattan has its share of B&Bs. Reservations should be made a few weeks in advance, with a deposit required. A cancellation fee may be levied. Most of the apartments listed have two-night minimums. Listings are divided into "hosted," meaning traditional B&B arrangements, and "unhosted," meaning that the people renting you the apartment will not be there. Most agencies offer a wide range of prices, depending upon the size and quality of the accommodation and the safety of its surroundings. Apartments in the West Village and the Upper East Side cost the most. Most agencies also list accommodations in boroughs other than Manhattan; these can be a particularly viable budget alternative in many cases.

New World Bed and Breakfast (675-5600 or toll-free: from U.S. and Canada, 800-443-3800; from Australia, 0014-800-125-496; from France, 1905-901-148; from Great Britain, 0800-891-696; from Japan, 0031-111-503, from West Germany, 0130-811-672). Over 100 listings, in all parts of Manhattan. Prices include fee; when you make your reservation, you must pay 25% of the total bill as a deposit. Refundable up to 5 days before your visit. Credit card payments accepted. Singles in guest rooms $55. Doubles $50-90, most around $80. Unhosted apartment $90-120.

Bed and Breakfast Network of NY Inc. (645-8134). Around 300 listings throughout the city. A 25% deposit required when you make your reservations. Deposits payable by personal check, but only cash or traveler's checks accepted for the bill. Hosted accommodations: singles $50-60, doubles $70-90. Unhosted apartments from $80. Weekly and monthly rates available.

Urban Ventures (594-5650). The oldest and most established agency in the city. A whopping 700 listings covering most neighborhoods. Booking fee of $20, or if booking with less than 5 days notice, one night's rent. Unhosted singles from $79. Hosted facilities $60-115.

Food

> *A native-born American who has spent the entire day in what he knows to be New York City and has not once stepped board a ship or plane, is almost invariably chagrined and disoriented by a menu that uses the French counterpart for the perfectly adequate English word grapefruit.*
> —Fran Lebowitz, *Metropolitan Life*

This city takes its food seriously. In New York, delis war. Brunch rules. Trendy dining has caught on. Supermarkets haven't—with so many bakeries, butcher shops, and greengrocers, who needs to stop and shop in a food mall? Don't be confused by the conflation of food with art. Certain eateries think they are galleries, while select delis look like museums. Assorted gourmet cooks pose as pushcart vendors. Sidewalk gourmands can stick with the old roving standbys on wheels (hot dogs, pretzels, roasted chestnuts), or try something more adventurous (knishes, shish kebabs, fajitas).

New York's restaurants do more than the United Nations to promote international goodwill and cross-cultural exchanges. City dining spans the globe, with eateries ranging from relatively tame sushi bars to wild combinations like Afghani/Italian, or Mexican/Lebanese. And international relations couldn't be easier with the massive numbers of places willing to deliver; in no other city can you pick up the phone and order a full Italian meal, a platter of sashimi, or a helping of Thai noodles that will appear on your doorstep 15 minutes later. Some restauranteur types have even put together a magazine for the members of the upper crust tired of the same old pizza deal who'd like to order in gourmet delicacies. The extra tax charged is a rip-off, but subscribers to *Dial a Dinner* are really paying to have a gent in tux and tails materialize at their threshold with a dish from a major New York restaurant.

Chinese restaurants spice up every neighborhood and even fill up a neighborhood of their own. For a taste of bell'Italia, cruise to Mulberry Street in Little Italy. For the truest in post-revolutionary Russian cuisine, make a trip to Brighton Beach, where the Soviet emigré community has built its lair. Many Eastern European dishes have become New York staples: the plump traditional dumplings called knishes make a great lunch; eat potato knishes with mustard, meat knishes with *yoich* (gravy), or *kasha* knishes (buckwheat groat) all by their delicious selves. Fill up on *pirogi,* Polish dough creations stuffed with potato or cheese and garnished with fried onions and sour cream; sample some spicy Polish *kielbasa* (sausage); or pig out on blintzes, thin pancakes rolled around cream cheese, blueberries, and other divine fillings. The bialy is a flat, soft, onion-flavored bagel cognate.

And of course there is always the bagel, a child of Brooklyn and one of that borough's greatest contributions to Western civilization. Bagels come in a rainbow of flavors—the most common being plain, egg, poppyseed, and onion—but only one shape. Exiles from the city often find bagel deprivation to be one of the biggest indignities of life outside of New York.

Those low on cash can take advantage of the inexpensive lunch specials offered by otherwise intangible restaurants—a large Hungarian lunch can be yours tor $5. Pizza bakes everywhere and runs cheap. Almost any local coffeeshop will serve you a full American breakfast with eggs, bacon, toast, coffee, and the works for $2-3.

Atriums and public parks provide idyllic urban milieux for picnics. Natives do their gazing and grazing in Central Park, tourists on the steps of the Metropolitan Museum. Many of the larger museums provide picturesque, artwork-filled cafés to facilitate your digestion.

New Yorkers dine later than most Americans. In New York you can find a restaurant open and serving dinner almost anytime between afternoon and midnight. Make reservations or arrive before 7pm to beat the hordes to the best tables in the house.

Follow your nose. Look before you eat. Read the writing on the menu on the wall. Don't judge a restaurant by its façade; quality is more than brick deep. Ask: where are the crowds? To fine old smells be true. Trust the clichés of restaurant dining and peek inside to gauge if the crowds have gathered to eat, to socialize, or just to watch the game on the large TV at the bar.

West Midtown

West Midtown sizzles with summer heat, booms with construction, and tempts with nocturnal promise, but has never promised anyone decent food at reasonable prices. Watch your step or you'll stumble onto some real sleaze emporiums. Around Times Square and the Port Authority Bus Terminal, fast-food chains outnumber drug dealers, tourists, and prostitutes—quite an achievement. In the Theatre District, the stretch of Broadway from Times Square to 52nd St., you'll run into plenty of good but overpriced restaurants, many of them Japanese.

After a hearty performance, stars tend to drift over to **Sardi's,** 234 W. 44th St., and take a seat on plush red leather, surrounded by caricatures of themselves and their best friends. If this exercise grows tedious, they may head west of Eighth Ave., to 46th St.'s "Restaurant Row," an appealing but expensive strip that has recently been liberated by the Guardian Angels. There, stars wander into **Joe Allen,** 326 W. 46th St., where they can gaze at posters of shows that closed in under a week. Farther uptown, beneath Carnegie Hall, artsy and businessy types down caviar and vodka at the **Russian Tea Room,** 150th W. 57th St.

Carnegie Delicatessen, 854 Seventh Ave., at 55th St. World-famous deli in a prime location. Eat elbow-to-elbow at long tables with regulars and celebrities and soak up the boisterous atmosphere. The incredible pastrami and corned beef sandwiches ($8.45) easily feed 2 people (but sharing costs you $2 extra). Neophytes shouldn't leave without trying the *gefilte* fish ($10.45). Open daily 6:30am-4am.

La Fondue, 43 W. 55th St., between Fifth and Sixth. The dark wooden tables and chalet decor might transport you to Lake Geneva. Grab some Grolsch beer and dip into the delicious cheese fondue ($9); don't miss sublime Swiss chocolate fondue with fruit ($5.75) for dessert. Open Mon.-Thurs. noon-midnight, Fri.-Sat. noon-12:30am, Sun. noon-11pm.

La Bonne Soupe, 48 W. 55th St., between Fifth and Sixth. Excellent meals in a "bistro" that doubles as a gallery for Haitian and French paintings. Small meals of aromatic soups served with bread, salad, dessert, and wine for $7. Open Mon.-Sat. 11:30am-midnight, Sun. 11:30am-11pm.

Ristorante Prego, 1365 Ave. of the Americas, between 55th and 56th. Fast-food pasta served on marble-top tables amidst a forest of green plants. Over 25 kinds of pasta. Every dish ($8.30) comes with a bowl of marinated fresh vegetables. Adequate portions. Open daily 11:30am-midnight.

Le Parisienne, 910 Seventh Ave. A typical diner. Great for a quick burger ($4.80) or a cup of coffee ($1). It's a short walk from here to Central Park—a fine location for digesting. Open Mon.-Sat. 6am-10pm, Sun. 7am-10pm.

Hard Rock Café, 221 W. 57th St. The trunk of a 1950s car dangles from the entrance. Brass doors lead into a vast space rife with expensive autographed guitars and trendy Trentonites. Burgers cost a hefty $7, but what can you expect from a restaurant that thinks it's an international t-shirt franchise? Open daily 11:30am-2am.

Sapporo, 152 W. 49th St. near Seventh Ave. Japanese version of a coffee shop. A favorite snack spot for Broadway cast members and the business luncheoning crowd. Sweet *oyako-don* (chicken with sauteed egg patty) served on sticky rice ($5) will fuel food fantasies for weeks after your first encounter. The *gomoku ramen* floats in a mind boggling broth ($5.25). Open Mon.-Fri. 11:30am-midnight, Sat.-Sun. 11:30am-11pm.

Ariana Afghan Kebab, 787 Ninth Ave. The owner has decked this narrow space with ornate textiles, Arabic calligraphy, and a neon map of his homeland. Palatable appetizers for the adventurous. Try the *Bandinjah Burani* ($2.50), an unusual spicy eggplant dish served with sour cream and bread. Entrees ($5-8) present a larger dilemma. Experiment with *chicken tandoori* ($6), wood charcoal-cooked chicken on a bed of rice, served with a salad. BYOB. Open Mon.-Sat. 11:30am-3pm and 5-10:30pm.

Hourglass Tavern, 373 W. 46th St. (265-2060), on Restaurant Row. A romantic, left-bank, surreal atmosphere. Watch time go by in the hourglasses on the wall. Generally Italian entrees; fine wine list. Open Sun.-Thurs. 5-11pm, Fri.-Sat. 5-11:30pm.

The Ground Round, 1501 Broadway, in Times Square. Escape the sleaze into a semi-fast-food joint. Burgers $6-7, decent deli sandwiches $5-6. Often packed with sea rubes and Marines on shore leave. Open daily noon-11pm.

YAKI Ten, 147 W. 42nd St., just east of Times Square. The exterior has transmogrified into a dragon with 2-ft.-long horns. Authentic Japanese food with great specials. For $6, you can get an 8-oz. teriyaki steak with soup, rice, and salad. Open Mon.-Sat. 11:30am-9pm.

Little Italy Pizza Parlour, 72 W. 45th Street (730-7575), corner of 45th and Sixth Avenue. All of the pizzerias on 45th St. claim to be world famous, but this one takes the pie. *Ambience* borrowed straight from Grandma's sitting room on Mulberry Street: painted plaster predominates. The walls shine with studio glossies of anonymous starlets, interspersed with sexy photos of beloved pies. Pizza by the slice $1.55, large Neapolitan pie $11.80, pie with everything and anything you want $21. Calzones clock in around $3.75. Open Mon.-Fri. 9:30am-7:30pm, Sat. 10:30am-6:30pm.

J.P. French Bakery, 54 W. 55th St., between Fifth and Sixth. Great croissants on the premises, plus a variety of conversation piece French breads and sandwiches. Croissants $1.05, $1.60 for the almond, coconut, and the chocolate varieties. Breads start at $1.60. Sandwiches with a variety of imported cheeses and meats $2.35-$6. Open Mon.-Fri. 7am-8pm, Sat. 7am-7pm, Sun. 7am-5pm.

China Regency, 850 Seventh Ave. For this part of town, the prices ring cheap. Pick up a spicy General Tsao's Chicken ($8.75) in tangy sauce. The snapshots outside commemorate meetings between the owners and Muhammed Ali, Henry Kissinger, Ted Carson, Buddy Hackett, and Péle. Open daily 11:30am-10:30pm.

Lindy's, 825 Seventh Ave. Diner food in a world-famous expensive restaurant. That's why a tunafish salad sandwich with sliced egg (called a "Woody Allen") costs $9.75. The menu, the centerfold of a food magazine, is drowned in trite jokes. If you happen to fall into this tourist trap, don't miss the most worthwhile (and not untouted) item there: the cheesecake ($4.25). Open Sun.-Thurs. 7am-midnight, Fri.-Sat. 24 hr.

Meson Sevilla, 344 W. 46th St., on Restaurant Row. Rich food for rich people. Try the *paella* ($13.50), yellow rice with carefully arranged seafood. The bar in the front can help you along in obtaining that perfect buzz only Spanish food can render. Open daily noon-midnight.

Lotfi's Couscous, 145 W. 45th Street (768-8738) on the 2nd floor. A taste of Morocco. Couscous comes served in a broth of saffron, cinnamon, and coriander ($10-13). All tangines (Moroccan stews served in a decorative bowl with cover) come highly recommended, especially the chicken with preserved lemons. ($11)Superb pastry, including the "snakes"—a cigar-like pastry filled with ground nuts and spices ($2.25). Moroccan tea parlor ambience enhanced by traditional tapestries on the walls and 1001 Morocco tourist posters in the hall. Soups $2.50, salads $3.75, entrees $10-12, desserts $2-3.50. Open Mon. noon-11pm, Tues.-Sat. noon midnight, Sun. 4-11pm.

Grigori's à la Russe, 315 W. 54th street (246-6341) between Eighth and Ninth. Though it specializes in catering and take-outsky, Grigori's is also a homey, makeshift restaurant devoted to upkeeping the traditional cuisine of Czarist Russia; no chicken perestroyka here. Russian women's shawls double as tablecloths, and absurdist canvases by contemporary Soviet artists stretch across the walls. For $8 you can buy a Czarist t-shirt, emblazoned with imperial eagle and all. Soups like borscht or Fish Sollanka $1.50-1.75. Vinaigrette or eggplant caviar salad $1.50-2 per ¼ lb. Entrees include *Golubfsky,* stuffed cabbage rolls with meat and vegetables ($2), *Teftely,* Russian meatballs in sour cream sauce, Chicken Kiev, and *Salmon Pojharski,* ground fresh salmon with fresh dill and lemon ($2.75). Of the pastries and pâté, *Goulibiac* (salmon baked in pastry; $2.75) and *Pelmeni,* Siberian meat dumplings (50 pieces; $7.50) are especially memorable. Open Mon.-Fri. 10am-7pm, Sat. noon-7pm.

East Midtown

New York has five "four-star" restaurants, four of them (La Grenouille, Hatsuhana, Lutèce, and The Quilted Giraffe) in this area. Tycoons dine here amongst skyscraping office buildings, art deco monuments, and high rents. But you can manage to eat here without an expense account. East Midtown houses more fast-food peddlers than any other part of the city. Picnicking is free in the area's green cloisters: try **Greenacre Park**, 51st St. between Second and Third; **Paley Park**, 53rd St., between Fifth and Madison; or **United Nations Plaza**, 48th St. at First Ave.

Dosanko, 135 E. 45th St., and many other locations around the city. Midtown: 423 Madison Ave., 10 E. 52nd St., and 123 W. 49th St. Plasticky Japanese restaurant with all the allure of McDonald's. The main dish here is *larmen,* a tubful of noodles and occasional vegetables, seasoned with butter or curry ($4.90). Six pork dumplings with rice and salad $5.70; marinated and fried chicken, served with green salad and sauteed vegetables, $6.05. Open daily 11am-9:30pm.

Horn and Hardart Co., 200 E. 42nd St. at Third Ave. The last of the automats—those places where you plunk some change in a slot and retrieve your sandwich from a hatch in the wall. Spotlights hang from the walls, a split-glass crystal ball reflects onto the ceiling, and 50s food-o-rama tunes evoke a time when one could dine, rollerskate, and boogie in the same place. Cafeteria serves timeless favorites like half a roast chicken ($5.10), homemade soup ($1.25), and pot roast ($6.50). Open daily 6am-10pm.

Crystal Gourmet, 422 Madison Ave., between 48th and 49th. Also 666 Washington Ave. at 55th St. The most bountiful salad bar in the tri-state area. Sushi, pasta vinaigrette, vegetables, and fruits in the chilled section; lasagna, chicken, and beef dishes in the hot one—all at $4.50 per pound. Open Mon.-Sat. 7am-7pm.

Flamingo Bay, 716 Third Ave. at 45th St. Painted in pop-art tropical pinks, turquoises, oranges, and yellows, this stop-and-sip joint serves refreshing mango, piña colada, and papaya drinks to start and no-nonsense, all-beef hot dogs to finish. Open daily 8am-7pm.

La Boulange, 712 Third Ave. at 45th St. Four chefs, including a bona fide French pastry handler, proffer an array of continental delicacies to eat in or take out. A typical soup list includes a *persillade,* fresh mussel soup, chicken curry, gazpacho, chicken consommé, watercress, and split pea and bacon (all soups $1.85 for a large bowl). Hot and cold sandwiches $3.50-5.25; entrees like stuffed veal or beef *bourgignon* $5. A look at one of the pastries is worth a thousand words. Open Mon.-Fri. 7am-6pm.

Hsin Yu, 862 Second Ave. (752-9039), at the corner of 46th Street. In the heart of the commercial area. The business crowd dominates at lunch but peters out at dinnertime. Interior decorator had no personality but food does. Poultry $7, specialties like szechuan lamb $7.25-11.50. The very unusual entree "all different kind vegetable" $6. Soups $1.20 to $4 for a double-feeding winter melon with ham. Open Mon.-Fri. 11:30am-10:50pm; Sat., Sun., holidays noon-10:50pm.

Zaro's Bread Basket, 46th and Lexington (972-1560). A busy purveyor of breads, cakes, salads, soups, pizza, and sandwiches in the heart of the business district. Choose from a fabulous selection of food and a plenitude of neighborhood atriums. Meat sandwiches $4.75-6, salad sandwiches $2.75-3.25. Funkomatic 8-oz. homemade salads $3.25-5. Great pizza $8 per pie. A large serving of the day costs $2. Open Mon.-Fri. 5:30am-8pm, Sat. 6am-6pm.

Au Bon Pain, 425 Lexington Ave. (599-8975). Salads, sandwiches, multiflavored croissants, and French breads by the yard. Sitting area upstairs. Croissants 40¢-$2.20, soups $2.20, sandwiches that last and last $3.75. Open Mon.-Fri. 6:30am-7pm, Sat.-Sun. 8am-4pm.

Chelsea

Don't let the chipwiches get you down—beyond the rows of yuppified refreshment stands, you can wine and dine for less. Eighth Avenue offers many options, including several—yes, you heard right—Latin and Chinese hybrid restaurants. This area also caters to connoisseurs of Cajun and Creole.

Kitchen, 218 Eighth Ave. Grab a burrito ($5.70) to go, stuffed with pinto beans, rice, and green salsa. Other mandatory take-out delights include a Cajun meatloaf sandwich on Italian flat bread ($4). Eye-opening daily specials. Open Sun.-Thurs. 11:30am-9:30pm, Fri.-Sat. 11:30am-10pm.

Sam Chinita Restaurant, 176 Eighth Ave. at 19th St. A melange of Spanish and Chinese food in a diner atmosphere. Try the yellow rice with chicken Latin style ($6). Open daily 11:45am-11pm.

Empire Diner, 210 Tenth Ave. at 22nd St. A self-consciously hip diner harkening back to the 1920s. Lounge on patio furniture and drink in the thick atmosphere and a decent bottomless cup of coffee ($1). Sophisticated beers. Open 24 hr.

Cajun, 129 Eighth Ave. White stucco, window gates, and a long red bar, New Orleans style. Charming food with a Louisiana drawl. Affordable lunch until 3pm. Brave the blackened chicken breast ($6.50). Open daily noon-midnight.

Singalong, 17 W. 19th St. Continuous live singing; the lyrics appear on video monitors to encourage patrons to join in. Try to swallow before bursting into song. Lunch Mon.-Fri. noon-3pm, Dinner Tues.-Sat. 7pm-1am, Fri. and Sat. club open until 4am, club cover charge $5.

La Favorita, 114 Eighth Ave. Another hybrid of Latin American and Chinese food, slightly cheaper than Sam Chinita down the block. Wild chicken rice Dominican style ($4.40) glows fluorescent yellow. Open daily 11am-midnight.

Daphne's Hibiscus Resaurant, 243 E. 14th St. Funky and floral restaurant specializing in authentic Jamaican cuisine. Excellent Chicken Hibiscus ($8.50) baked with tropical fruits and herbs. Live entertainment Fri. and Sat. 10pm-1am. Open Tues.-Sun. 11am-11pm.

Romeo's, 120 E. 15th St., corner of Irving. Quality Italian food. Chicken parmigiana with linguini $9, fettucini alfredo $8. Mon.-Thurs. noon-10pm, Fri.-Sat. noon-11pm.

Utopia-W-Restaurant, 338 Eighth Ave. at 27th St., in the pastel shadow of the Fashion Institute of Technology; the school's chic diner. Heavy-duty meaty burgers on toasted buns (cheeseburger with fries $4.40). Dinner comes with a complimentary glass of wine. Open daily 6am-9:30pm.

Café Il Faro, 325 E. 14th St. Linen tablecloths, candlelight, and reasonable prices. Soup $3.75; ziti siciliano $8.75.

America, 9 E. 18th St., between Fifth and Broadway. A massive pastel establishment, very 80s. Extensive menu with American regional cuisine. Most entrees $6.50-16. Open daily 11:30am-midnight.

Las Mañanitas, 322 E. 14th St. On the fancy side. Beef and cheese enchilada with lettuce, guacamole, rice, beans $9. Tortilla stuffed with beef $8. Live Mexican music Fri. and Sat. Mon.-Fri. Lunch 11:30am-4pm Dinner 4:30-11:30pm, Sat. and Sun. 3-11:30pm.

Mama's Fried Chicken, 353 E. 14th St. A fast food place that's not just another link on another dreary chain. By far the cheapest place to eat in the area. Good fried food; clean, no-frills ambience. Cheeseburger $2, 5 pieces of fried fish with chips $3.29. Open Mon.-Sat. 10:30am-1am.

Lower Midtown

Right across from Penn Station, Seventh Ave. between 33rd and 34th St. deals in fast food of every persuasion, from McDonald's to sushi. On Lexington's upper 20s, Pakistani and Indian restaurants battle for customers, some catering to a linen-tablecloth crowd and others serving take-out food. Between 14th and 34th St., the West Side becomes a dining wasteland, where meals soar in price with the exception of a few coffee shops and Chinese and Italian saviors. Some corner delis have salad bars where you can select from pre-prepared vegetable and noodle dishes with an Asian flavor and pay by the pound.

Sbarro, 701 Seventh Ave. at 33rd. Right smack in the chaos of Midtown. Appealing Italian fast food. Breakfast buffet: eggs, bacon, sausages, french toast, fresh fruit, biscuits, all you can eat $4. Slice of stuffed pizza $3. Chicken *parmigiana* hero $4.29. Open daily 8am-8pm.

King of China, 425 Seventh Ave. (564-6065), between 33rd and 34th. In the middle of an overwhelming row of fast food. Six barbecued chicken wings $1.65, three pan-fried dumplings $2. Open daily 10:30am-5:30pm.

Genroku Sushi, 366 Fifth Ave., between 34th and 35th. Beats the automat (see East Midtown) for funkiest mechanical gimmick. A conveyor belt surrounds the oval-shaped counter and parades the food in front of you; take what you like. Pick carefully: some of the dishes have been around the circuit one time too many. *Sushi, udon,* and *ramen.* Dishes $5.35. Soup $1.15. Open Mon.-Wed. and Fri. 11am-8pm, Thurs. until 8:30pm, Sat. until 7:30pm, Sun. noon-6pm.

Albuquerque Eats/Rodeo Bar, 375 Third Ave. and 27th. Take a wild guess at the theme here. Late-night country western entertainment. Dinner $5-14. Open daily 11:30am-3am, kitchen closes at 1am.

Noor Mahal, 102 Lexington Ave., between 27th and 28th. No relation to the Taj, as the atmosphere (or lack thereof) makes clear, but the least expensive quality choice in an area overloaded with Indian restaurants. Try the lunch special meat platter ($5) or an excellent and spicy vegetable *jalfrezi* with sauteed tomatoes, green peppers, and onions ($5.25). Open daily 11am-midnight.

Empire Szechuan Restaurant, 381 Third Ave., between 27th and 28th. One of a chain of tacky Chinese restaurants with reliably good food. Try the broccoli with garlic sauce or the Paradise Chicken. Lunch special around $5 (served Mon.-Fri. 11:30am-3pm). Open daily 11:30am-midnight.

Peso's Mexican Grill, 102 E. 25th St. at Park Ave. South. Franchise member with a sterile seating area. Quesadillas, chili, tacos, burritos, and nachos with no added salt, lard, or artificial ingredients. Best known for its homemade salsas (free) and Mexican pizza (layers of tortillas filled with black beans, red sauce, scallions, olives, tomatoes and 2 kinds of cheese, $5). Open Mon.-Fri. 11am-9:30pm, Sat. 11am-9pm, Sun. 4-9pm.

BA's, The Place on 24th Street, 6 W. 24th St. As its name indicates, this is virtually the only restaurant on the block. Its incongruous light wood exterior brightens a gloomy shadowed row of unmarked storefronts. Informal, neighborhood atmosphere, large bar. Caesar salad $4, fried clams with french fries or onion rings $8. Open Mon.-Fri. noon-9pm.

Upper East Side

Unless you feel like eating a large bronze sculpture or a lace dress, you won't find too many dining opportunities on Museum Mile along Fifth and Madison Ave., aside from a few charming cappuccino haunts, brunch breweries, and near-invisible ritzy restaurants. You will find mediocre food at extraordinary prices in posh and scenic museum cafés where you can languish among ferns and sip espresso between exhibits.

For less glamorous and more affordable dining, head east of Park Ave. Costs descend as you venture toward the lower-numbered avenues, though many do not escape the Madison pricing orbit. Hot dog hounds shouldn't miss the 100% beef "better than filet mignon" $1.50 franks at **Papaya King,** 179 E. 86th St. (369-0648), off Third Ave. Papaya King has been in business since 1933, and should not be confused with its West Side competitor, Gray's Papaya (see Upper West Side). These all-beef franks come endorsed by the prime beef queen herself, Julia Child. (Open

Sun.-Thurs. 8am-1am, Fri.-Sat. 9am-3am.) Another location, at 59th St. and Third Ave., makes delicious fresh-squeezed juices. For a real New York bagel, try **H&H East,** 1551 Second Ave. (734-7441), between 80th and 81st, which bakes them 24 hr., still using their original formula. Impervious to fads, H&H continues to deliver on their promise to put you in heaven. Don't feel confined to restaurant dining. Grocery stores, delis, and bakeries speckle every block. You can buy your provisions here and picnic in honor of frugality in Central Park.

Zucchini, 1336 First Ave. (249-0559), between 71st and 72nd. A nutrition-conscious triathlete runs this healthy establishment. No red meat, but fresh seafood, salads, pasta, and chicken dishes should satiate even practicing carnivores. A steaming loaf of whole-wheat bread precedes dinner. Rough brick walls laden with naturalistic renderings of fresh fruits and veggies. Most pasta and vegetable entrees (soup included) under $11. Convince the owner that you've won a running medal and earn an additional 10% off your meal. Open daily 10:30am-10:30pm, brunch Sat.-Sun. 11am-4:30pm.

TKO, 1286 First Ave. (734-2862) at 69th St. For those who can't imagine life without sports. A well-groomed barn, gracefully festooned with such sporting relics as a basketball signed by Michael Jordan. Barrels of peanuts strategically set at the greatest traffic points in the room. Multiple big-screen TVs run music videos and notable sports events. Frequented by well-toned young clientele, old bonecrushers, and sports celebs. Soups $2.25-3.50, sandwiches $5.50-9. Open Sun.-Thurs. 1:30pm-2am, Fri.-Sat. until 4am.

Afghanistan Kebab House, 1345 Second Ave. (517-2776), between 70th and 71st. Behind a simple, inconspicuous sign lurks one of the most rewarding restaurants in New York. Tender meats are broiled to perfection in a charcoal oven. Rich smells waft, subdued hues of Afghani rugs soothe, and soft Middle Eastern music drifts from an invisible source. Bring your own alcohol. Ask him about the establishment's fleeting first incarnation as New York's sole Afghani pizzeria. Youngish crowd, casual atmosphere, irresistable kebab. All kebab dishes $6.50-7.50, vegetarian entrees $6. Take out and free delivery ($10 minimum). Open Mon.-Sat. 11:30am-10pm.

Sarabeth's Kitchen, 1295 Madison Ave., also at 423 Amsterdam (496-6280). Once upon a time it was a darling local bakery. Then it got reviewed. There went the neighborhood: the few unassuming tables and a couple of walls of floral patterns have sprawled into a glossy duplex serving weekend brunches attended by half of Manhattan. Still, the pumpkin muffins ($1.25) are to die for. Gourmet dinner prices are steep, but brunch addicts should join the masses, put their name down an hour early, stroll around the neighborhood, and return to sink their teeth into dreamy "green and white" eggs ($6.75), scrambled with cream cheese and scallions. No relation to Dr. Seuss. Open Mon.-Thurs. 8am-3:30pm, Fri.-Sun. 9am-4pm and 6-11pm.

Jackson Hole Wyoming, 1611 Second Ave. (737-8788/9), between 82nd and 83rd. If East Side quicheries make you wonder where the beef is, it's here—in thick, juicy, virtually unfinishable ½-pound hamburgers (37 varieties, $4-7; add $2 for fries, lettuce, and tomato). Also at 64th St. between Second and Third, and most importantly on Madison Ave. at 91st St. Open Mon.-Thurs. 10am-1am, Fri.-Sat. 10am-4am, Sun. 10am-11pm.

Szechuan Hunan Cottage, 1433 Second Ave. (535-1471), between 74th and 75th. As soon as you enter this small restaurant, a glass of white wine is offered, along with a smile. Generous portions. Arrive early (6pm) to avoid waiting. Seafood entrees $7.50-9, vegetable entrees around $5.50. House special *chow fun* $6.50. Open Sun.-Thurs. noon-11pm, Fri.-Sat. noon-11:30pm.

ecco'la, 1660 third ave. (860-5609), corner of 93rd. if you don't mind waiting with the rest of the neighborhood, you're in for a lowercase fantasy. sit at paint-splattered tables and twirl your fork fast so you can admire equally daunting patterns on the plateware. shout over the roar of the crowd. ignore the unhappy acoustics and focus on your fettucine *alla contessa,* swimming in a divine lobster and avocado cream sauce, or a slew of other pasta dishes around $10. open daily noon-11:30pm.

Fagiolini, 334 Lexington Ave. (883-9555). Also at 1393B Second Ave. (570-5666). Hop down 2 steps into this narrow, sleek, taciturn Italian restaurant. The setting is trim and refined, elegant tables appointed in strict black and white. Fun mirrors in weathered gilded frames dispel the shadows of mannered propriety. Try the fried calimari or the *pollo arrosto* (roasted chicken). Respectable portions leave just enough stomach room for one of the heavenly desserts ($4.25). Open Sun.-Thurs. 5-10pm, Fri.-Sat. 5-11pm.

Camelback and Central, 1403 Second Ave. (249-8380) at 73rd St. A touch of Phoenix on the Upper East Side. Dine within adobe-like apricot-colored interior or join the crowds at outdoor tables. Arthur Ashe enjoys the service here often, as does Morley Safer. Diane Keaton and Robert Redford have also been sighted. Nouvelle-continental cuisine. Lunch entrees $6.50-9, soups and salads $3.25-6. At dinner, appetizers $3.25-6, light fare (burgers with fries, special salads) $7-10, pasta entrees $12. Brunch $13. Open Sun.-Thurs. 11:30am-3pm and 5-11pm, Fri.-Sat. 5pm-midnight. Brunch Sat.-Sun. 11:30am-4pm.

Mocca, 1588 Second Ave. (734-6470), between 82nd and 83rd. Best Hungarian dining in the country. Bring your immigrant cronies here and watch them turn nostalgic at the sight of stuffed cabbage or goulash. Clean, cozy, inviting, and run accordingly by Old World emigrés who serve much and charge little. Incredible $6 lunch deal includes soup, pancake, and full-fledged entree. Dinner comes complete with potato, vegetables, house salad, and several spicy ethnic jokes ($10-13). Open daily 11:30am-11pm.

Lenge 83, 1465 Third Ave. (535-9661). Enjoy fresh classic Japanese cuisine in a tidy, hospitable setting, where delicate paper lanterns cast light on a host of marvelous dishes. The menu features shrimp, sushi, beef, and chicken as well as countless exotic vegetable dishes. Entrees $7.50-13. Fresh salmon $9.50. Open daily noon-3pm and 5-11pm.

Gabriel, 1370 Lexington Ave. (369-9374), between 90th and 91st. An intimate, delightful neighborhood eatery. Gabriel's proprietors have a penchant for things angelic and for hand-crafted American folk art. The pleasantly unpredictable menu reflects the chef's latest great inspiration. Recurrent favorites include cold strawberry soup, gazpacho, and a battery of fresh pastas and salads ($5-8.50). Dinner entrees $7.50-14. Open daily 7am-11pm.

Sesumi, 222 E. 86th St. (879-1024), between Second and Third. Small, romantic and Japanese. One of New York's best-kept secrets. Inconspicuous outside, but a blizzard of ornate silk tapestries, paper lanterns, and winding greens inside, topped off by a full suit of samurai armor. Fresh food presented with a keen aesthetic sense. Entrees $9-12, sushi from $7.50. Open Mon.-Fri. noon-2:30pm and 5:30-11pm, Sat.-Sun. 4:30-11pm.

Mimi's Pizza and Ristorante, 1248 Lexington Ave. (861-3363) at 84th St. Also at 1049 Lexington Ave. (535-8400), between 74th and 75th. Pizza the way it was meant to be. Craved by New Yorkers, copied without success by impersonators (Mimmo's and Mimma's), and the favorite of at least one Brit in New York—Paul McCartney. Large pie $11, spaghetti with meatballs $6, veal parmigiana $7.50. If the pizzeria seems impersonal, dine in the cozy ristorante portion. Take out and free delivery. Open daily 11am-11pm.

Dumpling Queen, 206 E. 85th St. (249-0362), off Third Ave. Not a place to take your parents to show them that you've made it, but clean and filling enough to satisfy that late-night won-ton craving. No surprises on the menu, just good food at low prices. Soups $1-3.25, *dim sum* $1-4, seafood entrees $7-8, vegetarian entrees $5.50. Take out and free delivery. Open Mon.-Thurs. 11am-11pm, Fri.-Sat. 11am-11:30pm, Sun. noon-11pm.

Mumtaz, 1493 Third Ave. (879-4797), near 84th St. Informal but unusual setting, enclosed in heavy mauve drapes and submerged in conspiratorial semi-darkness. Traditional North Indian cuisine includes a smattering of spicier Southern dishes. When in doubt, resort to the tried and true basics—a multiplicity of kebabs and funky Indian breads will satisfy even the most critical of palates. Entrees $8-11, most desserts under $2, breads $2-3.50. Open daily noon-11:30pm.

Café Ernesto, 1427 Second Ave. (628-8315), between 74th and 75th. Regional Italian cuisine in a fun, informal setting. Try *chicken cacciatore* ($9) or revel in the glorious pastas ($7.50-10). Ask for a mug of cappuccino ($3) and a plump *cannoli* ($2) to learn what *la dolce vita* is all about. Open Sun.-Thurs. 11am-11pm, Fri.-Sat. 11am-midnight.

El Pollo, 1746 First Ave., between 90th and 91st. A chicken by any other name would not taste as good. Plump chickens soaked in secret spices, turned on a rotisserie, and topped with a hot green Argentinian sauce or a mild white Peruvian variant. The proprietors have even perfected the potato: try *papa rellena* ($2.75), a ball of fluffy mashed potatoes formed around a meat and olive nucleus and then deep-fried. Whole chicken $7, half chicken $4, fried sweet plantains $2. Open daily 11am-11pm.

Thai Express, 1750 First Ave., between 90th and 91st. Restaurant comes complete with a miniature shrine and two smiling photoportraits of the king and queen of Thailand. Sprays of fresh orchids at every table. Authentic menu; food fragrant with fresh cilantro and lemon grass. "Dinner box" ($9-11) includes soup, Thai garden salad, sweet and sour noodles, white rice, and a large entree. Noodle dishes $6-6.45. Open daily 6-10pm.

Dante's, 1640 York Ave., between 86th and 87th. Browsing room only in this aromatic kitchen, but the presence of delicacies makes up for the absence of chairs. For a divine movable feast, choose from gourmet sandwiches made with ingredients like *prosciutto, sopressata,* homemade mozzarella, and freshly baked Italian breads ($7); calzones ($3.75); mouthwatering salads ($2.50-5); pastas ($7-8); and Buffalo wings ($4). A fine selection of French and Italian pastries will soften the heart of Beatrice, the girl next door. Open daily 10am-10pm.

Indian City, 1690 York Ave. at 89th St. Warm, neighborhood feel. On Friday and Saturday nights, the prerecorded pluck of the sitar gives way to curried live jazz. (Sets begin at 10:30pm.) Chicken entrees $7-8, vegetarian vagaries $6, up and coming Indian breads $1.25-3.25. An extensive bar keeps spirits high. Open daily noon-11:30pm.

Pig Heaven, 1540 Second Ave., between 80th and 81st. New York's best disguised Chinese restaurant, with a pink corkscrew twist. Things porcine adorn the plates, the walls, and the minds of pig-happy patrons and critics. The list of "recommended by:" includes media hogs *N.Y. Times, N.Y. Magazine, Forbes, Esquire, Gourmet Magazine* and that great expert on porkbellies, the *Wall Street Journal.* While pig, glorious pig dominates the menu, choices aplenty can keep the pig off your plate. Tasteful barnyard decor. Open daily noon-11pm.

Caffè Bianco, 1486 Second Ave., between 79th and 80th. Sip gourmet coffee and pose here with a sandwich or a slice of memorable *tartuffo bianco.* The storybook garden in the back leaves just enough room for a few tables and a gurgling, penny-toss fountain. Toasted sandwiches with mozzarella, roast peppers, fresh mushrooms, or *prosciutto* $3.50-4.75. *Dolci* $2-3.75, *Gelati* $3.50. Open Sun.-Thurs. 11am-11pm, Fri.-Sat. 11am-1am.

Ottomanelli's Café, 1559 York Ave., between 82nd and 83rd. The East Side outpost of the vast and powerful Ottomanelli Empire that has supplied New York with meat and bake shops since 1900. No-frills setting, but extraordinary fresh-baked goods. An impressive coterie of bagels, breads, danish, and muffins 50¢-$1.25. Large iced coffee, a summertime must, $1. After 5pm, all danishes and muffins depreciate to 50¢. Open Mon.-Sat. 6:30am-3pm, Sun. 7:30am-3pm.

Burger Joy, 1332 Lexington Ave., between 88th and 89th. Put an 8-oz. burger on a pedestal and gild it 33 different ways. Toppings include bacon, cheeses, ham, cream cheese, avocado, grilled pineapple, and anchovies ($3.70-9.80). Side orders like *chili con carne,* onion rings, or fries $1.60-2.25. Also gourmet sandwiches, quiches, omelettes, and bagels. Open Mon.-Fri. 6:30am-9pm, Sat.-Sun. 6:30am-6pm.

Paris Croissant, 609 Madison Ave. (319-0828) at 58th St. A pleasant, hospitable café perfect for lunch or an informal snack. Fresh soups, innovative salads, quiche, pizza, and every member of the croissant species. Pastries 80¢-$2.50, salads $4.15 per pound. Take out downstairs, restaurant upstairs. Open Mon.-Sat. 7am-8pm, Sun. 8am-6pm.

Dumas Patisserie, 1330 Lexington Ave. (369-3900), between 88th and 89th. Everything you ever dreamed a French bakery should be: tortes, croissants, plentiful *pains,* notorious cheeses, and prosperous hams. Croissants 80¢, creamy layered Napoleons $1.60, excellent coffee, and sandwiches to write home about ($5-5.50). Open Mon.-Sat. 8am-6:30pm.

La Prima Strada, 1293 First Ave. (722-9333), between 69th and 70th. Delicious whole-wheat pizza to take out or to have delivered. Large plain pie $10, with 1 topping $12. Another location at 263 Amsterdam Ave. (496-7300). Both open 11am-midnight.

Creative Corn Company, 1275 Lexington Ave. (722-5514), between 85th and 86th. Popcorn flavored to taste like everything else, including corn. Order by color or by flavor. Open Mon.-Sat. 11am-10pm, Sun. noon-8pm.

Upper West Side

The Upper West Side stays up later than its austere counterpart to the east. Monthly rents have been heading up, "in" bars have been going out, and high-fashion boutiques have been moving in, but here, gentrification has not made for boredom. Old New York charms endure: refined Central Park West buildings with fancy names, outdoor Columbus cafés with fried zucchini and gleaming chrome, dollar-a-book Broadway bookinistes, Riverside views of sunset on the Hudson. If browsing in **Laura Ashley** or **Charivari** makes you tired, go haggle at the Columbus Avenue Street Fair, happen onto a hidden gallery, or wander down the tempting aisles of **Zabar's,** 2245 Broadway (787-2002), the deli that never ends.

At night, **Lucy's,** 503 Columbus Ave. (787-3009) at 84th St., always draws a crowd ready to make noise and conversation. Bring a friend, a book, or both to

Café La Fortuna, 69 W. 71st St. (724-5846), between Central Park West and Columbus Ave. Enjoy conversation and meditation over cappuccino ($2), inside or out in the backyard garden. The proprietor of these Old World cafés, a devout opera lover, has decorated the walls with autographed daguerrotypes of opera greats, ancient programs, and even thick victrola LPs, which on close inspection reveal the names of Caruso and Shalyapin.

Pizza Joint Too, 70 W. 71st St. (799-4444). The ultimate. Those in the know know to go. 132 varieties of pizza. Osh makes everything to order. Tell them Charlie sent you. $1.35 per slice. Open 23 hr., delivery until 4:30am. Open daily 6am-5am.

The Opera Espresso, 1428 Broadway (799-3050), between 64th and 65th. If you're in the neighborhood to hear some Wagner, drop by between the acts to grab an espresso. The patrons here may be snobs about Teutonic music, but few are snobs about Euro-style cafés. While the restaurant pays homage to the heritage of European cooking, it also tips its hat to the great tradition of the American diner. Vinyl seats, plastic covered menus, and shades of green and brown ground the wall-bound opera programs and candelabras in a distinctly American setting. Soups $2.75, no-surprise tuna, chicken, or roast beef sandwiches $4.25-8.75. Or try Italian-American favorites like linguini with tomato sauce ($6.50) or lasagna ($8.75). Sit at pleasant outdoor tables to admire the view of Lincoln Center and of the small, expensive portions served by Espresso's competitor to the right. Open Mon.-Sat. 7:30am-midnight, Sun. 8:30am-midnight.

Fellini's, 180 Columbus Ave. (986-6744) at 68th. An intimate retreat with whitewashed brick walls. Upbeat pastels and unbeatable pasta. Pasta dishes $10, sandwiches $7.50. Open daily noon-midnight.

Genoa, 271 Amsterdam (787-1094) at 73rd St. This tiny, family-owned restaurant serves some of the best food on the West Side. Wood beams, stucco walls, red candlelight, and Italian romance. Excellent pasta dishes from $9. Arrive before 6pm or wait in line with the rest of the neighborhood. Open Tues.-Sat. 5:45-10:30pm, Sun. 5:30-9:30pm.

Dan Tempura House, 2018 Broadway (877-4969) at 69th St. A bamboo-thatched awning hangs over a window display of exotic plants and fish. The cluttered, smoky atmosphere recalls the setting of a B-grade samurai flick. Come here to enjoy excellent Japanese dishes and plan a revenge mission against the murderers of your ninja master. Tempura dinners $9-11. Noodle dishes $5-7. Sushi and sashimi platters $9-12. Open Mon.-Sat. noon-2:30pm and 5-11pm, Sun. 4-11pm.

Rikyu, 210 Columbus Ave. (799-7922), between 69th and 70th. The food in this modestly but tastefully furnished Japanese restaurant lives up to the name, "happiness forever." Consume eternal happiness at one of three appetizing locations—in the main room, at the sushi bar watching the chef have his way with the fish, or in a kneel-as-you-eat *tatami* room. Noodle dishes $7-8, but come here for the seafood ($9-11). Sushi lunch combo $7. Open Mon.-Fri. noon-3pm and 5-11:30pm, Sat.-Sun. noon-11:30pm.

Diane's, 251 Columbus Ave. (799-6750), off 71st St. Large portions and reasonable prices make this brass-railed café a student hangout. Spice up a 7-oz. burger ($4) with chili, chutney, or your choice of seven cheeses (85¢ per topping). Sandwiches $3-5, omelettes $3.90, French onion soup $3. Great ice cream. Open daily 11am-2am.

The Blue Nile, 103 W. 77th St. (769-9191), between Columbus and Central Park West. The dress is up, but the setting is relaxed. The Northern Italian cuisine features delectable pastas and *antipasti.* Pasta $10-14; half-portions available. *Antipasti* $5.50-8. Open Mon.-Sat. 5pm-midnight, Sun. noon-10pm.

Museum Café, 366 Columbus Ave. (799-0150) at 77th St. Art meets life in the café's arrangement of natural foods. Patrons eat off white linen tablecloths draped over immaculate tables and gaze at an aquarium-like view of the Museum of Natural History. Glass walls enclose the sidewalk area and muffle the bustle of the city. Entree salads $9-11, pasta dishes $12-15, pizza $6-8.50. Open daily 11:30am-midnight.

Dallas BBQ, 27 W. 72nd St. (873-2004), off Columbus Ave. Also at 21 University Place (674-4450) at 8th St. Authentic Texas-style chicken and ribs on the same bill with tasty tempura and homey chicken soup. Mountains of food and oceans of noise in this often crowded restaurant. Early bird special (Mon.-Sat. 4-6:30pm, Sun. 2-5pm) features soup, half a chicken, cornbread, and potato for $8 per dining duo. ½-lb. burger $4.75, Texas-style chili $3 per bowl. Take out an entire barbecued chicken for $5. Open Sun.-Thurs. noon-midnight, Fri.-Sat. noon-1am.

Original Ray's Pizza and Restaurant, 462 Columbus Ave. (873-1135), between 82nd and 83rd. Despite the name, the distinctive coat of arms over the entrance, don't be fooled. Every branch of Ray's pretends to be the original one, and this one doesn't have high hopes. But the pizza does, made with tender loving care using Napoletan tomatoes, Wisconsin cheese, and fresh meat supplied by Napoli butchers. Large plain pie $11, with one topping $13.50. Just $1.50 for a slice the size of Manhattan. Take out and free delivery. Open daily 10am-3am.

Panarella, 513 Columbus Ave. (799-5784), between 84th and 85th. Outside Italian cinema, you'll never again find such a picture-perfect little restaurant. Upstairs and downstairs separate dining areas sparkle, posed amidst light blue walls painted with clouds. A tiny oak-and-glass bar sits inside; cozy, hospitable tables lounge outside. To match the light decor and spirit, the food arrives blissfully free of heavy, buttery sauces. Salads around $6.50, *antipasti* $4.50-7.50, and pasta dishes $7.50-11. Open daily noon-2am.

The Armadillo Club, 2420 Broadway (496-1066) at 89th St. If someone wanted to shoot a *Magnificent Seven* or *Adios Zapata* set circa 1990, this urban chic/Tex-Mex bistro, would furnish the perfect postmodern setting. A decorator has adorned the generous high-ceilinged space with Mexican-flavored cliché bric-a-brac: guitars, ponchos, quilts, horns, and weathered skulls. The designer's masterstroke is a 7-ft.-high, orange neon cactus mounted on a column in the center of the room. The menu croons with a heavy Texan drawl, sporting such regional staples as hot chili and barbecued chicken and beef. And no Tex-Mex meal would be complete without an Almodóvar-colored margarita. All entrees $7-12. Open daily noon-1am.

Caramba!!!, Broadway and 96th St. (749-5055). The 3 exclamation points signify that this is the third of many Carambas in this city. All guts, no-frills Mexican eatery the size of a small roller rink and about as loud. Good food, bountiful portions, and a festive atmosphere. All that's missing is a bull. Chili plate $9, "do-it-yourself" combos $10 for two items. Open Sun.-Thurs. noon-midnight, Fri.-Sat. noon-1am.

Empire Szechuan Kyoto Sushi, 2642 Broadway (662-9404), between 100th and 101st. Hungry scribes at the *New York Times* are all agog about this wonderful Chinese/Japanese eatery: the price is right, the food outstanding. On the Chinese side of the border, soups run $1.30-3.75, vegetarian entrees $6, chef's specials like lamb with Szechuan *ma la* sauce $8.25-11. All Japanese entrees in the $8-12 orbit. Take out and free delivery. Open Mon.-Sat. 11:30am-2am, Sun. 11:30am-1am.

Golden Eagle, 2731 Broadway (316-4847), between 104th and 105th. Delicious, homemade food, disarming cordiality. North America may be more technologically advanced, but when it comes to cooking, the Old World still has a few lessons to teach. The centerpiece counter displays fresh buffet offerings in two different gastronomic traditions—the Middle Eastern and the Mediterranean. Here, gyros and shish kebabs encounter hummus and felafel in a culinary summit of diner satisfaction. The French-Lebanese chef prepares the food according to generations-old family recipes which he politely declines to divulge. Sample the *mousaka,* a satiny, slithery melt of tomato-touched eggplant strips, or concoct a meal from a selection of three appetizers ($5). Gyro or kebab platters $6.50, felafel sandwich $2.75, burgers $3.25-5.55. BYOB. Open daily 8am-11:30pm.

Au Petit Beurre, 2737 Broadway at 105th. French café staffed by *garçons* with patent accents and frequented by a cosmopolitan student crowd along with ordinary neighborhood folks. Espresso $1.25, cappuccino $1.75. All this and homemade muffins too. Open daily 7am-midnight.

Popover Café, 551 Amsterdam Ave. (595-8555), between 86th and 87th. Sandwiches, salads, lemonade, and charm, starring not-to-be-missed popovers ($1.25; 50¢ extra for jam). Or try a cup ($3) or bowl ($4.50) of homemade soup. Open Mon.-Fri. 8:30am-11pm, Sat. 10am-11pm, Sun. 10am-10pm.

Chez David, 494 Amsterdam Ave. (874-4974) at 84th St. Pizza and Middle Eastern specialties, in their kosher incarnations. The fresh felafel is an ecumenical must. Open Mon.-Tues. 8am-1am, Wed.-Thurs. noon-10:30pm, Fri. 8am-4pm, Sat. 7pm-1am, Sun. sunset-midnight.

Café Bel Canto, 1991 Broadway (362-4642), between 67th and 68th. A 50-table café in a 3-story atrium. Sit in style amid vegetation and nurse that steaming mug of cappucinno ($2.50). Espresso $2. If you're up for hardier fare, Bel Canto will readily renew your pasta habit ($8-9) or build you a bountiful sandwich ($6-8). Open daily 10am-midnight.

Asmara, 951 Amsterdam Ave., between 106th and 107th. African curries seasoned with cardamom set alongside spicy spaghetti. Those who feel plagued by Miss Manners' distinctions between varieties of forks can let their fingers do the walking here; every dish arrives with *injera,* a soft pancake-like bread which leads a double life as food and utensil. To wash down the hearty, hot fare try *mes,* a heady wine made with honey and raisins ($2). Beef entrees $5.75-6.50, vegetarian $2-5. A menu short on vowels and long on spice. Open Mon.-Thurs. 4pm-midnight, Fri.-Sun. noon-midnight.

Indian Café, Broadway at 108th St. Cozy Indian joint. Vegetarian entrees $6-8, seafood like shrimp *muglai* (sauteed with fresh ginger and garlic in a creamy curry sauce with almonds) $9-10. Treat yourself to a mango shake for $2.25. Open daily 11:30am-midnight.

Obento Delight, 210 W. 94th St., between Amsterdam and Broadway. Eating in? Consider sending out for fresh Japanese food at prices so low you'd think the dollar had overcome the yen. *Miso* soup $1; *yakitori* (2 skewers of chicken and onion) $3; sashimi $7.50. Electrify your senses with flamed eel in tantalizing sauce grounded in a heaping bowl of rice. Delivery with a $7 minimum. Open daily 11:30am-11pm.

Mi Tierra, 668 Amsterdam Ave., between 92nd and 93rd. The first Mexican restaurant on the Upper West Side and still one of the best. Authentic Yucatecan and Venezuelan food served in a simple setting dotted with fleamarket-style toreador paintings. 3 enchiladas (beef, chicken, cheese, shrimp, or pork) $8.50-9.50. On the Venezuelan side of the border, investigate *carne ranchera,* steak chunks with tomato sauce, peppers, onions, and olives ($8). Open daily 11am-midnight.

Cleopatra's Needle, 285 Broadway (864-1410), between 92nd and 93rd. Cleopatra wouldn't deign to drop by this joint on her burnished throne, but lesser mortals will enjoy the generous portions of Middle Eastern cuisine. Hummus $1.75, entrees $8-11. Deli (with take-out) open daily 7am-11pm; restaurant daily 11am-midnight.

Zula Café and Restaurant, 1260 Amsterdam Ave. (663-1670) at W. 122nd St. On the Columbia scene. Instead of silverware use your hands and the sour, spicy *injera* in which you wrap the morsels. Beef and chicken dishes $6.75, lamb dishes $7.75-8.50. Espresso $1.50, cappuccino $1.75. Open daily noon-midnight; bar open until 4am.

Greenwich Village and SoHo

Here eatery owners come and go, fads rule briefly only to be suddenly deposed, followings build and then decline at an accelerated pace. As a result, the restaurants have tuned in to the hip. Every restaurant has a gimmick and a loyal crowd and engages in a daily struggle between the twin dynamos of quality and kitsch.

West Village

The network of zig-zagging streets between 14th and Houston St. west of Fifth Ave. remains lower Manhattan's bohemian headquarters. Try the major avenues for cheap, decent food. Wander by the posh row houses around Jane St. and Bank St. for classier bistro and café fare. The European-style bistros of **Bleecker Street** and **MacDougal Street,** south of Washington Square Park, have perfected the homey "antique" look. Amidst a clutter of collectibles, **Le Figaro,** 184 Bleecker St., at MacDougal, serves personal-sized pots of exotic brews sweetly complemented by homemade pastries. (Open Mon.-Thurs. 11am-2am, Fri. 11am-4am, Sun. 10am-2am.)

The Village comes to life late at night. Explore (with caution, and with companions) twisting side streets and alleyways where you can join Off-Broadway theatergoers as they settle down over a burger and a beer to write their own reviews, or drop into a jazz club with top-notch music to whet your appetite. If all this sounds too effete, sneak down 8th St. to Sixth Ave. to find some of the most respectable pizzerias in the city. The crucial question then becomes whether John's or Ray's makes the better pie.

John's Pizzeria, 278 Bleecker St. Read the writing on the wall—thank-you notes from former clients, including past U.S. presidents—but don't let them distract you too much from the pizza. Cooked in a brick oven, with a crisp crust and just enough cheese, pizza for 2 costs $7.75. If the place is full, they'll find room for you at **John's Too** next door. No slices; table service only. Open daily 11:30am-11:30pm.

Ray's Pizza, 465 Sixth Ave. at 11th St. Half of the uptown pizza joints claim to be the "Original Ray's." But any New Yorker will tell you that this is the real McCoy. The best pizza in town. Well worth braving the lines and paying upwards of $1.75 for a slice. Open Sun.-Thurs. 11am-2am, Fri.-Sat. 11am-3am.

Olive Tree Café, 117 MacDougal St. Middle Eastern food and endless stimulation. Charlie Chaplin films run continuously on the wide screen, and for a dollar per hour you can borrow chess, backgammon, and Scrabble sets, or doodle with colored chalk on the slate tables. Felafel $2.25, chicken kebab platter with salad, rice pilaf, and vegetable $7. Delicious egg creams only $1.75. Open daily 11am-3am.

Trattoria Due Torri, 99 MacDougal St., near Bleecker St. Cozy; you can see Chef Meshel cooking in the back. And eating his creations even beats watching him create. Fresh pastas $6-7, veal and chicken $7-8. Try the *Gnocchi Sorrentina*, or anything at all, but go. Open Sun.-Thurs. 12:30pm-midnight, Fri.-Sat. 12:30pm-2am.

West 4th St. Saloon, 174 W. 4th St. Do late supper with a rowdy crowd in this pub's brick-walled, brass-railed decor. Salads and sandwiches $6-8. Catch-of-the-day priced according to season. Open daily 11am-4am.

Eva's, 11 W. 8th St., between MacDougal St. and Fifth Ave. Refreshing, fast-service health food with a seating parlor. Massive meatless combo plate with felafel, grape leaves, and egg-plant $4.50. Open Sun.-Thurs. 11am-midnight, Fri.-Sat. 11:30am-1am.

The Temple in the Village, 74 W. 3rd St., off Broadway. Pay $2 per ½ lb. of all-natural high-fiber health food at the "Monk's Buffet." A quick meal here should restore any burnt-out traveler's vitamin deficiency. A shrine to tofu, eggplant, and soy bean creations. Open Mon.-Sat. 10:30am-9:30pm.

Villa Florence, 9 Jones St. (989-1220). Unpretentious, friendly neighborhood favorite. Brick walls, checked tablecloths, ceiling fans, and hearty food. The owner also runs the butcher shop next door; meat dishes are especially good. Pasta $7-10, Newport steak $9, Rainbow Salad (argula, endive, and radicchio) big enough for 2, $3.50. *Maria Tiramisu,* a trifle-like Sicilian dessert, $3. Open Tues.-Fri. 5-11pm, Sat. 4pm-midnight, Sun. 3-11pm.

Shima, 12 Waverly Place, northeast of Washington Sq. Dine whilst admiring a garden and small pond through the window. Weekday combo lunch features chicken or dumpling entree, vegetable, soup, rice, and fruit for $5.25. Lavish dinners under $12. Open Mon.-Fri. noon-2:30pm and 5-11:15pm, Sat.-Sun. 5:30-11pm.

Balducci's, 424 Sixth Ave. at 9th St. A gourmet Italian supermarket, carrying scrumptious delicacies and desserts. The prices may hurt but your belly will belch opera. Open daily 7am-8:30pm.

Mustafa, 48 Greenwich Ave. A fast-food Middle Eastern joint with tables and chairs outside. Down a felafel sandwich ($2.50) or its carnivorous counterpart, *schwarma* ($3.75). Open daily 11am-11pm.

Elephant and Castle, 68 Greenwich Ave. The avenue cuts diagonally northwest from Sixth Ave. at 8th St. Pleasant atmosphere makes this place consistently popular. Select from a page of omelette options ($5-7). The apple, cheddar and walnut creation proves especially exciting. Delectable sesame chicken with spinach and cucumbers $9. Open Mon.-Thurs. 8:30am-midnight, Fri. 8:30am-1am, Sat. 10am-1am, Sun. 10am-midnight.

Italian Home Cooking, 232 Bleecker St. at Carmine St. A tiny, friendly, perpetually crowded, manic restaurant. Pasta with verve and the best minestrone soup in town ($3.50). This place is so authentic that there's even an afternoon siesta. Open Mon.-Fri. 11:30am-3pm and 5-7pm.

Tutta Pasta, 26 Carmine St. A modern establishment with glass doors that are slid open in summer. The catch here is the fresh homemade pastas, including *tortellini, manicotti,* and *linguini* ($8). Open Mon.-Thurs. 11:30am-10:30pm, Fri.-Sat. 11:30am-11:30pm.

Ayaedeh, 33 Carmine St. (242-8729). Translates into "This is it." The chef stirs up unique Jamaican-inspired dishes. If the Rasta Pasta (spinach and tomato noodles in a thyme, basil, and mushroom sauce with plantains; $8.50), doesn't intrigue your taste buds, something else should. Experiment with oxtail or curried goat. BYOB. Open Tues.-Thurs. 11:30am-10:30pm, Fri.-Sat. 11:30am-11:30pm, Sun. 11:30am-10:30pm.

Murray's, 42 Cornelia St. (243-3289), off Bleecker St. A deli specializing in cheeses from Argentina, Greece, and Italy, among others, not to mention French Beaufort at a reasonable $7 per pound. Even if you're not hungry, go in to grab a smell. Open Mon.-Sat. 8:30am-6pm.

Caliente Cab Co., 61 Seventh Ave. A huge margarita glass and the rear ends of cabs adorn this clique-infested bar/restaurant. Those who live for beans should order the barbecued burrito ($7.25) or the Old Smokey Sandwich ($7). Open daily noon-3am

The Whitehorse Tavern, 567 Hudson Ave. Boisterous students and screaming waiters give life to Dylan Thomas's death site. A bar/restaurant with a historical claim to fame, heavenly food in the back, and the best burgers in the village ($4). Open Sun.-Thurs. 11am-2am, Fri.-Sat. 11am-4am.

Cheung Seng, 24 Eighth Ave. (691-7698). Unique Chinese food to take out or eat in. A quart of zesty chicken *lo mein* costs only $6. Open Mon.-Thurs. 11am-11pm, Fri.-Sat. 11am-midnight, Sun. noon-11am.

Tony Roma's, 450 Sixth Ave. north of 10th St. Part of a chain, this restaurant offers great ribs ($14). Try the onion rings served in a loaf ($4.50). Look for all-you-can-eat specials. Open Sun.-Thurs. 11:30am-10pm, Fri.-Sat. 11:30am-midnight.

East Village and Lower East Side

There are few frills but plenty of thrills on the lower end of the East Side, where pasty-faced punks and starving artists sup alongside an older generation conversing in Polish, Hungarian, or Yiddish. Observant Jews can't lose and slavophiles can only win in the delis and restaurants here. The Eastern European restaurants distributed along First and Second Ave. serve up some of the best deals in Manhattan. The **9th St Bakery,** 350 E. 9th St., and the **S&W Skull Cap Corporation,** 45 Essex St., sell inimitable New York bagels and bialys.

If you consider such delicacies at all bland you should hurry to one of the dozens of cheap Indian restaurants in the East Village, particularly concentrated on 6th St. between First and Second. Or you can try the newer, West Village-type restaurants that cater to a young and with-it crowd—often indistinguishable from their neighbors to the west.

Odessa, 117 Ave. A at 7th St. Beware of ordinary-looking coffee shops with slavic names. Lurking beneath the title may be an excellent, inexpensive restaurant serving Eastern European specialties. Choose your favorites from a huge assortment of *pirogi,* stuffed cabbage, kielbasa, sauerkraut, potato pancakes, and other delicacies for the combination dinner here. Spinach pie and small Greek salad $4.50. Open daily 7am-midnight.

Kiev, 117 Second Ave. Unparalleled *pirogi* and tons of heavy foods laced with sour cream and butter, generally under $5. Upscale deli decor. A popular late-night (and early-morning) pit stop for East Village club hoppers with the munchies. Open 24 hr.

Second Ave. Delicatessen, 156 Second Ave. at 10th St. The definitive New York deli; people come into the city just to be snubbed by the waiters here. Have a pastrami or tongue on rye for $6.50, a fabulous burger deluxe for $6.25, or Jewish penicillin (also known as "chicken soup") for $2.75. Note the Hollywood-style star plaques embedded in the sidewalk outside: this was once the heart of the Yiddish theater district. But while their art form is all but forgotten, such personages as Moishe Oysher and Bella Meisel have gained their foothold on immortality by being engraved in the pavement. Open Mon.-Fri. 8am-midnight, Sat.-Sun. 8am-2am.

East Village Ukrainian Restaurant, 140 Second Ave, between 8th and 9th. Pleasantly decorated, complete with chandeliers; excellent food at amazingly low prices. Cheese *pirogi* $4.50, stuffed cabbage with potato and mushroom gravy $5.25, kielbasa with sauerkraut $5, bowl of homemade soup $1.50, hot borscht with vegetables $1.75. Open Mon.-Fri. noon-11pm, Fri.-Sat. noon-midnight.

Tandoor Fast Food, 188 First Ave., between 11th and 12th. Spicy food with no frills, very cheap. Beef mushroom curry $5, homemade breads $1-2. Weekday lunch special (noon-3pm) $3.50. Open daily noon-midnight.

Veselka, 144 Second Ave. Yet another no-frills gem. Blintzes for $4.50, and if vous want to get fancy you can have an asparagus and mushroom crepe for $6. Open 24 hr.

The Cloister Café, 238 E. 9th St. Dive into your bowl of cappuccino in a restaurant with more stained glass per square foot than any place this side of Rome. Or lounge in an outdoor garden and sup from an inexpensive, quality menu with light dishes ($5-10). Open daily 11am-1am.

Hoki's Garden, 153 First Ave., between 9th and 10th. A darlink little Yugoslavian place, with outdoor seating in a courtyard. Barbecued chicken $6.25, rolled spinach pie $4.25. Open Mon.-Fri. 9:30am-10pm, later on weekends.

Kyber Pass Restaurant, 34 St. Mark's Place. A dainty place on the central artery of the East Village, serving Afghani food. Basically Middle Eastern curries, soups, and dumplings, but with a Chinese influence. Try *Bouranee Banjoun,* eggplant with mint yogurt and fresh coriander ($6.50) or *phirnee,* a delicate rice pudding with rose water ($2). Open daily noon-midnight.

The Life Café, 343 E. 10th St. The gimmick: old issues of *Life* magazine. Good gimmick. Café-style menu with most offerings around $7. Open daily 11am-1am.

Pizzapiazza, 785 Broadway at 10th St. Large, well-engineered innovation in pizza presentation. Try your pie Cajun, Californian, or Parisienne. Pizza from $6. Pasta, salad, burgers from $4.50. Open Sun.-Thurs. 11:45am-midnight, Fri.-Sat. 11:45am-1am.

The 11 Café, 170 Second Ave. at 11th St. The decor, not the seemingly random name, will plunge you into the tropics and prepare you for the cuisine of Venezuela. House specialty, stuffed tortillas, run $7-14. Open daily noon-4pm.

Passage to India, 308 E. 6th St. off Second Ave. Newer and classier than others on the block. Dine under chandeliers and brass-framed mirrors in British colonial style. Full *tandoori* dinner (soup, appetizer, main course, dessert, coffee) $12. Open daily noon-midnight.

Sugar Reef, 93 Second Ave., between 5th and 6th. Enough fake fruit to stock a plastic plantation; loud music to match the color scheme. Wide selection of appropriately garish drinks; entrees $6.50-14. Open Mon.-Thurs. 5-11:45pm, Fri.-Sat. 5pm-12:45am, Sun. 3-11:45pm.

Kosher mavens won't find much *traif* east of First Ave., especially south of East Houston St., where a Jewish community has stayed put since its turn-of-the-century immigrant days.

Ratner's Dairy Restaurant, 138 Delancey St. The most famous of the kosher restaurants, partly due to its frozen food line. Jewish dietary laws strictly followed; you will have to go elsewhere for a pastrami sandwich with mayo. But there's no better place to feast on fruit blintzes and sour cream ($8) or simmering vegetarian soups ($3.50). Open Sun.-Fri. 6am-11pm, Sat. 6am-2am.

Katz's Delicatessen, 205 E. Houston St., near Orchard. Classic informal deli, established in 1888. You'd better know what you want, because the staff here doesn't fool around. Have an overstuffed corned beef sandwich with a pickle for $5. Mail-order department enables you to send a salami to a loved one (or perhaps an ex-loved one). With testimonial letters from both Carter and Reagan, how could it be bad? (Don't think about that one too much.) Sun.-Thurs. 7am-11pm, Fri.-Sat. 7am-1am.

Yonah Schimmel Knishery, 137 E. Houston St. Rabbi Schimmel's establishment, around since the heyday of the Jewish Lower East Side, has honed the knish to an art, if not a religion. Kasha and fruit-filled knishes (from $1.75) available as well. Or try yogurt from a 71-year old strain. Open daily 8am-6pm.

Bernstein-on-Essex, 135 Essex St. Chinatown meets the Lower East Side, and presto—kosher Chinese food. Steep prices ($10 and up) and non-existent ambience. But observant Jews will travel for hours to indulge their palates here. An only-in-New-York establishment. This is the original "Waiter what time is it?"—"Sorry, not my table" restaurant. Open Sun.-Thurs. 8am-12:30am, Fri. 8am-3pm, Sat. 9:30pm-12:30am.

Ludlow St. Café, 85 Ludlow St. (353-0536) Hip. Exotic menu with funky, unusual South American-style dishes from $5. Intimate atmosphere, perhaps too intimate considering the live bands that play here every night. You're better off coming for lunch or brunch. Open daily 6pm-midnight.

SoHo

Like the residents, the restaurants here can prove surprisingly down to earth, but also may demonstrate an occasionally distracting preoccupation with art (some are practically indistinguishable from their neighboring galleries—but again, that holds true for the people too). Even the grocery stores get in on the act: **Dean and Deluca,** 560 Broadway, at Prince St., features gallery-quality art and gourmet-caliber food.

SoHo specializes in brunch; the ambience here has been custom-fitted to lazy Sunday mornings, and you can down your coffee and cantelope in any of a number of café/bar establishments. Prince St. and Spring St. run parallel to one another through most of SoHo, and together they account for many of the best and most affordable eating spots in the neighborhood.

Elephant and Castle, 183 Prince St., off Sullivan. Also at 68 Greenwich Ave. Popular with locals for its excellent coffee and creative light food. Perfect for brunch. Prepare to wait for a table. Dinner around $10, brunch around $8. Open Sun.-Thurs. 8:30am-midnight, Fri.-Sat. 8:30am-1am.

The Cupping Room, 359 West Broadway. Drinks, dinner, and coffee in a low-key atmosphere. A great choice for a weekend brunch on either Sat. or Sun., but arrive early or be prepared to wait. On the bright side, brunch is served from 7am to 6pm, and therefore difficult to miss. During the week, the Cupping serves a full breakfast and dinner menu. Entrees around $14. Light menu with salads and burgers ($7-8) also available. Open Sun.-Fri. 7:30am-1am; Sat. 7:30am-2am, but the kitchen still closes at midnight.

Fanelli's Café, 94 Prince St. A veeery mellow neighborhood establishment, where you can lounge on the sidewalk tables and savor your $2 beer. Burgers $6, steamed mussels $8. Open Mon.-Sat. 10am-2am, Sun. noon-2am.

Berry's, 180 Spring St., near Thompson St. A small, dark, homey place with simple American food, full bar, outdoor seating, and reasonable prices. Entrees around $8. Open daily 11:30am-3:30pm and 5:30-11:30pm. Kitchen closes at 10pm.

SoHo Kitchen and Bar, 103 Greene St., near Prince St. The quintessential SoHo hangout: sky-high ceiling, gigantic artwork, scores of wines by the glass, casual dress. Pasta around $9, sandwiches $7. Open Sun.-Thurs. 11:30am-2am, kitchen closes at 12:45am; Fri.-Sat. 11:30am-4am, kitchen closes at 1:45am.

Spring St. Natural Restaurant and Bar, 62 Spring St., at Lafayette. Vegetable dishes with an Asian influence, plus much seafood and "natural" poultry. Heavenly vegetable tempura $8.50. Open daily 11:30am-2am.

Tennessee Mountain, 143 Spring St. (tel. 431-3993). New Yorkers may be notorious for their sketchy knowledge of national geography, but isn't anyone bothered by the fact that this restaurant named for a southeastern state serves the Tex-Mex cuisine of the southwest? But no one could be bothered by the memorable frozen margaritas or barbequed ribs. Entrees $5.50-14. Open Sun.-Wed. 11:30am-11pm, Thurs.-Sat. 11:30am-midnight.

5&10, No Exaggeration, 77 Greene St. Listen to live piano music, look at jewelry for sale, eat European dishes, pay $7—or much, much more. Open Tues.-Fri. 5pm-1am; also weekend brunch. Two-drink minimum and $5 cover charge after 10pm.

New Deal, 152 Spring St., between West Broadway and Wooster. A fine option for those with a hankering for nouvelle cuisine (otherwise known as pretentious American food). You can avoid the steep *prix fixe* by ordering from a bistro menu that allows you to sample the chef's specialties at $6.50 per item. Or nurse one of the drink specials at the bar from 4-7pm. Open Mon.-Fri. noon-10:30pm, Sat.-Sun. noon-11:30pm.

Cowgirl Hall of Fame, 519 Hudson St. Antelope chandeliers and leather saddles. Barbecued chicken sandwich $5, buttermilk pancakes $5.25, fried chicken with mashed potatoes and gravy $7. Sunday brunch 11:30am-4pm (with children's brunch menu). Open Mon.-Fri. noon-11pm, Sat.-Sun. 5pm-midnight.

Chinatown

New Yorkers thrive on evenings and dawns in Chinatown, eating food just like Mom used to order in. Crowned by a red and gold pagoda, the neighborhood has nearly 200 restaurants cooking the best Chinese cuisine on the eastern seaboard. But they don't make dumplings for Trumplings—this insular community charges little for the best Asian food around. Try the *dim sum*—bite-sized hors d'oeuvres—served in almost every tea shop here. You may want to avoid the more commercial establishments which line Mott St. To reach Chinatown, take the Lexington Ave. IRT to Canal St., walk 2 blocks east on Canal to Mott St., go right on Mott, and follow the curved street toward the Bowery, Confucius Plaza, and E. Broadway. Explore the side streets along the way.

Fortify yourself for the trek through the crowded streets with a cup of Turtle Longevity Soup ($1.25) at **Maxim Bakery** on the corner of Canal and Mott St., or journey down Mott to Mosco St., where the proprietor of the **Hong Kong Cake Company** stand will gladly trade six coconut egg rolls or 20 bite-sized egg cakes for your single dollar. When you order in restaurants here, do it Chinese style; order one fewer dish than people at your table and share. You can always order more later.

Hee Seung Fung Teahouse (HSF), 46 Bowery. Large and hectic. Widely acclaimed *dim sum* dishes $1.50-1.75 (served 8am-4:30pm). Try sesame oil and ginger crispy fish and the *jung* (sticky rice wrapped in tea leaves). From the subway, walk east on Canal St. to the Bowery, then take a sharp left. Open daily 7:30am-2am.

Nom Wah Tea Parlor, 13 Doyers St., a curved side street north of Mott St. off the Bowery. *Dim sum* served all day ($1-2). Indulge yourself in the "simple imposing purity of steamed pork buns." Open daily 10am-8pm.

May May Gourmet Bakery, 35 Pell St., off Mott St. Countless interesting pastries (under $1) and fresh wontons ($3.75 for 10 pieces). Wash it all down with a ginger lemon coke ($1). Open daily 9am-7pm.

Lung Fong Bakery, 41 Mott St. Explore the racks for a quick nosh. Almond cookies cost 50¢, coconut squares 50¢, surprisingly tasty black bean paste (in the form of a cookie) 40¢. Open daily 8am-9pm.

Kam Kuo Food Corp., 7 Mott St. Multitudinous wonders grace this local supermarket. Explore the seafood section for a quick education in marine variety. Try a bag of dried *lychee* nuts ($2.50 per bag), raisin-like fruits with soft shells and pits. If you're up for a challenge, you can attempt to swallow an ancient egg ($1). Allegedly blackened from months spent beneath the earth, these eggs are considered delicacies. Open Mon.-Thurs. 9am-9pm, Fri.-Sat. 9am-10pm.

Petite, 1 E. Broadway, across the Bowery where Mott St. ends. The best seafood in Chinatown. *Soochow,* often called the Venice of China, has evolved a sweeter and less spicy cuisine than the more common Shanghai variety. Try the Szechuan baby shrimp ($7.25). Open Sun.-Thurs. 11am-9:45pm, Fri.-Sat. 11am-10:45pm.

Wai Tung, 13 Division St. The street cuts northeast from the Bowery, forming Confucius Plaza. Roasting chickens and slabs of pig hang in the window. Interesting barbecue roasts $7.25, ducks' feet and wings $5.25. Open daily 7am-11pm.

Do Noodle, 26 E. Broadway. Chef lunch special includes a rice plate or a huge bowl of soup and noodles (under $4). Open daily 10:30am-11pm.

Bo Bo, 20½ Pell St., off Mott St. Popular, clean, sweet-smelling restaurant. Offers every meat combination with asparagus ($6-$8).

House of Vegetarian, 68 Mott St. This chinese cuisine comes in a healthier form, cooked with soy, wheat by-products, and roots. Here they stuff dumplings with rice and veggies ($1.30) and would never try to pass off ketchup as a vegetable. Try *lo mein* with three different types of mushrooms ($3.75). Open daily 11am-10:30pm.

Pho Ha, 66 Bayard St., off Mott St. Tremendous servings of Vietnamese cuisine. Beef noodle soup the specialty ($3-4) but be sure to explore the makeshift dishes on the menu implanted in the tables. Open Mon.-Thurs. 10am-10pm, Fri. 10am-11pm, Sat.-Sun. 9am-11pm.

Mweng Thai Restaurant, 23 Pell St., off Mott St. If you're tired of Chinese, you can't go wrong with Thai. The curry comes in four different colors—good luck to those who choose hot green ($5). Don't neglect to ask for a pitcher of water. Open Tues.-Fri. 11:30am-11pm, Sat 11am-11pm, Sun 11am-10pm.

Hung Fat Restaurant, 63 Mott St. Late-night meals in a formica heaven, highlighted by a spicy Szechuan section. Try the *king po gai ding,* a tender, diced chicken dish with pepper and peanuts. Open daily 10am-5am.

Wohop, 17 Mott St. (962-8617). The main attraction is the hours. The downstairs section is more authentic than the cleaner, aboveground section. Good take-out. Most dishes under $5. Open daily 11am-5am.

Peking Duck House, 22 Mott St. This upscale place won eight stars from the *Daily News.* If someone else is picking up the bill, go for the *Peking Duck Extravaganza* ($27), the best in America. And don't overlook the fried spare ribs with honey ($7.75). Open Sun.-Thurs. 11:30am-10:30pm, Fri.-Sat. 11:30am-11:30pm.

Chinatown Ice Cream Factory, 65 Bayard St., off Mott St. Some say Chinatown natives give equal business to the Haägen-Dazs down the street, but this authentic homemade ice cream comes in flavors like ginger, lichee, papaya, green tea, red bean, and almond cookie. Cones $1.60. Open daily noon-midnight.

Little Italy

A chunk of Naples seems to have swum downtown into this lively quarter bounded by Canal, Lafayette, Houston and Bowery St. Raging Bull Robert De Niro stalked the *Mean Streets* here in 1973 and then returned a year later to cut a few slice-of-life scenes for the 1918 segments of *The Godfather Part II.*

Immortalized by Billy Joel, who used to hang in the local **ristoranti,** Mulberry Street is the main drag and the appetite avenue of Little Italy. From Spring St. down to Canal St., Chinese idiograms gradually take over. Italian restaurants cluster around Mulberry St. During the day, Little Italy keeps quieter than most districts of New York; at night, evening crowds clog the sidewalk cafés. Stroll here after 7pm to see the most street life. For the sake of variety and thrift, sup at a restaurant but get your just desserts at a caffè.

If you're around on the second Thursday in September, you could be lapping up lasagna and *prosciutto* at the **Feast of San Gennaro.** Mulberry St. goes wild as Little Italy toasts the Saint of Naples during a raucous 10 days of feasting and partying.

Assagio, 178 Hester St. (226-9197), off Mulberry St. The scarlet A on Hester distinguishes the spot. Dining at Assagio is a singular experience. Understated, elegant decor sets the stage for virtuoso performance by the chef. Spaghetti et al. $6-7.50. Chicken $8.50-10.75, veal $8-10.50. Open Sun.-Thurs., noon-midnight, Fri.-Sat. noon-1am.

Luna, 112 Mulberry St., between Hester and Canal St. Enter through the small kitchen—where a halo of steam inaugurates the generous platters of clams—to emerge into a narrow, somewhat haphazard dining room, furnished with stray photographs on hot blue walls. Veal *cacciatore* $9. Fresh pasta from $8. Open Sun.-Thurs. noon-11:30pm, Fri.-Sat. noon-12:30am.

Paolucci's, 149 Mulberry St. Family-owned restaurant with a penchant for heaping portions ($6-8). The boss watches you from the front wall. Appetizers $4-7, Chicken *cacciatore* with salad $10. Open Mon.-Tues. and Thurs.-Fri. noon-11pm, Sat.-Sun. noon-11:30pm.

Marionetta, 124 Mulberry St. Sit at sidewalk tables in the frenzy of things, or inside for something more intimate, and order some of the most inexpensive veal dishes in the neighborhood. Veal *parmagiana* $8.50-10.25, chicken *parmagiana* $8. Pasta $8-10. Lasagna $6.75. Open daily noon-2am.

Puglia Restaurant, 189 Hester St. Long tables mean fun and rowdy. Venture into 3 separate dining rooms, ranging from diner-like to warehouse-like. A favorite with New Yorkers and bold tourists. Monstrous plate of mussels $6, entrees $6.75-11.25. Live music nightly. Open Tues.-Sun. noon-1am.

Ballato, 55 E. Houston St., off Mott. Gracefully stemmed wire glasses and glistening chocolate-covered cherries greet you. Formerly a haunt of the beautiful people, now the breeding ground of impeccable Southern Italian cooking. Pasta $11.50, trout in olive oil $12.50. *Antipasti* $5.50-8. Open Tues.-Fri. noon-11pm, Sat. 4pm-midnight, Sun. 4-10pm.

Ruggiero's, 194 Grand St., off Mulberry St. A tidy, uptownish *ristorante* with outdoor seating in summer. Soups $4, pasta $8-10, including the intoxicating *penne alla vodka* made with fire water. Chicken dishes hatch for $11-12. Open daily 11:30am-midnight.

Villa Pensa, 198 Grand St., off Mulberry St. Little Italy's oldest, established in 1898. The 2-room terracotta pasta palace has hosted primadonnas like Rudolf Valentino and Enrico Caruso. Joe DiMaggio batted in countless spaghetti dishes, part of his strenuous diet that included dining in the company of Marilyn Monroe, who favored veal. Peter Falk walked out of this place because they would not serve scrambled eggs but came back later, shabby Colombo coat and all, and ordered pasta. The Big Man on Mulberry St., Billy "Italian Restaurant" Joel, wrote *Modern Woman* at one of the tables in the back. Traditional cuisine cooked to order. Spaghetti dishes $6.50-9.25, soups $2-4.50, fish $7.75 and beyond. Daily specials $10.50-11.50.

Angelo's of Mulberry St., 146 Mulberry St., between Grand and Hester. An old Little Italy stand-by, if a tad touristy. Upscale prices and quality. Pasta $11. Open Sun. and Tues.-Thurs. noon-11:30pm, Fri. noon-12:30am, Sat. noon-1am.

Ristorante Taormina, 147 Mulberry St., between Grand and Hester. No linoleum here; just large windows, graceful green plants, exposed brick walls, and blondewood fittings. Neapolitan fare at its best. Soups start at $4.75, specialties at $10. Open daily noon-11:30pm.

Il Fornaio, 132A Mulberry St. (226-8306). Though sausages and cheeses hang exhibitionist-style over the counter, the clean white-tiled interior, with its perfectly symmetrical jars and tins of olive oil and its absence of garishness, suggests that Il Fornaio is the new kid on the block. Perky, upbeat, reasonable menu. For lunch, mini-pizza costs $3. Hot sandwiches start at $4.50, pasta dinners at $5. Open Sun.-Thurs. noon-11pm, Fri.-Sat. noon-11:30pm.

Vincent's Clam Bar, 119 Mott St., off Hester St. A New York institution. Remarkable linguini with special sauce ($6.50) in a generic setting. A cornucopia of other linguinis, under equally unforgettable sauces. $6.50-13. Film and fiscal sharks prowl in Vincent's waters. Open Sun.-Thurs. 11am-1am, Fri.-Sat. 11am-3am.

Road to Mandalay, 380 Broome St., off Mulberry St. A rare Burmese pearl washed up on the Italian shores of Mulberry St. Refined Burmese cuisine, served in a cozy setting enhanced by baskets overflowing with fruit and vegetables. Start with the coconut noodle soup ($3.25), accompanied by the thousand-layered pancake, a delicate Burmese bread ($2.50). Entrees range from $7-9.50 with conversation-piece curry dishes laced with coriander checking in at $8. Open Mon.-Fri. 5-11pm, Sat.-Sun. 5pm-midnight.

Benito I, 174 Mulberry St. A small no-nonsense trattoria churning out genuine cuisine. For a memorable appetizer, order *mozzarella in carozza* ($6), and follow it up with *pollo scarpariello* ($11), a chicken beak and feather above the rest. Open Sun.-Thurs. noon-11pm, Fri-Sat. noon-midnight.

Paesano, 136 Mulberry St. (966-3337). Foresaking subtlety for pomp, Paesano embodies the Southern Italian soul. Everthing about this restaurant invites comparisons to big family reunions. Everyone seems familiar, portions are big enough to sink ships, and the piped tango seems a blood relation of the tune from *The Godfather.* White stucco and exposed brick straddle dark oak crossbeams wrapped in garlands and hung with hundreds of little Chianti bottles, diapered like babies in straw overalls. Pasta dishes $7, chicken $9-11, veal $10. Open daily 11am-midnight.

Caffè Sorrento, 132 Mulberry St. Part of a new breed of M-Street eateries, Sorrento takes exotica off the walls and puts it on the menu. Bring along an Italian-English dictionary to help you choose. Pasta $7.75, specialties (including veal and chicken) $6.50-10.75. Open daily 11am-midnight.

La Mela, 167 Mulberry St. If Little Italy believed in cult restaurants, La Mela would be the kingpin. Kitsch paintings and postcards dot the walls haphazardly: tables and chairs crop up here and there like mushrooms after a rain. Technically there's no menu; the boss talks you through your order. People travel from as far as Cleveland to sink their teeth into the famed *chicken scarpariello* ($10.50). A wide assortment of pasta and *gnocchi* $7-10. Equally rambunctious outdoor seating in their backyard, complete with a guitar-touting bard, the final mark of authenticity. The menu, a handwritten flyswatter of a paper bag, beckons: "Come in side please, for sure we will not disappointed you." Open daily noon-11pm.

Rocky's Italian Restaurant, 45 Spring St. at Mulberry. This Italian stallion punches out primo dishes a few blocks away from the heart of the action. When they shot *The Godfather III,* Rob Reiner and the rest came here to put away the chops. Billy Crystal and his uncle are regulars in this place that's been churning out consistently good Italian fare for over 20 years. Pasta $6.50-10 (some untangling may be required). For dessert, try their homemade Italian cheesecake, made with fresh ricotta tinted with anise ($3). Open Mon.-Sat. 11am-11pm.

Caffès

Caffè Roma, 385 Broome St. at Mulberry. Good caffès get better with time. A full-fledged saloon in the 1890s, Roma has kept its original furnishings intact: dark green walls with polished brass ornaments, chandeliers, and darkwood cabinets where liquor bottles used to roost. Since its saloon days, Roma has removed the imbibery and installed several elegant, Tuscan landscapes. The pastries and coffee, Roma's *raison d'etre,* prove as refined as the setting. Try the neapolitan *cannoli* or the baba au rhum ($1.20 to take out, $1.75 to eat in). Potent espresso $1.40; obligatory cappuccino, under a tiara of foamed milk, $2.25.

Caffè Biondo, 141 Mulberry St. Sip a $1.25 cup of espresso in a perfectly bare setting, touched up only by a few ancient relief fragments on the walls. Caffè corretto $2.25, cappuccino alla panna (with whipped cream) $2.50. *Cannoli* $2.25. Open daily noon-1am.

La Bella Ferrara, 110 Mulberry St. Named after the city that brought you turbo power, La Bella Ferrara maintains the dual imperatives of power and grace in their dynamic production of *dolci.* The largest selection of pastries around. Sleek glass and checkered tile. Pastries $1-3, cappuccino $2.50. Lunch special (soup and sandwich) $5.50. Open Sun.-Thurs. 9am-1am, Fri.-Sat. 9am-2am.

Ferrara, 195-201 Grand St. A slick emporium where hundreds of tempting pastries vie for your attention. The espresso bar has become one of the city's most popular places for cappuccino and others of its creamy species. In good weather the bar extends onto the sidewalk, where a counter dispenses authentic Italian gelati. Open daily 7:10am-midnight.

Lo Spuntino, 117 Mulberry St., between Hester and Canal. Not the flashy type. Gorgeous desserts compensate for lackluster decor. Try any one of the eclectic mousses. Espresso $1.50, double espresso $2.25. Little Italy's greatest ice cream—tiramiso and tartuffo ($3). Hours vary.

Caffè Napoli, 191 Hester St., at Mulberry. Like the mathematician Klein's bottle, Caffè Napoli has neither a separate inside nor a separate outside, but is a dynamic symbiosis of the two. People pour in and out, but most stick around long enough to polish off their desserts. Standard caffè prices. Open daily 10am-4pm.

Casa Dolce Caffè, 386 Broome St., just off Mulberry St. Just starting out, this place will probably receive the Rookie of the Year title for its fine performance in the pastry category, strong well-tempered espresso, friendly service, and reasonable prices. Espresso $1.50, cappuccino $2.25, iced espresso $2.50. Gelati in provocative flavors like hazelnut, *zabaglione,* and *zuppa Inglese* (literally, English soup) $3. Proprietors operate a video rental in the back room: videos piped onto the monitors Sat. nights. Open Sun.-Thurs. 11am-midnight, Fri.-Sat. 11am-1am.

Financial District

Bargain-basement cafeteria-style joints here can fill you up with everything from gazpacho to Italian sausages. Fast-food places pepper Broadway between Dey and John St., just a few feet from the overpriced offerings of the Main Concourse of the World Trade Center. In summer, food pushcarts form a solid wall on Broadway between Cedar and Liberty St., wheeling and dealing in a realm beyond hot dogs. Assorted vendors sell felafel and eggplant plates ($2.25), cheese nachos ($3) and chilled gazpacho with an onion roll ($3). You can sup or dine in Liberty park, across the street.

At the pedestrian plaza at Coenties Slip, between Pearl and South William St., you can choose among small budget restaurants. Munch on fish and chips at **Papaya Hut** here or select from a bounteous buffet at **The Golden Chopsticks** for $4 per pound.

North of City Hall, food kiosks fill St. Andrew's Plaza, a no-frills alternative for the local crowd of office workers doing lunch. At the South St. Seaport you can choose from a collage of food-booths; dine formally on exquisitely prepared salmon, or chomp casually on fried clams. Up Fulton St., between Cliff and William St., the cost of dining dwindles.

Frank's Papaya, 192 Broadway, at John St. Excellent value, quick service. Very close to World Trade Center. Hot dog 60¢. Open daily 5:30am-10pm.

Happy Deli, 181 Broadway, between John and Cortlandt St. A salad bar the size of a football field—choose your favorite greens at $4 per pound. Open 24 hr.

Main Food Pavilion, World Trade Center Main Concourse. Directly behind entrance to PATH trains. Central seating area surrounded by baking and delicatessing. Inexpensive fare, although you can do even better on the street. Croissant $1, cheese omelette $2.85.

Eat and Drink, 5 World Trade Center Main Concourse, near entrance to subway and PATH trains. A cafeteria with less-than-zero frills. Large slice of pizza $1.75. Chicken noodle soup $2. Open Mon.-Fri. 6:30am-4pm.

McDonald's, 150 Broadway at Liberty St. For the Wall St. McPower lunch. A double decker McPalace seating 250 at marble tabletops. A doorman in a tux and the strains of a baby grand piano greet you. Pick at grapes and strawberries with your breakfast, or down a pastry and espresso. Drop in on the new gift boutique on your way out. Open Mon.-Fri. 6am-11pm, Sat.-Sun. 8am-9pm.

Wolf's Delicatessen, 42 Broadway. A deli untainted by any trend in cuisine or decor that hit after the early 60s. Formica, pickles, no pretensions. Baked beans $1.10. Open Mon.-Fri. 6am-7:45pm, Sat. 6am-3:45pm.

Hamburger Harry's, 157 Chambers St. Gourmet burgers for the connoisseur; 7-oz. patty, broiled over applewood with exotic toppings, from $6. Mon.-Thurs. 11:30am-11:30pm, Fri.-Sat. 11:30am-1am, Sun. noon-11:30pm.

Kansas City Meat Exchange, 21 Beaver St. A hamburger joint that does not belong to a multinational chain! A humble Harry's. Burger $2.19, chicken on a bun $2.79. Simple seating upstairs. Open daily 10:30am-5pm.

Top Floor, Pier 17. Livelier than Fulton Market, with a better selection. Let's Make a Daiquiri (fresh fruit $3.75, no alcohol $2.50), South Philly steaks and fries (gourmet onion rings $1.81), The Salad Bowl (frozen yogurt and milkshake $2.75), Diner Dogs (foot-long hot dog $3.50).

Fulton Seaport Deli, 52 Fulton St. Select from the massive, high-quality salad bar at $3.79 per pound, then munch back at the seaport. Open 24 hr.

Topside Food Booths, Fulton Market, Fulton St. A partial survey of the highlights of this top-floor extravaganza: Everything Yogurt (pita bread sandwich $4), New York Pastrami Factory (Hebrew National hot dog $1.75), Fulton Market Fish and Clam Bar (6 oysters $6.50, fried shrimp on a bun $4.25), Burger Boys of Brooklyn (sirloin burger $3) Open daily 11:30am-9pm.

Jeremy's Ale House, 254 Front St. Garage-*cum*-Wall St. frat house. Old neckties and ladies' undergarments draped over exposed ceiling pipes. Chili $3.50. Open daily 10am-9pm.

Health Food Stores

The fitness craze of the 70s meets the ecological fixation of the 90s at these zones of purity, free from bodily contamination. They provide a wide range of escapes from the vicious chemical cycle. You can buy organic vegetables (grown without chemical additives), organic meats (from animals which have been allowed to move freely), and have not been pumped full of antibiotics, and "organic" cosmetics. Some stores have added natural juice bars, with an array of exotic fruit and veggie juices to choose from.

Whole Foods in SoHo, 117 Prince St., between Greene and Wooster St. A virtual supermarket of health foods, with a natural gourmet deli and salad bar, a fish department, and a macrobiotic department. Organic produce flown in weekly from California, the health food capital of the earth. Organic meats available. Open daily 9am-9:30pm.

Good Earth Natural Foods, 1334 First Ave., near 72nd St. Also at 169 Amsterdam Ave., at 68th St. Organic honey, complete lines of salt- and sugar-free products, staff nutritionists, and a juice bar. Open Mon.-Fri. 10am-7pm, Tues.-Thurs. 10am-7:30pm, Sat. 10am-6pm.

Integral Yoga Natural Foods, 229 W. 13th St., between Seventh and Eighth. Natural cosmetics, ecological household products, and a large selection of organically grown produce. Open Mon.-Fri. 10am-9:30pm, Sat. 10am-8:30pm, Sun. noon-6:30pm.

Vegetarian Paradise Health and Natural Food Co., 140 W. 4th St. at Sixth Ave. Chinese delicacies. Vegetarian *dim sum,* soy milk, pressed bean curd, homemade sauces. Open daily 11:30am-11:30pm.

Earth's Harvest Trading Company, 700 Columbus Ave. at 95th St. Herbs, homeopathic remedies, books. Open Mon.-Fri. 9:30am-7:30pm, Sat.-Sun. 10am-6pm.

Brooklyn

Downtown and North Brooklyn

Ethnic flavor changes every two blocks in Brooklyn. Downtown and Brooklyn Heights offer every dish you could ever want. Williamsburg seems submerged in kosher and cheap Italian restaurants, while Greenpoint is a borscht lover's paradise. Venture to find a restaurant that looks like it belongs in a foreign nation. Chances are you'll feel stuffed and wonder if the check is a joke.

Junior's, 986 Flatbush Ave. Extension (852-5257), just across the Manhattan Bridge. Lit up like a jukebox and adored for its roast beef and brisket, among other temptations. Entrees $8, complete dinner $15. Displaced New Yorkers drive for hours to satisfy their cheesecake cravings here (plain slice $3). Open Sun.-Thurs. 6:30am-1am, Fri.-Sat. 6:30am-3am.

Moroccan Star, 205 Atlantic Ave. (643-0800) in Brooklyn Heights. Entrenched in the local Arab community, this restaurant serves delicious and reasonably cheap food. Try the *pastello* ($8.75), a delicate semi-sweet chicken pastry with almonds. Open Sun. and Tues.-Thurs. 11am-11pm, Fri.-Sat. 11am-midnight.

Near East Bakery, 183 Atlantic Ave. (875-0016) in Brooklyn Heights. Stairs lead down to a stone basement, a Saharan atmosphere, and the most authentic meat and spinach pies ($1.10) in the borough. An entire loaf of fresh whole-wheat bread costs $1.40. Open Tues.-Sat. 9:30am-4:30pm, Sun. 9:30am-1pm.

Teresa's, 80 Montague St. (797-3996) in Brooklyn Heights. Good, cheap Polish food makes this place popular. Two pieces of stuffed pepper ($6) or some *pirogi* ($3.25) stuffed with cheese, potatoes, meat, sauerkraut, or mushrooms make for a filling meal. Open daily 7am-11pm.

Promenade Restaurant, 101 Montague St. (237-9796). A typical diner atmosphere with outdoor seating. A Romanian steak sandwich ($7) here serves as a fleeting pleasure. Open Mon.-Fri. noon-10:30pm, Sat.-Sun. 11:30am-10:30pm.

Milo's Restaurant, 559 Lorimer St. (384-8457) in Williamsburg. Subway: J or M to Lorimer St. In a neighborhood packed with Italian food this place stands out with its jukebox that plays 40-odd Sinatra tunes. Antipasto ($3) and several choices of pasta (under $5) will keep your budget healthy. Try the Napolitan specialty *capozzelle,* an entire lamb's head served with lemon wedges—bon appetit! Open Wed.-Sun. 11am-10pm.

Stylowd Restaurant, 694 Manhattan Ave. (383-8993) in Greenpoint. Subway: G to Nassau Ave. Polish cuisine in its best and cheapest form. Sample *kielbasa* (Polish sausage) with fried onions, sauerkraut, and bread ($4) or roast beef in homemade gravy with potatoes for $4. All other entrees served with a free glass of compote (fruit drink). Delicious potato pancakes $2.50. Open Mon.-Thurs. noon-9pm, Fri. noon-10pm, Sat. 11am-10pm, Sun. 11am-9pm.

Central Brooklyn

It would be impossible to name every great affordable restaurant in this area, but here are a few to get you started in the right direction:

El Castillo de Jagua, 148 Fifth Ave. at St. John Place in Park Slope. Subway: D to Seventh Ave. The deafening jukebox pumps out the newest Latino rhythms. Excellent, cheap food with great breakfast specials. Try a platter of *platanos* (fried bananas), the Latin American french fry. Open daily 7am-midnight.

Mexican and Lebanon Restaurant, 5709 Fifth Ave., in Sunset. Subway: R or N to 59th St. Tacos ($1.35) and enchiladas ($1.55) alongside baklava ($1.50). Open Wed.-Mon. 10am-10pm.

Kar Chang, 5605 Eighth Ave., in Brooklyn's new Chinatown in Sunset. Subway: R or N to 59th St. Wide variety of seafood includes frogs and snails. Clay pot casseroles ($7.50-10) and the best hot and sour soup in town ($1.50). If you're still hungry, grab a roast pork bun (50-60¢) at a nearby bakery. Open daily 10:30am-11pm.

Cafeteria of the Main Branch Library, Grand Army Plaza. Subway: #2, 3, or 4 to Grand Army Plaza. Unexciting food, but superior to McDonald's. "The Deal" provides 2 pieces of chicken, a quarter-pound of barbecue, a biscuit, cole slaw, and fries for $3.60. Open Mon.-Fri. 9am-5:30pm, Sat. 10am-5pm, Sun. 1-4:30pm.

Short Ribs, 9101 Third Ave., in Bay Ridge. Subway: R to 86th St. The best barbecue around, especially if someone else foots the somewhat hefty bill. Try the French onion soup served in a loaf of bread ($4). A solid meal with onion rings costs $10-15. Open Sun.-Thurs. 11:30am-11pm, Fri.-Sat. 11:30am-1am.

South Brooklyn

The shores of Brooklyn present a true dining dilemma: the choices are endless. Try knishes (Eastern European filled dough creations) on Brighton Beach Ave., Italian calamari (fried squid) in spicy marinara sauce along Emmons Ave. in

Sheepshead Bay, or tri-colored candy on Coney Island. Taste as many different things as you can. Your stomach, not your wallet, will feel it.

Mrs. Staul's Knishes, 1001 Brighton Beach Ave., at Coney Island Ave. World-famous knishes ($1.35; seniors $1.10) in twenty different flavors, including pineapple cheese. Grab a *hamantaschen* (a three-cornered, fruit-filled pastry) for dessert (90¢). Open Wed. 10am-7:45pm, Thurs.-Tues. 8am-7:45pm.

Sea Lane Bakery, 615 Brighton Beach Ave., underneath the El. The best Jewish bakery in Brighton. Try a little of everything or buy a whole loaf of honey cake, loaded with almonds and cherries ($4). Open daily 6am-9pm.

Lulu's Deli Restaurant, 107 Brighton Beach Ave., 1 block from Ocean Pkwy. Eighty years of preparing Hebrew National meats have made them a favorite among locals. The classic pastrami sandwich should be requested on rye with mustard. For a beverage, try Dr. Brown's Cream Soda ($1). The lunch special ($4) includes soup, entree, french fries, cole slaw, pickle, and a drink. For a nosh, grab a greasy but memorable potato pancake ($1). Open Tues.-Sun. 10am-10pm.

Primorski Restaurant, 282 Brighton Beach Ave. Popular with natives, this bright red and blue, diamond-shaped restaurant serves the best Ukrainian borscht ($1.70) in the hemisphere. Music, dancing, and shots of vodka ($1.60) destroy all chances of getting what you ordered since some of the waiters struggle with English to begin with. But don't worry, every dish is tasty. Eminently affordable lunch special ($4) available weekdays 11am-5pm, weekends 11am-4pm. At night, prices rise as you pay for entertainment too. Open daily 11am-midnight.

Nathan's, Surf and Sitwell Ave. in Coney Island. Nathan Handwerker became famous selling his hot dogs on the boardwalk for a nickel while the competition's were a dime. Seventy-four years later, a classic frank at Nathan's sells for $1.75. Unique french fries $1.55. Open Sun.-Thurs. 8am-4am, Fri.-Sat. 8am-5am.

Philip's Candy Store, 1237 Surf Ave., at the entrance to the D train in Coney Island. Everything the child inside of you wants. Famous for its salt-water taffy ($1.50 for a half-pound). Open daily 11am-4pm.

Jimmy's Famous Heros, 1786 Sheepshead Bay Rd., across the street from El Greco diner. Heros (around $5) are more than a meal and can be shared by two. Always ask for the works on whatever you order. Open Mon.-Fri. 8am-10pm, Sat. 6am-8pm, Sun. 6am-6pm.

Joe's Clam Bar, 2009 Emmons Ave., across the street from the bay. A bit expensive but the fish hail from the Atlantic and not from the toxic bay. Try the fried calamari ($12) and dip the chunks of chewy squid in mild or hot sauce. Raw clams served on the half-shell ($6 per dozen) are especially good when you drown them in lemon juice and crackers. Open daily 11am-1am.

Roll-n-Rooster, Nostrand Ave. and Emmons Ave., a half-mile walk east from Sheepshead Bay Rd. Twenty years of serving the best roast beef with cheese ($3.86) in New York have earned this semi-fast food joint a loyal following despite the plastic gas lamps and hollow stone walls. Open Sun.-Thurs. 11am-1am, Fri.-Sat. 11am-3am.

Queens

Reasonably priced and very authentic ethnic food is probably the best thing about Queens. Astoria specializes in discount shopping and ethnic eating. Take the N or R to Steinway St. and Broadway and browse all the way down to 25th Ave., or turn down Broadway and walk toward the Manhattan skyline. The number of Greek and Italian restaurants increases right around the elevated station at Broadway and 31st St., where you can catch the N north to Ditmars Blvd, for even more Astorian cuisine. In Flushing, you can find excellent Chinese, Japanese, and Korean restaurants, but always check the prices. An identical dish may cost half as much only a few doors away. Bell Boulevard in Bayside, out east near the Nassau border, is the center of Queens night life, and on most weekends you can find crowds of young bar-hopping natives here.

Roumely Tavern, 3304 Broadway, Astoria (278-7533). When in Astoria, do as the Astorians do. A taste of the Old Country, with Greek accents as authentic as the food. *Spanokopita* (spinach pie) appetizer $2.50, lamb stew $8.75. Open daily noon-1am. Take the R or G to the Steinway St. and Broadway stop in Astoria.

Waterfront Crabhouse, Long Island City (729-4862). Former home of the turn-of-the-century "Miller's Hotel," where the rich and famous escaping to Long Island by ferry passed through. Theodore Roosevelt, Grover Cleveland, and Lillian Russell all dined in this building, which lost its third floor in a 1975 fire. Today the crabhouse attracts its own big names, such as Dustin Hoffman and Ed Asner. Entertainment daily. Sliced shell steak $9. (Subway:#7 to Vernon Blvd. and Jackson Ave., make a right onto Borden and follow it to its end. Restaurant is one block from the water.) Open daily 12:30-11pm.

South River, 42-05 Main St., Flushing (762-7214). The little waterfall in the window says it all: pleasantly cheesy decor and traditional Korean food that immigrants swear by. Dinner entrees from $8.

Victor's Restaurant, 69-09 Roosevelt Ave. (tel. 651-9474), in Woodside. Filipino family-style dinner. Chicken special $7. Take the #7 to 69th St. in Woodside and walk to Roosevelt Ave. Open daily. Open Mon.-Thurs. 10am-11pm, Fri.-Sun. 10am-midnight.

Cyprella, 30-15 Broadway, (728-3718), in Astoria next to the elevated stop. Cypriot Greek specialties. *Souvlaki* $3.25, steak sandwich $4.50, *tzatziki* (yogurt, cucumbers, spices, and oil) $2.25. Unatmospheric, but the food more than compensates. Open daily until 2am. Take the N to Broadway and 31st St. in Long Island City.

Pastrami King, 124-24 Queens Blvd. (263-1717), near 82nd Ave., in Kew Gardens. The home-cured pastrami and corned beef among the best in New York. Take out a sprawling pastrami on rye for $6. (Take the E or F to Union Tpke. and Queens Blvd. in Kew Gardens.) Open daily 8am-11pm.

Galaxy Pastry Shop, 37-22 Ditmars Blvd., (545-3181), in Astoria. Experience unimaginably blissful sugary creations. Hypoglycemics can ascend to Mount Olympus. Honey-drenched baklava $1. Gorge yourself on Greek pastries at a squeaky-clean table inside the slickly mirrored shop, or lounge in the ample outdoor seating.

Empire Kosher Chicken Restaurant, 100-17 Queens Blvd. (tel. 997-7315), in Forest Hills. Cheap chicken prepared according to ancient Jewish laws of ritual purity by one of the major kosher meat manufacturers. Fried, roasted, or barbecued. (Take the R or the G to the 67th Ave. stop.) $5-7.25. Open Sun.-Thurs. 11am-9:30pm.

Rizzo's Pizza, 30-15 Steinway St., Astoria (721-9862). The restaurant is tiny, the seating makeshift, and the whole affair could easily go unnoticed in the endless row of discount stores and specialty shops lining Steinway. But the pizza deserves your attention: Sicilian rectangles based on a thin, crisp crust, and spread with an unforgettable tomato sauce. Ask for extra cheese and enter the gates of heaven. $1.10 per slice, $6.30 per 6-slice pie. Open daily, 11am-8pm. Take the R to the Steinway St. and Broadway stop and walk down Steinway St. toward 30th Ave.

First Edition, 41-08 Bell Blvd. (428-8522), in Bayside. Popular for ribs and fish, but "Lite Side" of the menu adds a spicy twist: hot Cajun chicken sandwich $9.

Marbella, 220-35 Northern Blvd. (423-0100) Refined Spanish cuisine. Entrees from $9. Take the #7 to Main St., Flushing, the last stop. Then take the Q12 bus to the restaurant, which is near the Adria Hotel.

Donovan's of Bayside, 214-16 41st Ave. (423-5178). The place to go for a midnight snack or a full meal. Open daily until 4am, late supper until 2am. American-style menu starts at $5. Take the LIRR to Bell Blvd., and walk down 41st Ave. past the 7/11.

Flushing Seafood Palace, 37-57 Main St. (886-1166). Extensive Chinese menu in a flashy pastel dining room. Neon sign, linen tablecloths and satisfying food at reasonable prices. Try broccoli in oyster sauce for $5.75.

Bronx

When Italian immigrants settled the Bronx, they brought their pots and pans with them, along with the centuries-old tradition of hearty communal dining. While much of the Bronx is a culinary wasteland, the New York *cognoscenti* soon discovered the few oases along Arthur Ave. and in Westchester where the fare is as robust and the patrons as rambunctious as their counterparts in Naples. Although it lacks the schmaltzy tourist veneer of Little Italy, the enclave on Arthur Ave., and along 187th St. brims with pastry shops, streetside cafés, pizzerias, restaurants, and ma-and-pa emporiums vending Madonna 45s and batallions of imported espresso machines. Established in 1910, **Ruggieri Pastry Shop,** under the dynamic leadership of Sam and Lurdes, produces mountains upon mountains of classic Italian pastries, though they're especially proud of their *sfogliatella*—a flaky Neapolitan pastry stuffed with ricotta. Those nostalgic for the groovy golden 50s will be glad to know that Ruggieri operates one of the last authentic ice cream fountains in New York. Drag your sweetheart here for a real malted or an egg cream. Ruggieri blends and bakes at 2373 Prospect Ave., at E. 187th St. (Open daily 8am-10pm.) Revel in elaborate French and Italian pastries to the tune of a warm cappuccino in **Egioio Pastry Shop,** 622 E. 187th St. An octogenarian with a modern flair, a trim, sexy interior, and inviting outdoor tables, Egioio makes the most perfect *gelato* in the Bronx. Finally, you can watch the rich and infamous stroll out of their limos and make a grand entrance into **Joe Nina's,** 3019 Westchester Ave., right under the subway platform of the #6 train.

Dominick's, 2335 Arthur Ave. (733-2807). Small authentic Italian eatery. Vinyl tablecloths and bare walls, but great atmosphere. Waiters won't offer you a menu or a check—they'll recite the specials of the day and then bark out what you owe at the end of the meal. Try the linguini dishes ($7) and the special veal and chicken *francese* dishes ($10). Open Mon.-Sat. noon-10pm, Sun. 1-9pm. Arrive before 6pm or after 9pm, or expect to wait at least 20 min.

Mario's, 2342 Arthur Ave. (584-1188), East Fordham. Five generations of the Migliucci *famiglia* have worked the kitchen of this celebrated Southern Italian trattoria. The original clan left Naples in the early 1900s and opened the first Italian restaurant in Egypt, then came to the U.S. and cooked themselves into local lore: Mario's appears on the pages of Puzo's pre-cinema *Godfather*. Celebrities pass through, among them the starting lineups for the Yankees and the Giants. A room-length couch embraces patrons with familial arms. Try *spiedini alla romana,* a deep-fried sandwich made with anchovy sauce and mozzarella. Notorious for pizza too. Traditional pasta $9-11, *antipasto* $5.50. Open Sun. and Tues.-Thurs. noon-11pm, Fri.-Sat. noon-midnight.

Pasquale's Rigoletto, 2311 Arthur Ave. (365-6644). A relative newcomer to the Arthur Ave. pasta scene, Pasquale's cooks with the best of them. As the name suggests, they do salve you with potent arias; if you have a favorite in mind, they'll gladly play it for you. (No Philip Glass or *Einstein on the Beach* here.) *Antipasti* $6-7, pasta $12, poultry $13-14. Open Sun.-Fri. noon-10pm, Sat. noon-2am.

Taormina Ristorante, 1805 Edison Ave. (823-1646). Hearty Italian fare in the shadow of the subway tracks. Combine any pasta with any sauce to suit your fullest farinaceous fancies. Though they won't meddle with the essentials of espresso themselves, they'll lend you a bottle of Sambuca or anise liquor to flavor the brew. Pasta $7.50-9, sandwiches $4.50-6.50. Chicken dishes from $10, veal from $12. Open Sun. noon-9:30pm, Mon.-Thurs. 11am-10:30pm, Fri. 11am-11:30pm, Sat. noon-11:30pm.

Pizza Putt Putt, 6027 Broadway (884-5041) at 244th St. A plasticky pizzeria done up in pink and turquoise that serves good pizza and calzones ($2.75) anyway. But the main draw here is the miniature golf course planted at the back of the restaurant (putter rental 50¢). Medium pizza $7.50, large $9.50 ($1 per topping). Open Sun.-Thurs. 11am-11pm, Fri.-Sat. 11am-1am.

Sights

> *Far below and around lay the city like a ragged purple*
> *dream, the wonderful, cruel, enchanting, bewildering,*
> *fatal, great city.*
>
> *—O. Henry*

Believe it or not, the classic sightseeing quandary experienced by New York tourists has been finding the Empire State Building. They've seen it in dozens of pictures or drawings, captured in sharp silhouettes or against a steamy pink sky as a monument of dreams. They've seen it towering over the grey landscape as their plane descends onto the runway, or in perspective down long avenues or from a river tour. But they can't see it when they're standing right next to it.

This optical illusion may explain why many New Yorkers have never visited some of the major sights in their hometown. When you're smack in the middle of them, the tallest skyscrapers seem like a casual part of the scenery. But no one—natives and tourists alike—knows what they're missing. Not all sights are as glaringly green and obvious as the Statue of Liberty. Sometimes you'll enter a more modest doorway to find treasures inside, and sometimes you'll need to take a long elevator ride to see what everybody's raving about. If it's your first time in the big city, you'll notice even more subtle attractions—the neighborhoods and personalities jumbled together on shared turf, the frenzy of throngs at rush hour, the metropolitan murmur at dusk. And if it's your hundredth time in the city, there will still be areas you don't know all too well, architectural quirks you've never noticed, and plain old doorways you have yet to discover and enter. Seeing New York takes a lifetime.

Sightseeing Tours

> *A bulger of a place [New York] is. The number of the*
> *ships beat me all hollow, and looked for all the world*
> *like a big clearing in the West, with the dead trees*
> *all standing.*
> —*Davy Crockett, Tour to the North and Down*
> *East . . . in 1834*

You'll get to know the city best by walking around, but you might want to take a quick official tour to get your bearings before returning to explore your favorite spots.

In spring and early fall, the **Museum of the City of New York** (534-1672) sponsors popular Sunday walking tours ($15) focusing on the city's history and architecture and moving at a leisurely pace. Sign up a few days in advance. The **Municipal Art Society,** at the Urban Center, 457 Madison Ave. (935-3960) near 50th St., leads $12-14 guided walking tours; destinations change with the seasons. Their free tour of Grand Central Station meets every Wednesday at 12:30pm underneath the Kodak sign at Grand Central and lasts an hour. Other tours follow Fifth Ave., take in the waterfront reconstruction units, or wander through ethnic neighborhoods. For those who'd like to see the unperfumed New York, the MAS also leads a series of environmentally conscious "Garbage" tours to the local recycling facilities and waste dumps ($15-17).

The Visitors Bureau distributes free brochures containing suggested outlines for touring the Big Apple by foot. Little American flags mark **Heritage Trail,** a do-it-yourself tour of lower Manhattan. Pick it up in the Financial District at Broadway and Wall Street.

The detail-oriented can enjoy a mass of more specialized tours. Imperial **Lincoln Center** sponsors guided tours of its theatres: The Metropolitan Opera House, New York State Theatre, and Avery Fisher Hall. Tours run daily from 10am to 5pm and last about an hour. (For information call 877-1800.) Artsy types should survey the vast resources of the library at Lincoln Center: a dance library, a theatre library, a film archive, and newspaper and magazine clipping files kept on prominent actors and directors. Every Thursday a free tour instructs the curious in the art of locating items in the library's mammoth gathering of musical soundtracks and movie scores. The tour also passes through the center's three art galleries. (For information, call 870-1630.) Historic **Carnegie Hall,** at 57th St. and Seventh Ave., opens its doors to tourists Tuesdays and Thursdays at 11:30am, 2pm, and 3pm. Tours cost $6, seniors and students $5, children $3. (For information, call 247-7800.) Clothes-minded types should consider the **Wholesale Shopping Tour** inside New York City's garment center. (For information, call (718) 377-8873.)

Rebels without a clue should inquire about the "Annual Walking Tour of Jimmy Dean's New York Hangouts," given the first Saturday of every June. An inveterate "Dean of Deanobilia" guides you through the free tour—just bring a handful of bus tokens. (For more information, call 244-8426.) To catch "glimpses of creative life in New York," contact Shella Sperber at 221-1111. She arranges pilgrimages to antique dealers, artists' garrets, and furniture showrooms on a full- or half-day basis. Excursions for individuals or groups begin at $20-25. For diehard tree-watchers, the New York park rangers conduct an extensive series of free tours of metropolitan greenery. The city has sprouted approximately 2.7 million trees, including 120 "Great Trees," distinguished by their size, age, species, location or association with notable events. (For information on these park jaunts, call 397-3081.) The

Guide Service of New York, 445 W. 45th St. (408-3332) offers specialized neighborhood tours, including both walking and bus excursions ($10-49), and **Sidewalks of NY** (517-0201), a series of unique walking tours with titles like "Famous Murder Sights" and "Ghosts of the Upper West Side." All tours cost $15 and last two hours. Make an appointment Monday through Friday. A recorded message will inform you of the next few forays.

Backstage on Broadway Tours, 228 W. 47th St. (575-8065), offers behind-the-scenes lectures at various Broadway theatres. Tour guides may be theatre celebrities; directors and actors have given past talks. The tours ($6) fill the house, so reserve well in advance. **Radio City Music Hall,** 50th St. and Sixth Ave. (632-4041), gives tours of its art deco palace every day and nearly every hour for a mere $6.50.

Call 265-2663 if you're interested in a $5 walking tour of the Upper West Side that bills itself as "Adventure on a Shoestring;" call 348-3854 if you'd like to pay $14 for an intensive architectural romp through Central Park South; call 718-951-7072 to reserve your spot in a $12 exploration of Jewish New York City through the Lower East Side.

The **Seaport Line** conducts boat cruises of New York's quintessentials for $12. Even the vessel has a sense of history—it's a copy of Twain's Mississippi steamboat. Three cruises per day run in the summertime and 1-hr. twilight cocktail cruises take place in May and June. For more information call 385-0791.

Circle Line Tours (563-3200) circumnavigates Manhattan island in a 3-hr. tour. Twelve cruises run daily 9:30am-4:15pm. Boats leave from pier 83 at the Circle Line Plaza. (Tickets $15, seniors $13.50, under 12 $7.50.) From May 26 to September 2, the Circle Line conducts romantic tours around Manhattan in the brassy light of sunset. You'll hear the sirens singing if you're not careful. Same rates as daily tour. Light snacks and cocktails served.

Joyce Gold's Tours, 141 W. 17th St. (242-5762). Ms. Gold has read over 900 books on Lower Manhattan, the subject she teaches at NYU and at the New School. Eighteen Sundays per year Joyce and a company of intrepid adventurers set out on trivia-filled area tours. Tours last 2-4 hr., depending on the subject, and cost $10. If you'd like to undertake a tour on your own, Ms. Gold's two books on the subject make an informative reference source: *From Windfall to World Trade Center* and *From Trout Stream to Bohemia.* (Both books cost $5 and inhabit travel sections of bookstores and museum bookshops.)

Gray Line Sight-Seeing, 800 Eighth Ave. (397-2600), between 53rd and 54th, offers 13 tours ranging from bus trips around Manhattan to historical explorations of upstate New York and gambling junkets to Atlantic City. The tour of the lower half of Manhattan ($15) runs about 2½ hr. and visits Times Square, the garment district, Herald and Madison Square, Greenwich Village, plus the World Trade Center, the U.N., Park Ave., and Rockefeller Center. Other notable tours include a stint through upper New York and Harlem ($14) and the grand tour ($23) that makes the city your oyster in under 5 hr. The launder-your-money voyage to Atlantic City costs $24. Arrive at the terminal ½ hr. in advance.

Harlem Spirituals, Inc., 1457 Broadway (302-2594), between 41st and 42nd, offers tours of upper Manhattan, including the "Spirituals and Gospel" tour, highlighted by trips to historical homes and participation in a Baptist service ($27 for 4 hrs., leaves Sun. at 9am). The "Soul Food and Jazz" tour ($60) runs from 7pm to midnight and features a filling meal at a Harlem restaurant. Call 24 hr. in advance for reservations. For a little less money, **Harlem, Your Way! Tours Unlimited, Inc.,** 129 W. 130th St. (690-1687), offers a similar package, without dinner, called the "Champagne Jazz Safari" ($25 on Wed. and Fri.-Sat. evenings). They also sponsor a 3-hr walking tour of Harlem for $25. Call 24 hr. in advance for reservations.

New York Big Apple Tours, Inc., runs 3-4 hr. tours of lower Manhattan $22, lower and upper Manhattan $27, and Harlem (including participation in a traditional gospel service) $27. Res-

Midtown

Lincoln Center

CENTRAL PARK

W. 62nd St.
W. 61st St.
W. 60th St.
W. 59th St.
Central Park S.
W. 58th St.
COLUMBUS CIRCLE
W. 57th St.

Carnegie Hall

W. 56th St.
W. 55th St.
W. 54th St.
W. 53rd St.
W. 52nd St.
W. 51st St.
W. 50th St.
W. 49th St.
W. 48th St.
W. 47th St.

Eleventh Ave.
Tenth Ave.
Eighth Ave.
Seventh Ave.

THEATER DISTRICT

W. 46th St.
W. 45th St.
W. 44th St.
DUFFY SQUARE
W. 43rd St.
W. 42nd St.
Convention & Visitors Bureau
TIMES SQUARE
W. 41st St.
Port Authority Bus Terminal
W. 40th St.
Broadway
Lincoln Tunnel
Dyer Ave.
W. 39th St.
W. 38th St.
W. 37th St.
Eighth Ave.
Seventh Ave.
W. 36th St.
Javits Convention Center
W. 35th St.
Macy's
W. 34th St.
W. 33rd St.
Ninth Ave.
General Post Office
Madison Square Garden
Eleventh Ave.
Tenth Ave.
W. 32nd St.
Penn Station
W. 31st St.
W. 30th St.

GARMENT DISTRICT

ervations required; call 410-4190. Tours leave from Sbarro Restaurant on Times Sq., at the corner of Seventh Ave. at W. 46th St.

Short Line Tours, 166 W. 46th St. (354-5122), runs similar tours for lower prices: upper Manhattan and Harlem ($14), lower New York ($15), and an exhaustive all-day tour of the metropolis ($32.50).

East Midtown

The commercial heart of New York thrives in the east 40s and 50s, a curious grid of skyscrapers, bankers, magnificent churches, and occasional moments of green. Here you can trace the history of the corporate complex as it evolved from the art deco of the Chrysler Building to the streamlined glass skin of the Jacob A. Javits Convention Center or the smooth granite façade of the IBM tower.

Midtown also sparkles with instances of pre-deco, most dramatically exemplified by the opulence of the Grand Central Terminal or the Central Research building of the New York Public Library. A smattering of 19th-century mansions lingers on in Midtown, including that occupied by Cartier at 52nd St. According to a New York legend, Morton F. Plant traded it with Pierre Cartier for a string of pearls, in a deal rivaling Minuit's purchase of Manhattan.

Although tarnished by city dirt and exhaust fumes, the Beaux-Arts **Grand Central Terminal,** 42nd to 45th between Vanderbilt Place and Madison Ave., still recalls some Eurosplendor of old. Mega-magnate Cornelius Vanderbilt stands embronzed at the center of the façade. Three frieze panels stretch across the Lexington side of the terminal, depicting quasi-Babylonian figures in a playful art deco tip of the hat to the ancient cartoonists.

The Main Concourse covers more ground than the nave of Notre Dame de Paris. Wander through this 100-ft. wide, 470-ft. long, 150-ft. high space or climb the stairs to gaze up at the vaulted ceiling covered with oak leaves (the Vanderbilt family's emblem), constellations of the zodiac, and 2500 stars that used to light up. The great arched windows onto the world measure 60 ft. tall and 33 ft. wide. Designers Reed and Stem constructed the building in 1913, assisted by Warren and Whitmore. Railroad engineer William Wilgus originated the multilevel organization of the traffic that flows daily through the terminal: trains, cars, subways, and over 170,000 visitors and commuters. The principal southern façade of the terminal is punctuated by a sculptural group by Jules Coutain entitled *Mercury, Hercules, and Minerva* (*Glory of Commerce, Moral Energy, and Mental Energy*). Don't forget to look up at the 13-ft.-wide clock, mounted below the sculpture, that was also designed by Coutain. The Municipal Society conducts guided tours of the terminal every Wednesday at 12:30pm, starting from under the Kodak sign in the Main Concourse.

The columns and arches of the **Bowery Savings Bank** at 110 E. 42nd St. between Park and Lexington, suggest that banking in New York City has taken on the status of a temple rite. Inside, limestone and sandstone walls frame a 160-ft.-long, 65-ft.-high banking room with a floor of fine French and Italian marble. Peek inside through the heavy portals; then take out a dollar bill and make a wish. Right next door at 122 E. 42nd St. hovers a gentle giant from Masters Sloan and Robertson—the **Chanin Building.** Note the textured, highly ornamental third-floor frieze and the gold and glitter art deco lobby, highlighted by operatic lighting design.

The New York skyline would be incomplete without the familiar headdress of the **Chrysler Building,** at 42nd and Lexington, built by William Van Allen as a series of rectangular boxes and topped by a spire modeled after a radiator grille. Other details evoke the romance of the automobile in the Golden Age of Chrysler Automobile Company: abstract car friezes, flared gargoyles at the fourth setback styled after 1929 hood ornaments and hubcaps, and stylized lightning bolt designs symbolizing the energy of the new machine. When built in 1929, this seductive if absurd building stood as the world's tallest, but the Empire State topped it a year later.

Forty-second St. also delivers the **Daily News Building,** the 1930 work of Raymond Hood with a little help from Howells. Above the entrance, an industrial-strength frieze tells the building's story. Inside, an immense globe rotates at the center of a grid, a brass analog clock keeps time for 17 major cities, and every breed of 'ometer graces the wall nearby. Frequent exhibitions breeze in and out of here.

Between 42nd and 43rd St. on Tudor Place hides the city's smallest and most charming park. A few benches, toylike gravel paths, and ancient oaks congregate in a refreshingly uncosmopolitan silence. Next door at 320 E. 43rd St., between First and Second, a landscaped plaza grows inside the **Ford Foundation Building.** Glass and rusted steel enclose a 12-story atrium dense with tropical vegetation. Down below sprawls a proper jungle, complete with 17 trees, 999 shrubs, 148 vines, and 21,954 ground cover plants (none of which have any numerical significance). The soothing echoes of the small central fountain counter the hum of business.

Ceremonial capital of the political world, the **United Nations** (963-7713) overlooks the East River between 42nd and 48th St. Designed in the early 50s by an international committee including Le Corbusier, Oscar Niemeyer, and Wallace Harrison (whose ideas won out in the end), the complex itself makes a diplomatic statement—part bravura, part compromise. You can take a one-hour guided tour of the **General Assembly** and the **Security Council,** which start in the main lobby of the General Assembly every half-hour from 9:15am to 4:45pm. (Open daily 9am-6pm. Admission $5.50, students and children $3.50. Visitor's Entrance at First Ave. and 46th.) Visitors must take a tour to get past the lobby. From September through December, free tickets to General Assembly meetings can be obtained in the main lobby about half an hour before sessions, which usually begin at 10:30am and 3pm Monday through Friday.

The U.N.'s other attractions include stained glass windows by Chagall in the lobby and a quasi-park set in a sculpture garden by the East River. You can enjoy the delightful promenade along, or rather above, the riverbank. Or just enjoy the irony of the musclebound Socialist Realist statue, of a man beating a sword into a plowshare, which the USSR gave to the U.N. in 1959, only three years after invading Hungary.

On Park Ave., between 44th and 45th, stands an indelicate monolith vaguely resembling an airplane wing section—the **Pan Am Building.** Opinions on the building remain split: some view it as an abysmal low of high modernism, a construction unworthy of its co-designer Walter Gropius (collaborator Pietro Belluschi might be blamed); others see it as an aging master's monument to turbulent modernity. The largest commercial office building ever built, it contains 2.4 million square ft. of corporate cubicles. Deep inside the lobby, right above the escalators, hangs an immense Josef Albers mural. In the building's other lobby, at E. 44th and Vanderbilt, an intriguing wire and light sculpture encloses what appears to be an energized atom.

In the shadow of the Pan Am bauhaus lies the Ivy League alma matrix, crowded with crusty old mansions emblazoned with commonplace clichés like *Lux et Veritas.* The **Yale Club,** at 50 Vanderbilt Ave. between 44th and 45th, also bears an inscription in English honoring patriot and Yalie Nathan Hale. The **Harvard Club,** built in 1894 by McKim, Mead & White, maintains a cool Georgian Ivy exterior at 27 W. 44th, between Fifth and Sixth. Inside, a mean game of high-stakes backgammon goes on, dominated by a player known only as "Doc." Across the street from the crimson club a bas relief of an arm and hammer announces the building of the **General Society of Mechanics and Tradesmen.** At 37 W. 44th St., next door to the ominous H club, floats the remarkable façade of the **New York Yacht Club,** shaped like the stern of a sailing-ship complete with three window bays, ocean waves, and dolphins. The club housed The Americas Cup from 1857 to 1983, when the title went down under.

Diamond Row, on 47th St. between Fifth and Sixth, resembles a medieval bazaar in its personable, vocal trade practices. The **Waldorf-Astoria Hotel,** at 301 Park Ave. between 49th and 50th, has kept an incomparable register: the Duchess of Windsor has soujourned here, along with King Faisal of Saudi Arabia, the late Emperor Hirohito of Japan, and every U.S. President since 1931. The lobby, accessible to most courteous mortals, seems to have slipped out of a silver screen film of the 40s. You can enter most unobtrusively from the Lexington entrance.

At 570 Lexington Ave. off 51st St. towers a 51-story pink marble extravaganza, enhanced with gold accents and stylized lightning bolts. The **General Electric Building,** built in 1931, used to house RCA. G.E., ever fearful that someone may steal the secret of its lightbulb, keeps security high, but you can at least enter the lobby. Peek inside the elevator if you can.

St. Bartholomew's Church, on Park Ave. between 50th and 51st, revisits the historical association between holy fathers and wholesome wine. The house of worship went up in 1919 on the former site of the Schaefer brewery. Some say you can still taste the evanescent barley in the holy water.

A taste of something else clean and refreshing, the **Seagram Building,** on Park Ave. between 52nd and 53rd, pioneered modernist architecture in New York. In 1958, designers Mies van der Rohe and Philip Johnson innovatively set the plaza and tower back 90 ft. from the building line.

Across the street, a pseudo-palatial structure by McKim, Mead & White serves as a **Racquet and Tennis Club.** The tireless trio constructed a more inspired work, the six **Villard Houses,** at the request of publisher Henry Villard. The landmark's subsequent owner, the archdiocese of New York, sold the houses to Harry Helmsley, who proceeded to incorporate two of them into his Palace Hotel. He restored the interiors to their turn-of-the-century rococo opulence, making them unnaturally shiny and overwrought. The Villards cluster at 451-455 Madison Ave., between 50th and 51st St.

St. Patrick's Cathedral, New York's most famous church, stands at 51st St. and Fifth Ave. Designed by James Renwick, the Gothic revival structure opened in 1879. Today it features high society weddings and the shrine of the first male U.S. saint, St. John Neumann. Artisans in Chartres and Nantes created the majority of St. Patrick's stained-glass windows.

On 53rd St. between Fifth and Sixth, umpteen street vendors hawk African statuettes, ritual masks, papyrus scrolls, and jewelry. At the end of this merchandizing gamut, on 53rd St. at Fifth Ave., stands the beguiling French Gothic **St. Thomas Church,** an architectural Long John Silver built in 1914 by Cram, Goodhue, and Ferguson; its Notre Dame-like construction lacks the second tower. It may be a high art invalid, but it joins the ranks of great French lopsided churches in the tradition of Chartres.

The interior of **Saint Peter's Church** 619 Lexington Ave. (935-2200) at 53rd St., reflects the postmodern collapse of the boundaries between art, image, faith, show, and media: along with its religious functions, the church serves alternately as a movie theatre, art gallery, concert hall, dramatic stage, and public information forum, performing the far-reaching social functions that great medieval churches once did. Instead of rekindling the mood of centuries past, Saint Peter's strives for a contemporary urban spirit and spirituality. The building stays architecturally in sync with its surroundings. The almost aerodynamic interior design does away with all gratuitous ornamentation. Blondewood furniture and cavernous white wall spaces complete the streamlined Bauhausian look. In the central hall, artist Arnaldo Pomodore has rendered a crucifix in rich, rust-colored bronze, incorporating a central, wedge-shaped "nail" into its otherwise homogeneous polished surface, making the violence of the crucifixion palpable.

The **Lever House,** at 390 Park Ave. between 53rd and 54th, may look like just another jolly glass giant but the people at the Landmarks Office will tell you otherwise. This structure exemplifies modernism as influenced by Le Corbusier. Raised off the ground on columns, the building supports a rooftop garden, a free façade on the outside of the structure, and a free plan on the inside. Along with the Seagram Building across the street, this Modern redefined the look and the shape of the city.

Leave modernity behind and head east for something completely Moorish, the **Central Synagogue** located at 652 Lexington Ave. off 55th St., built in 1872 by Henry Fernbach. The oldest continuously functional synagogue in the city, its brownstone façade conceals a colorful interior. The onion domes atop the 222-ft. towers make one nostalgic for a plate of *borscht.*

The shiny, slanted **Citicorp Center,** built on stilts, looks like a giant popsicle. The angled roof was intended for use as a solar collector that has yet to come to light. But the roof does support a gadget, called the Tuned Mass Damper, that senses and records the tremors of the earth and warns of earthquakes.

The story of the construction of St. Peter's Church at 54th and Lexington has a simple moral: faith pays. This pesky church virtually dictated the design of the Citicorp Center, ensuring that church and Corp would remain distinct and separate. Hugh Stubbins & Associates built both projects, but Massimo and Lella Vignelli originated St. Peter's tastefully space-age interior design. Known as the city's jazz ministry, St. Peter's stages notoriously hip, bee-bop vespers.

At Park and 56th, the **Mercedes Benz Showroom,** designed by Frank Lloyd Wright, showcases prestigemobiles. Stylish **135 East 57th Street,** a brand new 32-story office complex designed by the New York firm of Kohn, Pedersen, and Fox, bears the bronzed initials of Holland's NMB Bank. The front of the main building posed at the corner of 57th and Madison curves inward, creating an arc around four green marble columns capped by a complete circle. Just add water from a spar-kling fountain, gold trimmings on the green marble siding, and a first-floor arcade of art galleries and antique shops, and you get the building that has New York archi-tectural critics raving with joy. Downstairs on the gallery row christened **Place des Antiquaires,** you can visit **Beaumesnil, Ltd.,** 125 E. 57th St., a 17th-19th century European furniture outfit designed to simulate the interior of a French chateau. (Open Mon.-Sat. 11am-6pm.)

The **Fuller Building,** on Madison and 57th, displays the dark side of deco. The green granite **IBM Building,** at 590 Madison Ave. between 56th and 57th, brings you one of the city's best atriums, an airy space with comfortable chairs and a dense bamboo jungle. Back on Fifth Ave. at 56th St., you should have no trouble finding the swine amidst the pearls of the **Trump Tower.** Although the **Crown Building** dates back to the Golden Twenties, it has been overlaid more recently with coined goldleaf. At sunset the building appears enveloped in a cloak of fire. The monster at 9 W. 57th St. slants toward the bottom so much that it looks like a runway for an Olympic ski jump. Graphic designer Ivan Chermayev penned the hulking red 9.

The legendary **Plaza Hotel,** built in 1907 by Henry J. Hardenberg, struts its digni-fied Edwardian stuff on 59th and Fifth. Former guests and residents include Teddy Roosevelt, the Beatles, Solomon R. Guggenheim, Frank Lloyd Wright, Eloise, and the beautiful and damned couple F. Scott and Zelda Fitzgerald. Today, of course, the Plaza, oversized fountain and all, belongs to the hubristic Donald Trump. Double-billing as a forecourt to the Plaza Hotel and as an entrance to Central Park, the **Grand Army Plaza** bears the **Pulitzer Memorial Fountain** and an Augustus Saint-Gaudens gaudy gold equestrian statue of General Sherman. Those seeking a $4,500 stuffed giraffe or just a wonderful browse should stop in on the nation's largest toystore, **F.A.O. Schwarz,** at 767 Fifth Ave. (644-9400) between 58th and 59th. Imitate Tom Hanks and dance on the giant keyboard, or drive home in a $14,000 miniature convertible. (Open Mon.-Sat. 10am-6pm, Thurs. until 8pm, Sun. noon-6pm.)

The Empire State Building

> New York impressed me tremendously because, more
> than any other city in the world, it is the fullest expres-
> sion of our modern age.
>
> —Leon Trotsky

The Empire State Building (slurred together by any self-respecting New Yorker into "Empire Statebuilding") has style. It retains its place in the hearts and minds of New Yorkers even though it is no longer the tallest building in the U.S. (an honor now held by Chicago's Sears Tower), or even the tallest building in New York (now the upstart twin towers of the World Trade Center). It doesn't even have the best looks (the Chrysler building is more delicate, the Woolworth more ornate). But the Empire State remains the best-known and most-loved landmark in New York and dominates the postcards, the movies, and the skyline.

The limestone and granite structure, with glistening mullions of stainless steel, stretches 1,454 feet into the sky, and its 73 elevators run on 2 miles of shafts. High winds can bend the entire structure up to a quarter-inch off center. The Empire State numbered among the first of the truly spectacular skyscrapers, benefitting from the combination of Eiffel's pioneering work with steel frames and Otis's perfection of the "safety elevator." In Midtown it towers in relative solitude, away from the forest of monoliths that has grown around Wall Street. At festive times of year, the upper 30 floors light up in appropriate colors—from passion-red for Valentine's Day, to kelly green for St. Patricks Day.

The Empire State was built on the site of two famous 19th-century mansions belonging to the Astor family, a clan of prominent New York aristocrats. On this spot, Caroline Schermerhorn Astor created the "400" of New York's social elite, based upon how many well-connected people she could fit in her art gallery-ballroom here, snubbing scores of others in the process. Caroline's nephew, William Waldorf Astor, married a social climber who tried in vain to usurp Caroline's role as society queen. In revenge, William replaced the palatial residence next door to his aunt with the Waldorf Hotel in the 1890s and then took off to England. In under a year, a disgusted Mrs. Astor, the most spoiled of the crème de la crème, decided to move north to Fifth and 65th. In doing so, she joined a wave of millionaire migration toward Central Park, though she could not bring herself to ascend the risqueé heights of Andrew Carnegie, who ventured all the way up to 90th Street. By 1897, Caroline's son, John Jacob Astor, had built the Astoria Hotel beside the Waldorf. They were operated together, despite the family squabble, until 1929, when they moved uptown to make way for the Empire State Building. John Jacob Raskob, an entrepreneur who cut his education short to support his family, was responsible for the construction of the Empire State Building during the late 1920s, and managed to complete it in 1931 both ahead of schedule and under budget, circumstances that occasion openmouthed stares of awe from those familiar with the present state of the construction industry. The building quickly found itself in a perpetual limelight, especially as the city plunged into the Great Depression. The Empire State Building starred in the film classic *King Kong,* along with the jumbo-sized ape and his ravishing hostage. A series of tragic suicides beginning in 1933 brought the building some unwelcome attention, as did the tragic incident of July 28, 1945, when a disoriented bomber pilot crashed his B-25 into the 79th floor. A plaque on the observation deck commemorates this event.

The building is located on Fifth Ave. between 33rd and 34th (736-3100), walking distance from many Midtown hotels, as well as from Penn and Grand Central stations. (Observatory stays open daily 9:30am-midnight). When you enter the building, check out the lobby, a shrine of art-deco interior decoration right down to the mail drops and the elevator doors. Don't miss the singularly tacky series of 1963 illustrations depicting the Seven Wonders of the Ancient World (plus you-know-which New York skyscraper), done in "textured light." These are, to put it charitably, a failed experiment. Take the escalator down to the Concourse Level, where you can purchase tickets to the observatory. A sign here indicates the visibility level. On a day with perfect visibility you will be able to see 80 miles in any direction, but even on a day with a visibility of only 5 miles you'll still spot the Statue of Liberty. ($3.50, children and seniors $1.75.)

Once you buy your ticket, you can head back up the escalator to the lobby, where you will be shown to one of the marked "observatory" elevators. These will lift you rapidly up to the 80th floor, where gleeful bureaucrats will collect your tickets and put you on another elevator up to the main observatory on the 86th floor, 1050 ft. in the air. You can venture onto the outdoor observatory or opt to stay enclosed and temperature-controlled with the requisite coin-operated telescopes, candy machines, rest rooms, and snack bars at your disposal. This is the best place in the city to get your bearings, since you are pretty much in the center of the Manhattan street grid. Take a map with you, to get a sense of the size, shape, and architectural texture of the island. You may be particularly dazzled by the gorgeous view to the north which gives a feel for the monumental scale of the rectangle of greenery that is Central Park. You can get an even better view of the park from the somewhat stuffy, graffiti-ridden observatory on the 102nd floor. Take the elevator from the main observatory.

West Midtown

West Midtown brims with commercial life around Broadway and the major cross streets (39th, 42nd, and 59th), spills into a cluster of ethnic residential areas, and runs over at its edges into the patches of industrial sleaze along the Hudson River.

Lower Broadway maintains a frantic pace. Shoppers dart in and out of **Macy's** (the world's largest department store) and the electronic stores on 34th St. **Madison Square Garden** starts on Seventh and ends up on Eighth. Facing it on Seventh Ave., you can select from a wide world of plastic and styrofoam at a glut of fast food joints. Facing the Garden on Eighth Ave. looms the surreal immense main Post Office, its marble stairs sweeping past endless rows of doric columns. Digging a hole in New York won't send you plummeting to China. You're more likely to land on some tracks in the subterranean world of **Penn Station.**

At 40 W. 40th St. between Fifth and Sixth stands the **American Standard Building,** a 21-story building built in 1923. Raymond Hood's design combines Gothic detailing with art deco lines to form a stylized representation of the Tribune design. (Hood had coincidentally just won the commission to build the Chicago Tribune building). American Radiator, a heating equipment manufacturer, first owned this building, which in fact retains an uncanny resemblance to a glowing coal when lit up at night.

On the West side of Fifth Ave., between 40th and 42nd, reposes the **New York Public Library.** Mighty lions commonly called Patience and Fortitude guard the stairs. Grecian urns, sculptural groups and fountains (the one on the right represents Truth, the other Beauty) herald the even more resplendent ornamentation inside. Astor Hall wears garlands and rosettes; Gottesman Hall behind it flaunts an amazing ceiling. The murals designed by Edward Lanning on the third floor were executed as a part of a WPA project. The library's art collection, kept in the Edna B. Salomon room, showcases the work of Gilbert Stuart, Sir Joshua Reynolds, and Rembrandt Peale.

Carrère and Hastings erected the building in 1911 with the resources of two privately funded libraries—John Jacob Astor's general reference library (the first in the New World) and James Lenox's collection of literature, history, and theology. Samuel J. Tilden added a generous two million dollar bequest, Andrew Carnegie an even more generous $52 million donation for the establishment of the Public Library's 80 citywide branches. Free tours of the library take place Monday through Wednesday, at 11am and 2pm, starting from the Friends Desk in Astor Hall. For information call 661-7220. Note that this library, dedicated purely to research, doesn't lend out a thing. If you want to take a book out or do research in an upbeat atmosphere with less gloom and no intimidating lions, you're better off across the street at the main branch.

Head over to Seventh Ave. to reach the **Garment District.** Dodge the moving clothes racks and bins packed with striped and polka dotted polyester. Take a peek at the Garment Center Synagogue, 205 W. 40th St. Continuing along, you'll soon find yourself in the flickering streets of **Times Square,** at the intersection of 42nd St. and Broadway. This well-policed district takes good care of entertaining New York on Broadway stages and in first-run movie houses with neon lights, street performers, and porn palace after peep show after porn palace. The entire area is slated for multi-billion dollar demolition and reconstruction over the next few years: New York can no longer afford not to capitalize fully on the space. The first new building, the neatly polished **Marriott Marquis,** has already replaced two historic Broadway stages. A plethora of subway lines stop in Times Square (#1, 2, 3, 7, or A, C, E, Q, B, N, R, and S).

Just west of the Square, at 229 W. 43rd St., are the offices of the **New York Times,** founded in 1857, for which the square was named in 1904.

In the 20s, the **Algonquin Hotel,** located on 44th St. between Fifth and Sixth, hosted Alexander Woollcott's "Round Table," a regular gathering of the brightest luminaries of the theatrical and literary worlds, including Dorothy Parker and Robert Sherwood. The Oak Room still serves tea every afternoon, but now exclusively to Algonquin guests and their guests regardless of the arts circles they inhabit. Although Round Tablers favored the Rose Room, today's *literati* frequent Room 306. Inside the hotel, at the Blue Bar, original James Thurber drawings adorn the walls.

In the heart of the square, breathe the heady air of free enterprise. Watch the glow of the buildings recede into darkness against the high-juiced billboards as the sun sets. A stunning tile mosaic of New York adorns the Sweep Up New York building (on the island in the middle of the square); unfortunately it is layered with soot.

The **Theatre District,** once a solid row of marquees, stretches along Broadway from 41st to 57th St. Some of the theatres have been converted into movie houses or simply left to rot as the cost of live productions has skyrocketed. Approximately 40 theatres remain active, most of them grouped around 45th St. Between 44th and 45th, ½ block west of Broadway just in front of the Shubert Theatre, lies **Shubert Alley,** a private street for pedestrians originally built as a fire exit between the Booth and Shubert Theatres. After shows, fans often wait for hours at stage doors—generally labeled, several yards to the side of the main entrance—to get their playbills signed. The hardcore autograph collectors live outside **The Dramatists Guild,** 234 W. 44th St., their lives' work contained in weathered memorabilia notebooks. These collectors recognize even the vaguely famous. Watch them identify celebrities, undaunted by the heaviest of sunglasses. Farther west on 42nd St., past the seedy Port Authority Bus Terminal, lies **Theatre Row,** a block of renovated Off-Broadway theatres featuring some of the best work in town.

Nearby, the graffiti covered **Guardian Angels Headquarters,** off the corner of Eighth Ave. and W. 46th St., stands at the helm of posh Restaurant Row. The Angels spark controversy and keep watch over the neighborhood. Wearing red berets rather than halos, these angels are self-declared vigilantes and martial artists who have taken city crime into their own hands. Head angel Curtis Sliwa, like Batman with a nest of Robins, has made the streets of Gotham much safer. The angels carry no weapons. Still, some worry that their success has encouraged the likes of Bernard Goetz, the notorious "subway vigilante" and dubious hero of the early 80s, who shot some of his would-be muggers.

Up at 131 W. 55th St. stands a former Muslim temple converted into the **Manhattan Theatre Club.** Sickles and crescents still adorn each doorway. Four tiny windows facing Mecca occupy the vast limestone upper stories. Step inside, where the box office operates, to see the elaborate tile mosaics surrounding the elevators.

Between 48th and 51st St. and Fifth and Sixth Ave. stretches **Rockefeller Center,** a monument to the heights to which business can spur the arts. Raymond Hood and his cohorts did an admirable job of glorifying various business virtues through architecture. A wealth of art deco sculpture adorns the sunken plaza, which serves as a restaurant in summer and skating rink in winter. Thirty fine artists designed works for the lobbies and exteriors. 20,000 flowering plants complete frequent rotations about the center's periphery. Two acres of formal gardens crown the center's roofs. In the 70-story **RCA Building,** the most accomplished artistic creation in this complex, every chair sits less than 28 ft. from natural light. Nothing quite matches watching a sunset from the 65th floor as a coral burnish fills the room. Rockefeller Center is also home to **Radio City Music Hall,** at 51st St. and Sixth Ave. (757-3100). When completed, Radio City became the largest theatre in the world as well as the most endowed with gimmicky gadgets so appropriate for its original role as a variety theatre.

The lavish opening night festivities attracted celebrities like Charlie Chaplin, Clark Gable, and Arturo Toscanini. The premier performance incorporated 75 acts, including dancing horses and the Equine Rockettes (originally known as Roxyettes in honor of founder Roxy Rothafel.)

The hall later doubled as a movie theatre, and became the best place to preview a film in New York, and from 1933 to 1979 more than 650 feature films debuted here, including *King Kong, It Happened One Night, Snow White and the Seven Dwarfs,* and *An American in Paris.* The interior decorators here did not skimp. A Stuart Davis painting now in the Museum of Modern Art used to hang in the men's room. Tours of the Great Hall are given Monday to Saturday, 10am-4:45pm and Sunday 11am-5pm. Enter at 50th St. under the mosaic depicting the triumph of virtue over vice. Provocatively, the virtues of philosophy and hygiene take on equal significance in the mural.

Over on Sixth Ave., near 48th St., in the basement of the **McGraw-Hill Building** is the multi-media screen production *The New York Experience,* a sensational, sense-startling documentary on New York's history. (869-0345; shown every hr. on the hr. Mon.-Thurs. 11am-7pm, Fri.-Sat. 11am-8pm, Sun. noon-8pm. Admission $4.75, under 12 $2.90.) In the theatre lobby, stop by **Little Old New York,** a re-creation of Manhattan in the 1890s. (Free.)

Those hallowed Letterman halls lie just a few steps away, at 30 Rockefeller Plaza, and while you may not be asked to guest star on the show, you can take the momentous tour of the radio and television facilities of the **National Broadcasting Corporation.** (Open Mon.-Sun. 9:30am-4:30pm; admission $7.50; tickets available on a first come, first serve basis.) The **CBS Building,** a virtual cross between a skyscraper and a black hole, maintains an eerie and futuristic presence at 51 W. 52nd St. For greatest dramatic effect, view Eero Saarinen's smoke-colored granite tower from Sixth Ave.

Stroll along W. 53rd St. between Fifth and Sixth and take in a handful of master-pieces in the windows of the **American Craft Museum** and the **Museum of Modern Art.** A visit to the masterwork-studded sculpture garden, featuring the opuses of Rodin, Renoir, Miro, Lipschitz and Picasso, should improve your digestion if you happen to have brought lunch. (Garden open Mon.-Tues., Fri.-Sun. 11am-6pm; Thurs. 11am-9pm.)

First established in 1891, and saved in the 60s, **Carnegie Hall,** at 59th St. and 7th Ave., has become the central sound stage in New York. Tours are given Tuesdays and Thursdays at 11:30am, 2pm, and 3pm ($6, students $5). (See Music, Large Halls.)

Columbus Circle marks the top of West Midtown and the south west corner of Central Park. Check out the statuesque boy standing on a monumental ship (1898), a tribute to the seamen who died on the USS Maine. The Coliseum, the city's former convention center, now usurped by the Javits Center, has been converted into a parking lot. Its front has become an unofficial shelter for the homeless, protecting them from the winds whipping across the circle. Intense debate has flared up over the dimensions of the development that will replace the complex.

Hell's Kitchen is the name for the Midtown neighborhood that edges the Hudson, formerly a violent area inhabited by impoverished immigrants. Until the turn of the century, gangs and live pigs roamed its streets. A few housing acts and realtors later, the district's overcrowded tenements have been cleaned up and an artsier crowd has moved in; today multi-ethnic funk and unemployed actors have given the still dangerous area a new wanderlust. It is capped in the north by **Fordham University** (Columbus Ave. and W. 60th St.), a Jesuit college. One block south stands the low-Gothic **Church of St. Paul the Apostle.** A high relief above a sky-blue mosaic offsets the cold blackness of the exterior.

A two week takeover of CUNY's **John Jay College of Criminal Justice** (899 Tenth Ave. at 58th St.) in May 1990 ended with the building being violently re-claimed by the administration. Renovations have given the 1903 neo-Victorian building a post-modern atrium and an extension.

Farther south a black-striped building stands as the post-modern Tower of Baby-lon. AT&T (811 Tenth Ave. at W. 54th St.) has appropriately made this secure skyrise a safe place to control information—the private language of capital. Although a designer product and the work of highly acclaimed architect Philip Johnson, most connoisseurs of Manhattan's urban fabric agree that the **AT&T Building** does not reach out and touch anyone's heart. Built of a pinkish marble that looks like a Jersey stucco job, the building seems equally uninviting outside and in. In the only bright moment in the entire phonofiasco—Evelyn Longworth's statue *The Spirit of Communication,* better known as *Golden Boy*—an enormous youth supports a megalith globe that comes aglow ith the sun. The **AT&T Infoquest Center** (605-5555) an exhibition space dedicated to furthering the mystique of fiber optics, robotics, and computers, lurks right on the premises.

The **University Club** at 1 W. 54th St. another McKim, Mead & White opus, features a stern façade of rusticated brick and a lavish interior, open to the public by appointment only. This club set the style for all the collegiate dens that followed (247-2100).

New York's most influential congregation, including the Walcotts, the Livingstons, and Theodore Roosevelt, once prayed in the pews of **Fifth Avenue Presbyterian Church,** built in 1875 by Carl Pfeiffer. The church, after an exodus from 19th St., got re-ordained at its present location at 7 W. 55th St. off Fifth.

The **Samuel Paley Plaza,** Midtown Manhattan's idea of a landscaped public space, grants a quiet reprieve from the throttling metropolis. The park, complete with waterfall, nestles at 53rd and Fifth.

The **Museum of Broadcasting,** located at 1 E. 53rd St, will be relocating to more spacious quarters at 23 W. 52nd St. in the winter of 1991. If you can't visit the museum, at least you can catch the Hitchcock reruns flickering on multiple screens in the museum's Fifth Ave. storefront. But remember, it's bad for your eyes when it's dark outside.

Lower Midtown: Murray Hill, Madison Square, Union Square

Neither coldly commercial nor hotly trendy, lower Midtown, like the third little bear's bowl of porridge, seems just right. Neoclassical architecture and generously wide avenues create an aura of refinement around classy monuments like the Empire State Building. At the Madison Square intersection, four of the earliest skyscrapers form a sub-skyline, one of the city's hidden treasures.

Late 19th-century "robber barons" took the lead in transforming the U.S. from a rural backwater into the world's leading industrial nation, accumulating fortunes to put European monarchs to shame, and creating lower Midtown in the process. In the **Pierpont Morgan Library,** 29 E. 36th St. (685-0610), the former home of the financier and his son, J.P. Morgan, Jr., you can see a stunning library room and the elder magnate's office.

The omnipresent architectural firm of McKim, Mead & White naturally supervised the building of this low Renaissance-style palazzo of white marble, completed in 1906. The tree-shaded classical oasis may look familiar: it figured prominently in the movie *Ragtime.*

In 1924, J.P. Morgan, Jr. graciously opened the library to the public. Its permanent collection, not always on display, includes drawings and prints from Blake and Dürer, illuminated Renaissance manuscripts, manuscript of Dickens' *A Christmas Carol,* Napoleon's love letters to Josephine, and music handwritten by Beethoven and Mozart.

After taking in the exhibit, walk through the hall lined with medieval paraphernalia to a circular room, the former main entrance. The West Room on the right, Morgan Sr.'s opulent former office, contains a carved ceiling made during the Italian Renaissance. It was common (well, not *common*) in the early days of the century to import large elements from European buildings for incorporation into domestic architecture.

Pop into the library, a small but exquisitely planned space, its walls stacked with mahogany-colored bound volumes and encircled by a delicate balcony. Among the more notable items in the room: one of the three existing likenesses of John Milton, a fabulous 12th-century jewel-encrusted triptych believed to contain fragments from the Cross, and one of 11 surviving copies of the Gutenberg Bible, the first printed book. (Subway: #6 to 33rd St. Open Tues.-Sat. 10:30am-5pm, Sun. 1-5pm. Suggested contribution $3, seniors and students $1.)

The **Church of the Incarnation,** 205 Madison Ave. at 35th St., lurks just around the corner from the Morgan Library. A comprehensive collection of late 19th-century art fills its sanctuary. Built in 1864, the church contains stained glass by Tiffany, William Morris, and Sir Edward Burn-Jones (another pre-Raphaelite type), as well as work by Daniel Chester French and Augustus Saint Gaudens. An unimposing pink pamphlet near the entrance can guide you to the Church's art.

West on 34th St., Murray Hill refinement becomes Midtown chaos. The Empire State Building looms at 34th St. and Fifth Ave. Don't miss it (see Empire State Building). The chain of New York monuments continues west on 34th St. at Herald Square, home of **Macy's,** the largest store in the world. With nine floors (plus a lower level) and some two million square feet of merchandise, it occupies an entire city block. Macy's has come a long way from its beginnings in 1857, when it grossed $11.06 on its first day of business. The store sponsors the Macy's Thanksgiving Day Parade, a New York tradition buoyed by helium-filled cultural icons, as well as a generous share of marching bands, floats, and general hoopla. Santa Claus always marches last in the parade, signalling the arrival of the Christmas shopping season.

Don't worry about navigating. Although children, like Jamie Rosen, have been known to get lost in Macy's mazes, adults can get their bearings from the ubiquitous directories or the staffed information desk. And at Macy's, the only store in town with a Visitor's Center, a concierge will assist anyone looking for something specific. The concierge service (560-3827) will also make dining or entertainment reservations, provide information on upcoming entertainment events, and arrange for interpreters to accompany non-English speakers through the store. You don't have to spend a cent to take advantage of any of these services. The Visitors' Center obligingly sits on the balcony of the first floor. Those too busy making money to spend any of it themselves can hire otheres to spend it for them, using the "Macy's by Appointment" service. A staff of fashion consultants, home accessories experts, and corporate specialists act as consumer therapists, walking clients through the store if necessary to help them discover what they really want (for an appointment, call 560-4181).

In "On Location Video Studios," on the fifth floor,you can dominate the screen in any one of a number of ways (or all of them, if you've got the money). For $19, you can star in your own music video. The Video Family Album will make a production out of your family photographs for $60. A series of "On Location" videos will put you in exotic settings for $19: "Superhero" flies you over the New York harbor and into space, "Rap Around New York" plunks you in a graffiti-filled urban backdrop, and "Police Chase" sticks you in the middle of a car chase. Indulge in these and countless other scenarios. Children can star in their own animated videos. The "Center Stage" recording studio, on the fourth floor allows you to control audio technology. Select your favorite songs from their catalog and create your own tape for $13.

The **Toy Department** on the seventh floor has a working train set, complete with a tunnel through a mountain, as well as adult strategy games, stuffed penguins, and wind-up skunks. The basement shopping area, known as "The Cellar," specializes in domestic products, fully equipped with a bakery, butcher shop, candy store, delicatessen, cookie store, and pharmacy. (Open Mon. and Thurs.-Fri. 9:45am-8:30pm, Tues.-Wed. 9:45am-6:45pm, Sat. 10am-6:45pm, Sun. 10am-6pm. Subway: #1, 2, or 3 to Penn Station, or B, D, F, N, Q, R, S to Herald Sq.)

To avoid the roar of the midtown crowds, walk back east on 34th St. to Madison Ave., and then downtown. If you make a right onto 29th St. you will happen upon the **Church of the Transfiguration,** better known as "The Little Church Around the Corner," home parish of New York's theatre world ever since a liberal pastor here agreed to bury actor George Holland in 1870 when no other church would.

Check the stained glass windows: that may look like a scene from the Bible, but look again—it's from *Hamlet*.

Madison Avenue ends, appropriately enough, at **Madison Square Park.** The park, opened in 1847, originally served as a public cemetery, and in recent years has grown decidedly seedy. On the other hand, since developers have yet to sink their cranes into this area, a number of the landmark buildings from years past remain, forming a skyline in miniature. The area around the park, particularly to the south, sparkles with funky architectural gems.

The first of the old-but-tall buildings you will encounter, the **New York Life Insurance Building,** occupies the block at 26th St. and Madison Ave. Built by Cass "Woolworth Building" Gilbert in 1928, it wears its distinctive golden pyramid hat with an aplomb that should give modern box buildings pause. The site of P.T. Barnum's "Hippodrome," it was rebuilt by Stanford White (the one who's not McKim or Mead) and renamed "Madison Square Garden" in 1879. It soon became the premier spot for New York's trademark entertainment spectacles. In 1906, the husband of Stanford White's reputed mistress shot the prolific architect to death on the roof of this building. Its present-day descendant, with the same name, has moved to Penn Station.

The clock faces of the **Metropolitan Life Insurance Tower** survey the park from Madison Ave. and 23rd St. with charm. The tower, a 1909 addition to an 1893 building, also belongs to New York's I-used-to-be-the-tallest-building-in-the-world club.

Yet another distinguished club member, the **Flatiron Building,** has a dramatic wedge shape imposed on it by the intersection of Broadway, Fifth Ave., and 23rd St. counterpointed by delicate Renaissance detailing. One of the most recognizable and most photographed buildings in the world, it had its day in the sun in 1902, when it ruled over the skyline with its 20 stories. Currently the esteemed St. Martin's Press occupies some of its floors.

From here it's just a few increasingly off-beat blocks to **Union Square Park,** between Broadway and Park Ave. South, and 17th and 14th St. Before the Civil War, the area boomed with hoity-toity intrigue. Society types had long since disappeared from the neighborhood when the park became a focal point for New York's large radical movement early in this century, hosting the particularly popular Socialist Movement's May Day celebrations. Even the workers ultimately united with everyone else to abandon this park; in 1989 the city finally attempted to reclaim it. After some rebuilding and de-toxing, the park has improved, but retains an unsavory aftertaste.

Overlooking the park, a number of modern apartment buildings wear levitating party hats that glow at night. The **Zeckendorf Towers,** built in 1987, strut their haberdashery at 1 Irving Place, between W. 14th and 15th. The triangular caps seem to be an obscene echo of Cass Gilbert's pyramid-topped buildings, such as the nearby New York Life.

Make a left onto 14th St. to reach **Palladium,** at 126 E. 14th St., between Fourth and Third Ave. This former movie palace, converted into a disco in 1985 by Japanese designer Arata Isozaki, contains a mural by Keith Haring and a staircase with 2400 round lights (see Dance Clubs).

To get to the **Forbes Magazine Galleries** (206-5548), walk back along 14th St. past Union Square Park to 62 Fifth Ave. at 12th St. The holdings here, like those in the Frick Museum and the Morgan Library, were acquired by a multi-millionaire financier for his own amusement and then turned over to the public. Malcolm Forbes' irrepressible penchant for the offbeat permeates this 20th-century collection. Eclectic exhibits occupy the ground floor of the late magnate's publishing outfit: 12,000 toy soldiers arranged in various battle formations, a rotating exhibit of presidential paraphernalia (Reagan on "the secret of my success," and the opera glasses and stovepipe hat Lincoln was wearing when he was shot). A remarkable assemblage of documents relating to the dawning of the nuclear age include the map used on the *Enola Gay* to plot its course to Hiroshima and Nagasaki and the famous 1939 letter from Einstein to Roosevelt: "Recent work in nuclear physics has made it probable that uranium may be turned into a new and important source of energy."

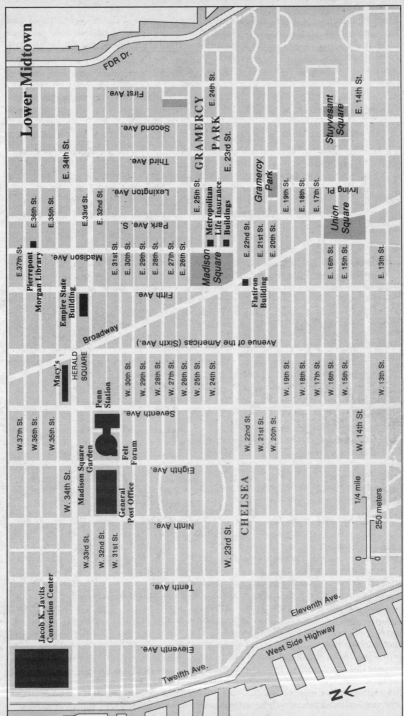

Forbes' collection of items produced under the direction of Carl Fabergé, the largest such assemblage in the world, contains a dozen of his exquisite Easter Eggs, made as gifts for the members of the Russian imperial family to present to one another. (Open Tues.-Sat. 10am-4pm. Free, but entry limited to 900 people per day, and ages under 16 must be accompanied by an adult.)

Chelsea

Clement Clark Moore of "Twas the night before Christmas" fame was more than just a long-winded poet with visions of sugarplums. He also owned and developed most of Chelsea during the mid-1800s. An example of his architectural work lives on at West 20th St.: **Cushman Row,** #406-418, in the Greek Revival style, with wrought iron railings.

These posh homes face the cathedral and the grounds of the General Theological Seminary (243-5150; entrance on Ninth Ave. between 20th and 21st; grounds open Mon.-Fri. noon-3pm, Sat. 11am-3pm, Sun. 2-4pm). Dean Eugene Hoffman erected this peaceful gateway in 1883 and called it "The Great Design." If you're lucky, you may catch some monks playing tennis. Take in the wonder of the fancy co-op at the **London Terrace Gardens,** spanning an entire block; it has occupied the area between 22nd and 23rd St. and Ninth and Tenth Ave. since 1929.

The historical **Chelsea Hotel,** on 23rd St. between Seventh and Eighth, has sheltered many a suicidal artist, including most recently Sid Vicious of the Sex Pistols. Edie Sedgwick made pit stops here between Warhol films and asylums. Countless writers, as the plaques outside attest, spent their final days searching for inspiration and mail in the lobby here. Many over-zealous fans beg the management to let them spend a couple of nights in their superstar's former room.

Chelsea's **flower district,** on 28th St. between Sixth and Seventh, grows most colorful during the early hours of the morning. Later in the day, if you wander around 27th St. and Broadway, you can witness the wholesale trading of cheap imports ranging from porn videos to imitation Barbie dolls to 100% human hair wigs.

A cool but expensive mixed drink over a game of pool at Chelsea Billiard (989-0096; 54 W. 21st St.) may hit the spot. The summertime drops afternoon (liberally defined as noon-7pm) pool rates from $10 to $5 per hour.

Upper East Side

> *Generally speaking, the weather is better on the East*
> *Side than on the West Side.*
> *—Fran Lebowitz*

Until the close of the Civil War, 19th-century jetsetters chose this part of town for their summer retreats, building elaborate mansions in garden settings. By the late 1860s summering uptown would not suffice. Landowners converted their warm-weather residences into year-round settlements, the building of elevated railroads soon brought in an influx of urban proletariat, and the East was won. In 1896, Caroline Schermerhorn Astor built a mansion on Fifth Avenue at 65th St. and the vanguard of high society, desiring proximity to Caroline and to Central Park, soon followed, including the Fiskes, Havermeyers, Armours, and that obscure jeweler Charles Tiffany. The Golden Age of the East Side high society epic progressed from 1895 to the outbreak of World War I. The old-money crowd conspired with improvements in technology to produce sumptuous mansions outfitted with elevators, intercoms, and theatrical plumbing devices. The new century saw a dramatic increase in the number of New York millionaires, prompting the rapid construction of luxurious apartment houses, especially along Park Avenue. Scores of the wealthy moved in and refused to budge, even during the Great Depression when armies of the unemployed pitched their tents across the way in Central Park.

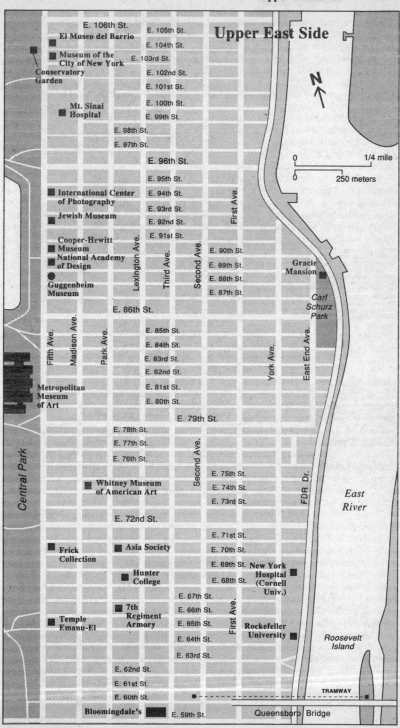

Upper East Side

E. 106th St.
El Museo del Barrio
E. 105th St.
E. 104th St.
Museum of the
City of New York   E. 103rd St.
Conservatory
Garden
E. 102nd St.
E. 101st St.
E. 100th St.
Mt. Sinai   E. 99th St.
Hospital
E. 98th St.
E. 97th St.
E. 96th St.
E. 95th St.
International Center   E. 94th St.
of Photography   E. 93rd St.
Jewish Museum   E. 92nd St.
First Ave.
E. 91st St.
Cooper-Hewitt
Museum   E. 90th St.
National Academy   E. 89th St.
of Design   E. 88th St.   Gracie
Guggenheim   E. 87th St.   Mansion
Museum
Carl
Schurz
E. 86th St.   Park
E. 85th St.
Fifth Ave.
Madison Ave.
Park Ave.
Lexington Ave.
Third Ave.
Second Ave.
York Ave.
East End Ave.
E. 84th St.
E. 83rd St.
E. 82nd St.
E. 81st St.
Metropolitan   E. 80th St.
Museum
of Art   E. 79th St.
E. 78th St.
E. 77th St.
E. 76th St.
Central Park
Second Ave.
E. 75th St.
Whitney Museum   E. 74th St.
of American Art   E. 73rd St.
FDR Dr.
East
River
E. 72nd St.
E. 71st St.
Frick   Asia Society   E. 70th St.
Collection   E. 69th St.   New York
Hunter   Hospital
College   E. 68th St.   (Cornell
Univ.)
E. 67th St.
7th   E. 66th St.   First Ave.
Temple   Regiment   E. 65th St.   Rockefeller
Emanu-El   Armory   E. 64th St.   University
Roosevelt
E. 63rd St.   Island
E. 62nd St.
E. 61st St.
E. 60th St.   TRAMWAY
Bloomingdale's   E. 59th St.   Queensboro Bridge

0   1/4 mile
0   250 meters

So it was that select hotels, mansions, and churches first colonized the primordial wilderness of the Upper East Side. Then the disciplined forest of limestone and red brick grew up between 1881 and 1932. The lawns of Central Park covered the land where squatters had dwelt; Fifth Avenue rolled over a stretch once grazed by pigs. These days parades, millionaires, and unbearably slow buses share Fifth Avenue. Its **Museum Mile** includes the Metropolitan, the Guggenheim, the International Center of Photography, the Cooper-Hewitt, the Museum of the City of New York, and the Jewish Museum, among others. Madison Avenue has been occasionally equated with the cutthroat advertising business, where artists, market psychologists, and salespeople conspire to manipulate America's buying habits. But these Jello-Pop jingle workshops are well concealed behind an unbroken façade of expensive boutiques and superb galleries. Check out the displays: the high-art and high-fashion windows of Madison afford endless hours of aesthetic enjoyment.

The stately boulevard of Park Avenue has been constructed around strict building codes. The Avenue Association oversees this area restricted to lofty residences, forbidding commercial developments in most zones—including businesses, stores, or even public buses or telephones. For the maintenance of the plush mid-street gardens, said association encourages donations from residents, who reap the benefits of the boulevard as they enjoy masses of yellow tulips, cute Christmas trees, and complimentary copies of an obnoxious magazine called *Avenue.* (Could there be any other avenue?) Foreign cultural missions or clubs dominate the non-residential sections. Landscaped green islands now bisect Park Ave. where railroad tracks once lacerated the thoroughfare. Here and there along the length of the avenue stand suspiciously old-looking, thoughtfully decorated churches. Admire the view down Park Avenue, its artbook-perfect perspective down the hazy indigo outline of star-scraping silhouettes in Midtown. Grittier Lexington Avenue injects a little reality into the idyllic East Side. Here and on Third, Second, and First Ave., you'll find the area's most vibrant crowds, a happening singles scene, and reliable public transportation. Farther north, highrise projects and grimmer urban settings replace the hardier party atmosphere of the 80s and 70s. At night it can be soothing to savor the quiet elegance of **Park Avenue** or **Fifth Avenue,** where liveried doormen guard the sidewalks, penthouse gardens overlook the cityscape, and polished lobbies seem always freshly mopped. Grand hotels approach senility here. One such old fogie, the 1927 **Sherry-Netherland,** wears daunting gargoyles.

At 60th St. and Madison Ave. stands the infamous **Copacabana Club** where Sammy Davis Jr. and Jerry Vale crooned in the 40s and Copa Girls like Lola danced with music and passion. Northwest of the Copa, at 1 E. 60th St., stands the **Metropolitan Club,** built by the dynamic trio of McKim, Mead & White on a commission from J.P. Morgan for his friends who had not been accepted at other clubs. Right next door to the Metropolitan sneers the mighty **Pierre,** another of the European-style hotels with many permanent residents.

Past residents of **810 Fifth Avenue** have included publisher Randolph Hearst and pre-presidential Richard Nixon. Dick could go upstairs to borrow butter and eggs from Nelson Rockefeller, a former shoeshine boy and owner of New York's only fully equipped bomb shelter. Also in the neighborhood, at 15 E. 61st St., you can see a rare, five-story example of English Regency style. At 21 E. 61st, you can plague your friends by discussing Camus at **Maxim's,** a transcontinental cousin of the Paris restaurant. Southeast of Maxim's at 47 E. 60th St. stands the **Grolier Club,** built in 1917 in honor of 16th-century bibliophile Jean Grolier. This Georgian structure houses a collection of fine bookbindings and a specialized research library. Exhibits present rare manuscripts, prints, and antique books. **Christ Church,** though built and decorated in the 1930s, manages to appear quite ancient. Ralph Adams Cram ornamented this Byzantine-Romanesque hybrid with Venetian mosaics and onion-rippled marble columns. Note the iconic panels (taken from an old Russian church) above the altar. (Open daily 9am-5pm for meditation, prayer and respectful viewing. Occasional classical church music concerts given; call 838-3036 for information.)

Between Lexington and Park on 63rd St., you'll find the **Society of Illustrators,** built in 1875. Moving down 63rd St. to Third Ave., you'll encounter another memorial to Donald Trump's formerly bottomless pockets—the **Trump Plaza.** Don't even bother throwing a coin into the waterfall to the left of the entrance. Antique and contemporary dolls take refuge at the **New York Doll Hospital,** located on Lexington Avenue between 61st and 62nd on the second floor. Some come whole, others in parts. Your parents have to put them together. (Open Mon.-Sat. 10am-6pm.)

Several blocks uptown at 163 E. 67th st. between Third and Lexington stands the **Park East Synagogue,** a richly ornamented house of worship executed in 1890 by Schneider and Herter in homage to Moorish architecture. A mutiny of mannerism consumes the porticos at 131 and 135 E. 66th St., counterpointing the otherwise dignified buidings. Occupying virtually an entire block, the **Seventh Regiment Armory** makes its stand between 66th and 67th on Park Ave. The Seventh Regiment fought in every major U.S. campaign from 1812 on, including a valiant outing for the cause of the Union in the Civil War. Masons laid the cornerstone of the Armory on October 13, 1877, and the rest of this crenelated, cartoon-like castle soon followed, built on the design of Charles W. Clinton, himself a veteran of the Seventh. Much of the original decoration and furnishing remain in place today. The rooms illustrate the multiform fancies of the Victorian period—a jumble of aestheticism tempered by an interest in Renaissance decoration. Inside, notable rooms were designed by the Associated Artists under the baton of Louis Comfort Tiffany. The Veterans' room and the adjoining library-turned-display-room for the Regiment's silver are especially noteworthy. Since the Armory still serves as an active military facility, you should call ahead if you'd like a tour (744-8180).

At 112 E. 64th St., between Lexington and Park stands the old Asia Society headquarters, designed by that most famous glass-blower/bricklayer of postmodernity, Philip Johnson. With this project—an obsidian shoebox—he pays homage to glass guru Mies van der Rohe whose Seagram Building set the tone for glass giants to come. At 2 E. 64th St., architect N. C. Melon revived the Venetian Renaissance style in the mansion that he built for coal magnate Edwin J. Berwind in 1896. At the height of his powers, Berwind's name had become virtually synonymous with coal: he was the sole supplier of fuel for U.S. warships.

On Fifth Ave. at the corner of 65th. stands **Temple Emanu-El,** (meaning "God is with us"), the largest in the U.S. Outside, Eastern details speckle the limestone and otherwise Romanesque structure. Inside, the nave bears Byzantine ornaments and seats 2500—more than St. Patrick's Cathedral. The 1929 temple built by Kohn, Butler, and Stein occupies the site of a mansion that once belonged to Caroline Astor.

The Sarah Delano Roosevelt Memorial House, actually a pair of identical buildings executed by Charles Platt in 1908, sweeps #45-47 E. 65th St. between Park and Madison. The powerful Roosevelt matriarch commissioned the constructions on the occasion of her son Franklin's wedding. In the bedroom on the fourth floor, Roosevelt recovered from polio in the early 1920s. He launched his political career in these buildings, now a community center for Hunter College students.

Richard Hunt designed the **Lotos Club** on E. 66th St. between Madison and Fifth, an organization of actors, musicians, and journalists. Red brick rises from a base of rusticated limestone, capped by a two-story mansard roof in a style best described as Second Empire meets wedding cake.

East 67th and 68th Street between Madison and Fifth furnish more examples of turn-of-the-century mansion architecture with a distinct French accent. At 45 E. 67th St. stands the former residence of poor little rich girl Gloria Vanderbilt, and the current address of ambassadors from Peru. **The Council on Foreign Relations,** the publisher of *Foreign Affairs,* hangs out at 58 E. 68th St. 680 Park Avenue (at 68th St.) served as the seat of the Soviet Delegation to the United Nations in the 40s and early 50s. Today, a gallery specializing in Latin American art occupies the building.

Landmark design work in a softer medium is on display at the **Giorgio Armani Boutique,** at 815 Madison Ave. at 68th St. No one can outfit a jazzman or a gangster like Armani—just ask Brian De Palma. Other fabric heavywieghts neighbor Armani along Madison: sensuous **Valentino** at 825, the Japanese-French flavored designs of **Kenzo** at 824, and Italian knit-whiz **Missoni** at 836.

The **Frick Collection** stands poised at 1 E. 70th St. on Fifth Ave. (see Museums). The contrived ambience of English-style luxury as interpreted by a New Yorker named Ralph has been conveniently summarized in the **Polo—Ralph Lauren** boutique quartered in a French Renaissance building at 867 Madison. The store's atmosphere—complete with a live string quartet—has been so meticulously orchestrated that you may feel that you're on location for the shoot of the *Great Gatsby.*

Hunter College, part of the City University of New York, presents its unsightly modernist façade to Lexington and its more attractive posterior to Park Ave., between 67th and 69th. At 117 E. 69th Street, between Lexington and Park, a large Georgian mansion built for a banker now plays host to Manhattan's most huggable celebrities—**The Muppets. The Asia Society,** 725 Park Ave. at 70th St., showcases an outstanding collection of Asian art assembled by John D. Rockefeller III (see Museums). The neoclassical **St. Jean Baptiste** stands on the corner of Lexington Ave. and 76th St. Twin towers *à la* Notre Dame flank a robust façade. Whites and Napeoleonic light blues color the place benign. Stained glass rarefies the light, devotional candles create the long shadows, and mosaics tell of miracles. The cavernous space feels oddly intimate. A bit removed from the mayhem of Madison where it once stood, **Sotheby Park Bernet Inc.** (606-7000) conducts its affairs and auctions at 1334 York Ave. near 72nd St. Viewings are open to the public, although admission to some auctions requires tickets.

On Madison Ave. at 75 St, box-shaped and brutalist, stands the **Whitney Museum of American Art**—a shape as aloof as some of the art that you will find inside (see Museums). You don't even have to enter the lobby to enjoy Alexander Calder's whimsical wirefest of acrobatics; peek through the window to let Calder convince you that all the world is a circus.

In 1912, Horace Trumbauer built a mansion for James B. Duke, the founder of the American Tobacco Company. His creation, a faithful replica of an 18th-century Bordeaux chateau, abides at 1 E. 78th St. off Fifth. The Duke's daughter, Barbara Hutton, donated the building to New York University. Many of the original furnishings have been preserved, including a portrait by Gainsborough. 'Round the corner, another limestone whimsy confronts the spectator with its sandcastle proliferation of ornament. McKim, Mead & White constructed the imitation Italian Renaissance impostor at 972 Fifth Ave. for financier Payne Whitney in 1906; it now houses the **French Embassy Cultural Services.** An earlier Renaissance palace courtesy of McKim, Mead & White stands at 25 E. 78 St. off Madison. They built it in 1898 for Stuyvesant Fish, New York's original upscale party animal.

Executed in a saucy Regency style, the **Junior League of the City of New York** occupies 130 E. 80th St. between Lexington and Park. Mott B. Schmidt, the architect of this mansion, also authored a Georgian house at 124 E. 80th St. Cross and Cross built the house at 116 E. 80th St., in a strict federal style chosen by owner L.S. Morris to honor his heritage—he was the direct descendant of a signer of the Declaration of Independence.

Even in death, celebrity New Yorkers manage to uphold their status, maintaining their coteries as they pass on to the Grand Ballroom in the sky. The grave roll call of the **Frank E. Campbell Chapel,** the world's most prestigious funeral chapel (at 1076 Madison Avenue at 81st St.), reads like Who Was Who on the American Mount Olympus: Elizabeth Arden, James Cagney, Jack Dempsey, Tommy Dorsey, Judy Garland, Howard Johnson, Robert F. Kennedy, Mae West, John Lennon, and Arturo Toscanini, just to name a pew.

The Metropolitan Museum of Art manifests its majestic presence at 1000 Fifth Ave. The largest in the Western Hemisphere, the Met's art collection encompasses some 33 million works. On its steps you can follow the navigation of the crowds and traffic along Museum Mile. **The Church of St. Ignatius Loyola,** at 980 Park Ave. off 84th bears a stern Renaissance-style façade that comes as a welcome relief after the superabundance of Gothic Ecclesiastical architecture.

Located in the far east, between 84th and 90th along East End Ave. lies the **Carl Schurz Park** named in honor of a many-hatted German immigrant who was a Civil War General, a Missouri senator, President Rutherford B. Hayes's Secretary of the Interior, and finally an editor of the *New York Evening Post* and *Harper's Weekly.* Gracie Mansion, the residence of New York's mayor, currently David Dinkins, occupies the north end of the park. To arrange a tour of the mansion call 570-4751. Tours, given on Wednesdays only, require reservations. (Suggested admission charge $3, seniors $1.)

Originally a German village, Yorkville (extending from the East River to Lexington Ave. from 77th to 96th St.) continued to welcome immigrants from the Rhine Valley over the first half of this century. The heavy German accent that once animated the local restaurant menus, beer gardens, pastry shops, and deli counters has thinned in the wake of newer chain stores and pizza parlors, but has not vanished. A few of the old faithfuls remain, keeping the *wiener schnitzel* and the tradition going. **Henderson Place** lines East End Ave. at 86th St.; this series of Queen Anne-style houses decorated with multiple turrets, parapets, and dormers could have been wrought from Legos. Ghostbusters beware—rumor has it that some of these houses are haunted.

All done up in reds, golds, and browns, the fanciful **Church of the Holy Trinity** all but hides from view at 316 E. 88th St. between First and Second. Behind this late 19th-century church lies a small heavenly garden. Known for its inspiring Dalton madrigal group concerts, the church keeps wonderful acoustics inside and wears a birthday-cake Gothic crown on top.

You can stop in at **Elaine's,** 1703 Second Ave., where Woody Allen makes the occasional appearance both on and off screen. But don't hold your breath. Still, media celebrities, gossips, and self-styled literati gather here. Elaine rules the place with an iron pan. The cuisine is allegedly Italian but you might not believe it if you tasted the food. If you don't look self-important, they might not let you in.

On 89th St. between Park and Lexington stands that celebrated educational shrine **The Dalton School.** Founded in 1920 by idealistic reformer Helen Parkhurst, the once-radical institution has since become Manhattan's most prestigious co-ed private school, notably featured in Woody Allen's *Manhattan.* Recently Dalton eliminated its nursery school program as many neurotic three year-olds and their parents considered it too competitive. While Dalton may be the only high school in the neighborhood that does not require its students to wear uniforms, some of them stick to a fashion-conscious regimen anyhow.

The prairie-white **Guggenheim Museum** on Fifth Ave. at 89th St. is the only New York building designed by midwestern plain builder Frank Lloyd Wright, an architectural apotheosis for architecture's sake (see Museums).

When Andrew Carnegie requested that Babb, Cook, and Willard construct "the most modest, plainest, and most roomy house in New York" on 91st and Fifth, he received a large but formulaic Renaissance-Georgian combo of red brick and limestone, situated in a luxurious garden. Within, dark oak paneling, textured wallpaper, and demure atriums create the perfect setting for a society ball. When Carnegie moved out, the Smithsonian moved in, relocating their National Museum of Design here at **The Cooper-Hewitt Museum** (see Museums).

The **National Academy of Design** building, on Fifth and 89th, serves as both a school and a museum for the academy established in 1825. Work by 11 of the 30 founding members lodges at the Metropolitan Museum. (see Museums).

The **Jewish Museum,** on 92nd and Fifth, a French Renaissance structure with a modern wing added in 1962, contains the country's largest collection of Judaica (see Museums). At 60 E. 93rd St. between Park and Madison stands the haughty French mansion that served as a retreat for Mrs. William K. Vanderbilt after her dramatic divorce. The **International Center of Photography,** the first museum in the world to have raised photography to the level of great art, maintains a rich permanent collection and operates workshops, photolabs, and a screening room.

The **Eighth Regiment's Armory** once occupied a square block between 94th and 95th St. and Park and Madison. Today only the façade survives, a red brick turreted expanse with rookish crenelation, arrow slits, and a yawning, semicircular gate. The demolished space within has been taken over by the **Hunter High School**—which was designed to match the armory's façade, prompting students to nickname it "The Brick Prison."

The **Synod of Bishops of the Russian Orthodox Church Outside Russia** now inhabits the 1917 Georgian mansion at Park and 93rd. The bishops scattered a few icons about but left the interior decoration virtually unchanged, save a former ballroom they converted into a cathedral.

Before Manhattan builders got wise and fireproof and turned to stone, they made all houses out of wood. A few of these mid 19th-century houses can be seen at 120 and 122 E. 92nd St. between Lexington and Park.

The **Islamic Cultural Center,** a mosque at Third Ave. and 96th St., has been precisely oriented by computer to face the holy city of Mecca. Meanwhile the tenacious Russian zealots continued their conquest of the Upper East Side with the construction of a **Russian Orthodox Cathedral of St. Nicholas** at 15 E. 97th St. The cathedral body has a polychromatic Victorian body but a spirit of authentic Rus', as manifested in its five onion domes. Louise Nevelson's 1972 steel sculpture *Night Presence IV* stands on the island of Park Ave. at 92nd St. From this same spot, you can the avenue with its manicured buildings and trees, stretching into the downtown horizon.

Central Park

> There is no greenery; it is enough to make a stone sad.
> —*Nikita Khrushchev, remark during visit to New*
> *York, October 1960*

Beloved Central Park has earned some moments in the sun. Recall Dustin Hoffman in *The Marathon Man,* running breathlessly through the park to escape from the hostile city, Laurence Olivier, and Olivier's instruments of torture. The park has staged grand dramas throughout its history from the heroics of its construction to ex-mayor Koch's "Silence the Ghettoblasters" campaign to Joseph Papp's popular Shakespeare in the Park festival.

The campaign for a public park in New York began in the mid-1840s with William Cullen Bryant, a vociferous editor of the *New York Evening Post,* and received support from the acclaimed architect Andrew Jackson Downing in his magazine *The Horticulturist.* The creation of the park became an issue in the mayoral campaign of 1851, with both candidates strongly in favor of the project. In 1853, the state authorized the purchase of land from 59th to 106th St. (The 106th to 110th St. addendum was purchased in 1863.) Unfortunately, Downing met his death by drowning and never got to design his dream project. The city held a competition to determine the new designer of the park.

The winning design, selected in 1858 from 33 competing entries, came out of a collaboration between Frederic Law Olmsted and Calvert Vaux. Olmsted and Vaux transformed 840 acres of bogs, cliffs, glacial leftovers, bone-boiling works, and pig farms into a living masterwork they called *Greensward.* The whole landscape took 15 years to build and 40 years to grow.

The Park may be roughly divided north and south at the main reservoir; the southern section affords more intimate settings, serene lakes, and graceful promenades, while the northern end has a few ragged edges. Nearly 1400 species of trees, shrubs, and flowers grow here, the work of distinguished horticulturist Ignaz Anton Pilat. When you lose yourself in the park, you need not get lost. Look to the nearest lamppost for guidance: check the four-digit small metal plaque bolted to it—the first two digits tell you what street you're nearest (89 for example), and the second two whether you're on the east or west side of the park (an even number means east, an odd west).

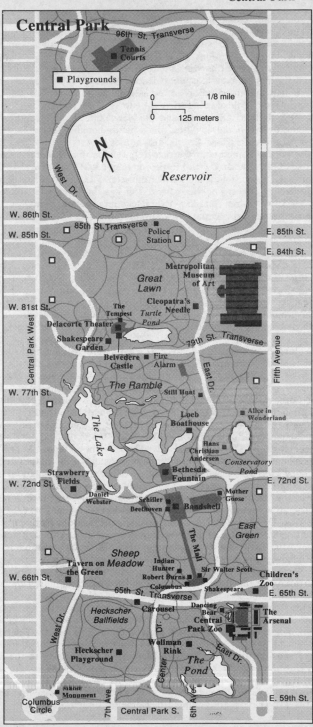

Central Park

96th St. Transverse

Tennis Courts

■ Playgrounds

0 _____ 1/8 mile

0 _____ 125 meters

Reservoir

West Dr.

W. 86th St.

W. 85th St. 85th St. Transverse E. 85th St.

Police Station E. 84th St.

Metropolitan Museum of Art

Great Lawn

Cleopatra's Needle

W. 81st St. The Tempest *Turtle Pond*

Delacorte Theater 79th St. Transverse

Shakespeare Garden

Belvedere Castle Fire Alarm

The Ramble

W. 77th St. Still Hunt

Alice in Wonderland

Loeb Boathouse

The Lake Hans Christian Andersen

Conservatory Pond

Strawberry Fields Bethesda Fountain

W. 72nd St. E. 72nd St.

Daniel Webster Mother Goose

Schiller Beethoven Bandshell

East Green

The Mall

Sheep Meadow

Tavern on the Green Indian Hunter

W. 66th St. Robert Burns Sir Walter Scott Children's Zoo

Columbus 65th St. Transverse Shakespeare E. 65th St.

Heckscher Ballfields Carousel Dancing Bear

Central Park Zoo The Arsenal

West Dr. Center Dr. Wollman Rink

Heckscher Playground East Dr.

The Pond

Maine Monument

Columbus Circle E. 59th St.

7th Ave. Central Park S. 6th Ave.

Central Park West

Fifth Avenue

East Dr.

While you should come here to play, you can observe some architectural and sculptural landmarks in the park. **The Arsenal** at Fifth Ave. and 64th St., the nerve center of the New York Parks system since 1848, once housed the National Guard. Bring all your burning questions to the friendly staff in this ponderous brick castle. Pick up the *Central Park Calendar* and a glossy broadsheet generically called the *Leaflet.* The former prints a seasonal calendar of events sponsored by the park, a handy park map, and information on recreational activities. The latter has similar listings but includes a calendar of the joint efforts of the park in conjunction with the Met, the Symphony Orchestra, and the New York Shakespeare Festival. Full information on recreational activities fills a handy booklet, *Green Pages* available at all information centers. The Arsenal also houses an Arts Gallery (360-8111), displaying the work of contemporary artists. (Open Mon.-Fri. 9:30am-4:30pm. Free.)

Constructed in 1934, the **Central Park Zoo** (439-6500) still attracts flocks of visitors. Come gaze at your fellow animals. (Admission $1, seniors 50¢, ages 3-12 25¢.) Above the archway, north of the main zoo, hangs the **Delacorte Musical Clock,** made in 1965 by Andrea Spaldini. Every half hour, bears, monkeys, and other bronze creatures perform a ritual hop and skip routine. At the **Children's Zoo** (408-0271), at Fifth Ave. between 65th and 66th, you can pet a barnyard full of ducks, goats, rabbits, and llamas. (Open daily 10am-4:30pm. Admission 10¢.)

Designed by Vaux in 1870 as a milk bar for mothers, nurses, and children, **The Dairy** has since become the Central Park Reception Center. Come here for information on Sunday tours and events. (Open Tues.-Sun. 11am-5pm, Fri. 1-5pm.) **The Chess and Checkers Pavilion,** a striped red brick concoction created by Robert Moses, realizes what Olmsted and Vaux called the *kinderberg*—the first ever children's playground. Today grandmasters and grizzled amateurs square off at the 24 outdoor boards and 10 indoor boards (indoor tables available on the weekends; open daily 11:30am-3:30pm.)

The Wollman Skating Rink doubles as a miniature golf course in late spring. (Open Sun.-Mon. 10am-5pm, Tues.-Thurs. 10am-9:30pm, Fri.-Sat. 10am-11pm. Admission $4, children $2.) Trade your putter for a pair of skates, and **rollerdance** to your heart's content without having to leave the building. Admission to the rollerrink costs $5, seniors $2.50, children $2, and renting skates costs $2.50. (Open same hours as miniature golf.) If you feel like horsing around, visit **The Friedsam Memorial Carousel** (879-0244), located at 65th St. west of Center Drive. (Open daily 10:30am-4:45pm, weather permitting. Admission 75¢.)

Erroneously called Sheep's Meadow even by those in the know, **Sheep Meadow,** the largest chunk of Greensward, exemplifies the pastoral ideals of the park's designers and today's teenage crowds. Sheep did graze here until 1934, but after that the Park could afford lawn mowers and so did away with the flock. North of Sheep Meadow lie the bowling and croquet greens. Inside Sheep Meadow lies the sheepish frisbee generation, getting suntanned or stoned in the noonday sun.

Along West Drive, at 67th St., stands the stirring **Seventh Regiment Civil War Monument,** sculpted by John Quincy Adams Ward in 1870. Although some bureaucrat deemed the Park "not an appropriate place for sepulchral monuments," the statue somehow got permission to stand. In subsequent years it became a prototype for Civil War monuments throughout the country. To the east of Sheep Meadow lies **the Mall,** surrounded by a dense arts and letters statuary. Off the southwest end of the Mall, you can see the first American statue placed in the park: **The Indian Hunter** (1869), by J.Q.A. Ward, in extraordinary, naturalistic bronze. At the **Hunt Memorial** at 70th St. on Fifth Ave., an elegant Beaux-Arts mish-mash, Bruce Price's architectural musings mingle with sculptural groups by **Daniel Chester French.**

The Terrace and **Bethesda Fountain,** the formal centerpieces of the Park, link the Mall with the Lake. Designed by Vaux and Jacob Wrey Mould, they swim in elaborate ornamental carvings of plants, birds, and park animals. Descending the grand central staircase, you can look through a noble arch and spy the 1865 statue of **The Angel of the Waters,** sculpted in Rome by Emma Stebins.

Located at 77th St. near the Lake, the graceful Balcony Bridge spans its stuff and features one of the most dramatic views from the Park: the Lake, the Ramble (a birdwatcher's paradise), and the heart of Midtown. The 1954 **Loeb Boathouse** (517-2233), a late but indispensible addition to the park, plies all necessary romantic nautical equipment. Its mighty rental fleet includes rowboats, swanboats, and even gondolas. (Open from late March daily 11am-5pm, weather permitting. Refundable $20 deposit; $6 first hr., $1.50 each additional quarter hr. Take gondola rides with an imitation Venetian gondolier in the evenings for $30 per ½ hour, up to five people. Reservations required: call 517-3623.) Those who weren't born water babies can rent a bike from the boathouse and make their own journeys on *terra firma*. (Bike rental open from late March daily 10am-6pm, in clement weather. First hr. $8-12. I.D. required. Call 861-4137.)

Model boats set sail daily on the Pacific swells of Conservatory Water. The formal basin, site of the yacht race in E.B. White's classic *Stuart Little,* vibrates in summertime with the impassioned joy of children and the dynamic progress of their intrepid vessels. The clouds and sails go by on golden afternoons here in the most enchanting part of the park. A statue of **Hans Christian Andersen,** a gift from wonderful Copenhagen in 1956, stands next to dreamchild **Alice in Wonderland,** with several of her friends—another gift from those dreamy Danes, given in 1959. Sadly, the Alice statue no longer shows a film at 11:00, but the Andersen statue has become a prime storytelling spot in the summer. (For information call 790-6442.) Storytelling, complete with puppets and marionettes, comes to the stage at **Heckscher Puppet House** (397-3162) and to the **Swedish Cottage Marionette Theater** (988-9093). People dressed as puppets engage in the mystical ancient rites of **folk dancing** (535-0673) at the King Jagiello Statue, at 80th St. They do-si-do on Saturdays and Sundays from 2pm-dusk, starting on March 31.

The high point of the Park, both literally and figuratively, is the **Belvedere Castle,** a whimsical fancy designed by the restless Vaux in 1869 as a scenic element. The castle of crossed destinies rises from the **Vista Rock,** commanding a view of the **Great Lawn,** the **Ramble,** and the **Winter Drive.** For many years a weather station, Belvedere Castle has been reincarnated as an education center and serves as the stronghold of those green knights—the **Urban Park Rangers**—who provide visitor and emergency services for the park.

Visit the **Delacorte Theatre** on midsummer nights to see **Shakespeare in the Park.** Come early: the theatre seats only 1,936 lucky souls.

The madras-clad crowd plays **croquet** in Central Park from May through November (*sans* flamingos) north of Sheep Meadow at 67th St. **Horseback Riding** operates out of Claremont Stables, at 175 W. 89th St. (724-5100). (Open Mon.-Sat. 6:30am-one hour before dusk, Sun. 6:30am-4pm. $27 per hour.) The NYC Audubon society (691-7483) outfits **bird-watching** expeditions in the spring, convening at 7:30am Monday and Wednesday at 72nd St. and Fifth Ave. The most popular place to run in the Park is on the track surrounding the Reservoir, where one lap measures 1.58 miles.

Upper West Side

An urban slum in the late 40s, the neighborhood west of Broadway cleaned up its act in the 50s. Ramshackle tenements met their bulldozers and constructions like Lincoln Center, the Lincoln Tower Apartments, and the campus of Fordham University shot up. Urban renewal has continued steadily since then, though at a less frantic pace, bringing with it antique stores, clothing emporiums, here-today-gone-tomorrow restaurants, and white-collar singles bars.

Central Park West, lined with apartment buildings with Old World names, makes for a soothing pre-theatre promenade. The original plan slated Broadway for residences and West End for businesses, but no one paid attention. Just the reverse happened, and Broadway became the principal and most colorful thoroughfare of the West Side. Today Broadway bursts with delis, theatres, and boutiques; here you can find chicken take-out with menus in Spanish and charismatic hawkers peddling

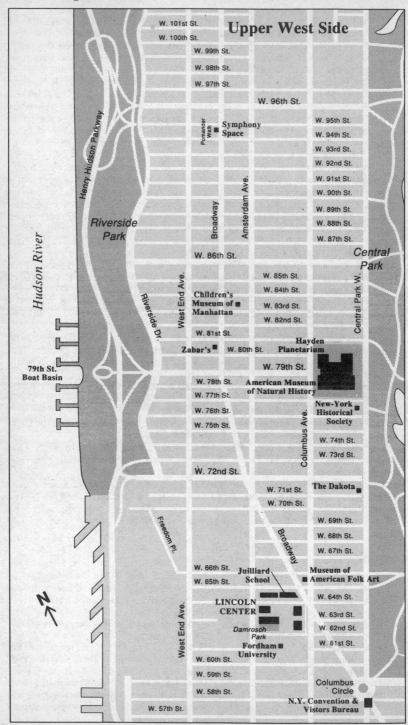

Upper West Side

W. 101st St.
W. 100th St.
W. 99th St.
W. 98th St.
W. 97th St.
W. 96th St.
W. 95th St.
W. 94th St.
W. 93rd St.
W. 92nd St.
W. 91st St.
W. 90th St.
W. 89th St.
W. 88th St.
W. 87th St.
W. 86th St.
W. 85th St.
W. 84th St.
W. 83rd St.
W. 82nd St.
W. 81st St.
W. 80th St.
W. 79th St.
W. 78th St.
W. 77th St.
W. 76th St.
W. 75th St.
W. 72nd St.
W. 71st St.
W. 70th St.
W. 69th St.
W. 68th St.
W. 67th St.
W. 66th St.
W. 65th St.
W. 64th St.
W. 63rd St.
W. 62nd St.
W. 61st St.
W. 60th St.
W. 59th St.
W. 58th St.
W. 57th St.

Henry Hudson Parkway
Riverside Park
Hudson River
Riverside Dr.
West End Ave.
Broadway
Amsterdam Ave.
Columbus Ave.
Central Park W.
Central Park
Freedom Pl.
Broadway
West End Ave.

Pomander Walk
Symphony Space
Children's Museum of Manhattan
Zabar's
Hayden Planetarium
American Museum of Natural History
New-York Historical Society
The Dakota
79th St. Boat Basin
Museum of American Folk Art
Juilliard School
LINCOLN CENTER
Damrosch Park
Fordham University
Columbus Circle
N.Y. Convention & Vistors Bureau

N

anything from used books to housewares of yesteryear. Broadway leads uptown to **Columbus Circle** at 59th St., the symbolic entrance to the Upper West Side and the end of Midtown. Set between Central Park and the **New York Coliseum,** a convention and exhibition complex slated for destruction in the near future, the Circle is distinguished by a statue of Christopher himself, a pigeon-marked creation by Gaetano Russo installed in 1892. At the corner of Central Park stands the 1913 **Maine Memorial,** the site of the failed Circle and Majestic theatres, maladroitly opened here in the 1900s.

At 1865 Broadway, off 61st, the **Bible House,** run by the American Bible Society, distributes the good book in nearly every tongue. Its exhibition gallery showcases rare and unorthodox bibles, plus a smattering of Gutenberg pages and some fragments of the Dead Sea Scrolls. (Gallery open Mon.-Fri. 9:30am-4:30pm. Free.)

Between 61st and 62nd, the 27-story edifice at 45 Broadway once served as the Columbus Circle Automatic Garage and has since become a College Board facility whose embellished walls celebrate the splendor of art deco.

For a taste of Paris on Central Park West, examine the art nouveau quarters of the **New York Society for Ethical Culture,** the 1910 creation of Robert D. Kohn.

The undistinguished modern façade of the **Museum of American Folk Art,** on Columbus between 65th and 66th, gives way to a cool interior, where you can rest on a bench once you've had your fill of 18th-century quilts. (See museums.)

Broadway intersects Columbus Ave. at **Lincoln Center,** the cultural hub of the city, between 62nd and 66th. The six buildings that constitute Lincoln Center—Avery Fisher Hall, the New York State Theatre, the Metropolitan Opera House, the Library and Museum of Performing Arts, the Vivian Beaumont Theatre, and the Juilliard School of Music—accommodate over 13,000 spectators at a time. Power broker Robert Moses masterminded this project in the 50s.

Avery Fisher Hall, designed in 1966 by Max Abramovitz, houses the New York Philharmonic under the direction of Zubin Mehta, who will hand over the baton in 1991 to Kurt Masur. Previous Philharmonic directors have included Leonard Bernstein, Arturo Toscanini, and Leopold Stokowski. (See Music below.) The **Metropolitan Opera House** vocalizes here behind a glass façade. Look in when the chandeliers light up and you'll see the Chagall murals spanning the lobby. The Metropolitan Opera shop sells gift books, posters, libretti, and boxes of cough drops used and autographed by Caruso.

The New York State Theatre plays house to the New York City Ballet and the New York City Opera. December is *Nutcracker* month. A pool with a Henri Moore sculpture leads to the **Vivian Beaumont Theatre,** built by Eero Saarinen in 1965. The combined terrace and bridge leads across 66th St. to the halls of the prestigious **Juilliard School of Music,** Pietro Belluschi's brutalist-inspired building. Here Itzhak Perlman and Pinchas Zuckerman fine-tuned their skills, and a drama major by the name of Robin Williams tried out his first comedy routines. For information on student concerts call 799-5000.

South of Juilliard, intimate **Alice Tully Recital Hall** makes a perfect setting for chamber music. Pietro "Brutalist" Belluschi built this one too. For concert information call 362-1911.

Another of New York City's armories holds the fort at 56 W. 66th St., between Central Park West and Broadway. The one-time bulwarks of the First Battery and the New York National Guard have become architectural props for the ABC television studios hidden behind the Fisher-Price fortress.

At 1 W. 67th St., poised between Central Park West and Columbus, stands the stately **Hotel des Artistes,** now a mass of luxury co-ops, originally designed to house bohemians who have gotten beyond the romantic garret stage of their lives. Built by George Mort Pollard in 1913, the building has quartered the likes of Isadora Duncan, Alexander Woollcott, Norman Rockwell, and Noel Coward. Here you will also find the chic Café des Artistes, run by jovial manager David Pogrebin.

In a city where residents have been known to coordinate art works with wallpaper patterns in the boudoir, it is hardly surprising that a synagogue should be built to match the neighboring arts center. Constructed in 1970 by the Talmudic tag team of Hausman and Rosenberg, the mannered and curvaceous **Lincoln Square Synagogue** at 69th St. and Amsterdam is a travertine cousin of Lincoln Center.

At 72nd St. and Broadway you will find the bowtie-shaped **Sherman Square.** In the north half of the cravate, **Verdi Square,** Giuseppe stares into space, hailed by four characters from his operas.

Cross 65th St. to reach **Central Park West,** a boulevard of graceful old apartment buildings. As Manhattan's urbanization peaked in the late 19th century, wealthy residents sought tranquility in the elegant **Dakota,** at 1 W. 72nd St. When built in 1884, someone thought the apartment house so remote from the heart of the city that "it might as well be in Dakota Territory." The idea caught on and became the building's official name, in a bizarre convergence of real estate and humor. Henry J. "Plaza Hotel" Hardenburg designed the luxury complex, which featured the first passenger elevators in the city. Take in the sprouting turrets, gables, and oriels. John Lennon's streetside murder here in 1981 brought notoriety to the already famous Dakota. In Yoko Ono's memorial to her husband, **Strawberry Fields Forever,** (across from the Dakota) 25,000 plants center around a mosaic that asks you to "Imagine."

Between 73rd and 74th, at 2109 Broadway, you'll find the grande olde dame of Belle Apartments, the famed **Ansonia Hotel.** The 16-story building bristles with heavy ornaments, curved Verona balconies, and towers, but it was its soundproof walls and thick floors that drew illustrious tenants like Enrico Caruso, Arturo Toscanini, and Igor Stravinsky. Theodore Dreiser did his own composing here while Babe Ruth, just a few doors away, meditated over his pinstripes.

Quartered in a formulaic French neoclassical building, the staff of the **New York Historical Society,** at 77th St. and Central Park West (873-3400), will help you uncover obscure facts about the past or provide pop trivia for the present. (See Museums.)

Between 76th and 77th on West End Ave. you will find a block of lively Victorian townhouses designed by mastermasons Lamb and Rich in 1891. It is rumored that former Mayor Jimmy "Gentleman Jim" Walker's mistress once occupied a flat at 76th and Broadway above the lowrise townhouses, and that the mayor had the block zoned off to prevent the building of highrises that might obscure the lovely view.

Dutch settlers constructed the **West End Collegiate Church and School,** 370 West End Ave., a reproduction of a Holland market building, in 1637. Robert Gibson overhauled it in 1893, using characteristically Dutch stepped gables and elongated bricks. **The Apthorp Apartments** at 2207 Broadway, featuring ornate iron gates and a spacious interior courtyard, have starred in a number of New York-based films: *Heartburn, Network, Eyewitness, The Cotton Club, The Changeling,* and *The Money Pit.* The apartments were built by Clinton and Russell in 1908 on a commission from William Waldorf Astor, who named them after the man who owned the site in 1763.

The American Museum of Natural History waxes as unwieldly as a prehistoric mastodon at Central Park West and 79th St. The central body of the museum, built in 1899 by J.C. Cady and Co., reeks of romanesque. At the main façade of the museum, on Central Park West, a Beaux-Arts triumphal arch honors Teddy Roosevelt. The figures standing atop the mammoth ionic columns commemorate intrepid researcher/writers Boone, Audubon, Lewis and Clark. At **Zabar's,** 2245 Broadway (787-2000), navigate your way through bricks of cheese, barrels of coffee beans, and cartons of caviar. Then stop at the deli. (Open Mon.-Fri. 8am-7:30pm, Sat. 8am-midnight, Sun. 9am-6pm.)

The **West Park Presbyterian Church** has been a fixture at Amsterdam Ave. and 86th St. since 1890. It exhibits a Richardsonian penchant for romanesque styling, with a rough-hewn red sandstone surface that makes it look like it just popped out of a clay oven. Strangely, pseudo-Byzantine doorways and capitals top off the romanesque half-baked look. And voilà—clichéd shrine becomes irreverent fun architecture.

On ever-ecclesiastical 86th St., you'll also find the **Church of St. Paul and St. Andrew,** dating from 1897. Check out the octagonal tower and the angels in the spandrells.

Central Park's Frederic Law Olmsted's other green contribution to Manhattan, **Riverside Park,** blossoms down the stretch from 72nd to 145th St. along the Hudson River. As in the case of Central Park, Olmsted had a little help from Calvert Vaux. The **Carrère Memorial,** a small terrace and plaque at 99th St., honors one of the city's great architects, John Merven Carrère, who died in an automobile accident. His partner, Thomas Hastings, designed the monument.

At 175 W. 89th St. stands the only surviving stable in Manhattan: the multi-story **Claremont Stables,** equine condos for high pedigree horses which also offer riding lessons (see Central Park). The appropriately named **Eldorado** apartments, on Central Park West between 90th and 91st showcase some flashy art deco detailing. Note all of the golds.

Originally a skating rink, the **Symphony Space** at 2537 Broadway has distinguished itself with brilliant if wacky programming. Their **Wall to Wall Bach** took a walk on the wild side, as did their gala birthday salute to contemporary classical music's *enfant terrible* John Cage. From the masters Carrère and Hastings comes the English Renaissance-style **First Church of Christ, Scientist,** on location at the corner of 96th and Central Park West. In the **Cliff Dwellers' Apartments** at Riverside and 96th St., art deco finds itself in the Arizona desert. Two great tastes that taste great together? You decide. Cliff dwellers' totemic symbols parade along the frieze.

If the faux turn-of-the-century barbershop window display of the Polo boutique has left you craving the real McCoy, check out the **Broadway Barber Shop** at 2713 Broadway, between 103rd and 104th. The gilt lettering on the windows has faded but the 1907 trappings remain intact. The stretch between 105th and 106th St. on Riverside Drive, peppered with Beaux-Arts townhouses, has been designated a historic district.

Harlem

> *Melting pot Harlem—Harlem of honey and chocolate*
> *and caramel or vinegar and lemon and lime and gall*
> *. . . where the subway from the Bronx keeps right and*
> *downtown.*
>
> *—Langston Hughes*

Half a million people are packed into the three square miles of Harlem's two neighborhoods. On the East Side above 96th St. lies Spanish Harlem, known as *el barrio* ("the neighborhood"), and on the West Side lies Harlem proper. It begins in the gentrified region known as **Morningside Heights** above 110th St. and stretches up to 155th. Both poverty-ridden neighborhoods thrive with street activity during the day. But in the more deserted sections, a tourist's new camera or clean eel skin wallet can quickly be turned into rocks of crack or just food for a family. Visit Harlem during the day. Even better, go there with someone who knows the area. But if you lack the necessary street wit or hip friend—and don't have a car—opt for a tour instead (see Guided Tours).

Harlem has played a proud and vital role in African American history and culture, particularly during the Harlem Renaissance of the 20s. In those years, northern Manhattan was the "end of the line" for blacks fleeing prejudice and poverty in the rural South. Ralph Ellison and James Baldwin, among others, produced novel after novel about life on these streets. The neighborhood has also spawned a host of different musical movements. Music fans of the 50s could easily find themselves paralyzed by confusion. In one bar Charles Mingus would be conducting orchestral tunes with only four pieces from his dancing bass, while next door the Bird would be blasting the newest in be-bop from a plastic horn, and across the street Billie Holiday would be reducing her audience to pools of tears.

In the 60s, the radical Black Power movement flourished here, and the Revolutionary Theater of LeRoi Jones performed consciousness-raising one-act plays in the streets. Nowadays, Harlem suffers from its image as America's quintessential black ghetto, but the area cannot be so easily stereotyped.

New York City's member of the Ivy League, **Columbia University,** chartered in 1754, is tucked between Morningside Drive and Broadway, and 114th and 121st St. Now co-ed, Columbia has cross-registration with all-female **Barnard College** across West End Ave. Ironically, this urban campus occupies the former site of the Bloomingdale Insane Asylum. The centerpiece of the campus is the magisterial **Low Library,** named after Columbia president Seth Low. Daniel Chester French's statue of the Alma Mater, stationed on the front steps of the building, became a rallying point during the riots of 1968. Tours of the campus are given Monday through Friday, leaving from 201 Dodge Hall (854-2845).

Columbia dominates the area east of Morningside Park and has developed it relentlessly, displacing some historically significant architecture and a few people in the process. Most recently, the university decided to acquire from the city the abandoned **Audubon Ballroom,** on 165th St. between Sixth Ave. and Broadway, and turn it into a genetics research center. This move sparked a controversy, since the place was the site of Malcolm X's assassination. The community has surrounded the doorway to the ballroom with plaques that demonstrate that they want a memorial there, not more Columbia University. The silver dome of the **Malcolm Shabazz Masjid Mosque,** where Malcolm X was once minister, glitters on 116th St.

Heading west of Columbia will take you to **Morningside Park,** a green patch that reaches up toward Amsterdam Ave. The **Cathedral of St. John the Divine,** between 110th and 113th, promises to be the world's largest cathedral when finished. Its floor area already surpasses that of Notre Dame and Chartres combined. Construction, begun in 1812, is still ongoing. At a stoneyard nearby, two dozen artisans carve blocks much as they would have done in the age of great medieval cathedrals. The original design called for a Byzantine church with some Romanesque ornamentation. Twenty years and several bishops later, Ralph Adams Cram drew up new designs that betrayed his admiration for French Gothic. The façade resembles Notre Dame, with its centerpiece rose window, symmetrical twin towers, and heavy arched portals. The nave measures 601 ft. long, the towers will be 300 ft. high, and the width will span 320 ft. The bronze door of the central portal was cast in Paris by M. Barbedienne, the same man who cast the Statue of Liberty. The church currently maintains an extensive secular schedule, hosting concerts, art exhibitions, lectures, theatre, and dance events. For information call 662-2133. (Church open daily 7am-5pm.)

The complex has a homeless shelter, a school, and countless other community services. The **Children's Sculpture Garden,** 112th St. and Amsterdam, crowned by a huge, grotesque fountain of a winged warrior on a smiling disc, explodes with spiralling jets of water. The Ring of Freedom surrounds the fountain, topped with small bronze sculptures created annually by schoolchildren. Enter the ground to the right of the main entrance to see the impressive stoneyard, where raw marble is chiseled for the renovation presently underway. Amble down the overwhelming central nave to see the altar dedicated to AIDS victims, a 100 million-year-old nautilus fossil, a modern sculpture for 12 firefighters who perished in the line of duty in 1966, and a 2000-lb. natural quartz crystal.

In Columbia's security shadow, non-denominational **Riverside Church,** on Riverside Ave. between 120th and 122th, attracts the likes of Nelson Mandela. Its well-known pastor, William Sloane Coffin, preaches revolutionary theology, supporting the struggles of the FMLN, ANC, and the fights against AIDS. Stop in for some spiritual contemplation or for a hair-raising elevator trip to the 20-story watch tower. (Open Mon.-Sat. 11am-3pm, Sun. 12:30-4pm. Donation $1.) The observation deck in the tower commands a wonderful view of the bells within and the expanse of the Hudson and Riverside Park below. You can hear concerts on the world's largest carillon (74 bells) twice daily. (Open daily 9am-5pm.)

Diagonally across Riverside Drive lies **Grant's Tomb** (666-1640). At one time, this was a popular monument, but stuck on the periphery of the city, it now attracts only the brave and the few. The massive granite mausoleum rests in peace on top of a hill overlooking the river. Inside, the black marble sarcophagus of Ulysses S. Grant and his wife Julia are surrounded by the General's career cronies cast in bronze. (Open Wed.-Sun. 9am-4:30pm. Free.) Take a rest on the Gaudi-inspired tile benches around the monument, added in the mid-70s. Or rest in the gazebo of Sakura Park, 122 St. and Riverside Drive. The building across the way, Columbia-owned **International House,** houses international graduate students.

Head east to the northwest corner of 120th St. and Broadway to see **The Union Theological Seminary,** an interfaith school of theology. Up Broadway, on the northeast corner of 122nd St., you'll find the **Jewish Theological Seminary.** Inside the main gate, you can rest in a small park with benches. Nearby on 126th St. between Old Broadway and Amsterdam, **St. Mary's,** a tiny religious establishment, dates from 1823 as does the pastor's white house.

125th Street, also known as Martin Luther King Jr. Boulevard, spans the heart of traditional Harlem. Fast-food joints, jazz bars, and the **Apollo Theater** keep the street alive day and night. The recently built **Harlem Third World Trade Center** on 163 W. 125th St. has drawn even more life to 125th. The former **Teresa Hotel,** on the northwest corner of 125th St. and Seventh Ave., has housed Fidel Castro and Malcolm X. The high balconies of the hotel—now an office building—once pounded with the rhetoric of Castro, who claimed that he considered the people of Harlem to be his people. An atypical tourist, Castro felt safer in Harlem than other parts of New York; still, eternally paranoid, he transported live chickens from Cuba for his meals.

Off 125th St., at 328 Lenox Ave., **Sylvia's** (966-0660) has magnetized all of New York for 22 years with enticing soul-food dishes. Sylvia highlights her "World Famous talked about BBQ ribs special" with her "sweet spicy sauce" ($10) served with collard greens and macaroni and cheese—and my is it good. (Open daily 9:30am-10:30pm.)

Sugar Hill (127th St. to 134th St. between Morningside Ave. and St. Nicholas Terrace) was at one time home to some of the city's wealthiest and most important gangsters. But today the striking buildings look as run down as the rest of Harlem, and the neighborhood is better known for the Sugar Hill Gang, the rap group that was born in its streets in 1979 and released the first real rap hit "Rapper's Delight."

Gothic **City College,** 138th and Convent (690-4121), took the mostly poor children of blacks and Jewish immigrants during the first half of the century and turned them into today's national leaders. Joseph Stein, author of *Fiddler on the Roof* and *Zorba,* went here. **Shepard Hall** looks like a church but a quick peek inside reveals the smell and feeling of all high-security public schools. The sharp angles of the **North Academia Center** on Amsterdam Ave. form an optical illusion if viewed from the south on Amsterdam Ave. This mutant of the early 1970s was designed with no windows, with the intent of extending students' attention spans—but unfortunately, the air conditioning doesn't always work so well. Recently, a wave of student protests against tuition increases culminated in students taking over a building and being granted their demands.

Attesting to the countless Dominicans who have settled in Harlem, the PLD (Dominican Liberation Party) headquarters stands on Broadway and 135th St. This party, along with 12 others, has nominated candidates for the upcoming Dominican presidential election. To the east on 135th St. and Lenox Ave., the **Schomburg Center,** a branch of the public library, houses the city's African archives and presents exhibits of local artists' work.

The one notable upper-class Harlem neighborhood occupies 138th St. between Seventh and Eighth: brownstones dominate **Striver's Row,** designed by David King in 1891. The **Renaissance,** 138th St. and Seventh Ave., once an important jazz hall and meeting place for white celebrities and later for leaders in the Black Power movement, now stands in piles of dust—its historic significance awaits the inevitable bulldozer. To the east stands the **Abyssinian Baptist Church,** 132 W. 138th St., where the oldest Congressman, Adam Clayton Powell Jr., once served as pastor. Hidden by Harlem's noisy urban life lie vestiges of the nation's more serene colonial past. Alexander Hamilton built his two-story colonial-style country home, **Hamilton Grange** (283-5154) at what is now 287 Convent Ave. at 141st St. (Open Wed.-Sun. 9am-4:30pm. Free.) Hamilton's furniture, however, has been moved to the Museum of the City of New York. The Georgian **Morris-Jumel Mansion,** in Roger Morris Park at W. 160th St. and Edgecombe Ave. (923-8008), served as Washington's headquarters for the battle of Harlem Heights in the autumn of 1776 and later became the home of Gouverneur Morris, U.S. minister to France during the Reign of Terror. (Open Tues.-Sun. 10am-4pm. Admission $2, seniors and students $1.)

Four buildings in **Audubon Terrace,** the Beaux-Arts complex at Broadway and 155th St., house the Numismatic Society Museum, the Hispanic Society of America, the Museum of the American Indian (see Museums), and **Boricua College,** a private Hispanic liberal arts college. The neo-Italian Renaissance courtyard has huge reliefs and sculptures. Diagonally across Broadway, you can wander around the graveyard that faces the Church of Intercession.

Spanish Harlem hugs the northeast corner of Central Park and extends to the 140s, where it is framed by the Harlem River. At the main artery on 116th St., the streets bustle with people selling fruit, shirts, and all sorts of unrecognizable chow. The famous ice man flavors ground-up ice with mango, papaya, coconut, or banana syrup to save you from the summer heat. Murals against crack span the walls, along with memorials to those killed by the drug. See this neighborhood from a car or with someone who knows the streets.

Washington Heights

Once upon a time it was an all-Irish enclave, but the sounds of rumba and calypso soon drowned out those of the pipe and drum, as Puerto Ricans and Latin Americans began to move into the neighborhood. Then black, Greek, and Armenian folk added their own tunes, as did a large Jewish community anchored around a cultural beacon, Yeshiva University. Unfortunately, Washington Heights has become one of the most drug-inundated areas in the city.

Come here during the day, for a taste of modern urban life with a heavy ethnic flavor. On the same block, you can eat a Greek dinner, buy Armenian pastries, purchase vegetables from a South African, and talk Talmud with a Jewish scholar from the Yeshiva. See the prices go down as the streets go up. Bargain-shop along trinket-ridden St. Nicholas Ave. or Broadway. Street vendors sell swimwear, Italian shoes, and household items for half the going rate. You'll find discount electronics stores here too.

The **United Church,** 4140 Broadway at 175th, may be the best example of architectural symbiosis between the Egyptian and Miami Beach schools. Originally Loew's 175th Street Theater, this old movie house now serves as a stage for the love-thyself sermons of Reverend Ike.

The **George Washington Bridge Bus Station,** on 178th St. between Broadway and Fort Washington Ave., resembles a huge Christmas tree cookie cutter. The **George Washington Bridge,** a 1931 construction by Othmar Amman, is a 14-lane suspension bridge once pronounced "the most beautiful bridge in the world" by Le Corbusier. Just beneath it lies **Fort Washington Park,** home to the **Little Red Lighthouse** and the remnants of the original fort. Originally constructed to steer barges away from Jeffrey's Hook, the lighthouse became the thinly disguised subject of Hildegarde Hoyt Swift's popular children's book, *The Little Red Lighthouse and the Great Grey Bridge.*

At 186th St. and Amsterdam Ave., surrounded by kosher bakeries and butcher shops, you'll find **Yeshiva University,** dating from 1886, the oldest Jewish studies center in the U.S. Its fanciful building bears Romanesque windows and colorful minarets. The journey north along Fort Washington Ave. (Third Ave. west of Amsterdam) takes you past a succession of mid-rise apartment buildings (c. 1920) to **Fort Tryon Park,** lovingly landscaped by Central Park's Frederic Law Olmsted. John D. Rockefeller donated this land to the city in exchange for permission to construct Rockefeller University. You can still see extant remains of Fort Tryon, a Revolutionary War bulwark. The park also contains a magnificent expanse of gardens and **The Cloisters,** the Met's sanctuary for Medieval Art (see Museums).

One block before the park, the **St. Francis Cabrini Chapel** shelters the remains of Mother Cabrini, the first U.S.-born saint and the patron saint of immigrants. Her body lies in a crystal casket under the altar, but above the neck you will only see a wax mask—her head lies in Rome. Legend has it that shortly after her death, a lock of her hair restored the eyesight of an infant who has since grown up into a Texas priest.

You can revisit a modest but charming 18th-century Dutch dwelling at 204th and Broadway. Donated to the city as a museum in 1915, **Dyckman House** has been restored and filled with period Dutch and English family furnishings. (Open Tues.-Sun. 11am-5pm. Free.)

Greenwich Village

In "The Village," bordered by 14th St. to the north and Houston to the south, bohemian indifference meets New York neurosis, resulting in the "downtown" approach to life. The buildings here do not scrape the skies, the street grid dissolves into geometric whim, and the residents revel in countercultural logic. Village people wear their slogans on their crotches and hang underwear in their galleries. The personal translates into the political, though even Village politics can sometimes be bourgeois.

"The" Village is the Greenwich one, which lies mostly to the west. The West Village is the virtual hometown of 19th- and 20th-century U.S. literature, with the exception of a short period of time when a bunch of stodgy New England types eloquently nudged their way into the spotlight. It all started with Tom Paine, who in 1808 had the common sense to live on Bleecker St. Herman Melville and James Fenimore Cooper set a few standards for American writing here, and Mark Twain and Willa Cather explored the U.S. heartland from their homes near Washington Square. Henry James was born on the square (not a half-block away, as New York University has incorrectly indicated) during the Village's high-society days, and Edith Wharton also lived in the neighborhood. John Reed, John Dos Passos, and e.e. cummings all made the Manhattan transfer straight from Harvard, as did James Agee later, and inhabited the first—and only—American Bohemia. At this time, Village rents were low, and many writers came here to begin their careers in poverty and obscurity. Eugene O'Neill created the Provincetown Playhouse in the West Village, and it created him in turn. Theodore Dreiser wrote here, as did Edna St. Vincent Millay and Thomas Wolfe. Even Tennessee Williams, James Baldwin, and William Styron found their way to small apartments in the area, and Richard Wright lived in the same building as Willa Cather, 35 years later.

Today, brownstone rents have taken a turn for the astronomical and young professionals have replaced young artists. Just about the only affordable housing here belongs to **New York University,** a huge landowner and one of the largest private universities in the world, with a "campus" scattered throughout the village. But the Village has not entirely sold out its old bohemian sense of fun—every year the wild **Village Halloween Parade** winds its way through the streets. If you ever wanted to see people dressed as toilets or carrots or giant condoms, this is your chance; if you're lucky, you may even receive a personal benediction from Rollerina, the city's cross-dressing fairy godmother on wheels.

The Villages of The City stay lively all day and most of the night. Those seeking a dull moment or two should head uptown immediately. Everyone else should experience the rich and strange atmosphere, stores, and people-watching.

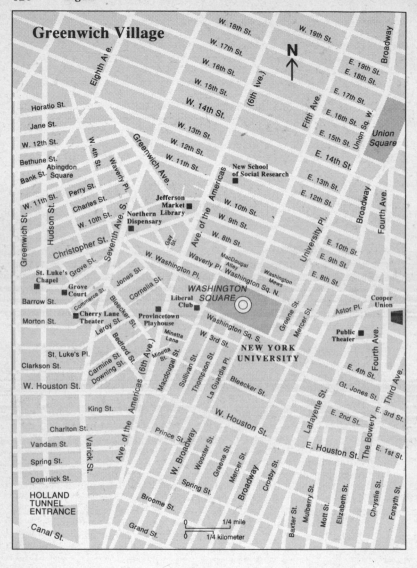

Greenwich Village

N

W. 18th St.
W. 17th St.
W. 19th St.
W. 16th St.
W. 15th St.
W. 14th St.
W. 13th St.
W. 12th St.
W. 11th St.
Horatio St.
Jane St.
W. 12th St.
Bethune St.
Abingdon Square
Bank St.
W. 11th St.
Perry St.
Charles St.
W. 10th St.
Greenwich St.
Hudson St.
Christopher St.
Eighth Ave.
Greenwich Ave.
Waverly Pl.
W. 4th St.
Seventh Ave. S.

E. 19th St.
E. 18th St.
E. 17th St.
E. 16th St.
E. 15th St.
E. 14th St.
E. 13th St.
E. 12th St.
Fifth Ave.
(6th Ave.)
Broadway
Union Square

Union Square

New School of Social Research

Jefferson Market Library
Northern Dispensary
Gay St.
W. 10th St.
W. 9th St.
W. 8th St.
Ave. of the Americas

Waverly Pl.
MacDougal Alley
Washington Sq. N.
Washington Mews
E. 10th St.
E. 9th St.
E. 8th St.
University Pl.
Broadway
Fourth Ave.

St. Luke's Chapel
Grove Court
Barrow St.
Morton St.
Cherry Lane Theater
Grove St.
Commerce St.
Jones St.
Cornelia St.
Bleecker St.
Liberal Club
Provincetown Playhouse
WASHINGTON SQUARE
Greene St.
Mercer St.
Astor Pl.
Cooper Union
Public Theater
Fourth Ave.

St. Luke's Pl.
Clarkson St.
W. Houston St.
Leroy St.
Bedford St.
Minetta Lane
Minetta St.
W. 3rd St.
Sullivan St.
Thompson St.
La Guardia Pl.
Bleecker St.
NEW YORK UNIVERSITY
Lafayette St.
E. 4th St.
Gt. Jones St.
E. 3rd St.
The Bowery
Third Ave.

King St.
Carmine St.
Downing St.
Ave. of the Americas (6th Ave.)
Charlton St.
Vandam St.
Spring St.
Dominick St.
Varick St.
W. Broadway
Prince St.
Wooster St.
Greene St.
Mercer St.
Broadway
Crosby St.
E. 2nd St.
E. Houston St.
E. 1st St.
W. Houston St.

HOLLAND TUNNEL ENTRANCE
Canal St.
Spring St.
Broome St.
Grand St.
Baxter St.
Mulberry St.
Mott St.
Elizabeth St.
Chrystie St.
Forsyth St.

0   1/4 mile
0   1/4 kilometer

Washington Square Park Area

> *I know not whether it is owing to the tenderness of early associations, but this portion of New York appears to many persons the most delectable. It has a kind of established repose which is not of frequent occurrence in other quarters of the long, shrill city; it has a riper, richer, more honorable look than any of the upper ramifications of the great longitudinal thoroughfare—the look of having had something of a social history.*
>
> —Henry James, *Washington Square*

Washington Square Park has been the universally acknowledged heart of the Village since the district's days as a suburb. The marshland here served first as a colonial cemetery (around 15,000 bodies lie buried there) and then as a revolutionary hanging-grounds (people swung from trees which still stand today), but in the 1820s someone who wanted to get away from all the death imagery decided to convert it into a park and parade ground. Soon high-toned residences made the area the center of New York's social scene.

Society has long since gone north, and New York University has moved in. The country's largest private university and one of the city's biggest landowners (along with the city government, the Catholic Church, and Columbia University), NYU has dispersed its administrative buildings, affiliated housing, and eccentric students throughout the Village. The university's signature purple banners concentrate around the park.

Washington Square Park has a recent history of seediness and drug trade. The mid-80s saw a noisy clean-up campaign which has partially reclaimed the park for more conventional and legal recreation, though you may encounter the occasional harmless individual sauntering along and hissing "smokesmokesmokes." Just say no. In the southwest corner of the park, a dozen perpetual games of chess wend their ways toward ultimate checkmate. The fountain in the center of the park provides an amphitheatre for comics and musicians of widely varying degrees of talent. Judge for yourself how well Beethoven's Moonlight Sonata translates to the steel drum. (Subway: A, D, E, F, K, or S train to W. 4th St.)

Across the street from the chess players, on the south side of the park, stands NYU's brick-arched **Vanderbilt Law School,** noted more for academic quality than for its architecture. Farther along Washington Square South you'll encounter the **Judson Memorial Baptist Church,** built in 1892 by that ubiquitous architectural firm McKim, Mead & White. Stained glass by John LaFarge panels the sanctuary. NYU's homely **Catholic Student Center** crowns the corner of Thompson St. and Washington Square South, neighboring the **Loeb Student Center,** an awkward shrunken likeness of the U.N. Building. On LaGuardia Place and Washington Square South looms a rust-colored monstrosity, the **Elmer Homes Bobst Library,** another hideous progeny of the university, which for a time wanted all of its buildings to look like this so that the "campus" would have a common theme. Luckily, NYU ended up opting for purple flags instead.

The north side of the park showcases some of the most renowned architecture in the city, called **The Row.** Largely built in the 1830s, this stretch of elegant Federal-style brick residences soon became an urban center roamed by 19th-century professionals, dandies, and novellalists. No. 18, now demolished, was the home of Henry James' grandmother, and the basic setting of his novel *Washington Square.*

Fifth Avenue splits The Row down the middle and arrives at its source, the grand **Washington Memorial Arch,** at the north side of the park. Some nostalgics built it in 1889 to mark the centennial of Washington's inauguration as president. The statues on top depict chameleonic George in poses of war and peace. For many years, you could rarely pass the arch without encountering a gaggle of blackleathered and pink-haired youth. Today they, and the punk lifestyle, have moved on.

A few steps up Fifth Ave. will bring you to **Washington Mews,** on your right, a quirky cobblestoned alleyway directly behind The Row. The boxy little brick and stucco buildings, originally constructed as stables, bear ivy and the tranquility and prestige that it endows.

Farther up Fifth Ave., on the corner of 10th St., rises the **Church of the Ascension,** a fine 1841 Gothic church with a notable altar and stained glass windows. (Open daily noon-2pm and 5pm-7pm.) Many consider the block down 10th St. between Fifth and Sixth. the most beautiful residential stretch in the city. This short strip plays out innumerable variations in brick and stucco, layered with wood and iron detailing. Ivy clothes the façades of many of the buildings, while windowboxes brighten others.

Balducci's, a legendary Italian supermarket, has been feeding Villagers for as long as anyone can remember. Enter its orgy of cheese barrels and bread loaves, live lobsters and chilled vegetables. (See Food.)

At 425 Sixth Ave. stands the landmark **Jefferson Market,** a Gothic structure complete with detailed brickwork, stained glass windows, and a turreted clocktower. Built as a courthouse in 1874, it occupies the triangle formed by the intersection of West 10th St., Sixth Ave., and Greenwich Ave. In an 1880s poll, architects voted it one of the 10 most beautiful buildings in the country. While they may have overstated the case, the remarkable structure did deserve redemption—it faced demolition in the early 60s. Carefully restored in 1967, the building reopened as a public library. Inside, the original pre-Raphaelite stained glass graces the spiral staircase. The brick-columned basement now serves as the Reference Room. An excellent pamphlet details the history of the site and the restoration. (Open Mon. and Thurs. noon-6pm, Tues. 10am-6pm, Wed. noon-8pm, Sat. 10am-5pm.)

If you leave the library, make a left onto 10th and cross the street, you'll see an iron gate and a street sign which says "Patchin Place" Behind the gate lies a tiny courtyard, little more than a paved alley. The buildings here, constructed around 1850, later housed writers e.e. cummings, Theodore Dreiser, and Djuna Barnes.

West Village

In the neighborhood west of Sixth Ave. (and east of Hudson Street), the gentrified avant-garde has taken up residence in 19th-century architecture, providing the perfect antidote to the sensory assault of commercial Midtown.

The West Village has a large and very visible gay population—this is the native territory of the Guppie (Gay Urban Professional). The twisting streets host a remarkable variety of alternative clothing stores, clubs, bookshops, video stores, and even car shops. Same-sex couples can walk together quite openly.

In the north, **Greenwich Avenue** will bring you to some of the most archetypal Village boutiques, as well as to choice cafés and restaurants, like **La Gran Café Degli Artisti,** 46 Greenwich Ave.

Christopher Street, the main byway to the south, swims in novelty restaurants and specialty shops. (Subway: #1, 2, or 3 line to Christopher St./Sheridan Sq.) The street also intersects with Sixth Ave. Christopher St. and Seventh Ave. intersect at tiny **Sheridan Square,** a carefully tended green traffic island-*cum*-park. Riots against the Civil War draft thronged here in 1863, during some of the darkest days of New York City's history; some protesters brutally attacked freed slaves.

A few street signs refer to Christopher St. as "Stonewall Place," alluding to the **The Stonewall Inn,** the transvestite club where 1969 police raids prompted the riots that sparked the U.S. gay rights movement. A plaque marks the former site of the club at 53 Christopher St.

Christopher St. runs into **Bedford Street,** a remarkably narrow old-fashioned strip. **Chumley's** bar and restaurant, at no. 86, between Grove and Barrow St. became a "speakeasy," in Prohibition days, illegally serving alcohol to literary figures named John such as Dos Passos and Steinbeck. As if in honor of its surreptitious past, no sign of any kind indicates that the neglected structure might be a commercial establishment.

One of the oldest buildings in the city, no. 77 Bedford St., on the corner of Commerce St., dates from 1799. Its handsome brick has tastefully faded. Next door, run-down, boarded-up no. 75½, constructed in a former alley, is the narrowest building in the Village: it measures 9½ ft. across. Edna St. Vincent Millay lived there in 1850.

Bedford St. crosses Commerce St., which nudges the **Cherry Lane Theatre** with its elbow. One of the top Off-Broadway houses, the Cherry Lane has staged numerous American premieres. Across the way stand a pair of identical houses known as the "Twin Sisters," separated by a garden. Completely unsubstantiated legend has it that they were built by a sea-captain for his spinster daughters who were not on speaking terms. At the other end of Bedford, look for the plaque near Seventh Ave. South marking the former home of Washington Irving, Jr.

Directly across Seventh Ave. from Commerce St. you will find **Bleecker Street,** a little Little Italy which occasionally closes for classic street fairs, complete with sausages, *zeppoli* (fried dough with sugar), and half the population of New Jersey. Bleecker St. will bring you back to Sixth Ave. at **Father Demo Square,** a colorful intersection with a liberal distribution of benches. Go one block over on Bleecker to reach **MacDougal Street,** a drag full of cafés and characters.

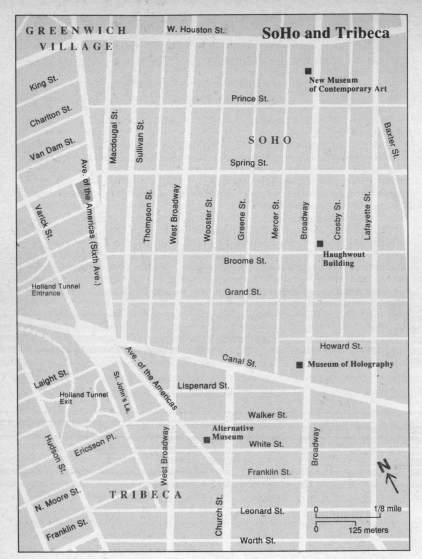

SoHo and TriBeCa

One day a Big Artist realized that if he took all of the
sewing machines and bales of rags out of a three-
thousand-square-foot loft and put in a bathroom and
kitchen he would be able to live and make Big Art
in the same place. He was quickly followed by other
Big Artists and they by Big Lawyers, Big Boutique
Owners, and Big Rich Kids. Soon there was a Soho
and it was positively awash in hardwood floors,
talked-to plants, indoor swings, enormous record
collections, hiking boots, Conceptual Artists, video
communes, Art book stores, Art grocery stores, Art
restaurants, Art bars, Art galleries, and boutiques sell-

*ing tie-dyed raincoats, macramé flower pots, and Art
Deco salad plates.*
                            —*Fran Lebowitz, Metropolitan Life*

The pompous character played by Nick Nolte in Martin Scorsese's chapter of failed flick *New York Stories* dwelled in SoHo with a vengeance. While established artists may not splatter paintings of city monuments to wafting strains of Puccini and Bob Dylan in their mega-lofts, many do live in the tiny district of SoHo (short for "South of Houston St."—pronounced HOW-ston), bounded by Houston, Canal, Lafayette, and Sullivan. The architecture here is American Industrial (1860-1890), notable for its cast-iron façades. Architects used iron to imitate stone and often painted it to look like limestone, lacing the columns and pediments with ornate detail. The iron frames made heavy walls unnecessary and allowed for the installation of vast windows. In 1962, the City Club called the area "the wasteland of New York," and soon it was slated for development. But residents fought against the construction of an expressway and in 1973 the city declared the neighborhood an historic district. **Greene Street** offers the best of SoHo's lofty architecture. Look up at the classic roof of No. 28-30, a bright blue building known as the Queen of Greene St. Its neighbor, No. 72-76, is actually two buildings designed to look like one, its Corinthian portico spread lavishly across five stories of painted metal. Once architects here made sweatshops look like iron palaces; now artists have converted factory lofts into studios. You can't pass half a block without going by a gallery, an experimental theatre, or a designer clothing store. High-fashion sorts pay dearly for the right look (up to $500 for a pair of pants). Excellent galleries line West Broadway, and although many come and go, you can count on top-quality work at **Vorpal,** 165 W. Broadway and **Leo Castelli,** 420 W. Broadway.

Ignore any condescending glances you may receive from the caretakers and feel free to explore some of the better side streets galleries: **Arte Brasilera,** 184 Prince St., specializes in Brazilian art; **Martin Lawrence,** 426-428 W. Broadway, in big-name modern; and **Ward-Nasse,** 178 Prince St. specializes in sculpture. You'll find another mass of galleries on Broome St.

A mind-twisting mural by Richard Haas covers the southeast corner of Prince and Greene St. Try to pick out which windows are real, which painted, almost more difficult than telling the mock cast-iron façades from the real thing. To the south, on a lot at Wooster and Spring St., a daily fair makes its presence felt. Browse around the extensive selection of international goods. The bargain hunt continues on Broadway with a wide selection of used clothing stores.

Ten years ago, TriBeCa ("Triangle Below Canal") was a wasteland. Today, Robert DeNiro has a grill in the neighborhood, and it doesn't take a genius to realize that this neighborhood bounded by Canal, Broadway, Chambers, and West St. is a farther south version of SoHo. But the new financial center and twin towers eclipse the southern sun. Observe the cast-iron edifices lining White St., Thomas St., and Broadway; the 19th-century federal-style buildings on Harrison St.; and the shops, galleries, and bars on church and Reade St. Duane St., TriBeCa's "Restaurant Row," has not cornered the market on good restaurants. For commercial goods, residents roam the streets of Hudson and W. Broadway. Between Chambers and Northmore St. stands Manhattan Community College, part of the City University system and a clear product of the 1980s.

Lower East Side

The old Lower East Side, once home mainly to Eastern European immigrants, extended from Hester to 14th St. Now this area has developed a three-way split personality, encompassing the part south of Houston (commonly considered the Lower East Side), the westernmost section (known as the "East Village"), and Alphabet City.

Between Houston and Canal lies the neighborhood that has most retained the character of the original Lower East Side. Toward the Bowery, crossing Delancey

St., bearded Hassidic shopkeepers ply their wares. Here are the remnants of the Jewish ghetto that inspired Jacob Riis' compelling work *How the Other Half Lives* and more recently the 80s epic musical *Rags* by Joseph Stein, Stephen Schwartz, and Charles Strouse. On **Orchard Street,** look for bargain clothes and wild fabrics; on **The Bowery,** for any lamp you've ever wanted; on **Allen Street** for shirts and ties. **Grand Street** specializes in underwear. Try the Orchard St. market on a Sunday morning for some real bargains. Off Delancey St., the Essex St. covered market looks like it just flew in from Northern Africa. **Schapiro's Winery,** 126 Rivington St., offers tours and taste tests Monday through Thursday from 11am to 4pm on the hour. On The Bowery (which comes from the Dutch *bouwerie,* or farm) check out Stanford White's **Bowery Savings Bank,** at Grand St., a repository of wealth ironically surrounded by many homeless people. Built in 1894, it has kept the original carved check-writing stands inside. You'd probably feel safe leaving your money here.

East Village

The East Village, a comparatively new creation, was carved out of the Bowery and the Lower East Side, as rents in the West soared and its residents sought accommodations elsewhere. Thus it was that Allen Ginsberg, Jack Kerouac, and William Burroughs eschewed the Village establishment to develop their "beat" sensibility east of Washington Square Park. Billie Holiday sang here during their time; more recently the East Village provided both Lou Reed and Madonna with their earliest audiences. The transfer of population has recaptured much of the gritty feel of the old Village, and the population here is less homogeneous than in the West, with older Eastern European immigrants living alongside new Hispanic and Asian arrivals. But it has been a difficult compromise, and many poorer denizens of the East Village feel they have been pushed out by the newcomers. These tensions have not been helped by glimmers of gentrification and rising rents in the East.

A fun stretch of Broadway runs through the Village, essentially dividing it east from west. But everyone and their grandmother knows about this browser's paradise. On summer weekends it overflows with shoppers known unaffectionately as the "B&T crowd," referring to the bridges and tunnels by which non-Manhattanites must reach the island.

Grace Church, constructed in 1845, asserts its powerful Gothic presence at 800 Broadway, between 10th and 11th. The dark, gorgeous interior has a distinctly medieval feel. Somehow, the birdsong echoes more than the street noise.

Antique stores flock around the church, especially on 10th and 11th St. Most specialize in large, high-priced pieces of furniture or architectural elements (Greek-style columns, eagle-shaped statues, tobacco-store Indians, and the like).

One of the world's most famous bookstores is **The Strand,** at the corner of 12th St. and Broadway, which bills itself as the "largest used bookstore in the world" with over 2 million books on 8 miles of shelves. (See Bookstores.) At **Forbidden Planet,** directly across Broadway, you can browse through European space toys, vintage Superman comics, and a complete line of "Dungeons & Dragons" fantasy paraphernalia.

Farther south on Broadway, the stores get funkier, with lots of "antique" (read: used yet expensive) clothing stores and accessory shops, where the trendy and their money are soon parted. Teeny-boppers trek miles for the fashion senses of **Unique Clothing,** 704 Broadway and **The Antique Boutique,** 217 Broadway. At Broadway and 4th St., you'll find another of the Village's spritual landmarks: **Tower Records,** a store with a musical inventory to rival the literary inventory of the Strand. At the "Personics" machine, you can mix your own tape from a preselected catalog of songs. You can listen to selections on headphones before making your decisions. Open late, Tower has become not only a popular hangout, but also a sudden bonding ground for people of similar musical taste: "Wow, you're into Maggot Brain? I *love* Maggot Brain! Were you at their last concert?" (See Record Stores.)

Walk one block east of Broadway on West 4th to reach Lafayette St. To your right will be Colonnade Row, with the Public Theatre across the street. "Colonnade

Row" consists of four magnificently columned houses, built in 1833, once the homes of New York's most famous 19th-century millionaires: John Jacob Astor and Cornelius "Commodore" Vanderbilt, as well as the Delano family (as in Franklin Delano Roosevelt). There used to be nine of these houses; the ones that remain, at 428-434 Lafayette St., are a bit on the grubby side. The **Public Theatre**, 425 Lafayette St. (598-7150), a grand brownstone structure, was constructed by John Jacob Astor in 1853 to serve as the city's first free library. After its collection moved uptown, the building became the headquarters of the Hebrew Immigrant Aid Society, an organization dedicated to assisting thousands of poor Jewish immigrants who came to New York in the early years of this century. In 1967, Joseph Papp's "New York Shakespeare Festival" converted the building to its current use as a theatrical center.

A walk up Lafayette St. will bring you to Astor Place, the name of both a small street and a large intersection. At 12 Astor Place, the street, you'll find *Astor Wine and Spirits* (674-7500), one of the city's largest and most reasonably priced liquor stores (Open Mon.-Sat. 9am-9pm.) Here you can also complement your new Village wardrobe with a distinctive trim at the largest haircutting establishment in the world: **Astor Place Hair Designers,** famous for its low-priced production-line approach to style. A total of 110 people (including a DJ) are employed in this five-level, 10,000 square-ft. complex at 2 Astor Place (475-9854; open Mon.-Sat. 8am-8pm, Sun. 9am-6pm; men's cut $10, women's cut $12).

Astor Place, the intersection, is distinguished by a sculpture of a large black cube balanced on its corner. If you and your friends push hard enough the cube will rotate, but somebody sleeping underneath may complicate the process. The whole intersection is a bizarre bazaar where a myriad of merchants position their possessions on the pavement. People try to sell virtually anything: new records, used underwear, aged red high-heeled shoes, hot stereo equipment, and four-year-old *Time* magazines. Note the subway kiosk, a cast-iron Beaux-Arts beauty which was built—believe it or not—in 1985 as part of a reconstruction of the station (the #6 train stops here).

Astor Place prominently features the rear of the **Cooper Union Foundation Building,** 41 Cooper Sq. (254-6300), built in 1859 to house the Cooper Union for the Advancement of Science and Art, a notable tuition-free technical and design school founded by the self-educated industrialist Peter Cooper. The school's free lecture series here has hosted practically every notable American since the mid-19th century. It's also the oldest standing building in the U.S. incorporating steel beams. Appropriately enough, its founder Cooper first rolled the steel rails that sped up railroad construction. In the basement of the building, the *Cooper Union Art Gallery* hosts changing exhibits on design and American history.

Stuyvesant St. angles off from Astor Place cutting north over 9th St., and terminates at Second Ave. and 10th St., right in front of the pretty **St. Mark's-in-the-Bowery Church,** 131 E. 10th St. (674-6377). The city's oldest church building in continual use, its body was built in 1799 on the site of a chapel in what used to be the estate of Peter Stuyvesant, the much-reviled last Dutch governor of the colony of New Amsterdam. He lies buried in the small cobblestoned graveyard here. Restored in the mid-70s, the church building burned to a near-crisp in a 1978 fire, and re-restoration was not completed until a few years ago.

Across from the church at 156 Second Ave. stands a famous Jewish landmark, the **Second Avenue Deli** (677-6606). This is all that remains of the "Yiddish Rialto," the stretch of Second Ave. between Houston and 14th St. that comprised the Yiddish theatre district during the early part of this century. The Stars of David embedded in the sidewalk in front of the restaurant contain the names of some of the great actors and actresses who spent their lives entertaining the poor Jewish immigrants of the city. Order sublime chicken soup or splurge on a pastrami sandwich while you watch the electronic stock-ticker, a new-fangled form of entertainment installed for the Wall Street clientele. (Open Mon.-Fri. 8am-midnight, Sat.-Sun. 8am-2am.)

St. Mark's Place, between Third Ave. and Tompkins Sq. Park at 8th St., is the geographical and spiritual center of the East Village. Architecturally unremarkable,

St. Mark's appeal lies in its vitality. St. Mark's is the East Village's answer to a small town's Main Street. People know one another here—sometimes they even stop to talk to each other. Dark little restaurants and cafés elbow for space with leather boutiques and trinket vendors. A Gap store sells its conventional color-me-matching combos across the street from a shop stocking "DEATH TO YUPPIE SCUM" T-shirts.

The **St. Mark's Bookstore,** 12 St. Mark's Place (260-7853), is a nice spot for browsing and has a particularly wide selection of art periodicals, as well as large sections of books on religion, mysticism, and philosophy. (Open Sun.-Thurs. 11am-10:40pm, Fri.-Sat. 11am-11:40pm.)

Alphabet City

East of First Ave., south of 14th St., and north of Houston, the avenues run out of numbers and take on letters. This drug-ridden area can be dangerous, especially at night, but efforts to regain control by the community seem to have made some headway. Last year, badgeless police beating squatters in **Tompkins Square Park,** at E. 7th St. and Ave. A, were captured on videotape, setting off a counter-violence movement. "Homesteaders" have grown gardens and painted murals in vacant lots. Visit the corner of E. 9th St. and Ave. C to see the controversial **Plaza Cultural,** a lot full of toys, flowers, kids—and graffiti. Graffiti artist Chico's tag seems particularly appropriate: *La Lucha Continua* (the struggle continues). City officials and private developers have declared *La Plaza* a "garbage filled lot" and plan to build on it. Another garden, up 9th St., even has chickens. The future of such homesteads is uncertain—the inhabitants of these makeshift homes live under the constant threat of eviction by police and developers. In one set-up on Ave. D between 4th and 5th, a man has set up a teddy bear gargoyle on the barbed wire fence that protects his homemade home and vegetables. Also worth seeing is the 3-D relief created by artist José de Diego on Ave. C between 7th and 8th.

Drugs have left many scars on this area, as the countless memorial murals attest. But some have suggested that intensified police action should not be the solution. A mural on a burnt-out former crack house, on Ave. C between 8th and 9th, pleads for the war on drugs to take place in the home, not on the streets. Read the neighborhood posters for an update on some of the current issues.

Public art adorns even religious institutions. On 5th St. between Ave. C and D lies the playground of the **San Isadora and San Leandro Hispanic Rite Catholic Church,** with its stunning mosaic incorporating mirrors, tiles, and faces. On the western wall of the playground, two parrots sit in a jungle of mirrors. You gotta love art.

Chinatown and Little Italy

Toward Mulberry St., several blocks south of the Village and just north of Canal St., lies **Little Italy,** a neighborhood that shrinks as Chinatown grows. Many young Italians are moving out. Meanwhile Italian neighborhoods flourish in Belmont, the Bronx and Bensonhurst, Brooklyn. Maybe that's why Martin Scorcese shot his film about Little Italy, *Mean Streets,* in Belmont. Nonetheless, alleged Mafia kingpin John Gotti still makes his way around to the few social clubs that remain here for a deal or a meal.

The restaurants cost, but a satisfying snack in one of the Italian delis on Grand St. shouldn't set you back too far. At **Umberto's Clam House,** 129 Mulberry St., "Crazy Joey" Gallo was slain in 1972 while celebrating his birthday; allegedly he offended a rival family. The old Police Headquarters, built as a monument against organized crime, at the corner of Center and Broome St., will soon be converted into a civic center.

Dotted with stores selling low-cost electronics and plastics, commercial **Canal Street** divides Little Italy and Chinatown. Only a few steps across Canal St. from Little Italy stand pagoda-topped phone booths, steaming tea shops, and firecracker vendors. New York's **Chinatown** has seven Chinese newspapers, over 300 garment

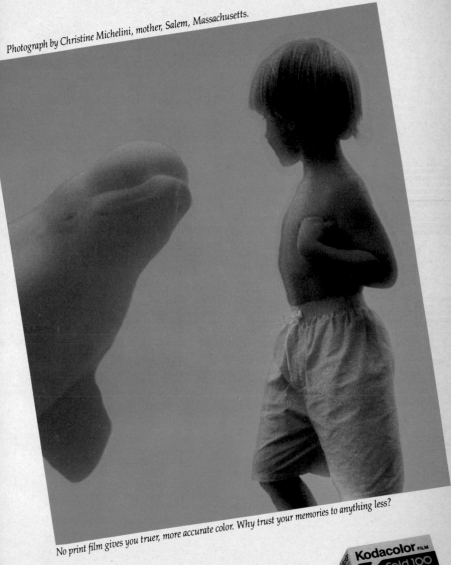

No print film gives you truer, more accurate color. Why trust your memories to anything less?

Show Your True Colors.™

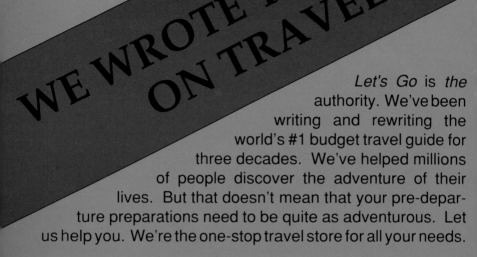

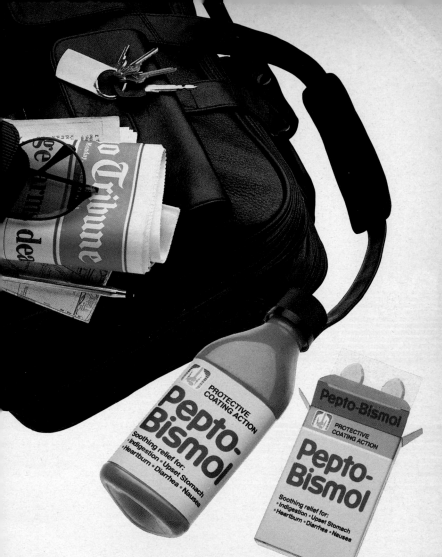

CARRY-ON RELIEF.

Chinatown and Little Italy

factories, and innumerable food shops, and houses the largest Asian community in the U.S. outside of San Francisco. For a trip in hybrid religions, check out the **Ling Liang Church,** 173-175 E. Broadway, resting place of a postmodern Christ surrounded by biblical blessings on a bed of red Chinese characters.

At the **Buddhist Temple,** 16 Pell St. off Mott St., the devout kneel in front of a porcelain statue, offering fresh fruit and shaking cans of incense. Visitors are welcome. The **Eastern States Buddhist Temple of America,** 64 Mott St., holds services at 8pm. Here Buddhists pray to *Kuinyin,* a multi-armed buddha who holds the symbol for Nirvana in his upper arms.

Secular Confucius stands firm and wise on the plaza dedicated to him on the corner of Division St. and the Bowery. The **Chinatown Fair,** 8 Mott St., features not only video games but two long-suffering chickens who for 75¢ are forced to play Tic Tac Toe or to dance: they "dance" enticed by food over a spinning turntable. The owner takes pride in this humane treatment, explaining that it is a great improvement over the hot plate they once used. Scholars should ascend to the **Oriental Enterprises Company,** 20 Pell St., a bookstore serving those literate in Chinese. They also serve free tea. Sit in reading chairs as you sip and translate or just admire the highfalutin calligraphy equipment.

Gift shops line the streets, doing their best to make sure that you don't go home without an overpriced miniature Buddha. During the Chinese New Year (in late Jan. or early Feb.), the area's frenetic pace accelerates.

Lower Manhattan

Many of the city's superlatives congregate in the southern tip of Manhattan Island. The Wall Street area is the densest in all New York. Wall Street itself measures less than a half mile long. This narrow state of affairs has driven the neighborhood into the air, creating one of the highest concentrations of skyscrapers in the world. Along with density comes history: lower Manhattan was the first part of the island to be settled by Europeans, and many of the city's historically significant sights lie buried in the concrete canyons here. Omnipresent Liberty Trail markers indicate the most significant spots.

Touring Lower Manhattan won't cost you. Parks, churches, temperature-controlled lobbies of cathedrals of commerce, and such highlights as the New York Stock Exchange and City Hall charge no admission. If you visit during the week, you'll see suspendered or high-heeled natives rushing to and fro, brandishing their *Wall Street Journals.*

Wall Street and the Financial District

> *A great city, Sir—replied the Little Gentleman,—a very opulent, splendid city. A point of transit of much that is remarkable, and of permanence for much that is respectable. A great money-centre.*
> —Oliver Wendell Holmes

In this district, you can see the two tallest buildings in the city, the street where America invests its wealth, and the building where the U.S. government was adopted.

Battery Park, named for a battery of guns the British stored there from 1683 to 1687, is a pretty chunk of greenery on the very southernmost toenail of Manhattan Island. The #1 train to South Ferry will let you off at the southern tip; the #4 and 5 will let you off at Bowling Green, just off the northern tip. You can take your morning constitutional here, admiring plaques and monuments on the way, or just inhaling some sea air. Usually mobs descend upon the park on their way to the Statue of Liberty ferry, to be preyed upon by sundry parasitic rip-off artiste peddlers. Try not to talk to strangers here.

Castle Clinton, the main structure in the park, contains the circular pavilion where you can purchase tickets for the Liberty or Ellis Island ferries (see Statue of Liberty and Ellis Island). More than just a glorified ticket booth, this structure was completed just before the war of 1812, as tensions between Britain and the newly independent United States were coming to a boil. It then stood in 35 ft. of water, connected by a drawbridge to the shore 200 ft. away. Not a single shot was ever fired from the fort, and by 1824 the city felt safe enough from British invasion to lease the area for public entertainment. In the 1840s, it got roofed over, and on September 11, 1850, 6000 people swarmed here for P.T. Barnum's famous presentation of Jenny Lind, "The Swedish Nightingale," an opera star so extraordinary that parents named their children after her. By 1855, enough landfill from nearby construction had accumulated to connect Castle Clinton to the mainland, and it became New York's immigrant landing depot. Between 1855 and 1889, more than 8 million immigrants passed through these walls. In later years, when Ellis Island had assumed this function, it turned into the site of the beloved New York Aquarium; then the aquarium moved to Coney Island and the building was left vacant. When the city declared the fort a national historic site in 1946, wreckers had already removed the second story, the roof, and other expansions, leaving the buiding at its present dimensions, the same as those of 1811.

As you look out at the water from Castle Clinton, you'll have a clear view of New Jersey (on your right), Ellis Island (dominated by a large brick building), Liberty Island (with you-know-who waving to you), Staten Island (directly behind the Statue of Liberty), and Governor's Island (to the left, a command center for the U.S. Coast Guard). A short walk south from Castle Clinton brings you to the **East Coast Memorial,** a large sculpture of a vicious-looking eagle in front of a number of granite monoliths engraved with the names of the dead. On the other side of the park, the sheer, elegant—and largely empty—wedge of 17 State Street dominates the skyline. Built in 1989, this leviathan building stands on the site of the house where Herman Melville was born in 1819. Melville soon got out of the house to pen his novelistic masterpiece *Moby-Dick* as well as "Bartleby the Scrivener," a maddeningly angst-ridden story of the life of a clerk in the 19th-century financial district. Behind 17 State Street, you can explore a new exhibit called "New York Unearthed," a museum of Manhattan archeology sponsored by the South Street Seaport. Excavators have discovered most of the items here during preparations for new construction in the downtown area. The huge green buildings on the water near 17 State Street are hard to miss even if you try; the Coast Guard Building and the Staten Island Ferry Terminal redefine dreadful. Across the street, a black skyscraper—New York Plaza, home of the Chase Manhattan Bank—redefines monolith.

Before this area was landfilled, State Street was the shorefront, and by the 1790s it had become the most fashionable residential street in Manhattan. But State St.'s domestic glamor has vanished today, though you can feel its former elegance in the **Church of Our Lady of the Rosary** and the **Shrine of St. Elizabeth Ann Seton.** They stand out like brick and wooden ghosts against an expanse of streamlined glass and steel. The shrine, originally the James Watson House, was built in stages from 1792 to 1805 in the Federal style and retains its original façade, its columns supposedly cut from ship masts. St. Elizabeth Ann Seton, canonized in 1975 as the first U.S.-born saint, lived here with her family from 1801 to 1803. The church next door dates from 1883, when it served as a shelter for Irish immigrant women.

If you walk up State St. along the edge of Battery Park, you will come to the **U.S. Custom House,** off the northwestern corner of the park. This gorgeous building, designed by Cass Gilbert, was completed in 1907, when the majority of U.S. revenues came from customs duties, and the majority of customs duties came from New York. Come inspect this palace of trade. Fort Amsterdam stood here in 1626, facing out into the harbor and defending the then-Dutch colony. In 1790, a Georgian mansion was built here as the presidential residence, but Washington never moved in because the United States capital moved to Philadelphia the very same year. (Washington, DC did not become the nation's capital until 1803.)

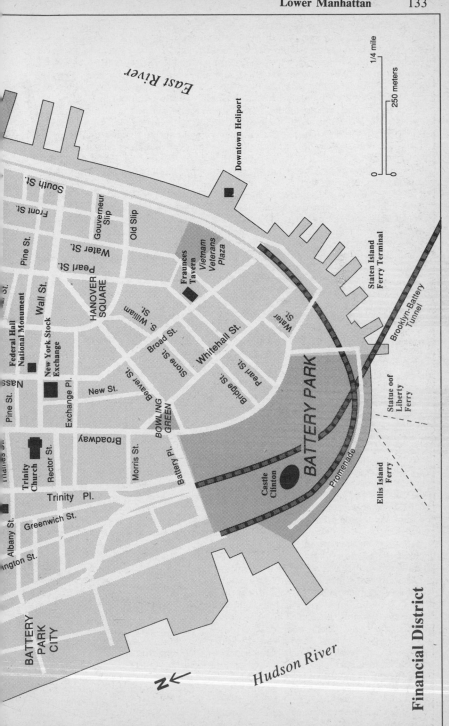

East River

Downtown Heliport

1/4 mile
250 meters

South St.
Front St.
Pine St.
Gouverneur Slip
Water St.
Old Slip
Pearl St.
Staten Island Ferry Terminal
Fraunces Tavern
Vietnam Veterans Plaza
Wall St.
HANOVER SQUARE
Brooklyn-Battery Tunnel
Federal Hall National Monument
New York Stock Exchange
S. William St.
Broad St.
Whitehall St.
Water St.
Nassau
Pine St.
Exchange Pl.
Stone St.
Pearl St.
Bridge St.
New St.
Beaver St.
BOWLING GREEN
BATTERY PARK
Statue of Liberty Ferry
Trinity Church
Rector St.
Broadway
Morris St.
Battery Pl.
Castle Clinton
Promenade
Ellis Island Ferry
Trinity Pl.
Albany St.
Greenwich St.
ington St.
BATTERY PARK CITY
Hudson River
N
Financial District

The Beaux-Arts masterpiece that stands here now combines Baroque and Renaissance inspiration with aggressively "relevant" decoration. All of the sculpture and artwork on the building relates directly to its function. The 12 statues on top of the façade represent the 12 great trading centers of the world ("Germany," the third statue from the right, became "Belgium" in the years before World War I). On the ground level, four large sculptures of enthroned women represent four continents. Daniel Chester French, who also seated Lincoln on his memorial in Washington, DC chiseled these zaftig symbols. Africa sleeps, her arms resting on a Sphinx and a lion, while a self-satisfied Europe holds the globe in her hands. America seems ready to leap forward out of her chair, carrying the torch of Liberty (although a Native American peeps ominously over her shoulder), and a distracted Asia rests on her throne of skulls. On the façade, observe the window arches, adorned with the heads of the eight "races" of the world, every column topped by the head of Mercury.

When the Customs Department moved to the World Trade Center in 1973, the building closed to the public so that no one could see the grand entrance or its rotunda, featuring a magnificent cycle of WPA-commissioned frescoes by Reginald Marsh depicting the travels of eight famous explorers. But the Federal Government's General Services Administration has decided to occupy the building once again and plans to reopen it to the public; it is currently undergoing intensive restorations.

The Customs House faces the egg-shaped Bowling Green, the city's first park. Here, colonists rioted in the 1760s against the taxes imposed by George III's Stamp Act. When George repealed the act in 1770, the forgiving New Yorkers commissioned an overbearing statue of the king on horseback and in 1771 protected the park with a gold-crowned fence made in England. But after the Declaration of Independence was read on July 9, 1776, in front of City Hall, the joyous if fickle populace raced to Bowling Green and tore down the statue, as well as the crowns on the fence. Bits of the statue later mysteriously surfaced in Connecticut. The 1771 fence still surrounds the park today.

A modest stone building across Broadway from Bowling Green says merely "United States Post Office—Bowling Green Station." Make an effort to go inside to see the **Cunard Building,** built in 1921 as the central headquarters for great transatlantic liners, which departed from nearby piers. The post office facilities are humorously swallowed up by the vast classical rotunda in the grand booking hall.

From the entrance to the post office, you'll have a good view of the Bull, poised to run from the tip of Bowling Green right up Broadway. The bull and bear have become the respective symbols of good and bad markets on Wall Street (some say because the bull attacks by raising its horns, but the bear by lowering its claws). The bull was the gift of an Italian artist who mischievously dropped it off in front of the New York Stock Exchange in the middle of the night last winter. Unamused brokers had it promptly removed, but for now it has been placed here as a compromise. For some, it may recall the Golden Calf.

Across from the post office stands 26 Broadway, a 1922 building that originally housed the offices of Standard Oil. Note how its façade curves along the edge of the street, but its tower aligns with the uptown grid; the street level and the skyline have been treated as two distinct elements.

Cross Broadway and walk back down the side of Bowling Green, on Whitehall Street. Between Stone and Pearl St. stands the **Broad Financial Center,** with one of the most whimsical lobbies in New York. Tapering pylons balance on surreal marble globes, and a wall-sized clockface stares over a sloping water-slide. Exit onto Pearl Street; at number 85 you will encounter a million-square-foot monster, the headquarters of Goldman Sachs. Dutch colonists wanting to recreate the traditions of their homeland created a canal here which ran through their settlement. It soon became putrid and filthy. The annoyed Dutch filled it in and created Broad Street.

To the right lies the pseudo-historic Fraunces Tavern block, an island of traditional and rather ordinary architecture in the sea of modern self-aggrandizement that is the financial district. The block contains structures built between 1719 and

1883, with many 20th-century additions and reconstructions. **The Fraunces Tavern Museum** (425-1778) stands on the site of one of George Washington's favorite New York hangouts. On this spot he said his final farewell to the officers of his victorious revolution. While some exhibits in the museum convey the spirit of old New York, the building itself is neither a restoration nor a genuine reconstruction of the original Fraunces Tavern, because no one knows what it looked like. Instead, the structure constructed between 1904 and 1907 is a piece of architectural guesswork, based upon generalizations about the typical tavern of the period. (Museum open Mon.-Fri. 10am-4pm; also Oct.-May Sun. noon-5pm. Suggested contribution $2.50, seniors, students, and children $1. Free Thurs.)

Continue up Pearl St. to Hanover Square, a paved-over intersection where you can find a place to sit. Note the statue of the Dutch goldsmith Abraham De Peyster, moved to this spot in the 1970s from Bowling Green. India House, a handsomely columned brownstone, faces the square; constructed in 1854 as the Hanover Bank, it has since become a private club.

Once the northern border of the New Amsterdam settlement, **Wall Street** takes its name from the wall built in 1653 to shield the Dutch colony from a British invasion from the north. By the early 19th century, it had already become the financial capital of the United States, and many a populist reformer used its name to refer to the entire financial district and its evil manipulations of the nation. Its mystique endures—Wall Street has become synonymous with the well-paid and high-pressured lives of the makers of million-dollar decisions.

At no. 55, Citibank has sprouted branch offices. This building once housed the Second Merchants' Exchange (1836-1854), the predecessor of the modern stock exchange. Its 16 Ionic columns, each weighing 41 tons and cut from a single slab of stone, were dragged here by teams of oxen. In 1863, it became the United States Customs House. Originally only three stories tall, the structure grew in 1909 when the firm of McKim, Mead & White added on the top four stories, and the **First National City Bank** moved in. A new row of smaller Corinthian columns gracefully complements the original façade. Citibank's branch offices occupy the main hall and the rows of tellers seem dwarfed by the magnificence of the space.

Across the street stands 48 Wall St., headquarters of the **Bank of New York,** originally founded in 1784 by Alexander Hamilton. This building, though constructed in the late 1920s, has somehow acquired tasteful colonial echoes. If you go quietly through the main entrance, you will probably be allowed to peek over the top of the sweeping marble staircases in the airy formal hall.

On the same side of the street hover the not-to-be-missed headquarters of the **Morgan Bank,** at no. 60—a veritable 52 stories of bizarre but eye-catching 1980s neo-neoClassicism. Some postmodernistes point out that the building itself resembles a column. Wander through its vast public atrium of white and gray marble and gaze at the mirrored white latticework ceiling. The overall effect is that of a front porch on steroids.

Just a bit farther down Wall St., at its intersection with Broad St. (which turns into Nassau St. to the north) cluster a mass of sights. Meet **Federal Hall** (264-8711) with its somewhat grotesque, larger-than-life statue of a tightly pantalooned George Washington on its steps. (Numerous historians have commented on the size of Washington's backside.) After 1703, this classical building housed the original City Hall, where the trial of John Peter Zenger helped establish freedom of the press in 1735 and the Stamp Act Congress met in 1765. It also served as the first seat of the constitutional government adopted in 1789; it was here that Washington was first sworn in (roughly on the spot where he stands today), that James Madison submitted the Bill of Rights to Congress, and that the House of Representatives and the Senate first met. Unfortunately, the original building was demolished in 1812. Its 1842 replacement functioned as a customs house until 1862, when a branch of the U.S. Treasury Department moved there. In 1955 it became a national memorial and its exhibits now include the illustrated bible Washington used at his inauguration, a 10-minute animated program called "Journey to Federal Hall," and models of the building's predecessor.

Walk across from Federal Hall to the **Morgan Guaranty Trust Company**, built in 1913. If you look closely at the Wall St. side of the building, underneath the fourth window over, you can see pockmarks in the stone wall that resulted from a lunch-hour explosion on September 16, 1920, when a bomb left in a pushcart went off. Conspiracy theorists, cynics, and experts suspect that it was detonated by an anarchist trying to destroy Morgan and his bank. The explosion killed 33 and injured 400, but the bank stood unscathed, and so did Morgan, who happened to be abroad at the time.

On the western corner of Broad St. stands the current home of the **New York Stock Exchange** (656-5167). (Open to the public Mon.-Fri. 9:20am-4pm.) The main building, constructed in 1903, has a relief sculpture in its pediment titled "Integrity Protecting the Works of Man," made by J.Q.A. Ward, the man responsible for the statue of Washington outside of Federal Hall. The Stock Exchange was first created as a marketplace for handling the $80 million in U.S. bonds issued in 1789 and 1790 to pay Revolutionary War debts. In the course of the 19th century, the Exchange became increasingly formalized, and the 1867 invention of the stock ticker revolutionized the market; the ticker recorded every stock sale and made transaction information instantly available to the public (and of course provided the necessary material for "ticker tape" parades). The stock market sizzled through the hot 1920s, only to collapse all of a sudden like a ruined cheese soufflé. After the crash of 1929 (morbidly nicknamed Black Monday) some ex-millionaires flung themselves out of windows, while others braved it through the Great Depression. The early 1980s saw another impressively "bullish" market, but its 1987 nosedive left many traders chastened.

To get to the visitors' entrance to the stock exchange, walk to the left, down Broad St. to no. 20, where someone should be distributing free admission tickets and letting groups in on the hour. Arrive early in the morning to ensure a convenient admission time. Tickets usually run out by around 1pm. Once admitted, you will be made to wait in a hellishly long line for the elevator—claustrophobes beware. Upstairs, you will pass through a metal detector, and cameras must be checked. Here you can see exhibits detailing the workings of the stock market and the history of the exchange, along with a wide-screen "experience theatre." But the real draw is the observation gallery, overlooking the zoolike main trading floor of the exchange. Under the 50-ft. ceilings of the 37,000-square-ft. room, you can observe frenetic activity from the glass-enclosed gallery while hearing recorded introductions to the floor activity in any of a number of languages. The visitors' gallery has been enclosed ever since 60s protesters invented creative ways to disrupt trading activity, like throwing dollar bills at the traders.

Observe the chaos of murmuring and milling in this paper-strewn pen, as people huddle around honeycomb banks of green video screens. The TV monitors, grouped in clusters called "trading posts," nearly outnumber the people. 1700 companies wheel and deal at the New York Stock Exchange, the world's largest with 79 billion shares of stock valued at $3 trillion. Note the telling color-coded jackets sported by the folks on the trading floor; you'll see brokers clad in yellow, reporters in navy, and pages in light blue. To your left, at the rostrum, the bell rings for opening at 9am and closing at 4pm. Don't forget your camera on the way out.

Around the corner, at the end of Wall Street, rises the seemingly ancient **Trinity Church** (602-0773). Its Gothic spire was the tallest structure in the city when first erected in 1846. Two other churches have stood on this site, and the Episcopal congregation here dates from 1696. The vaulted interior feels positively medieval, especially in contrast to the neighborhood temples of Mammon. You can also enter another era in the 2½-acre churchyard dating from 1681. Notice the graves of both Alexander Hamilton and Albert Gallatin, successive Secretaries of the Treasury. Hamilton, who served under Washington, committed himself to the development of the United States as a financial power, while Gallatin dedicated himself to the Jeffersonian vision of an agrarian republic. They now lie together, in a churchyard practically consumed by the vast financial establishment they nursed in its infancy. North of Trinity, on the same side of the street, stand 111 and 115 Broadway, the

Trinity and U.S. Realty Building. Gothic details lace the lobbies of these twins. With all the stained glass and gold leaf, you might as well be in a cathedral.

Walk up Broadway to Liberty Park, and in the background you'll see the twin towers of the **World Trade Center.** If you head toward them, skipping the first entrance, and go to the right, up Church St., you'll come to the main plaza on Church and Dey. In addition to two sculptures and a large fountain, the plaza offers ample seating space, daily lunchtime entertainment, and front-row views of the 1350-ft. tall towers (though actually you can see them from pretty much anywhere in New York). The sleekly striped 1973 shafts lilliputianize practically every other building in the city, and two instead of one betrays true architectural audacity. At 110 stories each, they provided 10 million square ft. of office space for their creator, the Port Authority of New York and New Jersey.

At Four World Trade Center, the Commodities Exchange Center (938-2018) does its thing on the ninth floor. The glass-enclosed visitors' gallery here overlooks the trading floor where gold, silver, sugar, coffee, and cotton change hands (not physically) from 9:30am to 3pm during the week. You can take free tours on weekdays at 10am, 11am, and 2:15pm, with slide presentations and lectures possible for groups by advance arrangement. The "floor show" can actually get more entertaining than the one at the Stock Exchange, since people here trade commodities in a bizarre brand of sign language which must be seen to be believed. Screen the Murphy-Ackroyd classic *Trading Places* for an introduction to the frenzy.

Two World Trade Center has the observation deck, and a banner to this effect hangs outside. When you enter the lobby, don't wait on the first line you see unless you want to get half-price tickets to a show (see Theatre). Around the corner sits the booth where they sell tickets to the very off-Broadway top of the building, music and lyrics by Port Authority. (Open daily 9:30am-11:30pm. Admission $3.50, seniors and ages 6-12 $1.75.) With a ticket, you can ride the elevator up to the 107th floor, where everyone ignores exhibits on trade history and economics in favor of the best view in New York. Unfortunately, looking out the window can be difficult, since the stainless steel "stripes" on the building walls preclude any panoramic "picture window" views. The architects opted to place much of the skeleton of the building on the outside, in order to leave large, unbroken spaces inside the building. You may want to use the coin-operated telescopes or diagrams of landmarks distributed throughout the observatory. From the north, the Citicorp Building looks particularly impressive, while the Citibank branch in Queens looks lost and diminutive. The green-capped Woolworth Building stands a bit to the north of the World Trade Center, and still looks attractive,even though its architects could scarcely have imagined that it would ever be appreciated from this angle. Note the gold-crowned federal court house and the hulking Municipal building bestriding the traffic of Chambers Street, topped off in a delicate wedding-cake fashion. And of course you'll see (as always) the frilly Chrysler Building and the chunky Empire State Building, flaunting their fancy outlines at the more mundane edifices of Midtown.

To the west glimmers the golden-hued **World Financial Center,** obviously designed to be seen from above. Its crisp glinting angles and smooth curves look more like an architect's model than a built reality. A flat New Jersey stretches across the river in the distance. To the south, you can see (from right to left) Ellis Island, Liberty Island (with the Lady looking tiny, but decidedly energetic), and Governor's Island, with Staten Island in the distance behind them. You can also see the entrance to the Brooklyn-Battery Tunnel: Look at the red paved area just north of Battery Park, where cars seem to disappear and re-appear from inside a boxy structure. To the east, the far-away Manhattan and Brooklyn Bridges steal the show. Still, it's hard to believe that the arches of the Brooklyn Bridge once overshadowed the rest of the New York skyline.

In good weather, the rooftop observatory opens. Unless you're terrified of heights, take the escalator up to this extraordinary experience. The top of the neighboring twin seems only a few feet away (though really it's farther away at the top than at the bottom, a fact that can be blamed on the curvature of the earth). You may have a distinct Burger-King feeling of violating the rules as you stand there, exposed to the elements, more than half a mile up in the sky. It doesn't get any higher than this.

The elevator will let you off one level below ground, cleverly ensuring that all tourists encounter the underground mall here, the largest in New York. If subterranean shopping fazes you, skip out of Hades and head back up the escalator to the plaza. Walk toward the Customs Building to the enclosed walkway which will take you to Battery Park City and the World Financial Center, a spanking-new complex built on property created by landfill from construction of the World Trade Center—these things seem to breed one another. The end of the walkway brings you up into the Winter Garden, the 1980s response to the eternal architectural dilemma of how to affect opulence. Its marble steps cascade into a glass-enclosed cavern of palm trees overlooking the Hudson River. Some Wintergardeners have planted requisite expensive restaurants here, plus novelty stores like the "Gallery of History," that vend tackily framed letters from Sir Isaac Newton and special prizes like signed photographs of Bush and Quayle. The "siteguides" in the complex—pressure-sensitive computer screen displays—tell you everything you always wanted to know about the World Financial Center but were afraid to ask. Outside lies the Battery Park City promenade, one of the best public spaces in New York, where you can hear regularly scheduled free summer music performances of everything from fiddle companies to string quartets on a vast scale. Walk to your right for a commanding view of the Twin Towers, and farther south for yet another glimpse of the Statue of Liberty. Two New York poets have inscribed their feelings about the city on the terrace here, and their words give new meaning to the rhetorical technique of "railing." Frank O'Hara explains, "One need never leave the confines of New York to get all the greenery one wishes—I can't even enjoy a blade of grass unless I know there's a subway handy, or a record store or some other sign that people do not regret life." Meanwhile, Walt Whitman gushes, "city of the World (for all races are here, all the lands of the earth make contributions here;) city of the sea! City of wharves and stores—city of tall façades of marble and iron! Proud and passionate city—mettlesome, mad, extravagant city!"

The best way to get back on the street is to return the way you came, back through the Wintergarden to the walkway to the plaza.

City Hall and South Street Seaport

The aura of 19th-century New York, bulldozed out of existence elsewhere, dominates this district. A number of magnificent municipal buildings stand nearby the rejuvenated South Street neighborhood.

The **Clocktower Gallery** (233-1096) stands at 108 Leonard St., between Broadway and Lafayette. The B, D, Q, and #4, 5, and 6 lines all stop on Canal St., and if you walk four blocks down Broadway or Lafayette you will come to Leonard. The avant-garde gallery resides in the former home of the New York Life Insurance Company, on the 13th floor. Not only can you see some of the city's more bizarre reinterpretations of "art" here, but you can climb inside the clocktower to observe its eye-boggling mechanism, as well as a fine view of lower Manhattan. (Open Thurs.-Sun. noon-6pm. Voluntary contributions.)

As you proceed down Lafayette to its intersection with Centre St., you can observe a group of sizable office buildings housing anonymous parts of the city bureaucracy. The pillared United States Courthouse at 40 Centre St., while unremarkable at street level, bears a gold roof that crowns the skyline. A bit farther down on Centre St., past a group of inexpensive food kiosks, the 1938 **Church of St. Andrew,** stands in the shadow of the overpowering Municipal Building. Enter the serene space of the church to take a look at the altar's dark wood pillars with gold capitals and carved cross set against a deep crimson curtain.

Its towering neighbor, **One Center Street,** also known as the **Municipal Building,** was completed in 1914. A bizarre free-standing colonnade distinguishes its enormous façade, while Chamber St. runs directly through its base. While fun-loving architects McKim, Mead & White outdid themselves on this one, creativity ultimately fails to soften the sheer power of the building's bulk. The Municipal Building presides over a busy intersection. Across the way, you'll find the **Hall of Records,** which also houses the Surrogate Court, with well-loved Judge Eve Preminger presiding. Two terribly municipal sculpture groups—"New York in Its Infancy" and "New York in Revolutionary Times"—grace the turn-of-the-century Beaux-Arts exterior. Twenty-four statues of notable New Yorkers also enliven the building. Come into the subdued marble entrance hall and step on the balcony to get closer to the unique curvy ceiling.

This building faces the infamous **Tweed Courthouse,** diagonally across Chamber St., on the northern edge of City Hall Park. Builders laid the foundations of the courthouse on a $150,000 budget in 1862 and finished it a decade and $13 million later. Most of this cash found its way into the corrupt political machine of the Tweed era, leading to a public outcry that marked the beginning of the end of the party's rule. Setting politics on the shelf, today you can admire the building's Victorian reinterpretation of the classical rotunda. The view from the ground floor affords an overview of the embellished space.

Exit from the other side of the Tweed Courthouse and you'll find yourself in **City Hall Park,** facing the rear of City Hall itself. Go around to the other side to observe the front of the building, which still serves as the focus of the city's administration. The colonial chateau-like structure, completed in 1811, may be the finest piece of architecture in the city. It illustrates the idea that good things come in little baby packages; you can stand only a few feet away and comprehend the entire two-story building. During its restoration in 1956, a durable limestone replaced the original marble and the northern side was refinished and improved (originally left rough due to the belief that the city would never really expand north of this point anyway). The vaulting rotunda here, while miniscule compared to the grand public spaces of lower Manhattan, wields a more restrained power. The winding stairs lead to the **Governor's Room,** originally intended for the use of said personage during his trips to New York, but now used to display a number of important early portraits, including ones of Jefferson, Monroe, Jackson, Hamilton, Jay, and Washington (who hated to sit for portraits since his false teeth caused him so much pain). On one side of the Governor's Room sits the City Council Chamber, which resembles a lavish schoolroom with its rows of darkwood desks. A curving gold-banistered balcony overlooks the room, and a massive allegorical painting adorns the ceiling. On the other side of the Governor's Room, down the short hallway to the right, lies the **Board of Estimate.** Crystal chandeliers complement white wooden pews and blue carpeting, reproducing the seal of the city. There is no admission fee, and the building officially opens to tourists on weekdays from 10am to 4pm, but public meetings here often run later (sometimes through the night) and can be interesting in their own right.

City Hall Park itself has been a public space since 1686. It has been home to an almshouse, a jail, and a public execution ground, and even a barracks for British soldiers. On July 9, 1776, George Washington and his troops encamped on the park to hear the Declaration of Independence. Today it has been prettily landscaped with gardens colored and shaped like flags.

At 233 Broadway, off the southern tip of the park, towers the Gothic **Woolworth Building,** one of the most sublime commercial buildings in the world. Erected in 1913 by F.W. Woolworth to house the offices of his empire of corner stores, it stood as the world's tallest until the Chrysler Building opened in 1930. The lobby of this five-and-dime Versailles is littered with Gothic arches and flourishes, its glittering mosaic ceilings complemented by carved caricatures: Note the one of Woolworth counting change and the one of architect Cass Gilbert holding a model of the building itself. Take one of the finely detailed elevators to the second-floor balcony, where you can get a closer look at the kitschy fresco of Queen Commerce receiving tribute from the subjects of the world.

A block and a half farther south on Broadway will bring you to **St. Paul's Chapel,** a parish of Trinity Church inspired by London's St.-Martin in the Fields. Constructed in 1766, with a spire and portico added in 1796, St. Paul's is Manhattan's oldest public building in continuous use. Gaze at the green churchyard and the surprising shades of the interior—baby blue, soft pink, and cream, with gold highlights. The human scale has its comforting effects—a sobering contrast to the arrogance of the two brash "World" centers nearby. You can see George Washington's pew and a memorial to Major General Richard Montgomery, killed in the famous 1775 attack on Québec.

If you head across Broadway again, and go east on Ann St., you will come to the **Nassau Street pedestrian mall,** a little-known and slightly seedy shopping district characterized by fabulous 19th-century architecture and tacky ground-level clothing stores. Packed with shoppers during the day, the area has acquired a nice gritty feel (in spite of the restored building painted pink and green). After dark, however, this seediness loses its charm. Make a right turn onto Nassau St. and walk down past John St. to Maiden Lane, where you will notice the atrociously turreted skyscraper at 2 Federal Reserve Plaza. The basement here, the downtown branch of the Whitney Museum of American Art, usually hosts small exhibitions of an extraordinarily high caliber, drawn from the Whitney's permanent collection. Don't miss this chance to see top-rate exhibits in easily digestible doses; admission to the temperature-controlled, quiet gallery is absolutely free. (Open Mon.-Fri. 11am-6pm. Gallery talks Mon., Wed., and Fri. at 12:30pm.)

Walking across Maiden Lane, you will encounter the **Federal Reserve Bank,** which occupies an entire block. Built in 1924, this neo-Renaissance building was modeled after the Palazzo Strozzi of a 15th-century Florentine banking family. More than 200 tons of iron went into the decorative treatment. This building stores more gold than Fort Knox, since many nations store their gold reserves here, in facilities sinking to five levels below the street. International transactions are frequently conducted merely by taking gold out of one room, and bringing it to another. Tours are available only by advance appointment (720-5000), but they're worth the trouble.

If you make a right onto Liberty St., you will see the **Chamber of Commerce Building** at no. 65, a 1901 Beaux-Arts showpiece with yet another grand entrance hall. A trip two blocks back up Nassau St. and right onto John St. will bring you to **St. John's Episcopal Methodist Church.** Established in 1766, St. John's is the oldest Methodist society in the country. (Sanctuary and museum of colonial memorabilia both open Mon.-Fri. 11:30am-3pm.)

To get to Fulton St. from here, make a left turn onto William St. and walk a block. A left onto Fulton will bring you past a large strip of moderately priced restaurants, and ultimately to the **South Street Seaport.** New York's shipping industry thrived here for most of the 19th century, when New York was the nation's prime port and shipping one of its leading commercial activities. Like many other waterfront areas of lower Manhattan, its size has increased considerably through the use of landfill. At the beginning of the 18th century, Water St. marked the end of Manhattan. Soon landfills had stretched the island to Front St., and by the early 19th century, to its present dimensions, with South Street bordering the water.

Zoning and development decisions made in the 70s rescued the neighborhood from a typical scenario of decay followed by rampant development, steering it in the alternative direction of homogenized commercialization. If you get a feeling of *déjà vu* as you walk the cobbled streets or wander among the novelty shops, that may be because the Rouse Corporation, which designed the rejuvenated area, also created similar gentrifications at Boston's Quincy Market and Baltimore's Harborplace.

The transformation succeeded, and the sleazy, fishy albeit historic seaside district turned into a ritzy Reagan-era playground. A fresh fish market became a yuppie meat market. Now the South Street Seaport complex has an 18th-century market, graceful galleries, and seafaring schooners. After 5pm, masses of crisply attired professionals fly out of their offices, ties trailing over their shoulders or sneakers lurking under their skirts, and converge here over long-awaited cocktails. The whole complex recalls a semi-formal frat party. Come observe the festive weekend atmosphere brought to you by the daiquiri-toasting Gucci-clad. And make sure to use the free and clean public toilets.

The intersection of Fulton, Pearl, and Water Streets begins the seaport with an abrupt transformation in tone, as car traffic gives way to street performers. To your left stands the paradoxically miniature Titanic Memorial Lighthouse. To the left on Water St., a number of 19th-century buildings have been splendidly restored and now house precious little shops. Maritime buffs should navigate toward the **Book and Chart Store,** and love of the printed word can be requited at **Bowne & Co.,** a restored 19th-century printing shop where employees demonstrate a working letterpress. On the Fulton St. side of this block, you can enter Cannon's Walk, a sparklingly clean alley around the back of these shops. Here you'll find the entrance to the **South Street Venture Theatre** (608-7889), where the *Seaport Experience,* a fun multi-media presentation about the area's nautical history, is screened hourly, mostly for the benefit of younger folk. (Admission $4.75, seniors $4, children 25¢.)

Back on Fulton St. to the right huddles a row of novelty shops housed in the famous Schermerhorn Row, the oldest block of buildings in Manhattan, constructed mostly between 1811 and 1812. When Peter Schermerhorn purchased this land in the 1790s as an investment, it was a "water lot," meaning that it was underwater, and the city sold him the right to create the land by filling it in. Schermerhorn's just-add-landfill purchase proved to be profitable, as this spot rapidly became the focus of much of New York's sea-related commerce. Come browse in the eminently browsable **Brookstone's,** where you can buy everything from leather bags to brass globes, foam rubber screwdrivers to mini-pool tables. At the **Museum Visitors' Center** here, you can buy tickets to many of the attractions at the Seaport. You can also purchase these tickets at Pier 16.

Across Fulton St. from Schermerhorn Row stands one of the foci of the seaport, the **Fulton Market Building.** On the ground floor, you can smell the wonders of "Market Hall," a collection of bakeshops and exotic grocery-type establishments. On the second floor you'll find the restrooms and Roebling's Bar and Grill, an over-priced but popular establishment. Do your own food thing at "Topside," on the third floor, a fun ensemble of small shops and food stands with large group seating areas. You can grab something from the Burger Boys of Brooklyn, while your friends pick up Chinese food from Wok and Roll or something light from Everything Yogurt. In front of Fulton Market, talented street musicians often perform, as do comedians or dangerous-stunt artists (sometimes the latter two can be hard to distinguish).

At the end of Fulton St., you can see the river suddenly in view, as the ghosts of deceased fish assault your nostrils. The odors come via the **Fulton Fish Market,** the largest fresh fish mart in the country, hidden right on South St. on the other side of the overpass. The city has tried to get the market to move, but it has been there for over 160 years, still operates at 4am, and has resisted all efforts. New York's store and restaurant owners have bought their fresh fish here by the East River ever since the Dutch colonial period. Between midnight and 8am you can see buyers making their pick from the gasping catch, just trucked here in refrigerated vehicles. Those with a stomach for wriggling scaly things may be interested in the behind-the-scenes tour of the market, given on the the first and third Thursdays of the month at 6am, except during the winter. (Advance reservations required; call 669-9416.)

On the other side of South St., you'll find the **Pier 17 pavilion** to your left, the **Pier 16 Ticketbooth** straight ahead, and a number of sailing ships docked to your right. At Pier 17 you can play on a three-story, glass-enclosed "recreation pier" filled with small shops, restaurants, and food stands. Highlights include The Sharper Image, New York's premier gadget and gizmo store for those with money to burn. Pick up a Japanese massage bed, a Cadillac-shaped stereo, or a digital-display exercise machine. Hats in the Belfry has a wonderful inventory, from the goofy to classy to plain outrageous, and The Weather Store sells only umbrellas and raincoats. But the most unique store here is **Mariposa, the Butterfly Gallery,** a store that sells works by an artist whose medium is butterflies, with different species arranged in different patterns. The results, while not always subtle, can be fascinating. Don't worry, all of the butterflies used have lived out their entire lifespan of thirty days.

The top floor eating complex here offers even greater selection than Fulton Market, and has a seating area with striking views of the Brooklyn Bridge (and of the vile AT&T Building). For marketplace information call SEA-PORT (732-7678).

The Pier 16 kiosk, the main ticket booth for the seaport, stays open from 10am to 5pm (open 1 hr. later on summer weekends). You can buy tickets here for some overpriced cruises, with predictably overstarched company aboard. The **Seaport Line's** authentic 19th-century paddlewheel steamboats (406-3434) offer one-and-a-half-hour day cruises departing daily at noon, 2pm, and 4pm (fare $12, students $10), and evening cruises to the live sounds of jazz, rock, and dixie ($15-20 depending on hour and day). Cruises leave from Pier 16. The air-conditioned boat circles around lower Manhattan to the Statue of Liberty, Ellis Island, and the World Trade Center. (The no-frills **Staten Island commuter ferry** gives you a similar view for 50¢, actually a sad spasm of inflation as it used to cost a quarter.)

The ticket booth also sells museum admission tickets, which can get you into many of the galleries located throughout the Seaport. At **The Seaport Museum Gallery,** back on Water St., small changing exhibits illustrate the growth of the city. **The Children's Center** also holds special exhibits in addition to regularly scheduled craft workshops. More sophisticated shows related to New York's seafaring past surface next door in the **Norway Galleries.** Museum admission price also includes the privilege of taking one of the several tours given daily at the Seaport. At 3pm, you can take an excellent "Walk Through the Back Streets," and get a sense of what the area used to be like before developers "saved" it as you meander through some of the unrestored parts of the seaport district. The tour departs from the Museum visitors' center. At 4pm, another tour leaves from the ticket booth itself. Unless you're spending a full day here, you may not want to spend the money on the ticket. For recorded information about the museums, call 669-9424. (Admission $6, seniors $5, students $4, ages 4-12 $3.) Finally, if you want to take a cruise as well as visit the museums (and line the seemingly bottomless pockets of the Rouse Corporation while you're at it) you can pay a combination fare ($15.25, seniors $13.50, students $12, children $7.50).

Parked in Pier 16, next to the ticket kiosk, you'll find the **Peking,** the second largest sailing ship ever built. You can get in with your Museum ticket or pay the $1 admission fee. The not-to-be-missed Peking, built in 1911 by a Hamburg-based German company, spent most of its career on the "nitrate run" to Chile, a passage which involves going around Cape Horn, one of the most dangerous stretches of water in the world. Powered purely by shifting winds and brute force, ships like the Peking are the culmination of 2000 years of sailing history. Technological advances made in the years following the Peking's construction made such ships obsolete.

On board, don't miss the 10-minute 1929 film of the ship during an actual passage around Cape Horn. This mind-boggling movie plays daily at 12:30, 2:30, 3:30, and 4:30pm. Also on board, you can see reconstructed living quarters, a photo exhibit about sailor life, and a stirring documentary about the Fulton Fish Market, shown daily at noon. Also at noon, or at 2 or 4pm, you can help the current crew raise one of the ship's 32 sails. On Sundays at 2:30pm, the staff demonstrates basic maritime duties.

Other ships seem docked for good in the seaport. Smaller ones include the *Wavertree,* an iron-hulled, three-masted ship built in 1885, and the *Ambrose,* a floating lighthouse built in 1907 to mark an entrance to the New York harbor. The *Pioneer* sailing ship gives two- and three-hour cruises on which you can assist with the sailing duties. Call 669-9400 for information.

The New York Harbor and the Brooklyn Bridge

You can stroll for a mile across the **Brooklyn Bridge.** To get to the entrance on Park Row, walk a couple of blocks west from the East River to the City Hall area. Ahead of you stretch the piers and warehouses of Brooklyn's waterfront; behind you, the cityscape that puts others to shame. The Gothically arched towers of New

York's suspended cathedral, the greatest engineering achievement of their age, loomed far above the rest of the city back in 1883, the products of engineering wizardry and 15 years of steady work. Plaques on the bridge towers commemorate chief architect John Augustus Roebling, who, along with more than 20 of his workers, died of construction-related injuries. But Roebling's son, Washington, took over the management of the job, achieving in the end a combination of delicacy and power that made other New York bridges look cumbersome or scanty.

Like all great bridges, this one has had its share of poetry and death. A Mr. Brody of 1920 fame leaped off the bridge, marking the first suicide. Locals say if he had dived and not belly flopped he might have lived. Obscure legal technicalities require all struggling city writers to pen an ode or two to these towering stone arches. You too can spin melancholy stanzas as you stroll across the walkway and observe the sun weaving through the constantly shifting cobweb of cables. Suspended above traffic, close your ears and imagine the bridge when only horse-powered vehicles took its path over the East River. Make sure to walk on the left. The right is reserved for bicycles, and you may be mowed down if you lose yourself in a tourist trance whilst gazing at the lower Manhattan skyline.

Battery Park City

Whatever the city tore up to construct the towering World Trade Center, it dumped west of West St. The 100 new acres were recently developed to form Battery Park City. Reached via the pedestrian overpass or a suicidal dash across West St., the area lies less than a mile from Wall St. With the stock market around the corner and the Statue of Liberty in full view, this neighborhood maintains the spirit of capitalism.

Cesar Pelli's World Financial Center towers with geometric shapes. Each of its 40-story towers has more footage than the 102-story Empire State Building because the buildings were built for computers requiring huge windowless rooms, not people who need a view to survive. Beneath the priceless electronics lies the glass-enclosed **Winter Garden,** an expanse of a dozen 40-ft. tall palm trees and expensive cafés. The garden points out onto the esplanade which takes you right out to the water.

Heading south will take you by a series of postmodern residences: along the esplanade you will pass sculptures by Fischer, Artschwager, Ned Smyth, Scott Burton, and Mary Miss, so new that they may be difficult to distinguish from the architecture. Soon you will reach the copper-topped 27-acre Battery Park, which harbors a unique downtown tranquility, removed from the swarming yuppies to the North and the blaring ship horns to the South.

The Statue of Liberty

The green lady standing in her bathrobe in the middle of New York Harbor might well be a monument to the lunacy of the city. In fact, she is merely Liberty. This copper statue, the absurd brainchild of the French sculptor Frédéric-Auguste Bartholdi, has come to stand as the most significant physical symbol of America. At 225 tons and 151 feet, she is nothing if not physical.

Bartholdi's classically detached statue (some have accused her of staring vacantly into the air) was intended to be a reserved representation of the ideal of "Liberty Enlightening the World," a gift from France to America. France would pay for the statue and the U.S. for the pedestal. Unfortunately, the word Liberty did not exactly roll off the lips of the "robber baron" millionaires of the 1880s, and little money was raised for the base that would support the statue. Congress declined to appropriate any funds for the effort, and the *New York Times* repeatedly implied that the whole transaction could only be a swindle. Things looked bleak for Liberty until newspaperman Joseph Pulitzer called upon the common people to do their duty, offering to print the names of all donors in his paper, *The World,* along with individual messages. The fervent notes included: "A lonely and very aged woman with limited means wishes to add her mite;" "Enclosed please find five cents as a poor office boy's mite to the pedestal fund;" and "We send you $1.00, the money we saved to go to the circus with." Pulitzer's populist campaign succeeded and even New York society came around to the idea in time to be well-represented at the lavish and eventful unveiling in 1886.

Women were officially barred from the opening ceremonies, but a group of determined suffragettes chartered a boat and sailed themselves over to the statue, interrupting speakers by shouting about the irony of a female embodiment of Liberty in a country where women could not vote. When this crisis passed, the moment to reveal the tricolor-veiled face of the statue approached. Bartholdi, stationed in the torch, was to pull a rope revealing the statue as soon as a young boy on the ground signalled that the long-winded fundraiser William M. Everts had finished speaking. But Everts had only gotten a few sentences into his speech when he stopped for a breath. The boy signalled, Bartholdi pulled, the tricolor dropped, Liberty was revealed, guns blasted, bands played, and the crowd cheered. Everts slunk away from the podium.

Lady Liberty's convenient placement in the harbor soon put her in a position of welcome for the boatloads of immigrants floating past, on the way to Ellis Island. This transformation in Liberty's symbolic role was described by Emma Lazarus' poem, "The New Colussus," ultimately inscribed in the statue's base. The lady in the harbor became a "Mother of Exiles:"

> *"Keep, ancient lands, your storied pomp!" cries she*
> *With silent lips. "Give me your tired, your poor,*
> *Your huddled masses yearning to breathe free,*
> *The wretched refuse of your teeming shore.*

While Lazarus' poetry may not be faultless, her reinterpretation of the statue's power has endured.

July 4, 1986 marked the centennial of the statue, and this time the ceremonies proceeded with impressive smoothness; the U.S. had learned a lot about show business in the intervening century. Ask any one of the hundred dancing Elvis Presley look-alikes who performed. The centennial also celebrated the completion of major restoration work—conducted by a joint French-U.S. team, of course. They replaced her torch, reinforced her wobbly arm (Bob Hope joked "I knew she was in trouble when I waved to her and she waved back"), and rebuilt her interior (the Port Authority of New York and New Jersey conducted an exhaustive analysis of traffic flow in the pedestal and statue). In the spirit of the statue, Chrysler Corporation Chairman Lee Iacocca ran a fundraising drive with a populist bent.

A few items of advice:
1) get here first thing in the morning;
2) get here first thing in the morning;
3) get here first thing in the morning.

Ever since her 1986 facelift, Liberty is the hottest date in town. Lines for the museums and observation points can be mind-bogglingly long, particularly during the summer. Try to eat before you arrive, because a cafeteria on an island will sink you for all you're worth, and who wants to pay $1.50 for a pretzel, anyway? The fun ferry ride over takes about fifteen minutes. In fair weather, go through the boat and up to the top level, where you can enjoy the breeze and the sunshine. Don't worry too much about getting a seat—once the boat starts moving everyone stands up anyway. On board, you can buy the paraphernalia of freedom, ranging from Statue of Liberty sunglasses ($3) to green foam rubber Statue of Liberty crowns ($2, but $1.40 in the gift shop on Liberty Island). Liberty seems to lend herself to franchising; for the unveiling ceremony in 1886, a man named Gaget brought three trunks of Liberty miniatures with his name on them over from the copper workshop where the statue was constructed. Hence the word "gadget," according to a team of etymologists in Harvard Yard.

As you pull up to the island, Liberty rises in elegant profile against a background of downtown skyscrapers and the Brooklyn Bridge, yielding in one fell swoop all of the glamorous clichés of New York. Here, you can take a closer look at the statue. Bartholdi used copper deliberately to achieve the patina effect which gives Liberty her peculiar hue. The seven rays on her crown represent the seven continents. The tablet she holds in her left hand says (in Roman numerals) "July 4, 1776," the date of the American Declaration of Independence. The base is almost as tall as the statue itself, which when first built stood as the tallest structure of her day. To resolve the practical problems of construction on such a grand scale, Bartholdi went to Gustave Eiffel, engineer extraordinaire, who would later design an obscure landmark in Paris and name it after himself. Eiffel, using funky bridge-building principles, devised an ingenious system of iron supports and a central "skeleton." The brilliance of Eiffel's solution is universally respected even today, and his technique was altered little during the 20th-century restoration.

Try to exit before you reach the boat docks, but if you don't want to miss any of the view, at least make sure you exit swiftly and go straight past the cafeteria, gift shop, and view of Ellis Island to the lines for the statue. Entire boatloads of huddled tourist masses arrive at once; every second counts. The line on the left leads to the crown (and then to the museums and observations decks on the way down), while the line on the right leads directly to the museums and observation decks. The public has not been allowed up to the torch since 1916.

The wait takes two to four hours. Check with the rangers to make sure you're standing in your line of choice. The observation deck line leads to the 10-story high pedestal, where you can enjoy a remarkable view—especially of the woman looming above you. The deck can be reached by hydraulic elevator. If you stand on the Crown Line, you get to climb 22 stories of steps (many of them teensy-weensy spiralling ones) to the seven tiny windows of Liberty's crown. From the glass nooks between the tiara tines, you can see the harbor far below—and maybe also some stars spinning around your head (or your life passing before your eyes). Senior citizens, younger tykes, or anyone with respiratory, heart, or leg problems should avoid this climb. Those who stop mid-statue and decide they never really liked the crown anyhow can take advantage of "bailout" points at various places in the climb. It is impossible to air-condition the statue, since she has such thin skin that water would condense on the outside, resulting in the rapid deterioration of her lovely green complexion. So the trip up the statue can be an object lesson in airlessness, as summer temperatures soar as high as 110°. One of the restorers wrote that the architectural team felt that a "grueling climb was an integral part of the visitor's experience" and should be preserved. This memorable ordeal may be for you.

You'll find two somewhat uneven exhibits in the pedestal of the statue: one on the history of the statue and one on the history of immigration. The immigration exhibit is being reorganized, as much of its collection has been transferred to the new museum at Ellis Island. You will probably want to spend some time exploring the pedestal, which was designed by well-known architect Richard Morris Hunt. From certain angles, this meticulously engineered classical complement overshadows even the green lady.

If you have some time before the next ferry departs and you're tremendously bored, stop in at the gift shop and cafeteria. In the former, you can buy everything from $70 Liberty hologram watches to 50¢ Statue of Liberty erasers. In the latter, see food names jumbled in a variety of languages by an indifferent staff. Fried fish and french fries cost $4, but you pay for precious little besides batter.

You can buy tickets for the ferry at Castle Clinton in the southwest corner of Battery Park, the "toe" of Manhattan Island (see Financial District Sights). Ferries leave for Liberty Island from the piers on Battery Park every half hour from 9am to 4pm, and the last ferry back runs at 5:15pm (in July and Aug. at 7pm). Tickets cost $4, (ages 5-11 $2, under 5 free).

Ellis Island

> *The only credential the city asked was the boldness*
> *to dream. For those who did, it unlocked its gates and*
> *its treasures, not caring who they were or where they*
> *came from.*
>
> —*Moss Hart*

Of 243 million U.S. citizens living today, 100 million descended from someone who passed through Ellis Island during its days as the main immigration center for the U.S., between 1890 and the 1920s. In its peak years, from 1900 to 1914, the island welcomed an average of 2000 new arrivals per day.

For years tourists could only gaze at the fog-shrouded island from afar, but a $140 million restoration effort culminated last fall in the opening of the island to the public. The museums and reconstructed facilities here have made the new Ellis Island one of New York's most popular tourist attractions.

Ellis Island, like its neighbor, Liberty Island, can be reached by ferry from Battery Park. You can buy tickets at Castle Clinton. Round-trip ferry fares include admission to all public parts of the island. On the ride over, enjoy the postcard-visionary views of lower Manhattan. The ferry docks in the same place as the boatloads of immigrants once did. (Tickets $6, seniors and children $3.)

On the 27½-acre island, you can visit the imposing main building that processed wave after wave of immigrants. Now known as the **Ellis Island Museum of Immigration**, it has been restored to the way it looked during the early 20s. Wander through exhibits on the histories of immigration and of the island, and see real immigrant baggage. At America's Family Album, an exhibit designed in 1986 by Kodak and formerly housed in the Statue of Liberty, you can match your last name to recent family photos of similarly named immigrants and their families. A nice idea, the exhibit will probably seem less pointless when enough time passes to make these people's clothes look funny. Another exhibit reviews the major contributions immigrants have made to America. The restoration has yet to be completed; an original dormitory, as well as the island's powerhouse and kitchen facilities, should be open by 1992, while a proposed convention center should be completed by the late 90s.

Roosevelt Island

This 3-mi.-long strip of land floating in the East River between Queens and Manhattan is the home of a growing state-planned community. Not the island itself, but the amusement-wracked tram ride over from Manhattan, draws visitors. It also drew international attention when Rutger Hauer hijacked it in the exciting pre-Rambo film *Nighthawks*. The place has more names than a Spanish nobleman. When Dutch settlers bought the property from the Canarsie Indians in 1637, it was called, of all things, "Long Island." The Dutch raised hogs here, thus the next title, "Hogs Island." By 1828, when the city purchased it from the Blackwell family, the island was referred to as Blackwell Island. The city built hospitals, prisons, and the New York City Lunatic Asylum here; Boss Tweed served time ont he island, and so did Mae West (for her role in a play called "Sex"). In 1921, the city christened the land mass Welfare Island, and in 1986 it was dubbed Roosevelt Island in honor of Franklin Delano.

The island has been the site of up to 26 hospitals, but only two remain today, caring primarily for chronically ill patients. By 1969, the residential building complexes of Eastwood, Island House, and Westview, completed under state supervision, provided housing for about 7000 people of mixed incomes. Now one of the nation's most successful planned and integrated communities, the island is virtually crime free. Procuring an apartment requires a wait of several years. In 1989, the subway link to Midtown Manhattan at 63rd St. opened, 14 years behind schedule, and further construction projects at "Southtown," and "Octagon" will soon complete the development of the island. Besides the subway and the tram, a bus runs from the Island over the Roosevelt Island Bridge to Queensboro Plaza.

Being there can't beat getting there. Even the historically significant buildings that grace the island stand inaccessible and completely neglected. But the tram endures, as an important commuter link to Manhattan and a beloved airborne landmark. Originally constructed in 1976 as a temporary alternative to subway service, the tram faces an uncertain future now that the subway has finally opened. One of the only publicly operated commuter cable cars in the world, it operates at an annual deficit of $1 million.

You can pick up the tram at 59th St. and Second Ave. Look for the big red cable cars next to the Queensboro Bridge. A round-trip ticket costs $2.50 and the ride takes about four minutes. (Cars run Mon.-Fri. every 15 min. 6am-2am, Sat.-Sun. 6am-3:30am.) As you hover, look to your right, downtown, and you can see the United Nations complex and the distinctive hats of the Chrysler Building and the Empire State Building. Once on the island, you can take the free mini-bus up Main St., but you will most likely find little of interest.

Brooklyn

In this hodgepodge of ethnic neighborhoods distinctly framed by avenues, each community has its own residential area and commercial zone clearly separated from one another. The Brooklyn-Queens Expressway pours into the Belt Parkway and circumscribes the borough. Ocean Parkway, Ocean Avenue, Coney Island Avenue, and diagonal Flatbush Avenue run from the beaches of Southern Brooklyn to Prospect Park in the heart of Brooklyn. Flatbush Ave. continues on and eventually leads to the Manhattan Bridge. The streets of Western Brooklyn (including those in Sunset, Bensonhurst, Borough Park, and Park Slope) are aligned with the western shore, not the south shore, and thus collide at a 45-degree angle with MacDonald Ave., which parallels Ocean Parkway and Central Brooklyn's other main arteries. In North Brooklyn, several avenues—Atlantic Avenue, Eastern Parkway, and DeKalb Avenue—travel from downtown far east into Queens.

The BMT and IRT both service Brooklyn, and all BMT lines end here. The IRT splits to service Flatbush Avenue and East New York. The J, M, and Z trains service Williamsburg and Bushwick and continue east and north into Queens.

Downtown and North Brooklyn

Fulton Street, the center of downtown, has recently transformed into an eight-block pedestrian shopping strip. The nearby **Williamsburg Savings Bank,** on the corner of Hanson St., is the borough's tallest building at 512 feet.

The **Dime Savings Bank,** 9 DeKalb Ave., presents a grand classical front, with monumental ionic columns beneath a triangular pediment, two reclining figures, and a majestic domed roof. Pass through the relief-set bronze doors—one of which displays a Cubist vision of the New York skyline—and enter a marble interior filled with its original turn-of-the-century furniture. **Abraham and Straus,** 420 Fulton St., is Brooklyn's premier department store. Unfortunately, the 1870s cast-iron interior was recently painted white. But you can still admire the vertical bands of brick on the 1929 art deco addition.

While a meal at **Gage and Tollner,** 372 Fulton St., would be out of the budgetarian's range, the restaurant's 1892 landmark interior—decorated with cherry wood paneling, mirrors and imitation leather called Lincrusta (invented by the guy who brought you linoleum)—is worth a peek. The original gas lamps still light up every evening.

The Romanesque Revival lives on at the **Brooklyn General Post Office,** 271 Washington St., and the nearby entrance to the **Eagle Warehouse and Storage Co.,** 128 Fulton St. Once a passageway for delivery wagons—check out the horse busts on the gates—the warehouse was recently converted into apartments. **Franklin House,** 1-5 Old Fulton St., another dramatic 19th-century building, was originally

Brooklyn

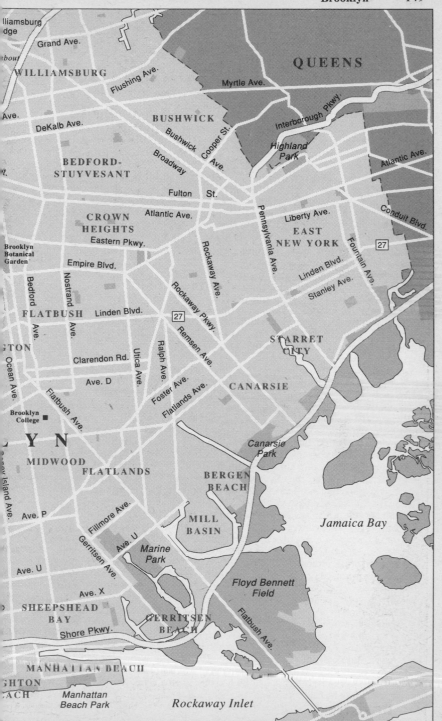

Williamsburg dge

Grand Ave.

bou

WILLIAMSBURG

Ave.

DeKalb Ave.

Flushing Ave.

BUSHWICK

Bushwick Ave.

Broadway

Cooper St.

QUEENS

Myrtle Ave.

Interborough Pkwy.

Highland Park

Atlantic Ave.

BEDFORD-STUYVESANT

Fulton St.

Atlantic Ave.

CROWN HEIGHTS

Eastern Pkwy.

Brooklyn Botanical Garden

Empire Blvd.

Bedford Ave.

Nostrand Ave.

FLATBUSH

Linden Blvd.

GTON

Ocean Ave.

Clarendon Rd.

Ave. D

Utica Ave.

Ralph Ave.

Flatbush Ave.

Brooklyn College

YN

MIDWOOD

FLATLANDS

Ave. P

ey Island Ave.

Ave. U

Fillmore Ave.

Gerritsen Ave.

Ave. U

Marine Park

Ave. X

SHEEPSHEAD BAY

Shore Pkwy.

MANHATTAN BEACH

GHTON
ACH

Manhattan Beach Park

Rockaway Pkwy.

Remsen Ave.

Foster Ave.

Flatlands Ave.

Liberty Ave.

Pennsylvania Ave.

EAST NEW YORK

Linden Blvd.

Stanley Ave.

Fountain Ave.

Conduit Blvd.

Atlantic Ave.

 27

STARRET CITY

CANARSIE

Canarsie Park

BERGEN BEACH

MILL BASIN

Floyd Bennett Field

GERRITSEN BEACH

Flatbush Ave.

Jamaica Bay

Rockaway Inlet

a hotel and now houses the Harbor View Restaurant. The newly renovated **Boro Hall,** 209 Joralemon St., sits on the edge of Columbus Park. Notice that Liberty, standing firmly with scales and sword on top of the hall, isn't wearing a blindfold—that's New York justice for you. (Tours Wed. at 12:30pm.)

Head down Atlantic Ave. into **Brooklyn Heights.** From Nevins St. to Smith St. you can "antique" to your heart's content. Between Clinton St. and Hicks St. you will find a Middle Eastern neighborhood (see Food) replete with *hookas* and spinach pies.

In 1814, when Fulton's invention of the steamboat made the development of Brooklyn Heights possible, rows and rows of now-posh Greek Revival and Italianate houses sprang up. To see the potpourri of styles that developed in Brooklyn and have come to represent 19th-century U.S. architecture, check out Willow Street between Clark and Pierrepont St. Numbers 155-159, in the federal style, are the earliest houses here (c. 1825). Observe the characteristic dormer windows that punctuate the sloping roofs. The hand-hammered leadwork and small glass panes date the original doorways. Greek Revival fans should heed the stone entrances of No. 101 and 103 (c. 1840) and the iron railings on No. 118-22. Numbers 108-12, built by William Halsey Wood in 1884, are Queen Anne-style houses. Note how deftly Wood exploits the characteristics of each material, pushing stone, stained glass, and slate to their individual capacities and unique limits. Wood, for some reason, used no wood.

The bronzed doors of **Our Lady of Lebanon Maronite Cathedral,** at Henry St. and Remsen St., are decorated with boats and churches that seem eerily prophetic, as they originally stood at the entrance to the main dining room of the grand French oceanliner the *Normandie.* Walk along the Promenade for a refreshing breath of sea air mixed with carbon monoxide from the cars shooting beneath you on the expressway. You can continue all the way to the towering Brooklyn Bridge for the mile walk into the metropolis. If you're driving, you can head west on Atlantic Ave. to the docks. On your right hovers one of the Watchtower buildings: Jehovah's Witnesses own much of the property in this area and print their publications here. Head south (left) on Columbia St. over trolley tracks and cobblestones. Follow the truck route signs to Van Brunt St. At the end of this street, deep in **Red Hook,** take in a dazzling view of the harbor and the Statue of Liberty. To the right stands a turn-of-the-century warehouse. If you turn around and take a right on Beard St., you will pass a number of lovely decaying industrial complexes. A left on Columbia St. followed by a right on Bay St. will bring you to a football field that draws young crowds for pick-up soccer games and white-clad Haitian immigrants for cricket.

Hassidic Jewish culture thrives as much as if not more in **Williamsburg,** north of downtown Brooklyn, than it does on Manhattan's Lower East Side. Men wear long black coats, hats, and sidelocks; women cover their shaved heads with wigs. The quarter is enclosed by Broadway, Bedford, and Union Avenues. Here, the austere Satmar cult celebrates Friday night and all day Saturday as their day of rest, *Shabbat.* If you intrude, you may feel unwelcome and conspicuous.

In recent years young artists have moved into ancient industrial complexes and converted them into lofts, and a hip SoHo-like bar scene has followed in their wake. **Peter Luger Steak House,** 178 Broadway (387-7400), internationally famed for its carnivorous menu, may sadden the budget traveler—it costs $50 per person.

Farther North, **Greenpoint** is the seat of a flourishing Polish community. The characteristic domes and triple-slashed crosses of the **Russian Orthodoxy Greek Catholic Cathedral of the Transfiguration of Our Lord,** Driggs Ave. and N. 12th St., loom over McGuiness Park. Kent Ave. and its side streets run along a seedy industrial zone and then beneath the Williamsburg Bridge to end beside the old Brooklyn Naval Yard, with its spectacular views of Manhattan.

If you venture east into the neighborhoods of Bedford-Stuyvesant, Brownsville and Bushwich, be forewarned. Low public funding, high unemployment, and inadequate public works have created a high-crime ghetto. The major sights here are burnt-out buildings, patches of undeveloped land, and stagnant commercial zones. Yet social consciousness spurts out from every pothole in these neglected streets.

Wall murals portraying Malcolm X, slogans urging patronage of black businesses, Puerto Rican flags, and leather African medallions all testify to a growing sense of racial and cultural empowerment.

On July Fourth weekend each year, an African cultural celebration is held on the grounds of the Boys and Girls School, 1700 Fulton St. From noon to midnight for several days, you can hear rocking reggae bands and the slamming beats of local rap musicians. The Boys and Girls School is a community-controlled public school, which grew out of the 1969 attempt at handing over control of the Ocean Hill-Brownsville School District to the community, a plan that was derailed by a teacher strike.

Central Brooklyn

Heading south on Flatbush Ave. will take you by the neighborhood of Park Slope, known for its fashionable shopping on Seventh Avenue and its magnificent brown-stones. Take a look on the corner of Sixth Ave. and Sterling St., at the graceful **St. Augustine Roman Catholic Church,** built in 1888 and adorned with owls. The attached academy around the block is drowned in graffiti and has a back entrance for "girls."

Continuing down Flatbush, enter **Grand Army Plaza;** you will be greeted by **Memorial Arch,** built in the 1890s to commemorate the North's victory over the South. In this plaza, you can also visit the Main Branch of the Brooklyn Public Library, where you can read or borrow any of 1,600,000 volumes. (Open Mon.-Thurs. 9am-8pm, Fri.-Sat. 10am-6pm, Sun. 1-5pm.) Take a look at the gold leaf façade or grab a bite in the cafeteria (see Food).

Frederick Law Olmsted designed **Prospect Park** in the mid-1800s and supposedly liked it even more than his Manhattan project, Central Park. Exercise caution in touring the grounds—crime has tarnished this area's reputation. In the northwest corner of the park, a bandshell holds concerts in late summer (718-643-3490). In the southeast corner of the park, you can see old Brooklyn preserved in **Leffert's Homestead Historic House** (open Wed.-Sat. noon-4pm, Sun. and holidays noon-5pm; 718-965-6505). The **1912 Carousel** nearby is scheduled to reopen in October 1990 (for more information, call 718-768-0227). And park officials hope that the **Zoo,** also currently undergoing renovations, will become the East Coast's premier children's zoo when it reopens. On the other side of the busy street, in the 50-acre **Botanical Gardens,** you can find specimens of almost all plants native to the city's climate. The sprawling grounds include the **Fragrance Garden for the Blind** and the **Cranford Rose Garden.** The annual springtime **Sakura Matsuri** (Japanese cherry blossom festival) draws visitors from around the world.

At Flatbush and Church Ave., you can see the oldest church in Brooklyn, **Flatbush Dutch Reformed Church** (c. 1654). Next door stands the second oldest high school in North America, **Erasmus High School.** Not a single brick can be moved from the school's center building or the Dutch Reformed will repossess it. Founding father-types Aaron Burr, John Jay, and Alexander Hamilton all contributed to the building of the school. On Flatbush Ave. and Clarkson St., down from Avi's Discount Center, you can spot the distinctive "tags" of graffiti artists Rock, Alan, Jew, and Picolo. Flatbush Ave. continues south through West Indian and Italian neighborhoods, past **Brooklyn College,** at Avenue H, a former site of P.T. Barnum's circus, and onwards to Far Rockaway.

The turn-of-the-century Manhattan aristocracy maintained summer homes in Victoria Flatbush (bounded by Coney Island, Ocean, Church, and Newkick Avenues). You can wander around Argyle St. and Ditmas Ave. to see some of the old mansions, but be careful to avoid the crack houses on Church Ave.

Farther west lies **Sunset,** a predominantly Latino neighborhood. Recently, new Chinese immigrants have begun to establish a community on Eighth Ave. between 54th and 61st St., alongside a well-established Arab population. The unique egg-shaped towers of St. Michael's Roman Catholic Church rise above the sidewalk on 42nd St. and Fourth Ave. Nearby, on the southwest corner of 44th St. and Fourth Ave., you can check out a famous graffiti piece by the infamous artist

"Dare." On 59th St. and Fifth Ave. stands Our Lady of Perpetual Help, where the new Archbishop of Brooklyn was ordained in May. Consumers flock to Fifth Avenue, which is lined by discount stores and odd hybrid restaurants. Stop in at **Oasis of Fifth Avenue,** 5104 Fifth Ave., for a *sabor de fruta batidas* ($1.50) in maney, papaya, mango, or guanabana flavor. (Open daily 8am-6pm.) Off the corner of 51st St. you will find a striking graffiti piece entitled "Crack Kills." If you are in a car, you can head down to First Ave. and explore the trolley-scarred streets, the setting for Vli Wedel's *Last Exit to Brooklyn.* Nearby, 19 huge white warehouses make up the six million square feet of **Bush Terminal,** the largest industrial park in Brooklyn. It is unsafe to explore this area on foot.

Racial tensions erupted last year in **Bensonhurst** after an African American youth, Yusef Hawkins, was slain there, resulting in a sea of anger, resentment, and media attention. The predominantly Italian neighborhood centers around 86th Street, which hosted the feet of John Travolta in the opening scene of *Saturday Night Fever.* The birthplace of disco still finds many Italians (calling themselves *couzines*) who frequent the area's Italian bakeries, pizza joints, and discount stores. Nearby Bay Ridge centers around Third Avenue, also called "Restaurant Row." If you're driving, venture down Shore Road and check out the mansions overlooking the Verrazano-Narrows Bridge and New York Harbor.

South Brooklyn

The D, B, F, N, R, and Q trains all plug into Stillwell Avenue Station at Coney Island, attesting to South Brooklyn's historic importance as a resort spot for the rest of the city. In the 1900s, only the rich could afford the trip here. Mornings, they bet on horses at the racetracks in Sheepshead Bay and Gravesend; nights, they headed to the seaside for fifty-dollar dinners. But the illegalization of gambling at horse races and the introduction of nickel-fare subway rides to Coney Island made the resort accessible to the entire populace. Summer weekends would see millions packed into the amusement parks, beaches, and restaurants. In the late 40s, the area began to lose its life. Widespread ownership of cars allowed people to get even farther away from the city, and a few devastating fires in Coney Island soon paved the way for the building of city projects throughout the area.

Some vestiges of this era linger. The **Cyclone,** at 834 Surf Ave. (718-266-3434), built in 1927, remains the most terrifying roller coaster ride in the world. Enter its 100-second-long screaming battle over nine hills of rickety wooden tracks—the ride's well worth three dollars. The 1920 Wonder Wheel ($2.50) has a special twist that surprises everyone, but make sure you get on a colored car. The El Dorado bumper car ($2.50), 1216 Surf Ave., is the only ride that still plays thumping 70s disco tunes; it offers a special "pay one price" option that isn't worth the money. If speed is not your calling, and you'd rather be a fish, head over to the **New York Aquarium** (718-265-3400) on Surf and West 8th St. The first beluga whale born in captivity was calved in these tanks. Watch a solitary brave scuba diver actually enter a tank full of feeding sharks. (Open daily 10am-4:45pm, holidays and summer weekends 10am-5:45pm. Admission $4.75, children $2, seniors free after 2pm Mon.-Fri.)

If you're driving, head west on Surf Ave. to the corner of West 15th, where you can see what remains of Steeplechase Park, a huge glass pavillion surrounded by mechanical horses. The Thunderbolt Coaster is still standing but now is overgrown with ivy and no longer runs. The landmark Parachute Jump, relocated to the edge of the boardwalk in 1941, once carried carts to the top and then dropped them for a few seconds of freefall before their parachutes opened. Once a year, on Puerto Rican National Day, a flag somehow gets tied to the top.

East of Coney Island, Ocean Parkway runs on a north-south line through half of Brooklyn. An extension of Olmsted's Prospect Park, this avenue was constructed to channel traffic to the seaside. Beyond the parkway lies **Brighton Beach,** nicknamed "Little Odessa by the Sea" because of the steady stream of Russian immigrants who moved there in the early 80s. Take a stroll down Brighton Beach Ave. or the parallel boardwalk along the sea. In late June and early July, old Eastern Europeans complaining about their doctor bills, young Spandex-clad girls listening to Top 40 music on their Walkmen, and middle-aged couples drowning their sunburns in Noxema are all blasted by the Blue Angels air shows. On the weekend of the Fourth of July, parachutists descend into cheering seaside crowds.

To the east lies **Sheepshead Bay,** named after the fish that has since abandoned its native waters for the cleaner Atlantic. Emmons Avenue runs along the bay and faces **Manhattan Beach,** a wealthy residential section of doctors and mafioso. You can go after some blues (as in the fish, not the music) on any of the boats docked here. (Boats depart daily 6am; trip $25.) Traditionally, a couple of dollars are collected from each passenger and the bundle goes to the person who lands the biggest fish.

If you have a car, you can drive east along the Belt Parkway, which hugs Brooklyn's shores. Stop off at **Plum Beach** for a more isolated sun and sand experience. At night, the parking lot here fills with big green Cadillacs and loving couples. Exit the Belt at Flatbush Ave. South, which leads to Queens and the Rockaway beaches. Turn left just before the bridge and you can drive around the immense abandoned air strips of Floyd Bennett Field. Here, you will also find information about Gateway National Park (718-338-3687).

Continuing on the Belt will take you to **Starett City,** based around Pennsylvania Ave. This development has its own schools, its own local government, and its own source of electricity and heat. Originally, rent here was based on how much each resident's salary allowed. But state legislators soon revoked this un-American policy.

Queens

Archie and Edith Bunker (and the employees of the Steinway Piano Factory) now share the brick houses and clipped hedges of their "bedroom borough" with immigrants from India, the West Indies, Thailand, Poland, Egypt, Argentina, and an atlas of origins. In this urban suburbia, the American melting pot bubbles away with a foreign-born population of over 30%. It is a land clad in oversized turbans and tight jeans, orange saris and pink stretch pants. Immigrant groups rapidly sort themselves out into neighborhoods where they try not to let the memory of their homeland die as they live "the American Dream."

These days, a borough president reigns over Queens, and moviehouses only roar with laughter when Eddie Murphy announces his plan to search for a blueblooded Queen there, but the name of the place did descend from royalty. The rural colony was baptized in 1683 in honor of Queen Catherine of Braganza, wife of England's Charles II. Not until the beginning of the 19th century did the small farms here begin to give way to industry, but by the 1840s the area along the East River in western Queens had burgeoned into a busy production center. In 1898, Queens officially became a borough of the City of New York, and with political linkage came physical growth. The building boom of the 50s effectively completed the urbanization of Queens, establishing it as the new Lower East Side, home to the immigrants of the late 20th century. Today, in this medley of distinct neighborhoods, you can trace the history of ethnic settlement from block to block. An area predominantly Korean one year may become mostly Indian the next. Even houses of worship change hands as neighborhoods evolve, and synagogues become churches and then transcendental meditation centers.

The city's tourism industry has not exactly devoted itself wholeheartedly to capitalizing on Queens' potential. In fact, this poor borough is universally ignored. You may be able to squeeze information out of the New York Convention and Visitors Bureau (212-397-8222). The **Queens Historical Society,** 143-35 37th Ave., Flushing (939-0647), can recommend personalized tours of historically important neighborhoods, such as Richmond Hill, Woodhaven, Long Island City, and Flushing. (Call Mon.-Fri. 9am-5pm). **The King Manor,** on Jamaica Ave. and 155th St. (523-1653), in Jamaica, was the colonial residence of Rufus King—a signer of the Constitution, one of the first two senators from New York State, and the first Ambassador to Great Britain. His son was Governor of New York. The mansion, set on an 11-acre

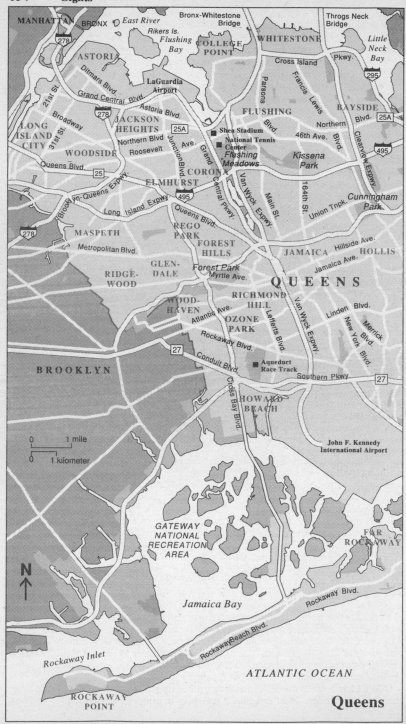

Queens

park, dates back to 1733 and contains examples of Georgian and Federal architecture. (Open Thurs. 1-4pm. Admission 50¢.) The restored **Onderdonk House,** at 18-20 Flushing Ave. (456-1776) in **Ridgewood,** is over 200 years old. (Open April 1-Dec. 6, Sun. 2:30-4:30pm; other times by appointment.) More recent architecture in Ridgewood also has a claim to fame; the neighborhood, founded 100 years ago when immigrants from Eastern Europe and Germany fled Manhattan tenements, has been declared a historic district. German architect Louis Berger designed 90% of the two- and three-story attached brick homes. For more information, write or telephone the Greater Ridgewood Restoration Corp., 20-40 Grove St. (366-8721), in Ridgewood.

More than anything else in the borough, the **Steinway Piano Factory,** at 19th Ave. and 30th St. (721-2600), puts Queens on the international map. The Steinways moved their famous operation out to Astoria in the 1870s, and, for quite a while, had the place to themselves. Their world-famous pianos continue to be manufactured in the same spot, in the same way; the 12,000 parts of the piano range from a 340-lb. plate of cast iron to tiny bits of the skin of a small Brazilian deer. Over 95% of public performances in the U.S. are played on Steinway grands. (Tours Fri. 9am-noon. Make reservations at least 2 weeks before you want to go. Tours are usually booked 1½ years in advance, but there are many cancellations, and you should try your luck.) If you're in the area, you can also drop by the **Steinway House,** at 18-33 41st St., the spacious mid-19th-century mansion that belonged to William Steinway. Also, on 20th Ave., between Steinway and 41st St., stands some of the pioneering affordable housing erected by the Steinways in the 19th century for their workers.

Orientation

To understand Queens' kaleidoscope of communities is to understand the borough. Just across the East River from Manhattan lies the Astoria/Long Island City area, the northwest region of Queens. **Long Island City,** noted as an industrial and transportation center, has recently acquired a reputation as a low-rent artist community. It remains to be seen whether the avant-garde will cross the river. **Astoria,** known as New York's Athens, is by some estimates the second largest Greek city in the world. It also supports a visible Italian population.

To the southeast, in the communities of Woodside and Sunnyside, new Irish immigrants are joining more established ones. **Sunnyside,** a remarkable "garden community" built in the 20s, commands international recognition as a model of middle-income housing. South of Sunnyside lies **Ridgewood,** a neighborhood founded by Eastern European and German immigrants a century ago. More than 2000 of the distinctively European attached brick homes there receive protection as landmarks, securing for Ridgewood a listing in the National Register of Historic Places.

Over to the east, **Forest Hills** and **Forest Hills Gardens** constitute some of the most expensive residential property in the city. The **Austin Street** shopping district imports the luxury of Manhattan. New York State Governor Mario Cuomo has a home in Forest Hills, as does former Vice Presidential Candidate Geraldine Ferraro. Just north of this area, the **Flushing Meadows-Corona Park,** site of the World's Fair in both 1939 and 1964, still attracts crowds, both for its museums and for its outdoor facilities. A little to the east, downtown, **Flushing** has become a "Little Asia" with a large Korean, Chinese, and Indian population, as well as a sizable number of South American immigrants. Many go to Bayside, east of Flushing, for bar-hopping in a relaxed, north shore atmosphere.

In the central part of the borough, industry booms in **Jamaica** and many of the middle-class neighborhoods to its southeast are primarily West Indian and African American. In the south shore of Queens, the site of mammoth Kennedy Airport, you can find "the Rockaways" and the large Jacob Riis Memorial Park, where a 1½-mil. boardwalk runs along the public shorefront. In rural eastern Queens, some sections might as well be in Nassau County.

Queens has neither the all-consuming grid of upper Manhattan, nor the angling chaos of the Village. Most neighborhoods here developed independently, without regard for an overriding plan. Most streets are numbered with at least a pretense of regularity, and usually streets and avenues run perpendicular to each other. But named streets sometimes intrude into the numerical system, and sometimes two different numbering systems collapse into one another (as in these consecutive thoroughfares in Long Island City: 31st Road, 31st Drive, Broadway, 33rd Avenue). On the bright side, residents usually give good directions.

Flushing

If you visit only one place in Queens, let it be Flushing. This is home to some of the most important colonial neighborhood landmarks, as well as to a bustling downtown and the largest rose garden in the Northeast. Transportation could not be easier: the #7 Flushing line runs straight from Times Square. Just get on and sit back for about half an hour, until you reach the last stop (Main St., Flushing) in the northeastern part of the borough. Manhattan it isn't, but the streets are usually congested. Walk past the restaurants, discount stores, and businesses, and soak in the atmosphere of Main St.'s crush of people and cultures.

Up Main St. toward Northern Boulevard stands **St. George's Episcopal Church.** The present structure was built in 1854 to replace the original, where signer of the Declaration of Independence Francis Levy was once a vestryman. Past the church about four blocks down and to the right, on Northern Boulevard, sits an inconspicuous shingled building at #137-16. This **Friends Meeting House** went up in 1694 and still serves as a place of worship for local Quakers (358-9636). Meetings are held here every Sunday morning, and the main room, a simple and severe hall, is open most Sunday afternoons. Come most soak in the serenity.

You can continue in the same historical vein down Northern Boulevard; pass the Town Hall, Union Street and "Lum's" to Bowne St, and then make a right. About two blocks down is the **Bowne House,** number 37-01 (359-0528). This low, unassuming structure, built in 1661, is the oldest remaining residence in New York City. But it has more going for it than age alone: here, John Bowne defied Dutch governor Peter Stuyvesant's 1657 ban on Quaker meetings—and was exiled for his efforts. Once back in Holland, Bowne persuaded the Dutch East India Company to order the colony to tolerate all religious groups, thus helping establish the U.S. tradition of freedom of religion enjoyed today by Buddhist and Hindu newcomers to Flushing. The house preserves the furnishings used by Bowne and his descendants, who resided in the house until 1945. (Open Tues. and Sat. 2:30-4:30pm, but staffing is erratic; you may have to wait for other people to arrive before receiving a tour. Admission $2, ages under 14 50¢.)

Next to the Bowne House lies a small park; if you walk through it and pass a playground on your left, you will come to the **Kingsland Homestead,** 143-35 37th Ave. (939-0647). This large, decrepit house, built in 1775, contains a permanent collection of antique china and memorabilia that belonged to the early trader Captain Joseph King. Although the pieces suffered some damage on the way to Queens, the collection merits a look. (Open Tues. and Sat.-Sun. 2:30-4:30pm. Donation requested.) In back of the house stands a somewhat offbeat attraction: a weeping beech tree, planted in 1849 by nurseryman Samuel Parsons upon his return from Belgium. The first of its species in North America, it hovers at a height of 65 ft. with a circumference of 14 ft. The venerably twisted patriarch weeps surrounded by a group of fine fledgling trees, and the neglected garden complements the charm of the cascading strings of leaves.

About five blocks down Main St., in the opposite direction from the #7 station, blooms the **Queens Botanical Garden** (886-3800), a public facility on a grand scale. (The Q44 bus toward Jamaica stops right in front of the garden.) Begun as a part of the 1939-40 World's Fair in nearby Flushing-Meadows Corona Park, the garden had to move when the park was being redesigned for the 1964-65 World's Fair. With the help of state-planning mastermind Robert Moses, the garden was relocated to its present site, where it now boasts a six-acre rose garden (the largest in the northeast), a 23-acre arboretum, and more than nine acres of "theme gardens." One of the more remarkable of these gardens, the **Wedding Garden,** encompasses a three-acre oasis with a rose-lined walk, flowering fruit trees, and a pool filled by a running stream. Park officials estimate that more than 10,000 romantic New Yorkers have trysted here on their wedding days. Make an effort to visit during the spring, when 80,000 color-coordinated tulips make their grand entrance. Lose yourself here for an afternoon or an entire day, and forget all about the concrete valleys of Manhattan. The garden stays open from dawn to dusk every day and charges no admission fee.

The **Historic Grove,** in **Kissena Park,** preserves nature on a more modest scale on Rose Ave. and Parsons Blvd. in Flushing. The grove here, only rediscovered in 1981, was planted in the 19th century as part of Parson's Nursery and contains many exotic tree species not indigenous to North America. Urban park rangers give walking tours (699-4204); you can call the Kissena Park Nature Center for more information (353-1047). From the #7 stop at Main St. you can pick up the Q17 bus in front of Model's. Take the Q17 down Kissena Blvd. to Rose Ave., and get out in front of Kissena Park.

Queens has hosted a pair of World's Fairs, both in Corona Park, a 1275-acre former swamp sliced out of the middle of the borough. Most of the present-day facilities are left over from the 1964-65 Fair. The crumbling concrete bears witness to the faded grandeur of the early 60s.Like downtown Flushing, the park is on the #7 line from Times Square; you can get off at the dilapidated 111th St. elevated station. Before leaving the platform, take a look at the large, pseudo-space-age, mushroom-shaped structures in the distance. Walk straight toward these, and you will come to a parking lot about five blocks down.

At first glance, the **New York Hall of Science,** at 111th St. and 48th Ave. (699-0675), may distress you; the building, futuristic back in 1964, stands on a neglected site, and its vision of the future has not aged well. But don't be deterred, because this "museum" merits a visit, especially if you bring children or anyone young at heart. In this hands-on museum, updated displays demonstrate a range of scientific concepts. Go to the second floor, where you will soon be as engrossed as any fifth grader in the participatory experience: climb into a distorted room, look at the veins in your own eye, reflect rainbows with prisms, or alter water waves by controlling the volume and frequency of a speaker. If you time your visit right, you may witness one of the regularly scheduled cow's-eye dissections performed by one of the young and spirited "Explainers" on the staff. (Open Wed.-Sun. 10am-5pm. Suggested admission $3.50, seniors and children $2.50. Free Wed.-Thurs. 2-5pm.)

To the left outside the building, across the parking lot and the overpass, lies the heart of the park and the **New York City Building.** The south wing houses winter ice skating (271-1996), and the north wing is home to the **Queens Museum** (592-5555). In the museum, you can see the "Panorama of the City of New York," the world's largest scale model, at 9335 ft. One hundred feet of New York corresponds to one inch on the model, which re-creates more than 850,000 buildings in miniature. This past summer, the panorama celebrated its 25th birthday with a number of updated models donated by architectural firms, some of them costing up to $10,000. The museum also shows contemporary exhibits as well as highlights from the '64World's Fair including "Formica's Kitchen of the Future" and a synthetic plastic raincoat. (Open Tues.-Fri. 10am-5pm, Sat.-Sun. noon-5:30pm. In summer, open until 8pm on Wed. Admission $2, students $1; seniors and children under 5 free.) As you exit the museum you may notice a 380-ton steel globe in the pavilion to your right. It's the "Unisphere," the centerpiece of the 1964 World's Fair. The fountain is drained and the foundation decayed, but the globe remains a sight to behold, and you can imagine what this place must have looked like 25 years ago, as women in bouffants and miniskirts and men in polyester turtlenecks perambulated. You may also notice **Shea Stadium,** another park property and home of the Mets, in the distance. As you explore the grounds, check out the games people play here: hop on a restored carousel from turn-of-the-century Coney Island at 50¢ a ride, get some sailing instruction (445-9202), play pitch-and-putt golf (271-3230), go cross-country skiing (271-1996). Or hang out in a playground accessible to disabled children.

Astoria and Long Island City

In Astoria, Greek, Italian, and Spanish-speaking communities mingle in lively shopping districts and a couple of top-flight cultural attractions. Astoria lies in the upper west corner of the borough, and Long Island City is just south of it, across the river from the Upper East Side. The N line services the area. A trip on the N to Broadway and 31st St. should take 20 minutes from Manhattan. As you climb down from the El stop you will find yourself in the middle of the Broadway shopping district, a densely packed area where your average block includes three specialty delis, a Greek bakery, and an Italian grocery. Revel in the discount shopping, but don't miss "Sculpture City" and the Isamu Noguchi Museum. Walk down Broadway for about 15 minutes toward the Manhattan skyline, leaving the commercial district for a more industrial area. At the end of Broadway, cross the intersection with Vernon Boulevard. **Sculpture City** poses right next to the steel warehouse. You may not believe your eyes at first: modern day-glo abstractions *en masse* in the middle of nowhere. The sign at the entrance says it all: "Sculpture City, Elevation—7 feet, Population—friendly." Wander among the 20-odd sculptures on this six-acre waterfront plot. Don't miss the Sound Sculpture right on the edge of the East River. Its tin drums and "vocal amplifier" face the water and ask the viewer to make as much noise as possible. You won't be able to miss the huge rainbow-colored fully-rigged ships, masts tilting out of the ground, stranded forever in the earth only a few feet from the river.

To the right of Sculpture City, two blocks down Vernon Blvd., stands the **Isamu Noguchi Museum** (204-7088), established in 1985 next door to the world-renowned sculptor's studio. Noguchi (1904-88) designed and built this space, one of the only world-class museums that presents a comprehensive survey of the work of a single sculptor. Inside 12 galleries display Noguchi's breadth of vision. Take a look at the model of his proposed "Sculpture to Be Seen From Mars" or his early design for the United Nations Playground. Don't pass over his most inspired and inspiring works, the smaller stone sculptures. Noguchi once said that he wanted "to look at nature through nature's eyes, and so ignore man as a special object of veneration"; he worked with stones not to make them into something else, but to help them reveal their true souls. The outdoor sculpture garden bears witness to his success. In "The Well," Noguchi left large parts of the boulder uncut, but bored a large circular "belly button" into the top, and water perpetually wells over the top and shimmers down the sides of the stone. You can (and should) touch its moving surface. The curators at the Metropolitan Museum liked this work so much, they commissioned one of their own. (Open April-Nov. Wed. and Sat. 11am-6pm. Suggested contribution $2. A shuttle service from Manhattan ($5), leaves from 725 Park Ave. at 70th St. Thurs.-Tues. every hr. on the half hr., 11:30am-3:30pm and returns every hour until 5pm; $5. An informative but very long guided tour kicks off at 2pm.)

If you still have the energy, you may want to visit the Kaufman-Astoria Studio's **American Museum of the Moving Image,** (784-0077). Head back up Broadway, past the El stop, and another five blocks, to 36th St. Make a right and walk 2 blocks through the residential neighborhood. This studio, part of a 13-acre plant with eight sound stages, is the largest studio in the U.S. outside of Hollywood. Since 1977 it has been the filming site of such major motion pictures as *Ragtime, Arthur, The Verdict,* and *All That Jazz.* Although the studios are not open to the public, the public can go to the left to find a museum, "dedicated to the art, history, and technology of motion picture and television." The screening room regularly shows vintage films and rare collections of shorts. The selections tend to be a bit on the scholarly side. A gallery with changing exhibitions occupies the ground floor, and a group of eclectic and not-entirely-successful permanent exhibits reside upstairs. Look in a Magic Mirror to see yourself as Marilyn Monroe, or gaze at a wall of Bill Cosby's Sweaters (he never wears one twice). Don't miss the video avalanche of cultural icons and entertainment excerpts, a reminder of how much cultural baggage lug we around with us: see Laurel and Hardy cut to the Muppets then cut to Fred

Astaire then cut to E.T. (Open Wed.-Thurs. 1-5pm, Fri. until 7:30pm, Sun. 11am-6pm, tours by appointment (784-4520). Admission $5, seniors and students $2.50.)

Hunter's Point

In Hunter's Point, a partly industrial and partly residential area, you can gain some perspective on Manhattan from across the East River. Take the E or F to 23rd St. and Eli Ave., the first stop in Queens. You'll come up from the subway right in front of the brand-new **Citicorp Building,** the tallest building in New York outside of Manhattan. Its sleek glass exterior looms above diminutive brick row houses, as if a butter-fingered planning official somewhere slipped, plopping a midtown monolith down on the wrong side of the river. But this is no mistake; as Manhattan development reaches its saturation point, companies must look elsewhere to do major construction.

To get to the cutting-edge museum/gallery **PS1** from the Citicorp Building, turn toward the Manhattan skyline and walk two blocks down, then make a left onto 21st St., go three blocks on 21st St., pass the park, and you will come to a red stone Victorian building, at 46-01 21st St. This is PS1—**Institute for Art and Urban Resources** (784-2084). The building housed the first public school in Queens; you can still see the word "Girls" cut into the stone lintel above the entrance. You must be buzzed in to this unconventional museum, a study in the haphazard. The partially restored, partially decayed hallways lead to some rooms that appear to be exhibition space and turn out to be empty, and to others that appear to be empty and turn out to be exhibition space. Besides providing inexpensive studios to lure artists out of Manhattan, PS1 hosts changing exhibitions of national and international standing. Recently a special exhibit in memory of the Chinese students killed by government soldiers in June 1989 in Beijing featured hundreds of door-sized panels, each designed by a different artist in materials ranging from goldfish bowls to candle-wax.

Most of the exhibits change, but you can see three permanent installations. Richard Serra created an untitled piece for the 1976 opening: he took an unusual room of exposed beams and bricks and left it completely intact, constructing only a channel in the floor that runs from one corner of the room to the other. Alan Saret's contribution, also designed for the opening, may be more accessible. Called "Fifth Solar Chthonic Wall Temple," its wall excavation records the movement of the sun as shadows move around inside the room. In James Turrell's well-known "Meeting," you can sit on high-backed benches in a room where the ceiling rolls back and watch the heavens shift colors at sunset. The design celebrates the interplay between natural and artificial light. The piece was inspired by Turrell's Quaker background. "Meeting" opens only at prime sunsetting time for two hours between 5 and 9pm. Call in advance for reservations. (Museum open Wed.-Sun. noon-6pm. Suggested donation $2.)

Long Island City commands an outstanding view of Manhattan and the East River. To get to the shorefront, walk toward the skyline. Go right on Vernon Blvd., and then make a left onto 44th Dr. The **East River Yacht Club** and its hoity-toity restaurant look out from the well-kept pier on a superlative view of Manhattan. To your right as you face the river lies the Queensboro Bridge, better known to Simon and Garfunkel fans as the 59th St. Bridge. Directly in front of you, on the southern tip of Roosevelt Island, you can see the romantically turreted ruins of 19th-century hospital facilities. Besides the conventional highlights of the Manhattan skyline (the angular Empire State Building, the art-deco Chrysler Building, the Twin Towers of the World Trade Center off in the distance to your left), you will have a fine view of the United Nations Complex, the wide gray tower facing out into the river, connected to a smaller domed annex with a satellite dish. The Citicorp Building stands out boldly directly behind you. You can take 45th Ave. back to the subway. On 45th, between 21st and 23rd St., take a look at the Hunter's Point Historic District. On first glance, the buildings here may only appear to be well-kept brownstone apartments: look more closely to see the facing of Westchester stone on these 10 Italianate row houses, excellent and rare examples of late 19th-century architecture.

Parks

You may not be able to find a parking space in Queens, but park space is easy to come by. While the Flushing-Meadows Corona Park complex does take up a lot of room, at 2868 acres (plus 9155 acres of marshes) the **Jamaica Bay Wildlife Refuge** (474-0613) in Broad Channel covers almost 10 times the area, spanning a surface about the size of Manhattan. The western half of the park dips into Brooklyn. Together, the Queens and Brooklyn facilities comprise one of the most important urban wildlife refuges in the U.S., which harbors more than 325 species of shore birds, water fowl, and small animals. (Open daily 8:30am-5pm. Free.) Environmental slide shows and tours are available on weekends. Call 474-0614 for information on one of the regularly given walking tours. To get there by subway from Manhattan, take the A or C lines to the Rockaways, exit at Broad Channel Station, walk west to Crossbay Blvd., and then north (right) about half a mile to the refuge. Or, easier still, take the G, R, E, or F line to Roosevelt Ave. in Jackson Heights and then the Q56 express bus to the Broad Channel stop. Either way involves a half-mile walk.

Also down in the Rockaways you can visit the Jacob Riis Park (338-3338), better known as **Rockaway Beach.** A famous boardwalk here has recently been refurbished, and stretches almost the entire length of the coast, from 149th to 169th St. This gorgeous beach offers good facilities but gets very crowded when the weather warms up. (To get there, take the #2 for about half an hour to Flatbush Ave., the last stop. On Nostrand Ave., you can pick up the Q35 bus in front of Lord's Bakery. Ask the driver to let you off at Riis Beach.)

In the central part of the borough, the **Alley Pond Park/Environmental Center** (229-4000) offers guided tours of natural trails in the park, a greenbelt of wetlands, woodlands, and marshes. (To get there, take the #7 to Main St., Flushing. The Q12 bus stops in front of the Stern's department sore on Roosevelt Ave.) The **Forest Park Ecocenter** and **Forest Park,** similar facilities, teem with wildlife and vegetation (520-3090). For information on horseback riding along park trails, call 261-7674 or 263-3500.

Finally, get a taste of Old New York at the **Queens County Farm Museum** (347-3276), at 73-50 Little Neck Parkway, in Floral Park on the Nassau Border. Built by Jacob Adriance in 1772 on 52 acres of land, this is the only working farm of its era that has been restored. (Open Sat.-Sun. noon-5pm, weekdays by appointment. Free.)

The Bronx

> *The Bronx?—No thonx.*
>
> *—Ogden Nash*

America has gotten to know the Bronx mostly through Hollywood thrillers like *Fort Apache: the Bronx.* Like Alcatraz, it has come to symbolize hell. Seen from the subway, it looms as an ominous landscape of identical, anonymous highrises, abandoned buildings staring onto the street with empty sockets of former windows.

But the Bronx offers more than urban decay. Bronx life, less glamorous than that of Manhattan, builds on a history of urban change squeezed into just over half a century. In addition to projects and burnt out tenements, the landscape sprouts suburban riverfront mansions, seaside cottages, colleges, 2000 acres of green parkland, and fading boulevards of grand apartment towers.

The only borough on the U.S. mainland, The Bronx took its name from the Bronx River, which in turn took its name from early Dutch settler Jonas Bronck who claimed the area for his farm in 1636. Until the turn of the century, most of the area consisted of cottages, farmlands, and wild marshes. Then the tide of immigra-

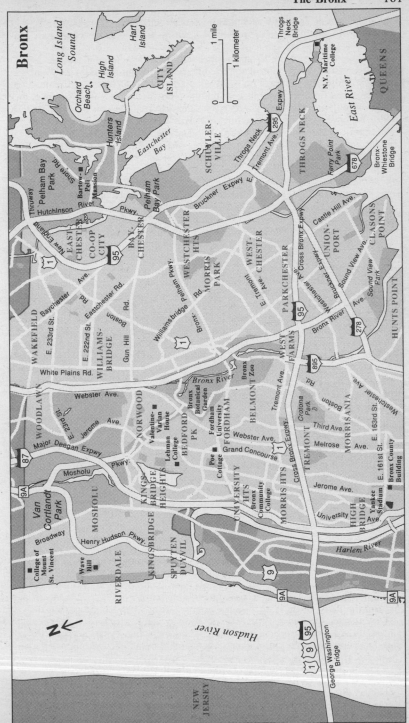

tion swelled, bringing scores of Italian and Irish settlers in its wake. The flow of immigrants has continued to the present day but these days the newcomers are Hispanic and Russian.

The southern part of the Bronx has become home to a large black and Latino population, with the exception of a predominantly upper-middle-class white enclave along the Hudson River just north of Manhattan known as Riverdale. The northern and eastern parts have stayed largely middle class, with single-family houses and duplexes along peaceful, tree-lined streets. Pelham Bay Park in the northeastern Bronx, the city's largest park, used to be a private estate owned by the Pell family. Bronx Park, which contains the Bronx Zoo and the splendid New York Botanical Garden, borders the banks of the Bronx River with the campus of Fordham University at its western edge. The subway will take you to The Bronx's attractions, but the ride takes a good while.

The wildest reason to come to the Bronx is the **Bronx Zoo,** also known as New York Zoological Park. The zoo husbands over 4000 animals, making it the largest urban zoo in the United States. While the zoo has some architecturally sound buildings, the animals along with everybody else prefer the 265-acre expanse where natural habitats have been created for their dwelling pleasure. While the Timber Rattlesnake has been sentenced to life in the Reptile House, more benign beasts like Indian elephants now inhabit the Wild Asia exhibit and White-Cheeked Gibbons treehop in the jungleworld.

Noteworthy naturalistic habitats include the Himalayan highlands, home to endangered snow leopards and fiery red pandas; Wild Asia, stalked by rhinos, antelopes and rare Sika Deer; World of Darkness, where Batman took lessons from the scores of bats and bushbabies; and the hands-on Children's Zoo, where kids do what animals do, including climbing a spider's web or trying on a turtle shell.

You can explore the zoo on foot or ride like the king of the jungle aboard the Zoo Shuttle/Safari Train that runs between the elephant house and Wild Asia. (Fare $1, children 75¢.) Soar into the air for an eagle eye's view of the zoo from the **Skyfari** aerial tramway that runs between Wild Asia and the Children's Zoo. (One-way ticket $1.25, children $1). If you find the pace a bit too Manhattan-like, just saddle a camel ($2). (Open Mon.-Sat. 10am-5pm, Sun. 10am-5:30pm. Admission Tues.-Thurs. free; Fri.-Mon. $3.75, seniors free, children $1.50.) If you're driving, take the Bronx River Pkwy. or (from I-95) the Pelham Pkwy. Subway Lexington Ave. #5 Express to E. 180th St. and transfer to #2 express to Pelham Parkway. Walk west to Bronxdale entrance to the zoo.

Across East Fordham Rd. from the zoo lies the labyrinthine **New York Botanical Garden** (220-8700). Remnants of forest and untouched waterways allow you to imagine the area's original landscape. The 250-acre garden, one of the world's outstanding horticultural preserves, serves as both a research laboratory and a plant and tree museum. Take in the 40-acre hemlock forest kept in its natural state (no doubt by the application of the Socratic method), the Rockefeller Rose Garden, the T.H. Everett Rock Garden complete with waterfall, the Native Plant Garden, and a Snuff Mill reincarnated as a café. At the westernmost tip of the Garden stands the **E.A. Haupt Conservatory,** built in 1902 to resemble the Great Palm House at Kew Gardens in England. (Conservatory open Tues.-Sun. 10am-4pm. Admission $3.50, students $1.25, children 75¢. Free Sat. 10am-noon.) Tours of the Conservatory take place year-round on weekends from 11am to 4pm, departing from the Palm Court. Tours sweep the garden grounds on weekends from April through October, at 1 and 3pm. Tours depart from the steps of the Visitor Information Center. If you go exploring yourself, get a garden map; it's a jungle out there for the mapless. (Garden Grounds open April-Oct. Tues.-Sun., 10am-7pm, Nov.-March 10am-6pm. Admission free; parking costs $4. Call 220-8779 for information.) Subway: D or #4 to Bedford Park Blvd. Walk eight blocks east or take the Bx26 bus to the Garden. Subway: the Metro-North Harlem line goes from Grand Central Station to the gardens (Botanical Garden Station), and includes admission ($7 round-trip, seniors $5, children $3.50).

Several universities have taken up residence in the Bronx. Begun in 1841 by John Hughes as St. John's college, **Fordham University** (579-2000) has matured into the nation's foremost Jesuit school. Robert S. Riley built the campus, a characteristic assembly of collegiate Gothic structures, in 1936. It spans 80 acres on Webster Ave. between E. Fordham Road and Dr. Theodore Kazimiroff Blvd. (Subway: C or D to Fordham Rd.)

The Herbert H. Lehman College, founded in 1931 as Hunter College, is a fiefdom in the CUNY empire. In 1980, the Lehmans went on to endow the first cultural center in the Bronx, **The Lehman Center for the Performing Arts,** on Bedford Park Blvd. West (between Jerome and Goulden Ave.), a 2300-seat concert hall, experimental theatre, recital hall, library, dance studio, and art gallery in one. (Subway: #4 to Bedford Park Blvd.)

En route to Van Cortlandt Park, consider looking in at the **Manhattan College** (920-0100), a 100-year-old private liberal arts institution that got its start as a high school. Starting from the corner of Broadway and 242nd St., take 242nd up, up, uphill. As you scale the steep, tortuous hill past Irish pubs and Chinese laundries, the college's quasi-federalist red brick buildings and chapel will come into view. The campus sprawls over stairs, squares, and plateaus, ideal for a life-sized game of Chutes and Ladders. The second staircase on campus brings you to a sheer granite bluff crowned with a kitsch plaster Madonna, a likely kidnapping victim for a suburban garden. Stamina-heads who make their way to the top of the campus can take in a cinemascopic view of the Bronx.

Across 1,146 acres of ridges and valleys in the northwest Bronx spreads the **Van Cortlandt Park** (430-1890), the city's third-largest jolly green giant. The park contains golf courses, tennis courts, baseball diamonds, soccer and football fields, kiddie recreation areas, and a large swimming pool. Anglers will adore the Van Cortlandt Lake; paleontologists will coo over the layers of evidence of the park's tumultuous prehistoric origins. The Cass Gallagher Nature Trail in the park's northwestern portion leads to rock outcroppings that have lingered since the last ice age as well as to the lairs of the park's little creatures. Stop by the Croton Aqueduct Trail, on the site of a former major city water source; the Old Putnam Railroad Track, which was once the city's first rail link to Boston and is now a hiker's trail leading past the quarry that supplied the marble for Grand Central Station; and the Indian Field, a recreation area laid on top of the burial grounds of pro-rebel Stockbridge Indians ambushed and massacred by British troops during the Revolutionary War.

Also inside the park stands the **Van Cortlandt Mansion** (543-3344), a city and national landmark built in 1748 by the prominent political clan that, like Rome's Cincinatus, divided their time between politics and farming. Early in the saga, George Washington made frequent visits here, including his 1781 meeting with Rochambeau to determine the final strategy of the war. It was from here that "wooden teeth" George commenced the triumphant march into New York City in 1783. Vague British nobility, aristocratic French, solitary Hessians, and continental Americans all showed up with their forces for a brief, historic sojourn.

Musty masonry and peeling paint add a few flakes of authenticity to this repeatedly restored mansion. The strange *gorbels* placed above the windows reveal the Dutch heritage of the builder; grimacing countenances like these showed their faces frequently in Holland, but rarely in the New World—in fact, this is their sole recorded public appearance in the Western Hemisphere. The house has another unique possession—an antique dollhouse, the oldest in the U.S. (Museum open Tues.-Fri. 11am-3pm, Sun. 1-5pm. Scheduled public tours occur Fri. 1-3pm and Sun. at 2pm. The park and the mansion can both be reached by subway—IRT #1 or 9 to 242nd St.) The 1758 **Valentine-Varian House** (881-8900), the second oldest building in the Bronx (Van Cortlandt got there first), has become the site of the Museum of Bronx History under the auspices of the Bronx County Historical Society. The museum, at Bainbridge Ave. and E. 208th St., functions as an archive, profiling the borough's heritage. The house has retained few period furnishings and negligible ambience. The enthusiastic Historical Society also maintains the **Edgar Allan Poe Cottage,** built in 1812 and furnished in the 1840s. The macabre writer and his tubercular wife lived here from 1846-48 but only three objects in the entire place actually belonged to them. Here he wrote *Annabel Lee, Eureka*, and *The Bells,* a tale about the neighboring bells of Fordham, later parodied in John Michael's witty tax return saga, "The Bills." The museum displays a slew of Poe's manuscripts and other morbidabilia. (Open Wed.-Fri. 9am-5pm, Sat. 10am-4pm, Sun. 1-5pm. Admission $1.) Another prominent local showcase, the **Bronx Museum of the Arts** (681-6000), at 165th St. and Grand Concourse, set in the rotunda of the Bronx Courthouse, exhibits works ranging from loan shows of old masters to new local talent. (See Museums.) At the **Bronx Community College Hall of Fame** at University Ave. and West 181st St. (220-6920), you can pay homage to the bronze busts of 102 great Americans set on beds of granite and weeds, sculpted by Epimethean Americans Daniel Chester French, Frederic MacMonnies, and James Earle Fraser. Predictably, McKim, Mead & White designed this turn-of-the-century hall.

Wave Hill, 675 W. 252nd St. (549-2055), a pastoral estate in Riverdale, commands a breathtaking view of the Hudson. Samuel Clemens, Arturo Toscanini, and Teddy Roosevelt have all resided in the Wave Hill House. Donated to the city over 20 years ago, the estate currently offers concerts and dance amidst its greenhouses and spectacular formal gardens. (Open daily 10am-4:30pm, Wed. until dusk, Sun. until 7pm. Free Mon.-Fri., Sat.-Sun. $2, seniors and students $1.)

Pelham Bay Park has over 2100 acres of green saturated with fun activities for the entire family. The omniscient Park Rangers lead a variety of history- and nature-oriented walks for creatures great and small (call 430-1890 for a schedule). Located inside the park, the **Barton-Pell Mansion Museum,** a Federal house on grounds that could have been manicured by Madge herself, has sweeping views of the Long Island Sound and prize-winning formal gardens landscaped in 1915. The interior decorator was not unfond of the Empire/Greek Revival style. (Open Wed. and Sat.-Sun. noon-4pm. Closed one month in summer. Admission $2, seniors and students $1.)

For a sniff of New England in New York, visit **City Island,** a community of century-old houses and sailboats, complete with a shipyard. The **City Island Historical Nautical Museum** and the **North Wind Undersea Institute** (885-0701) may not promise something for everyone but can chart a tour better than Julie McCoy any day. The ancient mariner's heart will be warmed at the sight of a 100-year-old tugboat, antiquated diving gear, exotic sea shells, and bundles of whale bones. (Open Mon.-Fri. 10am-5pm, Sat.-Sun. noon-5pm. Admission $3, seniors, harpoonsters, and children $2.) To get there, take IRT #6 to Pelham Bay Park and then board the #21 bus right outside the station. Get off at the first stop on City Island.

Sports fans and stadium fanatics will enjoy a visit to historic **Yankee Stadium,** on E. 161st St. at River Ave., originally built in 1923. Frequent remodeling has kept the aging stadium on par with and often technologically ahead of more recent constructions. The Yankees played the first night game here in 1946; the first message scoreboard tallied points here in 1954. Inside the 11.6-acre park (the field itself measures only 3.5 acres), monuments honor Yankee greats such as Lou Gehrig, Joe DiMaggio, Ernest Hemingway, Casey Stengel, and Babe Ruth. (Subway: C, D, or 4 to 161st St.)

For a visit to an authentic Bronx neighborhood where time seems to have stopped around 1960, take the "Appian Road" to **Arthur Avenue,** the Bronx's Little Italy. Follow Southern Boulevard to 187th St., past a row of uniform highrises, and make a right turn, and you'll suddenly find yourself surrounded by two-story row houses, winding streets, and pastry shops; here, old men sit at outdoor tables, slamming dominoes, and neighborhood priests conduct masses in the language of Dante. Outside the poignantly furnished Church of Our Lady of Mt. Carmel, at 187th and Belmont, stand a pair of hokey ecclesiastical shops where you can buy a statuette of your favorite saint. The portable martyrs come in all sizes and every color of the rainbow.

Arthur Avenue itself is home to some of the best homestyle southern Italian cooking in the world. At **Dominick's,** between 186th and 187th, boisterous crowds at long communal tables put away pasta without recourse to ordering, prices, or menus. For the same dish on three different days you may pay three different prices, but you'll never leave kvetching. (Subway: C or D to Fordham Rd.)

Staten Island

In 1524, 32 years after Columbus patented the New World, a Florentine named Giovanni Da Verrazano sailed into New York Harbor and entered the history books as the godfather of what would later be known as Staten Island. The name (originally *Staaten Eylandt*) comes courtesy of Henry Hudson, who plied his sail in the neighboring waters while on a voyage for the Dutch East India Company in 1609. In 1687, the sportive Duke of York sponsored a sailing contest with Staten Island as the prize. Manhattan won and has since called the island its own.

In 1713, a public ferry started running from Staten Island to the rest of the city, providing the only link between the two communities—until 1964, when builder Othmar "George Washington Bridge" Amman spanned the gap between the islands with a 4260-ft. suspension baby, the **Verrazano Bridge.**

Traffic flows more easily between Manhattan and Staten Island now that there's a bridge, but the two boroughs exchange nothing save the barest cordiality. Life takes its sweet time on Staten Island, as residents move along winding streets among colonial-style houses enveloped in foliage. The rustic, almost enchanted atmosphere appears unchanged despite the surge of new settlements. The Manhattan-spirited Verrazano Bridge still seems like a far-away fantasy.

Getting there is 70-80% of the fun. The unforgettalbe ferry costs 50¢ per round trip, the bargain of the century. Along the way you're treated to memorable views of Manhattan's skyline, Ellis Island, the Statue of Liberty, and Governor's Island, all captured within the dramatic expanse of the harbor.

While bus gates beckon right near the harbor you should call your destination to verify directions before setting out. The upstart borough has not deigned to place information booths in the ferry stations. Staten sightseeing may tire you; the island's hills, a sight for citysore eyes, can be tough on city feet. The attractions here do not come as a set, and you may get that Sisyphisian feeling of eternally traveling uphill.

Just up the hill from the terminal, the second street on the right is Stuyvesant Place, site of the imposing Federalist **Town Hall,** with a clocktower, and the **College of Staten Island,** the local colony of the City University of New York system. Its main building, a white institutional construction in the style of a Florentine palazzo, makes an attractive landmark inside and out. In the back courtyard, from randomly placed patches of greenery, rises a sculpture of enigmatic Frank D. Paolo—a "public man"—and a terrace with views of the harbor.

The **Staten Island Institute of Arts and Sciences,** at 75 Stuyvesant Place (727-1135), contains displays of natural history and fine arts as well as nifty dioramas on Native American life. (Open Tues.-Sat. 10am-5pm, Sun. 2-5pm. Suggested donation $2, seniors, students, and ages under 12 $1.)

Visible from virtually everywhere on the island, the **Verrazano-Narrows Bridge** has the distinction of being the world's longest suspension bridge, measuring 60 ft. longer than San Francisco's Golden Gate Bridge. Between the epic bridge and the impossible hills, San Franciscans will feel right at home.

At 1000 Richmond Terrace, the **Snug Harbour Cultural Center** has been designated a National Historic Landmark District. A former mariners' lair, it includes 26 architecturally significant buildings and the **Newhouse Gallery,** which showcases the work of contemporary U.S. artists. (Open Thurs.-Fri. 1-5pm, Sat.-Sun. noon-6pm.) Also on the premises is the free **Staten Island Children's Museum** (448-2500; grounds open daily 8am-dusk). The **Staten Island Botanical Garden** occupies 28 acres of the Cultural Center's 80-acre spread. The garden stays open daily until dusk. (Free.)

If the zoos of the concrete jungle have not appeased your crocodile cravings, visit the **Staten Island Zoo** (442-3101), in Barrett Park at Broadway and Clove Rd. For

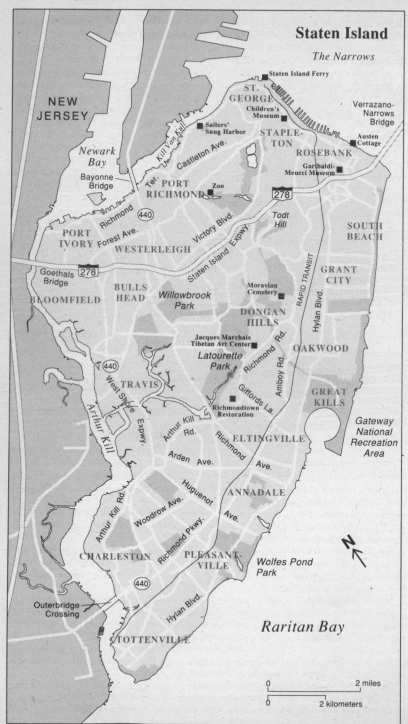

Staten Island

The Narrows

NEW JERSEY

Staten Island Ferry

ST. GEORGE

Children's Museum

Verrazano-Narrows Bridge

Sailors' Snug Harbor

STAPLE-TON

ROSEBANK

Austen Cottage

Newark Bay

Castleton Ave.

Bayonne Bridge

PORT RICHMOND

Zoo

Garibaldi-Meucci Museum

278

Todt Hill

SOUTH BEACH

Richmond

PORT IVORY

Forest Ave.

WESTERLEIGH

Victory Blvd.

Staten Island Expwy.

RAPID TRANSIT

GRANT CITY

Goethals Bridge

278

BULLS HEAD

Willowbrook Park

Moravian Cemetery

DONGAN HILLS

Hylan Blvd.

BLOOMFIELD

440

Jacques Marchais Tibetan Art Center

OAKWOOD

Latourette Park

Richmond Rd.

TRAVIS

West Shore Expwy.

Giffords La.

Amboy Rd.

GREAT KILLS

440

Arthur Kill Rd.

Richmondtown Restoration

Gateway National Recreation Area

Arthur Kill Rd.

Richmond Ave.

ELTINGVILLE

Arden Ave.

ANNADALE

Huguenot Ave.

Woodrow Ave.

Richmond Pkwy.

CHARLESTON

PLEASANT-VILLE

Wolfes Pond Park

440

Hylan Blvd.

Raritan Bay

Outerbridge Crossing

TOTTENVILLE

N

0   2 miles

0   2 kilometers

$1 you can toy with some of the world's finest reptiles—an unmitigated object of pride for the islanders. (Open daily 10am-4:45pm. Free Wed.)

Built to resemble a Tibetan temple, an illusion abetted by its hilltop placement, the **Jacques Marchais Center of Tibetan Art** displays the finest collection of Tibetan art in the Western Heathzensphere (see Museums). The Vanderbilt saga comes to an end at the Moravian Cemetery, on Fichmond Rd. at Todt Hill Rd. in Donegan Hills. Commodore Cornelius Vanderbilt and his clan lie in this ornate crypt, built in 1886 by Richard Morris Hunt. Central Park's Frederic Law Olmsted obliged with the landscaping. Unfortunately, the crypt can be viewed only from the outside.

The divine comedy of Staten Island, commenced in 1524, continued in the mid-1800s when Giuseppi Garibaldi, an Italian patriot and one of the trio behind Italy's reunification, took refuge on the island following his defeat at the hands of Napoleon III. He settled in an old farmhouse in Rosebank and proceeded to amass enough memorabilia to make the place into a museum: the **Garibaldi-Meuci Museum** (442-1608), is located at 420 Tompkins Ave. (Open Tues.-Fri. 9am-5pm, Sat.-Sun. 1-5pm. Free.)

Richmondtown Restoration, encompassing 26 buildings, is a labor of love; here authentic dwellings of 17th- to 19th-century villagers have been painstakingly reconstructed to their original condition. Founded in the late 17th century, Richmondtown used to be the county seat of Staten Island. The **Voorlezer's House** (1696) stands at the head of the class as the oldest surviving elementary school in the U.S. (None of the duncecaps survive.) At the General Store (1840) and the Boehm-Frost House (1750), you can see the tools of the restorer's craft. **The Staten Island Historical Society Museum** occupies a former county clerk's building constructed in 1848. The exhibits include early American trades and crafts. (Open Wed.-Fri. 10am-5pm, Sat.-Sun. and Mon. holidays 1-5pm. Admission $2, seniors $1.50, children $1.)

The only peace conference ever held between British forces and U.S. insurgents transpired on Staten Island in the **Conference House.** At the Sept. 11, 1776 summit, British commander Admiral Lord Howe met with three Continental Congress representatives—Benjamin Franklin, John Adams, and Edward Rutledge. Located at the foot of Hyland Blvd. in Tottenville, the house has become—what else?—a National Historic Landmark. Inside, you can see period furnishings and refresh your knowledge of Revolutionary War minutiae. (Admission $1, seniors and children 50¢. Guided tours by appointment Wed.-Sun. 1-4pm.)

Museums

Come witness a culture collecting itself. Stand under a life-sized replica of a great blue whale at the **American Museum of Natural History.** Control a 900-ft. aircraft carrier at the **Intrepid Sea-Air-Space Museum.** Enter the world of the 2000-year-old Egyptian Temple of Dendur or of Van Gogh's 100-year-old *Café at Arles* at the **Metropolitan Museum of Art.** Relax alongside Monet's *Water Lilies* at the **Museum of Modern Art.** MoMA and the Guggenheim are neck-and-neck in the most browsable giftshop category. At the Asia Society you can hobnob with a celebrated author over an informal cup of tea; aboard *The Intrepid,* the whole family can spot-fly a squadron of real jets.

New York museums' peaceful indoor atriums, spacious marble courts, intriguing sculpture gardens and not-*always*-mobbed cafés conspire to reinforce the image of museum as equal opportunity public space. Museum-goers set out to defend this democracy of art last summer when they joined the nationwide efforts to combat the philistine practices of Jesse Helms and his ilk. Rallies descended upon the steps of the Met, recording artists made an anti-censorship hit single, and thousands signed petitions urging Congress to do the right thing.

During the annual **Museum Mile Festival** in June, Fifth Avenue museums keep their doors open till late at night, stage popular interest exhibits, involve city kids in mural painting, and fill the streets with the gritty lyricism of jazz.

Most museums request a donation instead of setting a fixed admission charge. No one will throw you out or even glare at you for giving less than the suggested donation. Recently the Met has extended its hours so you can stay longer or take a break and come back for more. (Always keep your pin.) Most museums have regular, weekly "voluntary contribution" (read: free) times.

Know that New Yorkers use "museum" as a verb; they go "museuming." You can too.

The Metropolitan Museum

In 1866, a group of eminent Americans in Paris enthusiastically received John Jay's proposal to create a "National Institution and Gallery of Art." They probably never imagined that one day their project would span 1.4 million sq. ft. and house 3.3 million works of art, mounted on a hill of steps, crawling with popsicle and hot dog vendors. But whatever their vision, the New York Union League Club pressed hard under Jay's leadership, rallying civic leaders, art collectors, and philanthropists to the cause. In April 1870, the Metropolitan Museum showed its first collection, containing 174 paintings (mostly Dutch and Flemish), and assorted antiquities.

After a nomadic start, the museum finally came to settle at its present location in Central Park at 82nd St. and Fifth Ave. on March 30, 1880. Although Frederic Olmsted, the designer of Central Park, was somewhat peeved at the intrusion of the building onto his landscape, different stages of construction continued for over a century. In the Lehman Wing, you can still see the west façade of the first building, a Ruskinian Gothic structure designed by Calvert Vaux and Jacob Wrey Mould. In 1902, Richard Morris Hunt, Richard Howland Hunt, and George B. Post erected the neoclassical façade. The Hunts also designed the magnificent central pavilion. McKim, Mead & White contributed the north and south wings, while Kevin Roche, John Dinkeloo & Associates created the Lehman Wing (1975), the Sackler Wing (1978), the American Wing (1980), the Rockefeller Wing (1982), and the Lila Acheson Wallace Wing (1987)—a high-tech glass curtain. The museum (879-5500) is located at Fifth Ave. and 82nd St.

Practical Information

Having caught your breath, your first stop should be the **Visitors Center,** located at the Information Desk in the Great Hall. Stock up on brochures—make sure to grab a copy of the floor plan and the latest museum calendar, containing descriptions of current exhibits, a handy Practical Information section, and a schedule of concerts, lectures, and other special events. In the Great Hall, the **Foreign Visitors Desk** distributes maps, brochures, and assistance in French, German, Italian, Spanish, Chinese, and Japanese. For information on handicapped access or on services for sight and hearing-impaired visitors, call Disabled Visitors Services (535-7710). **Wheelchairs** are available upon request at coat check areas. **The Museum Cafeteria** is open Sun. and Tues.-Thurs. 9:30am-4:30pm, Fri.-Sat. 9:30am-8pm. The overpriced **Museum Restaurant** (570-3964) is open Sun. and Tues.-Thurs. 11:30am-3:30pm, Fri.-Sat. 11:30am-8pm.

You can rent **recorded tours** of the museum's exhibitions. Or you can be led around by one of sundry multilingual guides. For tour information go to the Recorded Tour Desk in the Great Hall. **Gallery tours** in English roam daily. Inquire at the Visitors' Center for schedules, topics, and meeting places. For recorded information on upcoming **concerts** and **lectures,** call 535-7710. Single tickets go on sale one hour before the event.

Admission is free to members, as well as to children under 12 accompanied by an adult. Suggested donation $5, seniors and students $2.50, but the emphasis here should be on the word "suggested"—you can pay as little as a quarter to get in. The museum is open Sun. and Tues.-Thurs. 9:30am-5:15pm; Fri.-Sat. 9:30am-8:45pm. You can write to your favorite painting at 1000 Fifth Ave., New York, NY 10028-0198. For recorded information call 535-7710.

The museum's holdings sprawl over three floors. The **ground floor** houses the Costume Institute, European Sculpture and Decorative Arts, the well-hoarded Robert Lehman collection, and the Uris Center for Education, where public lectures, films, and gallery talks take place. The **first floor** contains the extensive American Wing, the Arms and Armor exhibit, Egyptian Art, more European sculpture and decorative arts, Greek and Roman Art, Medieval Art, Art of the Pacific Islands, Africa, and the Americas, the Lila Acheson Wallace Wing with its footloose collection of 20th-century art, plus all the information facilities, shops, and restaurants. Finally, the **second floor** brings you more of the American Wing, Ancient Near Eastern Art, Asian Art, a collection of drawings, prints, and photographs, yet another dose of European painting, sculpture, and decorative arts, a Greek and Roman Art encore, more Islamic art, Musical Instruments, the second installment of 20th-century Art, and the R.W. Johnson Recent Acquisitions Gallery. Got all that? There will be a quiz.

Don't rush the Metropolitan experience; days can be spent here. No one ever "finishes" it. If you only have a few hours, the Greeks and Egyptians should keep you occupied. The dawn of civilization doesn't disappoint. Or dip into one of the funkier smaller collections.

Collections

The **American Wing** houses one of the nation's largest and finest collections of American paintings, sculptures, and native decorative crafts. The paintings cover almost all phases of the history of American art from the late 18th to the early 20th century. You can get some celebrated glimpses of early America in Matthew Pratt's *The American School,* Gilbert Stuart's regal portrait of George Washington, Bingham's pensive *Fur Traders Descending the Mississippi,* and the heroic if precariously perched *George Washington Crossing the Delaware* by Emanuel Gottlieb Leutze. Nineteenth-century painting virtuosi include Thomas Eakins and Winslow Homer. Particularly memorable is Eakins' haunting *Max Schmitt in a Single Scull,* depicting his melancholy friend resting the oars of his scull on Philadelphia's Schuykill River. But the pearl of the collection is Sargent's *Madame X,* a stunning portrait of a notorious French beauty, Mme. Gautreau, who allegedly consumed small doses of arsenic in the fashion of the time to give her skin the proper classic, marble-like pallor.

In the Charles Engelhard Court pose numerous examples of neoclassical and Beaux-Arts sculpture, chiseled by such masters as Daniel Chester French, Frederick Remington, John Quincy Adams Ward, and Augustus Saint-Gaudens.

The samples of decorative art date from the early colonial period to the beginning of the 20th century and include furniture, silver, pewter, glass, ceramics, and textiles. Twenty-five period rooms document the history of American interior design. Note the especially fun, sinuously curved Victorian tête-à-tête—an "S"-shaped love seat that looks like a pair of Siamese armchairs, joined at the seam. Art nouveau fans will gush at the ample selection of Louis Comfort Tiffany's glasswork, while palladins of American modernism can pay their respects at the Frank Lloyd Wright Room, ingeniously designed to be an integral and organic part of the natural world outside the windows, manifesting Wright's concept of total design.

The collection of **Ancient Near Eastern Art,** located on the second floor, covers artwork produced from 6000 BC to the Arab conquest in 626 AD, which comes from ancient Mesopotamia, Iran, Syria, Anatolia, and a smattering of other exotic lands. Gaze at Sumerian stone sculptures, Anatolian ivories, Iranian bronzes, and Sasanian silver and goldwork. Notice that the *Human-Headed Winged Lion,* an Assyrian limestone palace gateway piece, has five legs. Viewed from the front, the beast stands firmly in place; viewed from the side, it appears to stride forward.

The **Arms and Armor** collection contains more than 14,000 weapons—both functional and ceremonial—gathered from around the world. The collection presents outstanding examples of the armorer's, swordsmith's, and gunmaker's craft. Come here on your next major D & D quest.

The **Asian Art** collection gathers together painting, sculpture, architecture, and decorative arts from China, Japan, Korea, India, and Southeast Asia. Notable holdings include philosophical-minded Japanese screens, Stone and bronze Indian deities, and Ming dynasty furniture. The *Yashoda and Krishna* sculpture, a strangely moving work, depicts a cowherdess, Yashoda, breastfeeding the infant Krishna: according to legend, newborn Krishna was exchanged for a cowherding couple's baby in order to prevent his death at the hands the wicked King Kamja. To witness the subtle workings of yin and yang in Chinese architecture, direct your sandals to Astor Court, modeled on a Ming scholar's garden. Here light meets dark and hard balances soft; the architect re-creates the harmonies of nature.

A garden of sartorial delights awaits you at the *Costume Institute*. The collection includes fashionable dress and accessories as well as traditional regional costumes from Europe, Asia, Africa, and the Americas. The space age meets the royal cobblers of the Far East in an odd 1600 Venetian shoe concoction called *Chopins,* which rest on stilts as tall as 18-in. Understandably, walking in these was no picnic, and the fashionable females who wore them had to rely on the support of their servants to get from A to B. Art meets garment in the elongated, vertically dynamic Art Nouveau trousers of Charles Frederick Worth and in the minimalist geometric cuts of Yves Saint Laurent, imprinted with Mondrian's colorful rectangles.

The **Drawings, Prints, and Photographs** collection, particularly strong in Italian and French works from the 15th to the 19th centuries, does not stay on permanent view due to the fragility of the works, but regular exhibitions profile the collection. The highlights of the collection include Leonardo's *Studies for a Nativity,* Michelangelo's *Studies for a Libyan Sibyl* (which he later realized on the ceiling of the Sistine Chapel), drawings by Rubens, Rembrandt, and Goya, and assorted modern prints.

The **Department of Egyptian Art** occupies the entire northeast wing of the main hall, spanning thousands of years—from 3100 BC to the Byzantine Period (8th century AD)—and containing a galaxy of artifacts, from earrings to whole temples. You can see the Tomb of Perneb, the Lord Chamberlain of the Fifth Dynasty. Sun gods now smile upon the Temple of Dendur, through a shrine of glass. It looks much as it did back when Isis was worshiped in here, before the days of Shazam. Preserved in entirety, the temple was a gift from Egypt to the United States in 1965 in recognition of the U.S. contributions to the preservation of Nubian monuments. And of course there are plenty of mummies on hand to keep the kids happy.

Bring along your art anthologies to compare the illustrations with the originals, nearly 3000 of which congregate here in the museum's astounding hoard of **European Paintings.** The Italian, Flemish, Dutch, and French schools dominate the collection, but British and Spanish works make an occasional cameo appearance.

The Italian paintings date as far back as the early Renaissance and include works by Giotto, Fra Filippo Lippi, Botticelli, Piero di Cosimo, Andrea del Sarto, Simone Martini, Perugino, Raphael, Giovanni Bellini, Titian, Tintoretto, and Paolo Veronese. Make sure not to miss Bronzino's *Portrait of a Young Man,* one of the greatest works by this master of mannerism. You can peruse an entire room devoted to the canvasses of elder and younger Tiepolo. Dad preferred large historic or allegorical subjects, such as his monumental *Triumph of Marius.* Junior settled for lighter fare, often depicting unadorned contemporary scenes, as in *A Dance in the Country,* a meditation on the pleasures of aristocratic life in 18th-century Veneto. Of the North Italians represented in the collection, the canvasses of Andrea Mantegna are the most poignant. The *Adoration of the Shepherds,* painted when the artist was barely 20, illustrates the prodigy's gift for drafting impeccable detail and capturing facial expressions.

The Spaniards are here with instantly recognizable selections from El Greco (like the brooding *View of Toledo,)* Murillo, Riberra, and Goya. Goya's portrait of Don Manuel, an innocent-eyed boy in red vestments, is shot through with allegorical innuendo. The magpie that the boy holds by a string (a favorite pet since the Middle Ages) refers to Christian symbolism, in which birds represent the soul. Cats, personifying evil, stare menacingly at the bird, while caged birds, symbolizing innocence, are separated from the cats by thin gilded bars.

In the Flemish quarters, you'll find Jan Van Eyck's *Crucifixion* and the macabre *Last Judgement*, where an undernourished Christ presides over the heavens as reptiles munch on writhing sinners in the Hades below; Memling's portraits of Tomasso Portinars and his Wife; Hieronymus Bosch's *The Adoration of the Magi*, populated with his usual quirky types; and the almost too-famous Bruegel the Elder's *The Harvesters*, a piece that haunts nearly every anthology of Western painting. You can also drop in on Peter Paul Rubens. Note his famous and characteristic portrait of himself, his wife Helena, and their son Peter Paul, Jr. Don't miss the voluptuous, Baroque *Venus and Adonis* in which the artist captures the tender moment of parting between lovers, one immortal, the other about to encounter death.

The Dutch make a strong showing, somewhat eclipsed by a tour de force from Rembrandt, whose most emblematic *chiaroscuro* canvasses gather at the Metropolitan. Here are *Flora*, the *Toilet of Bathsheba*, *Aristotle with a Bust of Homer*, and a *Self Portrait*, one of nearly 100 that the artist executed throughout his career before dying in poverty. The Metropolitan is also one of the foremost repositories for the works of yet another esteemed Dutch master of light, Johannes Vermeer. Of less than 40 widely acknowledged Vermeer canvasses, the Museum can claim five, including the celebrated *Young Woman with a Water Jug*, the *Allegory of Earth*, and the hauntingly expressive *Portrait of a Young Woman*, with enigmatic eyes and high forehead *à la* Mona Lisa.

The English are represented by the like of Joshua Reynolds, Thomas Gainsborough, John Constable, and J.M.W. Turner, since the collection concentrates on the 18th and 19th century. Note Gainsborough's *Mrs. Grace Dalrymple Elliott*, a portrait of tremendous insight. Some of these canvasses run the gamut from florid to flaccid to forgettable. The English masters lack Italian monumentality and Dutch sensitivity, but they can capture a dull countryside or a stodgy ship at dusk like no one's business.

The French contingent of the European collection may be the most comprehensive section of the museum. Jean Clonet represents the 16th century. The 17th century brings the mannered and eloquent paintings of Georges de la Tour; note especially the remarkable *Penitent Magdalen*, with Mary Magdalene at the moment of conversion, her face lit up by a bright flame. Then come the mythological and allegorical tableaux of Nicholas Poussin and Claude Lorraine, followed by the pastoral subjects of Watteau. The 18th century ushers in the sensitive scenes of Greuze, the great painter of mythologized nudes and the favorite of Mme. de Pompadour; the portraits of François Boucher Fragonard, another diarist of dames; and the monumental classicism of Jacques Louis David. The latter's *Death of Socrates* protested against the injustices of the Old Regime and became a symbol of the Republican virtues of the French Revolution as well as a manifesto of neoclassical style. The 19th century heralds in the academic neoclassicism of Ingres, the nascent romanticism of Eugène Delacroix, the unvarnished social commentary of André Daumier (for example, in *Third Class Carriage*, where the human horrors of industrialization mark the faces of weary working-class travelers), the lyrical naturalism of Courbet, and the artful patriotism of Bastien-Lepage. His Joan of Arc is not a historical relic but a living symbol of French *esprit*, painted during the Franco-Prussian War. The rest of the 19th century belongs to the brand-name Impressionists, present here in great numbers and all shades of pastel. Notable moments include Cézanne landscapes, still lifes, and one of the five extant versions of the *Card Players*—the favorite painting of Russian supremacist Kasimir Malevich. Renoir and Degas live here too, in all their saccharine sweetness. You can see Gauguin's familiar Tahitian canvasses, one with an unusual twist: in *La Orana Maria*, a winged angel lurks amidst the traditionally semi-clad women and tropical fruit. The central duo, a mother and a small child, have halos above their heads. This is a wonderfully Gauguin variation on the theme of annunciation. The name of the painting means "I hail thee, Mary"—the first words of the angel Gabriel at the Annunciation.

Van Gogh makes a showing with one of his self portraits, the swirling, mossy, possibly drug-induced *Cypresses*, and the first of a duet of *Irises*, painted during his sojourn in the asylum of Saint Paul in Saint-Rémy.

The **European Sculpture and Decorative Arts** department contains about 60,000 works, ranging from the beginning of the Renaissance to the early 20th century. The collection covers eight areas: sculpture, woodwork, furniture, ceramics, glass, metalwork, horological and mathematical instruments, tapestries, and textiles, emphasizing French, English, Italian, German, and Spanish art. The collection also features entire rooms from palaces and great houses: the 16th-century patio from Velez Blanco, Spain; several lavish salons from 18th-century French mansions; and a pair of English neoclassical rooms designed by Robert Adam.

If you have to pick from the Italian sculptures on display, choose della Robbia's blue and white glazed terracotta relief *Madonna and Child*, hanging by the admission desk in the Great Hall. Also high on your list should be the delightful smaller bronzes like Gagini's *Boy Removing a Thorn* or a *Rearing Horse* modeled on Leonardo's drawings. Again on a diminutive scale—but no small masterwork—is *Bacchanal: A Faun Teased by Children*, by Gian Lorenzo Bernini, son of one of Rome's greatest pre-baroque sculptors and architects. Bernini conveys poignantly the exultation in the face of an inebriated faun.

The collection of French sculpture should not disappoint you too much. The featured sculptors include Monnot, the gently rococo Lemdyne, Houdon (the portraitist of Diderot and other Encyclopedists), the Romantic Barye, and Carpeaux, whose intensely and moving *Voolino and his Sons* (1865-67) illustrates the story from Canto XXXIII of Dante's *Inferno* of how the Pisan traitor Voolino, his sons, and his grandsons were imprisoned and then killed by starvation. The pose, the face, and the anatomical intensity of Voolino bespeak Carpeaux's reverence for Michelangelo.

The museum's holdings of **Greek and Roman Art** span several millenia and the sweep of both empires. In addition, the collections illustrate the pre-Greek art of Greece and the pre-Roman art of Italy. Cypriot sculpture, Greek vases, Roman busts, and Roman wall paintings number among the ancient treasures here. Don't miss the tiny *Seated Harp-Player*, a simple but moving Cycladic statuette that influenced 20th-century styles. Remarkable amidst nubile and perfectly proportioned Greek youths strolls the 2nd-century BC statue of an old, tired woman on her way to the market—a notable departure from myth toward realism.

The museum offers the most comprehensive exhibition of **Islamic Art** on permanent view anywhere in the world. Outstanding possessions include glass and metalwork from Egypt, Syria, and Mesopotamia, royal miniatures from the courts of Persia and Mughal India, and classical carpets from the 16th and 17th centuries. The abstract, decorative geometry of Arabic lettering, captured on parchment and pottery, appears strangely modern. Meticulous, wizardly ornamentation adorns Iranian pottery and earthenware. You can see an intact mid-14th-century Iranian *mihrab* (a niche in a house of worship that points in the direction of Mecca), covered entirely in blue glazed ceramic tiles.

The **Robert Lehman Wing**, which opened to the public in 1975, houses the extraordinary collection assembled by the Lehman clan. Rich in Italian paintings from the 14th and 15th century, the holding also profiles Dutch and Spanish canvasses, notably those by Rembrandt, El Greco, and Goya. French painters from the 19th and 20th century take up a few walls here, with special appearances by Ingrès, Renoir, big-name Impressionists, and color-biased Fauves. The department also has a celebrated collection of drawings which includes rare early Italian doodles, plus works of Dürer, Rembrandt, and Flemish masters. Among the decorative art objects here, you will find the famed Botticelli *Annunciation*, the melancholy *Madonna and Child* by Venetian master Giovanni Bellini, Memling's *Annunciation* and *Portrait of a Young Man*, El Greco's strangely vertical *Saint Jerome as a Cardinal*, Corot's mythical *Diana and Actaeon*, an erotic Balthus nude modeled after the frescoes of Piero della Francesca, and a Rembrandt drawing of the Last Supper, based on the Da Vinci original.

The newish **Jack and Belle Linsky Galleries** emaphasize precious and luxurious objects. The highlights of the collection include canvasses by Lucas Cranach the Elder, Rubens, and Boucher; more than 200 rococo porcelain figures from such renowned factories as Meissen and Chantilly; exquisite 18th-century French furniture; and 37 bronze statuettes and utensils, including a lively Romanesque monk/scribe astride a dragon. Don't leave without taking in the beauty of Crivelli's *Madonna and Urilo with Two Angels* set below symbolic Christian fruit, the playfulness of Bacchiacca's *Leda and the Swan,* and the romp and revelry of Jan Steen's *The Dissolute Household.*

Although a large portion of the museum's **Medieval Art** holdings sojourn in the Cloisters, the main building retains over 4000 works covering the period from the fall of Rome to the beginning of the Renaissance in the 16th century. You can wander from early Christian to Byzantine, migration, Romanesque, and Gothic. Take note of the multiform devotional pieces that include plaques, reliquary casements, triptychs, statuettes, and service vessels fashioned from ivory, silver, and painted enamel.

The gallery of **Musical Instruments** showcases some of the most important things that have ever gone plunk, selected for technical and social importance as well as for tonal and visual beauty. The collection features a wide variety of exotic noise-makers from the Middle Ages and the Renaissance, rare violins and harpsichords, and some non-Western specimens. Music lovers can enjoy the sights if not the sounds of a Stradivarius violin, a pair of guitars formerly owned and played by Andrés Segovia, a number of sumptuously painted spinnets and Virginals, Florentine Bartolomeo Cristofori's pianoforte from 1720 (the oldest piano in existence), an elegant Indonesian sesando, shaped like a shell from sections of palm leaf, and vigorously painted Korean percussion instruments.

The arts of **Africa,** the **Pacific Islands,** and the **Americas** populate the **Michael C. Rockefeller Wing.** The African collection is especially robust in bronze sculpture from Nigeria and wooden sculpture by the Dogan, Bamana, and Senufo of Mali. From the Pacific, major works include sculpture from Asmat, from the Sepik provinces of New Guinea, and from the island groups of Melanesia and Polynesia. A group of Eskimo and Native American artifacts tells the story of the arts of this country. While most of the artifacts here originally had religious or ceremonial purposes, some native rituals collapsed the tenuous boundaries between ceremony and real life. Take, for example, the New Guinean *Mlois Pole,* intended literally as a headrest whence enemy crania would be prominently displayed during a ceremonial feast.

Since its inception, the museum has been reluctant to invest in controversial modern art; the Museum of Modern Art had to be built to house those works that the Metropolitan would not accept. But in 1967, the museum relented, establishing the **Department of 20th-Century Art** that has opened its walls to canvasses of Picasso, Bonnard, and Kandinsky. The Americans flex the most muscle in this terrific collection, with paintings by The Eight, the modernist works of the Stieglitz Circle, abstract expressionism, and color field paintings. Highlights include Picasso's ponderous, pondering *Gertrude Stein;* Modigliani's *Juan Gris;* Balthus' stilted *The Mountain;* and Braque's post-cubist *Le Gueriden.* The great American works include Charles Demuth's bold *I Saw the Figure 5 in Gold;* Grant Wood's primitive realist *The Midnight Ride of Paul Revere,* painted from a bird's eye perspective; Thomas Hart Benton's heroic realist *July Hay;* and Jackson Pollock's almost figurative *Pasiphae.* Abstract expressionism is seen through the eyes of Willem de Kooning, Robert Motherwell, and Richard Poujette-Dart. Rejecting the emotional, gestural approach of pure expressionists, Ellsworth Kelly and Frank Stella proclaimed color the supreme element and drastically simplified form, sometimes eliminating it altogether, to give bright hues unimpeded play. Roy Lichtenstein and James Rosenquist represent the Pop Art movement of the 60s.

The **20th-Century Sculpture** section rests in the stone, steel, and bronze of Brancusi, Archipenko, Giacometti, David Smith, and Isamu Noguchi.

The Museum of Modern Art (MoMA)

A virtual Picasso warehouse, MoMA commands one of the most extensive post-Impressionist collections in the world. Founded in 1929 by scholar Alfred Barr in response to the Met's reluctance to embrace contemporary work, MoMA tells the story of the Modernist attack on the foundations of European art. Cesar Pelli's 1984 structural glass additions to the 1939 museum building flood the masterpieces with natural light.

Past the admission desk lies the Abby Aldrich Rockefeller Sculpture Garden, an outdoor space with a fountain, a drooping willow, and one of the finest assemblages of modern sculpture in the world, featuring Rodin, Matisse, Picasso, and Moore. Indoors, to the right, a small space presents changing exhibitions by contemporary artists. Nearby, the overpriced Garden Café somehow manages to command a following. To the left, the Education Center sponsors video presentations and gallery talks. The escalator descends to the René de Hanoncourt Galleries, where MoMA stages its major exhibitions. The museum has hosted some momentous shows in the past, but little can overshadow the permanent collection. Also on the lower level, the new Roy and Niuta Titus Theaters screen films. Pick up afternoon film tickets at 11am or evening tickets starting at 1pm in the theater lobby.

The main painting and sculpture exhibits occupy the second floor. In Impressionist Gallery 1, you can gaze at the mesmerizing swirls of Vincent Van Gogh's *Starry Night,* one of the best-loved treasures of the museum, as well as Van Gogh's complementary *Portrait of Joseph Roulin* of 1889. The curlicues of this postman's beard match the improbably floral wallpaper. Also reposing here, Henri Rousseau's famous *Sleeping Gypsy* of 1897 renders a crisp, elegant vision of mythic serenity: a lion, a gypsy, a mandolin, the moon. Four paintings unmistakably by pointillist Georges Pierre Seurat dot the walls.

In Gallery 3, you can find Vienna artist Gustav Klimt's famous vision of *Hope II,* a cascade of golden women painted in 1907. In its neighbor, *The Park,* the same artist seems quite the Impressionist, depicting a carpeting of treetops on a canvas filled with leaves, pure form and color. Only the tiny little brown trunks at the bottom of the canvas give the painting any representational content. In the next room you will encounter a gaggle of Picassos, including the 1904 piece *Two Acrobats with a Dog,* notable for its use of conventional techniques of depicting reality. These didn't last long.

At the far end of Gallery 4, turn left to enter the world-famous Water Lilies Room. Picture windows overlook the sculpture garden and let in a mass of natural light, and you can lounge on cushioned benches and observe Claude Monet's 1920 evocation of water, sky, cloud, shadow, and light. The more closely you examine the shimmering liquid and ghostly reflections, the further it dissolves into mere dashes of color—random, rough, and unmasked brushstrokes, a pure blur which couldn't possibly represent anything, yet does.

Return from the haze to Picasso by going back through Gallery 4, to numbers 7 and 8, the heart of the Cubist movement. Picasso's 1921 *Three Women at the Spring* presents chunky, thick, unreal women in loose togas; you can sense his Cubist explosion about to occur. It happened in *Three Musicians,* a painting done in the same year. In this one, reality has been completely dismantled into its component parts—the pieces acquire meaning solely by their context.

The works in Galleries 10 and 11 abandon overt content once and for all, in favor of a liberating use of pure form and color. Thus the revolutionary declaration of Kasimir Malevich's "I've-even-got-past-cubism" *Suprematist Composition: White on White.* Marc Chagall, who left the academy he founded in Vitebsk after disagreements with Malevich, imagined a folkloric dreamscape, with floating peasants and flying cows highlighted against candy-colored wedges, as in his 1911 work *I and the Village,* or his 1912 *Cavalry.* His fantasies inspired the surrealist movement.

The museum's comprehensive assortment of the works of Piet Mondrian inhabit Gallery 13, containing 11 canvasses painted from the 1910s to the 30s. Mondrian's work explores a shocking disappearance of the subject, a *reductio ad absurdum* of the Cubist translation of the subject into its geometric parts: here, the parts are translated into the subject. The canvasses feature a series of triumphantly unnatural grids, with crisp squares of red, yellow, and blue on a glowing white background.

In *Broadway Boogie Woogie,* the lines themselves have been subdivided into the squares and rectangles that form them.

Past the stairwell, in airy Gallery 14, you can observe the celestial joy of Henri Matisse's 1909 *Dance (First Version).* The next room contains 14 canvasses by Swiss painter and etcher Paul Klee, with his characteristically giggly squiggles and irreverent geometry. Klee once said his fantasy works were efforts in "taking a line for a walk."

In Gallery 16, a large platform bears a wide sampling of the sculptures of highly polished Romanian Constantin Brancusi. The works seem entirely abstract and inaccessible upon first glance, but examine their titles: a thin gray slab of marble is indeed a *Fish.* Later, larger works by Picasso dominate the rest of the room. A 1930 *Seated Bather* is a grotesque distortion of the female subject. The plaster sculpture of the *Head of a Woman* evokes Picasso's world in 3-D. The fabulously deformed subject somehow appeals to the viewer's gaze.

The exhibits in the next galleries get curiouser and curiouser, leading up to six paintings from the 1920s by the Spanish surrealist Joan Miró. His explosion of reality, no longer geometric and not quite fluid, hovers somewhere in between a landscape of sexually charged curves, bulging balloons, and mustache whips. The final room of this section drowns in surrealism. Observe René Magritte's *The False Mirror,* a 1928 close-up of the human eye with the sky reflected in the center, clearly the source of the CBS News' logo. Also note Salvador Dali's acid-triptychtock images of *The Persistence of Memory,* with its signature melting timepieces.

On the left, the photography exhibit features changing series of contemporary photographers, while the permanent collection provides a survey of the still-developing canon of daguerrotypical art. You may want to seek out Ray K. Metzker's *Composite Nude #2* of 1966, consisting of 120 negatives of nude profiles arranged in rows, effecting a film-like union of motion, shape, and subject.

The Drawings department and the exhibit of Prints and Illustrated Books occupy the third floor, but even more impressively the painting and sculpture collection continues, beginning at Gallery 23. The first rooms cover the major developments in abstract expressionism during the war-torn first half of the 20th century, but they hang in the shadow of Henri Matisse's 1952 *Swimming Pool,* a paper-cut mural that originally covered the walls of his dining room. The museum constructed a special room specifically to display this work, with its blue bodies cavorting joyously in a band of white water.

Matisse employed similar formal techniques (which he developed as a result of a debilitating condition that restricted his movement) in his remarkable *Memory of Oceania* of the same year, a great chaos of color and shape—disordered joy. Return to hard-core expressionism with Ad Reinhardt's *Number 87.* It seems to be black-on-black, but on closer examination you can tell its true colors: deep violet on dark blue on black.

Jackson Pollock's fabled layers of squirts can be viewed in the next room, as can the canvasses of his contemporary Willem de Kooning, who made color his subject. On a somewhat less radical note, Andrew Wyeth's 1948 icon *Christina's World,* banging a chord in the American spirit, sits in an alcove just before the stairwell.

Look on the other side of the stairwell for the museum's exhibits of contemporary art. First you will encounter Edward Kienholz's enigmatic *Friendly Grey Computer—Star Gauge Model #54,* a 1965 fortune-telling computer in a rocking chair. Its message: *computers sometimes get fatigued and have nervous breakdowns, hence the chair for it to rest in. If you know your computer well, you can tell when it's tired sort of blue and in a funky mood.* Indeed. In a far corner of the gallery, a room contains Richard Serra's *Circuit II,* one of his trademark rusted steel creations of bleak industrial vision.

On the fourth floor, you can take in the scale models of great architectural works by modernist Le Corbusier, the Frank Lloyd Wright chairs, and the fascinating assemblage of *chaise longues* (enough to equip the office of every psychoanalyst in New York).

Before leaving, stop in at the Museum Bookstore (708-9700), where you can pick up books related to current exhibitions, 50¢ postcards, and excellent posters. The MoMA Design Store (767-1050) across the street sells high-priced chairs, easels, sinks, pails, and bicycles.

The museum is located at 11 West 53rd St. (708-9400; exhibition information 708-9480; film information 708-9490). Subway: E or F to Fifth Ave. Open Fri.-Tues. 11am-6pm, Thurs. 11am-9pm. Gallery talks Mon.-Fri. at noon, 1pm and 3pm; Thurs. 5:30 and 7pm. Admission $7, seniors and students $4, ages under 16 free when accompanied by adult. Thurs. 5-9pm pay if you wish.

The Guggenheim Museum

For the museum-goer accustomed to the stern neoclassical proportions of venerable repositories of beauty, the Solomon R. Guggenheim Museum will be a welcome surprise. Every New York-bred child dreams of skateboarding down the Guggenheim's spiralling hallway. Designed by Frank Lloyd Wright in 1959, the circular building houses Solomon Guggenheim's collection of 20th-century abstract and non-objective paintings, which was originally gathered at the Museum of Non-Objective Painting. The permanent collection pays special homage to the art of Mondrian and the influential Dutch movement of De Stijl.

You may want to start at the top and survey the art downhill, beginning on the sixth ramp with Impressionism and post-Impressionism. Van Gogh, Renoir, and Toulouse-Lautrec are all represented, often by "minor" paintings. The mysteriously jocund *Football Players* (1908) is a refreshing break from Degas' interminable ballet dancers.

Picasso is here in full force, from his early naturalistic works to his Braque-betrothed analytical cubism and Matisse-like colorful still lifes.

From the fifth ramp down to the rotunda, the winding path follows a dazzling succession of 20th-century *isms:* cubism, expressionism, primitivism, constructivism, surrealism, and even the little-known "rayonism"—cubist Impressionism *à la Russe*. The roll call of artists reads like a Who's Who in the 20th-century avant garde: Chagall, Delaunay, Kandinsky, Klee, Arp, Modigliani, Mondrian, Kokoschka, and Leger. Note the monumental *Great Parade* (1954), Leger's definitive work.

Renew your familiarity with the innards of your car by examining Picabia's machinist paintings of carburetors. Fans of the dragon-slaying St. George can try to locate his figure—on horseback, lance in hand—in several of the Kandinskys on display. For Kandinsky, St. George embodied the spiritual and prophetic forces that would one day overcome the darkness and ignorance of the modern world. Kandinsky celebrates messianic ideas again in his stylized depictions of the Russian troika, a potent image that he borrowed from another great Russian visionary, Gogol.The collection includes several other Russian painterly titans—Malevich, Larionov, and Chagall. Don't miss Chagall's well-known cubo-primitivist *Green Violinist*.

Modigliani mavens will be delighted to find one of the artist's controversial *Nudes,* a series so shocking when first exhibited in 1917 that the show was closed.You can visit some classic postmodern creations here as well: the eerie worlds of Francis Bacon, the mirthful objects of Alexander Calder, the Pop Tart art of Roy Lichtenstein, and the abstract expressionist canvasses of Rothko and de Kooning.

The collection features several important pieces of sculpture, including the notorious nose from Giacometti's gaunt and haunted period and Brancusi's seal disguised as a piece of sausage. Unfortunately, the museum will be closed until the fall of 1991 for renovations and the construction of a 10-story annex. The permanent collection will be in exile until that time, parcelled into theme shows for European and Asian consumption.

The museum is located at 1071 Fifth Ave. (360-3500; bookshop 360-3525). Subway: #4, 5, or 6 to 86th St. (Open Tues. 11am-7:45pm, Wed.-Sun. 11am-4:45pm. Admission $4.50, seniors and students $2.50. Free Tues. 5-7:45pm.)

The Frick Collection

Pittsburgh steel industrialist and robber baron Henry Clay Frick left his house and art collection to the city, and the museum retains the elegance of his French "Classic Eclectic" white marble chateau. It showcases Old Masters and decorative arts in an intimate setting, making a refreshing break from the warehouse feel of New York's larger museums. You may want to buy the written guide to the Frick, which can lead you informatively from room to room ($1). Paintings have not been comprehensively labeled in this most private of collections.

The collection has some natural highlights. Two of the 35 Vermeer paintings extant hang in the South Hall: *Officer and Laughing Girl* and *Girl Interrupted at Her Music,* both suffused by a uniquely warm light. The Octagon Room has Fra Filippo Lippi's 15th-century *Annunciation,* a work of great spiritual power and luminous coloring. A number of early works also hang in the anteroom, including El Greco's *Purification of the Temple* as well as an anonymous 15th-century *Pietà* with a coldly surreal tone à la Salvador Dali. Bruegel's painting *The Three Soldiers* counts Charles I and Charles II of England among its previous owners.

In the Dining Room, feast your eyes on Thomas Gainsborough's 1783 masterpiece *The Mall in St. James's Park.* In this work the painter melds his love of nature with his mastery of the elaborate vanity of 18th-century portraiture. Leaves and gowns swish about the canvas complementing one another, as if corsets were the most natural thing in the world. In the Living Hall hang El Greco's *St. Jerome* clasping his Latin translation of the Bible, Titian's pensive *Portrait of a Man in a Red Cap,* and Giovanni Bellini's extraordinary *St. Francis in the Desert,* a 15th-century masterpiece of symbolic naturalism. The Library walls display Gainsborough and Reynolds portraits, a Constable landscape, a Turner seascape, a Gilbert Stuart likeness of George Washington, and a benign Henry Clay Frick surveying his domain. In the largest room in the Frick, the West Gallery, three works represent Rembrandt: the *Polish Rider,* owned by the last king of Poland; *Nicholaes Ruts,* one of Rembrandt's earliest portrait commissions; and his 1658 *Self-Portrait,* one of a series of over 60 such meditations painted during his lifetime, a masterwork of sensitive insight. Also note the works by Van Dyck (an elegant 1620 portrait of a close friend), Vermeer (an unfinished rendition of the opening of a letter), and Velazquez (a famous portrait of King Philip IV of Spain, painted in the town of Fraga following his military victories there against the French). Goya's *The Forge,* with its depiction of blacksmiths at work, is a most appropriate piece in the art collection of a steel industrialist. Perhaps the workers managed to sneak their way into this predominantly aristocratic collection because of their association with their previous owner, King Louis-Philippe of France. The Enamel Room contains a collection of Limoges enamels from the 16th and 17th centuries, as well as a spiritually penetrating evocation of Satan in Duccio di Buoninsegna's 1308 *The Temptation of Christ on the Mountain.*

The Oval Room has fine Gainsborough portraiture as well as an entrancing life-size terracotta sculpture of *Diana the Huntress,* executed in 1776 by Jean-Antoine Houdon. The East Gallery holds some more notable 19th-century work, including portraits by Whistler with unusually descriptive names: *Symphony in Flesh Color and Pink, Harmony in Pink and Grey,* and *Arrangement in Black and Brown* should be easy to tell apart. A fine Goya portrait of a young *Officer* pouts here. Downstairs, basement galleries added in 1977 feature special exhibits.

After walking through the least exhausting museum in New York, you can relax in the cool Garden Court and watch the fountains of water stream from the mouths of the little stone frogs.

The museum is located at 1 E. 70th St. at Fifth Ave. (288-0700). Subway: #6 to 68th St. Open Tues.-Sat. 10am-6pm, Sun. 1-6pm. Admission $3, students and seniors $1.50. No children under 10 admitted, and children under 16 must be accompanied by an adult. Group visits are by appointment only. Coats, cameras, and large handbags must be checked in the coat room.

The Whitney Museum

The 1966 futuristic fortress by Marcel Breuer makes a fitting setting for the premier museum devoted solely to American art. At the onset of the 20th century, as progressive American artists found it virtually impossible to sell or exhibit their work, Gertrude Vanderbilt Whitney became the leading patron of U.S. art until her death in 1942. She organized the museum's opening in 1931. Today the museum's predominantly 20th-century collection numbers some 8500 paintings, sculptures, drawings, and prints. Turn right as you enter to see the ebullient shapes of Calder's *Circus,* one sculptor's fantasy world. A periodically shown videotape allows you to see these many-hatted dolls put on a 3-ring sword-swallowing extravaganza, with a little help from their creator.

The second floor's somewhat dank space hosts changing shows, as does the airier area on the fourth floor. The third floor contains the permanent exhibition "20th Century American Art: Highlights from the Permanent Collection," as well as the theater used by the Film and Video Department, showing independent, noncommercial film and video.

Catch the highlights from the "Highlights" collection. Don't miss Ad Reinhardt's *Abstract Painting, Number 33.* Andy Warhol pops up with his *Ethel Scull, 36 Times,* a silkscreen multiple portrait. Jasper Johns' *Three Flags* of 1958 explores levels of American symbolism. And admire the rich strokes of color and of genius in Robert Rauschenberg's 1960 *Summer Rental + 2.* George Segal is represented by a characteristic life-sized white plaster sculpture, a monument to the mundane: *Walk, Don't Walk* presents the viewer with a street-corner, three people, and an electric street sign. Willem de Kooning's *Woman on Bicycle* and Jackson Pollock's *Number 27* hang side by side. Georgia O'Keeffe's *Flower Abstraction* of 1924 overwhelms the room with its oversized presence.

The Store Next Door is next door, at 943 Madison Ave.; it sells all sorts of artsy things, including books, postcards, and jewelry. (Open Sun. noon-6pm, Wed. and Sat. 10am-6pm Tues. 10am-8pm.)

The museum is located at 945 Madison Ave. at 75th St. (information 570-3676; special tours 570-3652; films 570-0537). Subway: #6 to 77th St. Museum open Tues. 1-8pm, Wed.-Sat. 11am-5pm, Sun. noon-6pm. Admission $4, seniors $2, students free. Free Tues. 6-8pm. Weekend gallery talks at 2 and 3:30pm. Free tours of third floor collection Tues. and Sun. at 1:30, 3:30, and 6:15pm; Wed.-Fri. at 1:30 and 3:30pm.)

The Cooper-Hewitt Museum

Since 1976, Andrew Carnegie's regal Georgian mansion has been the setting for the Smithsonian Institute's National Museum of Design. Pieces from the museum's vast permanent collection are culled into topical and fascinating shows on aspects of contemporary or historical design.

Many guest exhibits sojourn here. Recent shows have featured legions of intricate porcelain cups, saucers, and bowls from Denmark and a breezy review of contemporary designer fabrics. The Cooper-Hewitt has often done justice to the offbeat, in funky exhibits like "The Outdoor Chair" (a collection of creative sitting receptacles in the museum's backyard), or their delightful history of the pop-up book, including works dating from the 16th century.

This design museum has an impressive design itself. Cast-iron archways alternate with intricately carved ceilings and an operatic staircase, and everything basks in the pale, gilded glow of muted candelabras.

The museum is located at 2 E. 91st St. (860-6894) at Fifth. Subway: IRT #4, 5, or 6 to 86th St. Open Tues. 10am-9pm, Wed.-Sat. 10am-5pm, Sun. noon-5pm. Admission $3, seniors and students $1.50, under 12 free. Free Tues. 5-9pm.

American Museum of Natural History

The largest science museum in the world, in a suitably imposing Romanesque structure guarded by a statue of Teddy Roosevelt on horseback. Play Tarzan to a stationary herd of elephants in Akeley Memorial Hall or fancy yourself an intrepid anthropologist as you survey artifacts from Central America and Asia. The notorious *Star of India* shines in the Guggenheim Hall of Minerals but *Gaslight's* Gregory Anton and his gem-dazzled ilk morbidly obsess over the surfeit of sparklies in the Morgan Memorial Hall of Gems. Admire the largest unexploded Pop Rock on earth here—the 34-ton *Ahnghito,* the largest meteorite ever retrieved. Or seek audience with the greatest king of them all—the 45-ft.-long *Tyrannosaurus Rex.*

The museum is located at Central Park West (769-5100), at 79th to 81st St. Subway: Central Park West IND to 81st St. Open Sun.-Tues. and Thurs. 10am-5:45pm, Wed. and Fri.-Sat. 10am-9pm. Suggested donation $4, children $2. Free Fri.-Sat. 5-9pm.

The museum also houses **Naturemax** (769-5650), a cinematic extravaganza on New York's largest movie screen, four stories high and 66 ft. wide. Admission $4, children $2; Fri.-Sat. double features $5.50, children $3. The **Hayden Planetarium** (769-5920) offers outstanding multi-media presentations. Seasonal celestial light shows twinkle in the dome of the **Theater of the Stars,** accompanied by astronomy lectures. Admission $4, seniors and students $3, children $2. Electrify your senses with **Laser Rock** (769-5921) on Fri.-Sat. nights. Admission $6.

Other Major Collections

Museum of American Folk Art, 2 Lincoln Center (496-2966), on Columbus Ave. between 65th and 66th. A modest but pleasant historical record of American aptitude for needlework, embroidery, painting, smithing, and weather-vaning. The museum provides special programs for children and crafts demonstrations for all ages. Folk dancers and storytellers often materialize to liven up the place. The gift shop will make you reconsider throwing away that unwanted piece of wood. Open daily 9am-9pm. Free.

Museum of Broadcasting, 25 W. 52nd St. (752-7684), between Fifth and Sixth. Boob tube bric-a-brac now vastly expanded in a new building. Select your favorite from over 40,000 classic radio and TV programs (as well as 1000 commercials) to enjoy on one of 100 individual monitors. Special screenings can be arranged for groups. Monthly retrospectives focus on legendary personalities and landmark shows. Open Tues. noon-8pm, Wed.-Sat. noon-5pm. Tours Tues. at 1:30pm. Suggested admission $4, students $3, seniors and ages under 13 $2.

The Cloisters, Fort Tryon Park, upper Manhattan (923-3700). Subway: IND A through Harlem to 190th St. From the train station take a right and head through the park. Buses leave regularly from the Metropolitan Museum's main building. In 1938, Charles Collen brought the High Middle Ages to the edge of Manhattan in the form of this offshoot of the Metropolitan Museum, building a monastery from pieces of 12th- and 13th-century French and Spanish cloisters, and adding a new tower. Retreat to the air-conditioned Treasury to admire the Met's rich collection of medieval art. See 15th-century playing cards with symbols based on dog hunting instead of hearts and clubs. Examine the countless books drawn by neurotic monks who detailed intricately the sensational 3-D biblical scenes carved in boxwood miniature. Gaze at the priceless Unicorn Tapestries, or wander through airy archways and manicured gardens installed with European treasures, like the ghoulish marble fountain in the Cuxa Cloister. (Open March-Oct. daily 8:30am-5:15pm, Nov.-Feb. Tues.-Sun. 9:30am-4:45pm. Donation, which includes admission to the Metropolitan Museum of Art's main building.)

Museum of Holography, 11 Mercer St. (925-0526), just north of Canal St. The most important institution in the development of this new art form that bends light, using a laser to create a 3-D image. Simple holograms now appear on most credit cards, but they are a far cry from the stunning works in this collection. A must-see for art-lovers with an open mind. The main floor has 2 galleries with changing exhibitions and selections from the permanent collection. Downstairs, check out a new interactive workshop. Open Tues.-Sun. 11am-6pm. Admission $3.50, seniors and students $2.50.

International Center of Photography, 1130 Fifth Ave. (860-1778) at 94th St. Subway: Lexington Ave. IRT #6 to 96th St. Housed in a landmark townhouse built in 1914 for *New Republic* founder Willard Straight. Historical, thematic, contemporary, and experimental works. Open Tues. noon-8pm, Wed.-Fri. noon-5pm, Sat.-Sun. 11am-6pm. Admission $3, seniors and students $1.50. Free Tues. 5-8pm. Midtown branch at 77 W. 45th St. (869-2155). Open Mon.-Fri. 11am-6pm, Sat. noon-5pm. Free.

The Jewish Museum, 1109 Fifth Ave. (860-1889, recorded information 860-1888), at 92nd St. Subway: Lexington Ave. IRT to 96th St. The permanent collection of over 14,000 works details the Jewish experience around the house and throughout history and ranges from antiques and ceremonial objects to contemporary masterpieces by Marc Chagall and Frank Stella. Numerous exhibitions trace the threads of history and culture of Jewish communities dispersed around the world; other exhibitions examine Jewish themes in contemporary art, as in the recent "Gardens and Ghettoes: the Art of Jewish Life in Italy." Open Sun. 11am-6pm, Mon., Wed. and Thurs. noon-5pm, Tues. noon-8pm. Closed Fri.-Sat., major Jewish holidays, and some national holidays. Admission $4.50, seniors, students, and ages 6-16 $2.50. Free Tues. 5-8pm.

National Academy of Design, 1083 Fifth Ave. (369-4880), between 89th and 90th. Founded in 1825 to advance the "arts of design" in America: painting, sculpture, architecture, and engraving. Currently the academy hosts exhibitions, trains young artists, and serves as a fraternal organization for distinguished American artists. The Academy is home to the fourth largest collection of American art in the country. The collection includes paintings, sculptures, drawings, prints, and architectural designs. Winslow Homer, Frederic Edwin Church, John Singer Sargent, Thomas Eakins, and others represent the 19th century in the permanent collection. The impressive assortment of contemporary artists and architects includes Isabel Bishop, Richard Estes, Robert Rauschenberg, Robert Ventura, and Philip Johnson. The permanent collection is supplemented by regular exhibitions exploring the history of American design and its European influences. The Academy is quartered in a 19th-century dollhouse mansion, remodeled by Ogden Codman in 1913. Inside you will find all the ingredients of a classic townhouse: checkered floors, ornate ceilings, columns, and, of course, a winding Cinderella staircase. In the petite ballroom on the first floor, a *Venus de Milo* replica rises proudly from a four-wheel pushcart. Open Tues. noon-8pm, Wed.-Sun. noon-5pm. Admission $2.50, seniors and students $2.

Brooklyn Museum, 200 Eastern Pkwy. at Washington Ave. (638-5000). Subway: IRT #2 or 3 to Eastern Pkwy. The collection of folk art draws from sources as wide-ranging as indigenous New York (brownstone "sculpture" and period rooms) and the People's Republic of China. Changing exhibits display celebrated and unusual works, with superb painting shows. The Egyptian collection is considered third only to those of Cairo and the British Museum. On long-term loan are the "lost" Williamsburg murals. Products of Roosevelt's 1930s Works Project Administration, 200 of the abstract works originally resided in public housing throughout Williamsburg. Years of neglect and layers of paint later, the murals were widely assumed to be ruined. But recently several well-known artists' creations have been rediscovered and restored.

Smaller and Specialized Collections

American Craft Museum, 40 W. 53rd St. (956-3535), across from MOMA. Subway: IND to 53rd St. The museum's *raison d'être* is to exhibit and interpret fine craft pieces by artists working in all contemporary media, from brooches to grandiose tapestries. Even a three-story atrium did not prove too cumbersome for this collection. Five times per year, the museum contrives ingenious, fun exhibitions around particular subjects or materials. Past shows have included "Made with Paper," "American Glass Now," and the no-holds-barred "Plastic as Plastic." Open Tues. 10am-8pm, Wed.-Sun. 11am-5pm. Admission $3.50, seniors and students $1.50. Free Tues. 5-8pm.

Museum of the American Indian, at Broadway and 155th St. (283-2420), in Harlem. Subway: #1 to 157th St. Since 1916, the world's largest and most comprehensive collection of Native American artifacts, though in recent years the museum has been faced with demands by Native American groups for the return of their art. The duck decoys from the Archaic period (8000-1000 BC) call into question any pretensions to reality by modern fake ducks. A North American pipe collection reveals the widespread use and cultural diversity of tobacco smoking. The Mesoamerican collection is light, but the Alaskan masks, with their bugged-out, trippy wind chimes, make up for it. Open Tues.-Sat. 10am-5pm, Sun. 1-5pm. Admission $3, seniors and students $2.

AT&T Infoquest Center, 550 Madison Ave. (605-5555), at 56th St. An interactive exhibition that attempts to explain the information age, sponsored by the pseudo-monopoly with the soothing voice. Everything you wanted to know about photonics, microelectronics, and computer software, plus 40 interactive computer displays and 2 robots. But were afraid to ask. Open Tues. 10am-9pm, Wed.-Sun. 10am-6pm. Free.

China House Gallery, 125 E. 65th St. (744-8181), between Park and Lexington. Part of the China Institute. Ever-changing exhibitions borrowed from museums aroung the world. Open Mon.-Fri. 10am-5pm. Free.

IBM Gallery of Science and Art, 590 Madison Ave. (745-6100), at 56th St. User-friendly exhibits covering a wide range of art. Previous exhibits have included 18th-century painting and the use of computers in excavating Pompeii. Meet fun, interactive mainframes or see the permanent show titled "Mathematica: A World of Numbers and Beyond." Highlights include a probability machine demonstrating a "Normal Distribution Curve," a Mobius Strip, and optical illusions. Open Tues.-Sat. 11am-6pm. Free.

New Museum of Contemporary Art, 583 Broadway (219-1222), between Prince and Houston St. Dedicated to the destruction of the canon and of conventional ideas of "art," the New Museum supports the hottest, the newest, and the most controversial. Interactive exhibits, video tricks aplenty. Many works deal with the politics of identity—sexual, racial, and ethnic. And once a month an artist herself sits in the front window and converses with passersby. Open Wed.-Thurs. and Sun. noon-6pm, Fri.-Sat. until 8pm. Suggested donation $3.50; artists, seniors, and students $2.50; ages under 12 free.

The New-York Historical Society, 170 Central Park West (873-3400), at 77th St. Permanent collection and special exhibits celebrate urban history and culture in New York City and throughout America. The hyphen in the name, which dates back to 1804, recalls the original spelling of "New York." The historical society takes special pride in preserving and documenting every possible historical object, no matter how trivial. As a result of such care for the simplest human things, the collection achieves an unusual kind of personal warmth. Everything from scraps of ancient "New-York" advertisements to the merchandizable majesty of Tiffany lamps can be found here, preserved for posterity. Open Tues.-Sun. 10am-5pm. Admission $3, seniors $2, children $1.

Studio Museum in Harlem, 144 W. 125th St. (864-4500). Subway: Broadway IRT to 125th St. A permanent collection of avant-garde work (mostly by African Americans who have lived in Harlem) complemented by special exhibits. Open Wed.-Fri. 10am-5pm, Sat.-Sun. 1-6pm. Admission $2, seniors and students $1; seniors free on Wed.

Ukrainian Museum, 203 Second Ave. (228-0110). Exhibits of Ukrainian history, design, and folk art, strongest in textiles. Seasonal exhibits on crafts related to Christmas and Easter, including an extraordinary collection of Easter eggs, decorated in intricate traditional patterns using batik techniques. Upcoming special exhibits include a show of avant-garde book designs from the constructivist period. Open Wed.-Sun. 1-5pm. Admission $1, seniors and students 50¢.

Guinness World of Records, 350 Fifth Ave. (947-2335), located in the Concierge Level of the Empire State Building. Subway: #6 to 33rd St. If the world around you seems a little too normal, don't fret; this exhibit will reassure you that life is thankfully much wackier than your next-door neighbors Bob and Barb would have you believe. Replicas of the world's tallest, shortest, oldest and most foiblesome individuals on display. A computer entertains with fun factoids on the world's oddest animals, including the hen who took to heart the Lord's command to be fruitful and multiply, laying 371 eggs in 264 days. The Guinness laser-disc juke-box will rock you into nostalgia with historic recordings of legendary hits from the Beatles to Presley. Open daily 9am-8pm, with extended hours during peak season.

The Asia Society, 725 Park Ave. (288-6400), at 70th St. The Asia Society brings you the best of the East. Exhibitions, musical performances, popular and independent Asian cinema, an acclaimed "Meet the Author" series, and informative cultural symposia on topics such as Buddhist art or the political survival of Cambodia. Open Tues.-Sat. 11am-6pm, Sun. noon-5pm. Admission $2, seniors and students $1.

Kostabi World, 544 W. 38th St. (268-0616), off Eleventh Ave., in a 3-story former stable across from the Javits Center. Kostabi's world is a bustling factory of modern merchandizable art, in which an entire crew of multimedia artists realizes the inspirations of the master schemer. Kostabi signs all the works himself, which explains how he has managed more than 33 one-person shows in the last few years. Unfortunately, only the gallery is open to the public. Open daily 10am-6pm.

New York Public Library, at the Central Research Building, Fifth Avenue and 42nd St. (869-8089). Items in the collection range from a Gutenberg Bible to a 1939 Warsaw telephone directory, from Thomas Jefferson's handwritten version of the Declaration of Independence to T.S. Eliot's typewritten manuscript of *The Wasteland,* all available for reference and study. The Library also sponsors special exhibitions, on display in the foyer of the main building. Open Mon.-Sat. 10am-6pm. Admission (to the exhibits) $2, $1 seniors and students.

Intrepid Sea-Air-Space Museum, Pier 86 (245-0072), at 46th St. and Twelfth Ave. Bus M16, M27 or M106 to W. 46th St. Housed in a veteran World War II and Vietnam War aircraft carrier, *Intrepid* is dedicated to the military art. Pioneers Hall shows mock-ups, antiques and film shorts of flying devices from the turn of the century through the 20s. For a thrill, see the wide-screen film that puts the viewer on a flight deck as jets take off and land—a Navy glory-flying gimmick, but breathtaking nonetheless. Technologies Hall exhibits recount the exploration of the depths of the ocean and the far reaches of space. Come admire large rockets, complex weaponry, and other artifacts of 20th-century warfare, or become more intimate with aircraft on the Intrepid's 900-ft. flight deck. Open Wed.-Sun. 10am-5pm. Admission $6, seniors $5, children $3.25.

Museum of the City of New York, 103rd St. and Fifth Ave. (534-1672), in East Harlem next door to El Museo del Barrio. Subway: IRT to 103rd St. Originally located in Gracie Mansion, the museum moved to its own, roomy, neo-Georgian quarters in 1932. It tells the story of New York City through historical paintings, Currier and Ives prints, period rooms and furnishings, Duncan Phyffe furniture, Tiffany silver pieces, ship models, and a quorum of exquisitely made toys and dolls. Hosts frequent puppet shows for children, lectures and concerts for adults. Suggested contribution $4. Open Tues.-Sun. 10am-5pm, Sun. 1-5pm.

El Museo del Barrio, 1230 Fifth Ave. (831-7272), in East Harlem. Subway: Lexington Ave. IRT to 103rd St. The only museum in the U.S. devoted exclusively to the art and culture of Puerto Rico and Latin America. Begun in an East Harlem classroom, the project has blossomed into a permanent, significant museum that features video, painting, sculpture, photography, theater, and film. Permanent collection includes pre-Columbian art and *Santos de Palo,* hand-crafted wooden saint figures from Latin America. Open Wed.-Sun. 11am-5pm. Suggested contribution $2, seniors and students $1.

Nicholas Roerich Museum, 319 W. 107th St (864-7752), between Broadway and Riverside Drive. Subway: #1 or 9. A friend and close collaborator of Stravinsky on Diaghilev's *Ballets Russes,* Nicholas Roerich painted, philosophized, archaeologized, studied things Slavic, and founded an educational institution to promote world peace through the arts. Located in a stately old townhouse, the museum brims with Roerich's landscapes, books, and pamphlets on art, culture and philosophy. Free. Open Tues.-Sun. 2-5pm.

Alternative Museum, 17 White St. at Sixth Ave. (966-4444). Founded and operated by artists for nonestablished artists. New visions, social critique, and funky productions are the name of the game. Poetry reading and folk/jazz/traditional concerts, with an emphasis on the international and the unusual. Free. Open Tues.-Sat. 11am-6pm.

Jacques Marchais Center of Tibetan Art, 338 Lighthouse Ave., Staten Island (718-987-3478). Take bus #74 from Staten Island ferry to Lighthouse Ave, then turn right and walk up the hill. Who would have imagined that you can discover the East on Staten Island? Begun in 1947 on a bequest of Mrs. Jacques Marchais, the museum houses the largest private collection of Tibetan art in the Western Hemisphere. Art and artifacts of other Asian cultures also well represented. Tours, lectures, and classes on everything from Tibetan family rituals to origami. Set amid dramatic cliffs, the museum, itself a replica of a Tibetan monastery, exudes serenity. A few hours here and you may convert. Open April-Nov. Wed.-Sun. 1-5pm.

American Museum of Immigration, Liberty Island (363-3200). Located at the base of the Statue of Liberty, the museum chronicles the history of immigration from the arrival of the Dutch onward. Documents and memorabilia trace the conception and creation of the statue Her original torch is here on display. Free. Open daily 9am-5pm.

Goethe House, 666 Third Ave. (472-3960) at 41st St. Subway: #6 to 42nd St. Exhibits the work of German artists and concentrates on German themes. Open Tues. and Thurs. noon-6pm, Wed. and Fri. until 5pm.

Parsons Exhibition Center, at Parsons School of Design, 2 W. 13th St. (741-7572) at Fifth Ave. Smorgasbord of design arts features illustrations, photography, student art and computer art. Open Mon.-Fri. noon-6pm.

Museum of Colored Glass and Light, 72 Wooster St. (226-7258), between Spring and Broome St. Subway: #6 to Spring St./Lafayette St. Go west on Spring and turn left on Wooster St. Don't just sit in the dark; come see glass panels, made from thousands of delicately colored fragments, that channel, refract, and diffuse light and startle the imagination. Created by Raphael Nemeth, these compositions reflect the breakthrough of a new medium into the seemingly exhausted world of art. Nemeth, dissatisfied with the reflective poverty of natural light, uses 10,000 volts of pure electricity to highlight the artwork. It's worth the charge; admission $1. Open daily 1-5pm.

Hall of Fame for Great Americans, 181st St. (220-8366) and University Ave. Located on the grounds of City University of New York in the Bronx. Spurning the flimsiness of wax, this poignant albeit decrepit hall features nearly 102 bronze busts of America's immortals, among them Alexander Graham Bell, George Washington Carver, Abraham Lincoln, Booker T. Washington, and the Wright brothers. Free. Open Mon-Fri, 10am-5pm.

Schomburg Center for Research in Black Culture, 515 Lenox Ave. (862-4000), at 135th St. The world's largest collection of documentation on black history and culture includes more than 15,000 hours of taped oral history. Shows by African and African-American artists. Free. Open Mon.-Wed. noon-8pm, Thurs.-Sat. 10am-6pm.

Knoedler Gallery, 19 E. 70th St. (794-0550), between Madison and Fifth. The oldest New York-based art gallery, founded in 1846, the Knoedler stocks the same contemporary lumina-ries you'll find at the Whitney Museum—Richard Diebenkorn, Robert Motherwell, Robert Rauschenberg, and Frank Stella: all this and exciting exhibitions too. Open Tues.-Fri. 9:30am-5:30pm, Sat. 10am-5:30pm.

The Center for African Art, 54 E. 68th St. (861-1200), off Fifth Ave. Permanent exhibitions and frequent visiting shows profile African history and culture through art. Recent exhibits have included *Wild Spirits,* featuring menacing Shaman artifacts, and a show of portraits by black artists around the world. Also conducts scholarly research and organizes guided expedi-tions to Africa. Open Tues. 10am-8pm, Wed.-Fri. until 5pm, Sat. 11am-5pm, Sun. noon-5pm. Admission $2.50, seniors and students $1.50.

Museum of Bronx History, at Bainbridge Ave. (881-8900) and 208th St. Run by the Bronx Historical Society on the premises of the landmark Valentine-Varian House, the museum presents historical narratives of the borough of Bronx. Exhibitions change regularly; call for schedule. Open Sat. 10am-4pm, Sun. 1-5pm; Mon.-Fri. 9am-5pm by appointment. Admission $1.

The Bronx Museum of the Arts, at 165th St. and Grand Concourse (681-6000). Set in the rotunda of the Bronx Courthouse. The museum focuses on young talent, collecting works on paper by minority artists and sponsoring twice-yearly seminars for local artists which cul-minate in group showings. Open Sat.-Thurs. 10am-4:30pm. Suggested admission $1.50, sen-iors and children $1.

Black Fashion Museum, 155-157 W. 126th St. (662-1320). Founded in 1979, the BFM main-tains a permanent collection and mounts two yearly exhibits devoted to garments designed, sewn, or worn by Blacks from the 1860s to the present. Alongside the creations of popular contemporary black designers you'll find two slave dresses, an inaugural gown designed for Mary Todd Lincoln by Elizabeth Keckley, a dress made by Rosa Parks, and costumes from Broadway musicals like *The Wiz.* Open by appointment Mon.-Fri. noon-8pm. Donations wel-come.

City Gallery, 2 Columbus Circle (974-1150), in the Visitors Center at 58th and Broadway. Subway: #1, 9, or B, D, A. A gallery devoted to depicting the metropolis at its finest and at its direst. From the nuts that hold together New York bridges to the nuts who design the city's skyscrapers, they've got it covered. Open Mon.-Fri. 10:30am-6pm. Free.

Whitney (branch), Equitable Center, at Seventh Ave. and 51st St. (554-1000) A prodigious Roy Lichtenstein mural spans the lobby. The small museum can be covered in a leisurely half hour, but first-rate works make every minute worthwhile, from Lichtenstein's 2/3-D sculpture *Gold Fish Bowl* to the eternally refreshing Calder. (Open Mon.-Wed., Fri., 11am-6pm, Thurs. 11am-7:30pm, Sat. noon-5pm.)

Godwin-Ternbach Museum, at Queens College, Kissena Blvd. (997-5759 or 520-7179) in Flushing. Founded in 1981, the museum has a permanent collection of 2000 objets d'art, rang-ing from the ancient to the abstract. Its Klapper Library Art Center hosts changing exhibi-tions. Currently undergoing renovations, scheduled to be completed in the summer of 1991.

Chung-Cheng Art Gallery, Sun Yat Sen Hall, at St. John's University (990-6161, ext. 6582), Union Tpk. and Utopia Pkwy. in Jamaica, housed in a pagoda-like building on the campus of St. John's. Specializes in Asian arts.

Living Museum Building 75, Creedmoor Psychiatric Center, 80-45 Winchester Blvd. (464-7525) in Queens Village. This sprawling multi-media art installation has been created by the patients of the psychiatric center, under the guidance of artist-in-residence and Museum Di-rector Bolek Gracznski. The only museum in the country devoted entirely to the work of the mentally ill. A unique opportunity for the contemplation of the meaning of "insanity." Tours by appointment.

International Design Center of New York, 29-10 Thomson St. (392-3682 or 937-7474), Long Island City. Set of chic designer showrooms, complete with an atrium, located in the shell of two former factory buildings. Works from the world's finest contemporary furniture, fash-ion, and interior design firms.

Galleries

The city overflows with small galleries. Some focus on buying and selling, others on exhibiting small-scale shows. While gallery-hopping can be great fun, bear in mind that many of the commercial galleries have an elite image to maintain, and may not be the most accommodating places in the world for tourists not planning to shell out $5000 for a 200-lb. granite porcupine. Always ask before invading the premises, especially if you travel in a pack of two or more.

SoHo is a wonderland of galleries, with a particularly dense concentration lining Broadway between Houston and Spring St. The 79 different establishments in this two-block stretch can keep you busy for a while. Madison Ave. between 84th and 70th has a generous sampling of ritzy showplaces, and another gaggle of galleries festoons 57th St. between Fifth and Sixth. Most of these places are open from Tuesday to Saturday, from 10 or 11am to 5 or 6pm.

Pick up a free copy of the *Gallery Guide* at any major museum or gallery; it lists the addresses, phone numbers, and hours of virtually every showplace in the city, and comes equipped with several handy maps to orient you on your art odyssey. Extensive gallery information can also be found in the "Art" section of *New York* magazine as well as in the omniscient "Goings on About Town" in *The New Yorker.*

Sindin, 1035 Madison Ave. (288-7402) at 79th St. Master graphics, prints, and etchings by Picasso, Miró, Matisse, and Rivera. Open Tues.-Sat. 10am-5:30pm.

Solomon & Co., 959 Madison Ave. (737-8200) at 75th St. Painting and sculpture by Calder, Christo, Dubuffet, Francis, Rivera, Warhol. Open Mon.-Sat. 10am-5:30pm.

Saidenberg, 1018 Madison Ave. (288-3387). Leger, Masson, Matisse, Picasso, Popova, Rodchenko. Open Tues.-Fri. 10am-5pm, Sat. 1-5pm.

La Boetie, Inc./Helen Serger, 9 E. 82nd St. (535-4865). "Avant-Garde Work on Paper." Drawings, watercolors, and collages by Matisse, Miró, Leger, Klee, Schwitters. Open Tues.-Fri. 10am-5:30pm.

Barry Friedman, 1117 Madison Ave. (794-8950). A deliciously diverse European sampler—Russian constructivism, purism, kineticism, and Italian futurism, plus objects and furniture from the Wiener Werkstatte, Bauhaus, De Stijl, and art deco movements. Open Mon.-Sat. 10am-6pm.

Magidson Fine Art NYC, 1070 Madison Ave. (288-0666). Works by Albers, Calder, Francis, Johns, Lichtenstein, Haring, Combas, Picasso, Chagall, and Miró sojourn in this small but intensely exciting gallery space. Open Tues.-Sat. 10am-6pm.

Eduard Nakhamkin Fine Arts, 1055 Madison Ave. (570-2666). Come here to see what glasnost is all about. Irreverent, witty Soviet art, hot from the cold country. Large and bold. Open Tues.-Sat. 10am-6pm.

Pasquale Iannetti, 946 Madison Ave. (472-4300). Fine original prints and drawings by Rembrandt, Dürer, Renoir, Toulouse-Lautrec, Picasso, Miró, and Matisse. Open Tues.-Sat. 10am-6pm.

Isselbacher, 41 E. 78th St. (472-1766). Late 19th- and 20th-century master prints: Vuillard, Toulouse-Lautrec, Matisse, Picasso, Chagall, Klee, Kandinsky, Alechinksky, Beckmann, and Bonnard. Open Tues.-Fri. 10:30am-5:30pm.

Mark Milliken Gallery, 1200 Madison Ave. (534-8802). Contemporary American crafts presented in a casual atmosphere. If you think that folk art means embroidery and spoon carving, you'll be surprised. A kinder, gentler avant-garde. Open Mon.-Sat. 10am-6pm.

Circle Gallery of Animation and Cartoon Art, 780 Seventh Ave. (765-6975). Tired of highbrow art? Visit your favorite feather-brained friends. Stills and acetate shots galore plus posters, prints, and manuscripted comics. And that's not all, folks. Open Mon.-Fri. 10am-9pm, Sat. 1-9pm, Sun. noon-6pm.

Entertainment

Theatre

*When you are away from old Broadway you are only
camping out.*

—George M. Cohan

If you think, wandering through Times Square for the first time, that you've just
stepped onto the set of *Guys and Dolls* or *42nd Street,* you pretty much have. Nowhere do the distinctions between theatre and life collapse as absurdly and calmly
as in New York. If the actors seem to be missing their cues, perhaps it's time you
bought a ticket for the real thing. The lullaby of old Broadway still lulls the weary.
Thirty-four official Broadway playhouses cluster between Sixth and Ninth Ave.,
41st and 48th St., most of them concentrated on 45th and 46th, right by Times
Square's neon suns.

You can still get a feel for the Broadway of the past by stopping in on a weepy
revival or two. *Fiddler on the Roof* and *Gypsy* have both come back to remind everyone how it's done. Today, rising production costs and ticket prices—along with dis-
integrating musical tastes—have changed the face of Broadway. But don't despair
if you've dreamt of some Ethel Merman and you arrive to find her understudy, a
plume of floating dry ice. There's more to Broadway than spectacle and gimmick:
some shows still bother to tell a story and have a few great characters and even
a tap dancer or two—or a hundred. Others continue a strong tradition of dramatic
comedy; some (don't tell) even innovate.

Broadway tickets cost about $50 each, when purchased through regular channels.
TKTS sells half-price tickets to Broadway shows on the same day of the performance. TKTS (Times Square Theatre Center) has a booth in the middle of Duffy
Square (the northern part of Times Square, at 47th and Broadway). They will usually come to about $25 each (plus $1.50 service charge per ticket), paid in cash or
traveler's checks. Tickets usually go on sale after 3pm for evening performances
(curtain usually at 8pm), and at 10am for Wednesday or Sunday matinees. The line
can be long, snaking around the traffic island a few times, but it moves quickly.
Arrive before selling time. To see what shows are on sale, you can peek at the board
near the front of the line, where the names of the shows are posted. Then consult
a copy of *The New Yorker* for superior short descriptions of currently running
shows, or try *The New York Times.*

You may prefer to wait on line downtown, where TKTS has an indoor branch
in the lobby of 2 World Trade Center. The lines are usually shorter here. (Booth
operates Mon.-Fri. 11am-5:30pm, Sat. 11am-3:30pm.) You can also obtain matinee
tickets here one day before the show. TKTS has a third branch in Brooklyn, at
Court and Montague St. (Open Tues.-Fri. 11am-5:30pm, Sat. 11am-3:30pm.)

You can get a similar discount with "twofers,"(i.e. two fer the price of one) ticket
coupons that float around the city at bookstores and libraries and such, and can
always be found at the New York Visitors and Convention Bureau. They are usually
for the old Broadway warhorses—shows which have been running strong for a very
long time.

For information on shows and ticket availability, call the **NYC/ON STAGE hotline** at 587-1111, **Ticket Central** between 1 and 8pm at 279-4200, the **Theatre Development Fund's** toll-free number 800-STAGE-NY (782-4369), or the **New York
City Department of Cultural Affairs** hotline at 956-2787.**Off-Broadway** theatres are
a group of smaller theatres, mostly located downtown. Officially, these theatres have
between 100 and 499 seats; only Broadway houses have over 500. Off-Broadway
houses frequently offer a more offbeat or countercultural group of shows, with
shorter runs, though sometimes Off-Broadway shows run for long periods of time

or make the transition to Broadway houses. Tickets run from $10-20. The best of these theatres, many of them vanguards in the development of U.S. playwriting, huddle around the Sheridan Square area of the West Village. They include the **Circle Rep,** at 161 Sixth Ave. (807-1326), the **Circle in the Square Downtown,** at 159 Bleecker St. (254-6330), the **Lucille Lortel,** at 121 Christopher St. (924-8782), the **Cherry Lane,** at 38 Commerce St. (989-2020), and the **Provincetown Playhouse,** at 133 MacDougal St. (477-5048). Eugene O'Neill got his break at the Provincetown. Elisa Loti made her U.S. debut at the Actors Playhouse. You can buy tickets to the larger Off-Broadway houses at the TKTS booths. Off-Off-Broadway is not a comical designation (at least not deliberately) but an actual category of theatres, where shows play limited engagements at lower ticket prices.**The Public Theatre,** 425 Lafayette St. (598-7150), has become inextricably linked with founder Joseph Papp, one of the city's leading producers and favorite sons. The six theatres here present a wide variety of shows; the theatre is in the middle of presenting its Shakespeare Marathon, which includes every single one of the Bard's plays down to *Timon of Athens.* The Public Theatre saves one quarter of the seats for every production to be sold at its **Quixtix** for half price on the day of performance (until 6pm for evening performances, and 1pm for matinees). Quixtix also has free tickets to rehearsals, which can prove quite entertaining (or inhumanly boring).

Papp also founded the **Shakespeare in the Park** series, a New York summer tradition which practically everybody in the city has attended (or attempted to, anyway). From June through August, Papp presents two Shakespeare plays at the Delacorte Theatre in Central Park, near the 81st St. entrance on the Upper West Side, just north of the main road there (861-7277). The glorious outdoor amphitheatre overlooks Belvedere Lake and its mini-Dunsinane. Top-notch productions—plus the opportunity to perform Shakespeare in the great outdoors—attract the most important actors around. Recent performances have included *The Taming of the Shrew* with Morgan Freeman and Tracey Ullman, and *Richard III* with Denzel Washington. To acquire free tickets, wait in line at the Delacorte Theatre (you should get there by noon; 2 tickets per person).

The city also boasts the widest variety of ethnic theatre in the country. Although the days of the Lower East Side's Yiddish theatre are long gone, the **Jewish Repertory Theatre,** 344 E. 14th St. (505-2667), continues to produce notable shows (in English). The **Repertorio Español,** currently housed in the Gramercy Arts Theatre at 138 E. 27th St. (889-2850) presents many of its productions in Spanish. Neither the **Negro Ensemble Company** (246-8545) nor the **Pan Asian Repertory Theatre** (245-2660) has a permanent home, but both perform frequently at various locations. For something completely different, visit the **Yueh Lang Shadow Theatre,** 34-41 74th St. (476-6246) in Jackson Heights, Queens, where two-dimensional colored calfskin figures animate classical Chinese literature.

New York has birthed the most exciting and controversial developments in alternative theatre, including that elusive amalgam called "performance art," a combination of stand-up comedy, political commentary, theatrical monologue, and video art, starring the likes of J.J. Doonesbury. Beside the Brooklyn Academy of Music's famous Next Wave festival, a number of Manhattan institutions specialize in this distinctive art form, including **The Kitchen,** at 512 W. 19th St. (255-5793), **Franklin Furnace,** at 112 Franklin St. (925-4671), **Performance Space 122 (P.S. 122),** at 150 First Ave. (477-5288), and the **Theatre for the New City,** at 155 First Ave. (254-1109). **LaMama** at 74A E. 4th St. (475-7710), the most venerable of the lot, helped Sam Shepard get his start.

Broadway Houses

Ambassador Theatre, 215 W. 49th St. (541-6490), between Broadway and Eighth. Built on a slant. Spencer Tracy played here in *The Last Mile* in 1930. In *The Straw Hat Revue* (1939), Danny Kaye, Jerome Robbins, and Imogene Coca parodied the rest of the shows playing on Broadway, anticipating *Forbidden Broadways* to come.

Belasco Theatre, 111 W. 44th St. (354-4490), between Sixth and Seventh. Built in 1907 by David Belasco, a producer extraordinaire who acted, designed, and directed—and fervently believed in spectacle. He equipped the place with an elevator stage that could lower for set changes and a backstage elevator that would ascend to his private apartments. In 1935, the legendary Group Theatre brought Clifford Odets' *Awake and Sing* to the Belasco. The Group Theatre proved the most politically explicit act on Broadway, and four decades later nude revue *Oh! Calcutta!* exploded here as the most sexually explicit.

Booth Theatre, 222 W. 45th St. (246-5969), between Broadway and Eighth. Designer Herts dressed it up in early Italian Renaissance in 1913 and Melanie Kahane modernized it in 1979. Kaufman and Hart's *You Can't Take It With You* opened here, as did Noel Coward's *Blithe Spirit.* Ntozake Shange's poetic *For Colored Girls Who Have Considered Suicide When the Rainbow is Enuf* lasted 742 performances.

Broadhurst Theatre, 235 W. 44th St. (247-0472), between Broadway and Eighth. Designed in 1917 by Herbert J. Krapp, the man who churned out these theatres at the top of the century. Helen Hayes crowned the place with her legendary performance in *Victoria Regina* back in 1935. *Grease* first rocked here, as did *Godspell.* And *Dancin'* hoofed here for 3 years. Ian McKellan played Salieri to Tim Curry's Mozart and Jane Seymour's Constanze in the American premiere of *Amadeus.*

Broadway Theatre, 1681 Broadway (247-3660), between 52nd and 53rd. Built as a movie-house in 1924, with a whopping capacity of 1765. Its first theatrical venture, *The New Yorkers* by Cole Porter and Herbert Fields closed in 20 weeks—it was hard to sell tickets for $5.50 during the Depression. Benefits, featuring Irving Berlin's *This Is the Army* with a cameo by Irv himself, raised money for the Emergency Relief fund during World War II. Soon Oscar Hammerstein did a jazzed-up all-black *Carmen.* A few operas and dance troupes later, the stage saw another musical: *Mr. Wonderful.*—starring Sammy Davis Jr. and Sr. Soon *The Most Happy Fella* dropped in, *The Body Beautiful* dropped out, and Les Ballets de Paris, the Beryozka Russian Dance Company, and the Old Vic flew in to do Shakespeare. Then Ethel Merman brought musical comedy belting back with *Gypsy.* In 1972, *Fiddler on the Roof* ended its run here, breaking previous records with its tally of 3242 performances. Harold Prince revived Leonard Bernstein's *Candide* with labyrinthine staging and multi-level seating, and went on to stage *Evita* here. Here Anthony Quinn starred in the revival of *Zorba.*

Brooks Atkinson Theatre, 256 W. 47th St. (719-4099), between Broadway and Eighth. Designed in 1926 as the Mansfield by very busy architect Herbert J. Krapp. In 1930, *The Green Pastures* opened here, setting southern blacks amidst Old Testament events; it played 640 performances and won the Pulitzer Prize. Marc Blitzstein's revolutionary *The Cradle Will Rock* opened here during a tumultuous snowstorm on December 26, 1947. In the 50s, the struggling theatre served as a TV playhouse. Then in 1960, it was named for the much-loved *New York Times* theatre critic and Harvard grad who had retired from reviewing plays that spring. John Steinbeck's *Of Mice and Men* was revived here with James Earl Jones as Lenny. Ellen Burstyn and Charles Grodin conducted their annual fling here in *Same Time, Next Year* for 1453 performances.

Circle in the Square Theatre, 1633 Broadway (239-6200), between 50th and 51st. Most delightfully in the round, a charming hotbed of things Shavian and Shepardian. Modeled after the downtown theatre by the same name but half the size, it opened with *Mourning Becomes Electra* in 1972. The circular stage has brimmed with sand for Tina Howe's *Coastal Disturbances* and has been strung up with laundry for a recent production of *Sweeney Todd.* Much Molière moseys here.

Cort Theatre, 138 W. 48th St. (239-6200), between Sixth and Seventh. Built in the style of Louis XVI, with a lobby of Pavanozza marble and 999 seats. Katharine Hepburn made her debut here in 1928 in *These Days,* which closed in a week, but later returned in the 50s to star in a blockbuster run of *As You Like It.* Grace Kelly made her first Broadway appearance here too.

Edison Theatre, 240 W. 47th St. (302-2302), between Broadway and Eighth. A pretty small house, dwelling in the Edison Hotel. The long-time home of *Oh! Calcutta!*

Ethel Barrymore Theatre, 243 W. 47th St. (239-6200), between Broadway and Eighth. In 1927 a celebrated actress was blithely appearing in a Maugham play at another theatre when playwright Zoe Atkins approached her and promised that the Shuberts would build her a theatre if she would agree to do a play called *The Kingdom of God.* Ethel Barrymore read and liked it, and soon found herself starring in this play and a series of others. Alfred Lunt, Lynn Fontanne, and Noel Coward appeared here in Coward's *Design for Living.* Described as "a kettle of venom" by Brooks Atkinson, Claire Booth Luce's scathing play *The Women,* with a cast of 40 females, nonetheless ran for 657 performances. *A Streetcar Named Desire* opened here in 1947, starring Jessica Tandy and Marlon Brando, followed by a string of successful straight plays: *Bell, Book, and Candle; Tea and Sympathy; The Desperate Hour;* and *Look Homeward Angel,* which won Ketti Frings the Pulitzer Prize. Lorraine Hansbery's acclaimed *Raisin in the Sun* opened here in 1959, starring Sidney Poitier.

Eugene O'Neill Theatre, 230 W. 49th St. (246-0220), between Broadway and Eighth. Using the Georgian style, Krapp designed this one too, when it was born as the Forrest Theatre back in 1925. In 1959, it was renamed in honor of playwright Eugene O'Neill who had died in 1953. Arthur Miller's *All My Sons* opened here, as did his *A View From the Bridge.* A slew of musicals have come and gone here, followed by a host of Neil Simon plays and some sterner-stuff.

Golden Theatre, 252 W. 45th St. (239-6200), between Broadway and Eighth. Built by Krapp, commissioned by the producer whiz Chanin brothers who wanted the 800-seat space to accommodate intimate artistic work. When *Angel Street,* a strange piece of Victoriana, opened here, skeptical producers ordered only three days' worth of *Playbills*—and the show proceeded to run 1293 performances. Some revues swept through—highlighting Mike Nichols and Elaine May, Yves Montand, and finally the likes of Peter Cook and Dudley Moore in *Beyond the Fringe.*

Imperial Theatre, 249 W. 45th St. (239-6200), between Broadway and Eighth. Built in 1923, it entered the big leagues with *Oh, Kay!* by the Gershwins, with a book by P.G. Wodehouse and Guy Bolton. Rodgers and Hart, and George Abbot, conflated American musicals with Russian ballet in their 1935 hit *On Your Toes.* Cole Porter's *Leave It To Me* introduced to the Broadway stage Mary Martin and a chorus boy named Gene Kelly. Martin returned in *One Touch of Venus,* a show by unlikely collaborators Kurt Weill, S.J. Perelman, and Ogden Nash. Ethel Merman proved there's no business like show business in *Annie Get Your Gun.* Doing what came naturally, Merman managed 1147 performances. *Fiddler on the Roof* opened here on September 22, 1964. *Cabaret* had a brief stint, followed by *Zorba,* followed by *Minnie's Boys,* a musical about the Marx Brothers. *Pippin* opened here in 1972 and ran for 1944 performances. Michael Bennett brought his *Dreamgirls* here in 1981.

Helen Hayes Theatre, 240 W. 44th St. (944-9450), between Broadway and Eighth. It opened in 1912 with only 299 seats and was soon appropriately christened the Little Theatre. Originally designed to stage intimate and noncommercial works, it didn't do too well commercially and closed. It served as New York Times Hall from 1942-1959 and as the ABC TV Studio from 1959-1963, but then went on to host the long-running comedy *Gemini* and Tony Award-winning *Torch Song Trilogy.*

Lunt-Fontanne Theatre, 205 W. 46th St. (575-9200), between Broadway and Eighth. Built in 1910 as the Globe. Carrière and Hastings engineered the seating plan and equipped the place with an oval ceiling panel that could be removed in fair weather. Fanny Brice dazzled here in the *Ziegfield Follies of 1921. No, No Nanette,* featuring hit song "Tea for Two," was a hit here in the 20s. The Globe went dark during the Depression, and then became a moviehouse. In 1957, the City Investing Company fixed it up and named it after dashing drama couple Alfred Lunt and Lynn Fontanne. The restored house hosted new musicals *The Sound of Music* and *The Rothschilds,* and revivals *A Funny Thing Happened on the Way to the Forum* and *Hello, Dolly!* Sandy Duncan flew here as *Peter Pan.*

Lyceum Theatre, 149 W. 45th St. (239-6200), between Sixth and Seventh. The oldest of the lot, designed by Herts and Tallant back in 1903, topped by a 10-story tower with scene shops, carpentry studios, and extra dressing rooms galore. It faced demolition in 1939; playwrights George S. Kaufman and Moss Hart chipped in with some friends and bought it in 1940 and sold it to the Shubert Organization in 1945. *Born Yesterday,* with Judy Holliday, opened here in 1946. *Look Back in Anger* stormed over from England in 1957. In 1980 the 1939 flop *Morning's at Seven* was revived here—and won a Tony Award.

Majestic Theatre, 247 W. 44th St. (239-6200), between Broadway and Eighth. The largest legit theatre in the district and the last of what was formerly the Chanin chain. Rodger and Hammerstein's *Carousel* opened here, as did their short-lived *Allegro* and their hot ticket *South Pacific* which ran 1925 performances. *Camelot,* with Julie Andrews and Richard Burton, charmed Broadway for 873 performances.

Mark Hellinger Theatre, 237 W. 51st St. (757-7064), between Broadway and Eighth. On April 22, 1930, it opened as a Hollywood Theater moviehouse. It became the 51st Street Theatre in 1936. In 1940, Laurence Olivier and Vivian Leigh were Romeo and Juliet here, but soon the movies started playing again. Then in 1949, Anthony Farrell bought the place and named it for Broadway columnist Mark Hellinger. The 50s saw revues and a smattering of Gilbert and Sullivan. Then musical comedy reared its feathered head, starting in 1955 with *Plain and Fancy,* a musical about the Amish. In 1956, *My Fair Lady* won innumerable awards and ran for 2717 performances. *On A Clear Day You Can See Forever* opened here, as did *Jesus Christ Superstar.*

Martin Beck, 302 W. 45th St. (246-0102), between Eighth and Ninth. When built in 1924, it was the only Byzantine-style American theatre. The Abbey Irish Theatre Players descended here in 1932 with classics like *Juno and the Paycock* and *Playboy of the Western World.* Katharine Cornell played Juliet here to Basil Rathbone's Romeo and Orson Welles' Tybalt. Joshua Logan set *The Cherry Orchard* in the deep South in his *The Wisteria Trees.* Tennessee Williams found his way here with *The Rose Tattoo,* starring Maureen Stapleton and Eli Wallach, and *Sweet Bird of Youth,* starring Geraldine Page and Paul Newman. Liz Taylor made her Broadway debut in *The Little Foxes* here in 1981.

Minskoff Theatre, 200 W. 45th St. (869-0550), at Broadway. Not as streamlined as its neighbor, the Gershwin, but equally high-tech. Its 1621 seats have been built 35 ft. in the air. It opened on March 13, 1973, with a revival of *Irene* starring Debbie Reynolds. Nureyev pirouetted through here with the Murray Lewis Dance Company in 1978—followed by a series of short-lived musicals: *The King of Hearts,* a *West Side Story* revival, and *Can-Can,* an extravaganza that closed after 5 days.

Music Box Theatre, 239 W. 45th St. (246-4636), between Broadway and Eighth. Cute, charming, built in 1921 by Sam Harris and Irving Berlin to house Berlin's *Music Box Revues,* this stage braved the Depression with French comedy *Topaze* by Marcel Pagnol, *Once in a Lifetime* by Kaufman and Hart, and Noel Coward's "Mad Dogs and Englishman" ditty sung by Beatrice Lillie in *The Third Little Show.* Music Box production *Of Thee I Sing* became the first musical comedy to win the Pulitzer Prize. The house saw songless metaplay *Stage Door,* starring Margaret Sullavan, and equally straight production *The Man Who Came To Dinner,* which arrived and lingered for 739 performances at the end of the 30s. Soon romantic comedies had upstaged revues, and the house known as the Music Box churned out tuneless *I Remember Mama,* introducing the young Marlon Brando to the stage; Tennessee Williams' *Summer and Smoke;* and William Inge's *Bus Stop. Sleuth* mysteriously endured for 1222 performances, *Deathtrap* for 1609. Irving Berlin maintained a lively financial and emotional interest in the theatre until he died.

Nederlander Theatre, 208 W. 41st St. (921-8000), between Seventh and Eighth. Originally the National Theatre, it opened in 1921. Noel Coward and Gertrude Lawrence trod the stage in a group of plays called *Tonight at 8:30.* Orson Welles and John Houseman transported their Shakespearean productions from the smaller Mercury Theatre. Here Sir John Gielgud and Lillian Gish starred in a failed production of *Crime and Punishment* and star Paul Muni played Clarence Darrow in didactic courtroom drama *Inherit the Wind.* Here Edward Albee premiered his successful *Who's Afraid of Virginia Woolf*—starring Uta Hagen and directed by Alan Schneider—and his more obscure *Tiny Alice.* The Royal Shakespeare Company's *A Midsummer Night's Dream* directed by Peter Brook, came to visit, as did Tom Stoppard's *Jumpers* and Harold Pinter's *Betrayal.* By late 1980 the National-turned-Billy Rose-turned-Trafalgar got dubbed *The Nederlander* in honor of late theatre owner David Tobias Nederlander.

Neil Simon Theatre, 250 W. 52nd St. (757-8646), between Broadway and Eighth. Built in 1927 as the Alvin Theatre by tireless designer Herbert J. Krapp, who gave it a capacity of 1400. In 1934, it hosted Cole Porter's *Anything Goes,* starring Ethel Merman as Reno Sweeney, which blew everyone away. The Lunts' *The Taming of the Shrew,* staged for the Finnish Relief Fund, was soon followed by Pulitzer Prize-winning *There Shall Be No Night* by Robert E. Sherwood, about Russia's invasion of Finland. Lighter fare soon came to the Alvin, in the form of long-running *A Funny Thing Happened on the Way to The Forum* and Stoppard farce *Rosencrantz and Guildenstern Are Dead.* The 70s brought a gaggle of successful musicals—*Company, Shenandoah,* and *Annie.* In 1983, the Alvin was renamed the Neil Simon.

Palace Theatre, 1564 Broadway (757-2626) at 47th St. Sarah Bernhardt, Ethel Barrymore, you name it, they played at the Palace. Once a vaudeville haunt for Houdini, W.C. Fields, and the Marx Brothers, the Palace became a movie house with few spells of musical theater from the 30s to the 50s. Then in 1965, James Nederlander restored it. *Sweet Charity* with Gwen Verdon, choreographed by Verdon's husband Bob Fosse, moved in for a couple of years. Joel Grey starred here, in *George M!* and *The Grand Tour.* Lauren Bacall stopped by to be *The Woman of the Year,* later followed by the more outrageous men of the year in *La Cage aux Folles.*

Plymouth Theatre, 236 W. 45th St. (239-6200), between Broadway and Eighth. Built in 1917. Krapp designed it to seat 1000. Thornton Wilder's *Skin of Our Teeth* emerged here in 1942. A British invasion began with *Equus, Piaf,* and *The Real Thing;* English visitors completely reconstructed the house for the Royal Shakespeare Company's Dickensian 8-hr. marathon *Nicholas Nickleby* which won Tonys for inspiring actor Roger Rees and directors Trevor Nunn and John Caird.

Richard Rodgers Theatre, 226 W. 46th St. (246-0102), between Broadway and Eighth. Prolific architect Herbert J. Krapp sloped the seats L-Z upward so short people in the back would no longer suffer. Here *Finian's Rainbow* charmed Broadway with an Irish lilt—725 performances worth. *Guys and Dolls* opened here in 1950, won 8 Tony Awards, and lasted 1194 performances. Audrey Hepburn transmogrified into Jean Giraudoux's lyrical sprite in *Ondine* in 1954. The 60s brought the new musical *1776*, the 70s, a revival of *No, No, Nanette*. In 1975, Sir John Gielgud directed Maggie Smith in a revival of *Private Lives* and Bob Fosse staged the hit *Chicago*. The 80s brought the sizzling musical *Nine*, based on Fellini's *8½*.

Theatre Royale, 242 W. 45th St. (239-6200), between Broadway and Eighth. Designed by Krapp. This house seats over 1000 and caters mostly to musicals. Tennessee Williams' first Broadway play, *The Glass Menagerie*, moved here from the Off-Broadway Playhouse, starring Laurette Taylor. Julie Andrews made her debut in *The Boy Friend*, a 1954 take-off on 1920s musicals. Thornton Wilder's *The Matchmaker*—which previously flopped as *The Merchant of Yonkers* and later got musicalized as *Hello, Dolly!*—opened here in 1955. Mary Tyler Moore took the man's role in *Whose Life Is It Anyway?* to kick off the gender confusion of the 80s.

St. James Theatre, 246 W. 44th St. (246-0102), between Broadway and Eighth. Built in 1927. Seats 1600 in a Georgian interior. Here "April in Paris" was first sung and Hamlet first soliloquized on the American stage. John Houseman produced, and Orson Welles directed, Richard Wright's chilling *Native Son* here. *Oklahoma!* whirled through in 1943, dazzling New York, running for 2248 performances and launching the careers of Rodgers and Hammerstein. Yul Brenner first took the Broadway stage here in *The King and I* in 1951. Show-offs Laurence Olivier and Anthony Quinn even traded rolès at whim in their remarkable production of Anouilh's *Becket*. *Hello, Dolly!* took the St. James stage from 1964-70, winning 10 Tony Awards. Joseph Papp brought his musical version of *Two Gentleman of Verona* here. Then the St. James started hosting actual musicals again: a '76 revival of *My Fair Lady*, late 70s productions of *On the Twentieth Century* and *Carmelina*, and the 3-ring hit *Barnum* which outlasted them all with 854 performances. Mostly for musicals.

Shubert Theatre, 225 W. 44th St. (246-5990), between Broadway and Eighth. Built in 1913 by Lee and J.J. Shubert in memory of their deceased brother Sam, the Shubert exemplifies Venetian Renaissance design, complete with murals by Lichtenauer. Paul Robeson played Othello here in 1943, with Uta Hagen and José Ferrer. 1932 brought *Americana*, with its depression song, "Brother, Can You Spare a Dime?" Katherine Hepburn thrilled audiences with *The Philadelphia Story* for 417 sold-out performances. *A Chorus Line* opened and closed here after its record-breaking run.

Gershwin Theatre, 1633 Broadway (246-0102), between 50th and 51st. A vast shrine of postmodern art nouveau. It started up in 1972 as the Uris, hosting *Porgy and Bess*, *Sweeney Todd*, and the *Pirates of Penzance* that had inhabited Central Park for the summer. Both *The King and I* and *Mame* got revived here.

Virginia Theatre, 245 W. 52nd St. (977-9370), between Broadway and Eighth. On April 13, 1925, President Coolidge pushed a button in Washington, D.C. that set the floodlights flowing over Shaw's *Caesar and Cleopatra* starring Helen Hayes and Lionel Atwill. Next, Lunt and Fontanne came here with Shaw's *Arms and the Man*. Edward G. Robinson graced the stge in 1927 in Pirandello's *Right You Are If You Think You Are*. Eugene O'Neill's 5-hr. *Mourning Becomes Elektra*, complete with dinner intermission, premiered here. But a series of flops forced the Theatre Guild to lease out the place as a radio playhouse from 1943-50. The American National Theatre and Academy (ANTA) then took over, and started sponsoring experimental productions and straight plays such as *J.B.*, *A Man For All Seasons*, and a revival of *Our Town* with Henry Fonda.

Walter Kerr Theatre, 225 W. 48th St. (582-4022). Built in a record 66 days in 1921 as the Ritz, and only recently christened the Walter Kerr in honor of the gentle critic. It soon became the WPA Theatre, and the Federal Theatre Project staged a number of works here, including *Pinocchio* and T.S. Eliot's *Murder in the Cathedral*. Renovated in the spirit of the 20s by Karen Rosen, the dormant space reopened in 1983 with the juggling, entertaining *Flying Karamazov Brothers*.

Winter Garden Theatre, 1634 Broadway (245-4878), between 50th and 51st. It opened in 1911 as a hall "devoted to novel, international, spectacular and musical entertainment." Al Jolson first appeared in blackface here. The Winter Garden has always been graced by new musical successes, from *Wonderful Town* to *West Side Story* to *Funny Girl*. Here Zero Mostel revived *Fiddler on the Roof*, Angela Lansbury revived *Gypsy*, and the multimedia blitz *Beatlemania* revived Beatles nostalgia. Most recently, set designer John Napier clawed the place apart to create his fantasy dumping ground for *Cats*.

Off-Broadway Houses:

Actors Playhouse, 100 Seventh Ave. S. (691-6226).

American Place Theatre, 111 W. 46th St. (247-0393).

Astor Place Theatre, 434 Lafayette St. (254-4370).

Chelsea Theatre Center, 407 W. 43rd St. (541-8394).

Cherry Lane, 38 Commerce St. (989-2020).

Circle in the Square downtown, 159 Bleecker St. (254-6330).

Circle Repertory Company, 99 Seventh Ave. S. (924-7100).

Colonnades Theatre Lab, 428 Lafayette St. (673-2222).

Criterion Theatre, 1514 Broadway (354-0900)

CSC Repertory Theatre, 136 E. 13th St. (477-5808).

Douglas Fairbanks Theatre, 432 W. 42nd (239-4321)

Ensemble Studio, 12 W. End Ave. (664-9882)

Harold Clurman Theatre, 412 W. 42nd (695-3401).

Hudson Guild 441 W. 26th (760-9800).

John Houseman Theatre, 450 W. 52nd (564-8038).

Lamb's, 130 W. 44th (997-1780).

Lucille Lortel, 121 Christopher St. (246-0102).

Manhattan Theatre Club, 131 W. 55th St. (246-8989).

Orpheum, 126 Second Avenue. (477-2477).

Playhouse 91, 316 E. 91st St. (831-2000).

Playwrights Horizon, 416 W. 42nd St. (279-4200).

Promenade Theatre, 2162 Broadway (580-1313).

Provincetown Playhouse, 133 MacDougal St. (477-5048).

Public Theatre, 425 Lafayette St. (598-7150).

Ridiculous Theatrical Company, 1 Sheridan Square (260-7137).

Roundabout/Stage One, 333 W. 23rd St. (242-7800).

Roundabout/Stage Two, 307 W. 26th St. (242-7800).

Samuel Beckett Theatre, 410 W. 42nd. St. (594-2826).

Sullivan Street Playhouse, 181 Sullivan St. (674-3838).

Theatre of Saint Peter's Church, Lexington Ave. and 54th St. (751-4140).

Westside Arts Theatre, 407 W. 43rd St. (541-8394).

Village Gate, Bleecker and Thompson St. (475-5120).

Opera and Dance

Lincoln Center (877-1800) does for New York culture what Paris does for Jacques Brel. For a full schedule of events, write Lincoln Center Calendar, 140 W. 65th St. 10023; or call the Lincoln Center Library Museum (870-1630).

The **Metropolitan Opera Company** (362-6000), opera's highest expression, plays on a Lincoln Center stage as big as a football field. During the regular season (Sept.-May Mon.-Sat.), if you don't fear heights or mind risking a nosebleed, get upper balcony seats for $11-15. But standing room in the orchestra can't be beat at $10—stand next to the opera freaks who've brought the score with them and follow along. In the summer, watch for free concerts in city parks (362-6000).

At right angles to the Met, the **New York City Opera** (870-5570), under the direction of Beverly Sills, mounts performances of old warhorses—many in translation—and of new U.S. works. Its recently introduced English "supertitles" have set trends on the American opera scene. "City" now offers a summer season and keeps its ticket prices low year-round ($7-55; standing room, back row, top balcony $5). Call to check the availability of rush tickets on the night before the performance you want to attend, then wait in line the next morning.

The **Light Opera of Manhattan (LOOM)**, 316 E. 91st St., between First and Second (831-2000), sticks to Gilbert and Sullivan and similar oldie-but-goodie operettas. (Tickets $17.50-20, students $12.) Check the papers for performances of the **Amato Opera Company**, 319 Bowery (228-8200), and the **Bel Canto Company**, which perform in churches around the city.

When the city opera isn't using the New York State Theatre (877-5570), the late great George Balanchine's **New York City Ballet**, the oldest dance company in the U.S., steps in. (Performances Dec.-Jan. and May-June. Tickets $6-46, standing room $4.) **American Ballet Theatre** (477-3030), Balanchine's greatest rival, dances at the Met during the late spring and for about two weeks in summer. Under Mikhail Baryshnikov's guidance, ABT's eclectic repertoire has ranged from Kirov grand-style Russian to experimental American.

The **Alvin Ailey American Dance Theatre** (997-1980) bases its repertoire of modern dance on jazz, spirituals, and contemporary music. It often takes its well-integrated moves on the road, but always performs at the **City Center** in December. Tickets ($15-40) can prove difficult to obtain. Write or call the City Center weeks in advance, if possible. The **Martha Graham Dance Co.**, 316 E. 63rd St. (838-5886), performs original Graham pieces during their October New York season. The founder of modern dance, Graham revolutionized 20th-century movement with her psychological, rather than narrative, approach to choreography. (Tickets $15-40.) Keep an eye out for performances of the **Merce Cunningham Dance Co.**, and the **Paul Taylor Dance Company**, usually in spring. Two companies in Queens specialize in traditional ethnic folk dance: the **Ballet Folklorica de Dominican Republic**, 25-28 89th St. (651-8427) in Jackson Heights, and **The Yori African Dance Ensemble**, 89-21 169th St. (657-4264) in Jamaica.

Half-price tickets for many music and dance events can be purchased on the day of performance at **Bryant Park**, on 42nd St. (382-2323) between Fifth and Sixth. (Open Tues. and Thurs.-Fri. noon-2pm and 3-7pm, Wed. and Sat. 11am-2pm and 3-7pm, Sun. noon-6pm.) Monday concert tickets are available on the Sunday prior to the performance. Call the above number for daily listings.

Music

You need only wander through the subway stations to hear a Romanian accordionist, a Caribbean *marimba* player, or a gypsy guitarist. Every ethnic group that has come to New York has brought centuries of musical heritage with it. Inherited from Storyville and New Orleans, jazz came into its cool in the smoke-filled caverns of 52nd Street, now known as "Swing Street." It was in New York that John Cage translated random data into musical scores. More recently, the hardships of urban life below the poverty line has given birth to rap music.

Musicians advertise themselves vigorously; you should have no trouble finding the notes. Begin with the ample listings in the *New York Times, The New Yorker*, or *New York* magazine. Below is a partial list of the city's vast offerings. Keep in mind that many events, such as park or outdoor music, are seasonal.

The **Lincoln Center Halls** are alive and bopping with the sounds of music. **Avery Fisher Hall** paints the town ecstatic with its annual Mostly Mozart Festival, featur-

LET'S GO Travel

1991 CATALOGUE

LET'S PACK IT UP

Let's Go Pack/Suitcase:
Lightweight and versatile. Carry-on size
(24" x 14" x 10"). Hideaway suspension (internal
frame). Waterproof Cordura nylon. Lifetime
guarantee. Detachable day-pack.
Navy blue or grey.
10014 Suitcase   **$144.95**
Free shoulder strap and
Let's Go travel diary.

Passport/Money Case:
Zippered pouch of waterproof nylon.
7 1/2" x 4 1/2". Navy or grey.
10011 Passport Case   **$6.50**

Undercover Neck Pouch:
Ripstop nylon and soft Cambrelle. 6 1/2" x 5".
Two separate pockets. Black or tan.
10012 Neck Pouch   **$6.95**

Fanny Pack:
Pack cloth nylon. Three compartments.
Charcoal or Marine Blue.
10013 Fanny Pack   **$13.95**

Let's Go Travel Books:
Europe; USA; Britain/Ireland;
France; Italy; Spain/Portugal/Morocco; Greec
Israel/Egypt; Mexico; California/Hawaii; Pacif
Northwest; London; New York City.
1016 Specify USA; Europe   **$13.**
1017 Specify Country   **$12.**
1018 Specify New York or London   **$9.**
This is $1.00 off the cover price!

**International Youth Hostel Guide for
Europe and the Mediterranean:**
Lists over 3,000 hostels. A must.
10015 IYHG   **$10.**
FREE map of hostels worldwide.

Sleepsack: (Required at all hostels)
78" x 30" with 18" pillow pocket. Durable
poly/cotton, folds to pouch size. Washable.
Doubles as a sleeping bag liner.
10010 Sleepsack   **$13.**

LET'S G⊕® Travel
We wrote the book on budget travel

1991-1992 American Youth Hostel Card

(AYH): Recommended for every hosteler, this card is required by many hostels and brings discounts at others. Applicants must be US residents. Valid internationally.

10022	**Adult AYH (ages 18-55)**	**$25.00**
10035	**Youth AYH (under age 18)**	**$10.00**
10023	**Plastic Case**	**$0.75**

FREE directory of hostels in the USA.

ET'S SEE SOME I.D.

91 International Student ntification Card (ISIC): Provides counts on accommodations, cultural events, fares and, this year, increased accident/ dical insurance. Valid from 9/1/90–12/31/91.

020	**ISIC**	**$14.00**

EE "International Student Travel Guide" d insurance information.

91 International Teacher Identification rd (ITIC): Similar benefits to the ISIC.

024	**ITIC**	**$15.00**

EE "International Student Travel Guide" and urance information.

91 Youth International Education change Card (YIEE): Similar benefits the ISIC. Available for non-students under age of 26. Valid by calendar year.

021	**YIEE**	**$14.00**

EE "Discounts for Youth Travel."

Eurail Pass: the best way to travel Europe.

First Class

10025	15 Day	**$390.**
10026	21 Day	**$498.**
10027	1 Month	**$616.**
10028	2 Months	**$840.**
10029	3 Months	**$1042.**

Flexipass

10030	5 Days within 15	**$230.**
10031	9 Days within 21	**$398.**
10032	14 Days in 1 month	**$498.**

Eurail Youth Pass (Under 26)

10033	1 Month	**$425.**
10034	2 Months	**$560.**
10036	15 days in 3 months	**$340.**
10037	30 days in 3 months	**$540.**

Child Passes (age 4-12) also available.

All Eurail Pass orders include FREE: Eurail Map, Pocket Timetable and Traveler's Guide.

LET'S G® Travel
One source for all your travel needs

LET'S GET STARTED

PLEASE PRINT OR TYPE. Incomplete applications will be returned.

International Student/Teacher Identity Card (ISIC / ITIC) application enclose:
   ❶ Dated proof of current FULL-TIME status: letter from registrar or administration
      or copy of transcript or proof of payment.
   ❷ One picture (1½" x 2") signed on the reverse side.
      Applicants must be at least 12 years old.

Youth International Exchange Card (YIEE) application enclose:
   ❶ Proof of birthdate (copy of passport or birth certificate).
      Applicants must be age 12 – 25.
   ❷ One picture (1½" x 2") signed on the reverse side.
   ❸ Passport number _____ ❹ Sex: M   F

Last Name_____First Name_____

Street_____
            Continental U.S. Addresses only. We do not ship to P.O. Boxes
City_____State_____Zip Code_____

Phone (   )_____—_____Citizenship_____

School/College_____Date Trip Begins_____/_____/_____

ITEM NUMBER	DESCRIPTION	QUAN-TITY	UNIT OR SET PRICE		TOTAL PRIC
			Total Price		
			Total Shipping and Handling		
			Optional Rush Handling (add $9.95)		
			Mass. Residents (5% sales tax on Gear, Books & Maps)		
				TOTAL:	

Shipping and Handling
If your order totals: Add
Up to 30.00 $2.00
30.01 to 100.00 $3.25
Over 100.00 $5.25

Please allow 2-3 weeks for delivery.
RUSH ORDERS DELIVERED WITHIN ONE WEEK OF OUR RECEIPT.
Enclose check or money order payable to
Harvard Student Agencies, Inc.

LET'S GO® Travel

Harvard Student Agencies, Inc. Thayer Hall–B Cambridge, MA 02138
(617) 495-9649   1-800-5LETSGO

ing stellar performers like Itzhak Perlman, Acia de Larrocha, Jean-Pierre Rampal, and Emanuel Ax. Show up early; major artists and rising stars often give half-hour pre-concert recitals, free to ticketholders. The festival runs from July 1 to August 26. **The New York Philharmonic's** regular season commences in mid-September. To charge tickets, call CENTER CHARGE at 874-6770 (Mon.-Sat 10am-8pm, Sun. noon-8pm). For other information call 799-9595.

Alice Tully Hall serves up an eclectic mix of music, dance, theatre, video, and performance art. Composer Philip Glass is a regular here. Founded four years ago, the Serious Fun! Series brings you a universe of oddities. The summer '90 season erupted with the world premiere of John Moran's *The Manson Family: Helter Five-0*—a multi-media opera conflating the Charles Manson saga with the 1970s TV series "Hawaii Five-0." Box office open Mon.-Sat. 11am-6pm, Sun. noon-6pm. For information call 362-1911; for tickets CENTER CHARGE at 874-6770.

The main course at the **Metropolitan Opera House** is serious opera, though it dabbles in other mediums. Come summertime, you can catch some of the world's greatest touring dance companies at the Met. (Box office open Mon.-Sat. 10am-8pm, Sun noon-6pm.) Credit card and sales information 362-6000.

The New York City Opera loads its bases at the **New York State Theatre.** Summer '90 repertoire highlights included Mozart's *Le Nozze Di Figaro* and Herr Sondheim's **A Little Night Music.** (Box office open Mon. 10am-7:30pm, Tues.-Sat. 10am-8:30pm, Sun 11:30am-7:30pm.) For information call 870-5570.

For the price of an orchestra seat at the New York Opera, you can take yourself and your eight closest friends to the **Lincoln Center Plaza, Damrosch Park,** or the **Guggenheim Bandshell** to hear jazz, salsa, and big band delights. (Fountain Plaza concerts cost $5.) Free shows featuring international dance troupes, comedy outfits, and Lincoln Center's trip down memory lane with their new midsummer Night Swing Dancextravaganza. Held late June to late July at the Lincoln Center every Wednesday to Saturday night, the LC invites couples and singles to tango, swing, shimmy, or foxtrot. Some even do the lindy hop. The Center provides dance floor, café, and bands fronted by Old Ironside's Illinois Jacquet, Tito Puente, Panama Francis, and Pe De Boi. For information call 877-2011.

Come summertime, the **New York Philharmonic** heads for the parks (July 30-Aug. 20). Zubin Mehta and his band bring transport the classics to the great outdoors, holding concerts in all five boroughs. For information call 800-376-2721. **Central Park Concerts/Summerstage,** at 72nd St. in Central Park (east of the Bandshell), includes nearly 30 free music, dance, and opera events, along well as the spoken words of distinguished writers and a video drive-in. Summer 1990 brought David Byrne, Buddy Ivy, Donizetti, Joyce Carol Oates, and Lawrence Ferlinghetti, and introduced New York to the evocative sounds of Senegal's Baaba Mall and Zaire's Papa Wemba, the father of "rumba rock." The **Coca Cola Concert Series** (399-4444) brings types like Tears for Fears, Tracy Chapman, Frank Sinatra, Fleetwood Mac, and Anita Baker to **Jones Beach** (tickets $22.50; concerts at 8pm).

Carnegie Hall, Seventh Ave. at 57th St. (247-7800), one of the greatest musical auditoriums in the world, profiles opera singers, jazz singers, instrumental soloists, and symphony orchestras from Beatles to Bernsteins. (Tickets usually $15-30; prices vary.)

In the heart of Rockefeller Center, entertainment palace **Radio City Music Hall** (247-4777) has a bill of great performers that reads like the invitation list to the Forbes Anniversary bash: Ella Fitzgerald, Frank Sinatra, Billy Crystal, Jane Fonda, Diana Ross, and Sting, among others. (Box office at 50th St. and Ave. of the Americas. Open Mon.-Sat. 10am-8pm, Sun. 11am-8pm.) Tickets range from $20 to $1000 for the "Night of 100 Stars."

Radio City comes to the riverfront with their newest outdoor amphitheatre—the **Reebok Riverstage** at Pier 84. In a dramatic new design, the audience now faces the river as the sunset and boat beacons shed natural lighting. Rock groups give concerts there, along with jazz, reggae, and occasional comedy specials. Reebok Riverplace gleams at Twelfth Ave. and 43rd St., but tickets ($17 in advance, $19.50 day of the show) must be purchased at the Radio City box office.

Beacon Theatre, 2124 Broadway (496-7070) at 75th St., hosts special films, dance groups, international performing arts groups, and mainstream soul and rock artists. Knowledgeable critics like M. Scott Krivan consider the magnificent auditorium, decorated by Walter Ablschlater, to be the next best concert hall after Radio City's. **Madison Square Garden,** Seventh Ave. and W. 33rd St. (563-8300), America's premier entertainment facility, hosts over 600 events and nearly 6 million spectators every year, as wells as the Knicks and the Rangers (see Sports). Regular MSG offerings include exhibitions, trade shows, rock concerts, boxing matches, rodeos, dog, cat, and horse shows, circuses, graduations, tennis games, and the odd presidential convention.

The following music schools host frequent concerts: **Bloomingdale House of Music** 323 W. 108th St., (663-6021), just off Broadway, and the **Greenwich House Music School,** 120 Claremont Ave. (749-2802), just off the intersection of Broadway and W. 122nd St. Students and professional musicians give many free performances; tickets, when required, range from $8-12.

The landmark **Town Hall** (840-2824), an elegant pavilion with excellent acoustics, hosts a wide variety of cultural events. Tenacious trio McKim, Mead & White designed the place in 1921. Joan Sutherland made her debut here. The Town Hall, located at 123 W. 43rd St., between Sixth Ave. and Broadway, has a seating capacity of 1498.

Museums do their bit for metropolitan music. The **Metropolitan** posts a schedule of performances covering the sound spectrum from traditional Japanese music and Russian balalaika to all-star classical music recitals. Some concerts are free with museum admission; others charge $10 and up for tickets. For ticket information or a brochure, call Concerts and Lectures at 535-7710. **The Frick Collection** hosts occasional Sunday afternoon chamber music concerts, with music piping into the idyllic garden court. You can sit back in the lush, marmoreal setting and imitate Cicero listening to the Muses in a Roman courtyard. Or you can just enjoy the music. For information call 288-0700. Free concerts come to the garden of the **Cooper-Hewitt Museum** (860-6868) from June through August. (See Museums.)

Founded in 1859, the **Brooklyn Academy of Music (BAM)** has compiled a colorful history of magnificent performances: here Pavlova danced and Caruso sang while Edwin Bootz waxed quizzical as *Hamlet* and Sarah Bernhardt played *Camille.* BAM is the seat of the Brooklyn Philharmonic. Its fleeting opera season lasts from March to June. In 1990 BAM performed Mozart's *La Finta Giardinera* and Kurt Weill's *The Seven Deadly Sins.* Opera tickets cost $15-60. The annual Next Wave Festival has floated artists like Philip Glass and Laurie Anderson into the spotlight. The Brooklyn Academy of Music stands at 30 Lafayette St., between Felix and Ashland Place. Charging $4, a Manhattan Express Bus makes the round trip to BAM from 51st and Lexington for each performance. To get to the Academy by subway, take the #2, 3, 4, 5, or D, M, or Q to Atlantic Ave. Take B, N, or R to Pacific and you'll be one block from BAM.

Cultural life on the Upper East Side revolves around **The 92nd Street Y,** located on Lexington Ave. The Y's Kaufmann Concert Hall seats only 916 people and offers an intimate setting unmatched by New York's larger halls, with flawless acoustics and the oaken ambience of a Viennese salon. The Y is the home of the **New York Chamber Symphony** under the fiery direction of Gerard Schwartz. The Chamber Symphony's repertoire covers everything from Telemann and Rameau to the works of contemporary masters like Pijton, Diamond, and Stravinsky. In addition, the Y hosts a panoply of world class music. The Distinguished Artists Series, dating back to the late 30s, has featured all the big names from Segovia and Schnabel to Yo-Yo Ma, Alfred Brendel, and Schlomo Mintz. Other notable series include Chamber Music at the Y, Mastersingers, Fascinatin' Rhythm featuring too hot to touch jazz, Brandenburg Festival, Young Concert Artists for the up-and-coming properties, and annual installments of the decade-long restrospective of the music of Franz Schubert (series currently in its fourth year.) Other events include the running series of literary readings produced by the 51-year-old Poetry Center and the most provocative lecture forum in New York. For further information call 996-1100.

Quartered in Abraham Goodman House at 120 W. 67th St. between Broadway and Amsterdam, the **Merkin Concert Hall** offers eclectic, ethnic, and contemporary music alongside more conventional selections. A typical week at the Merkin might include love songs and laments spanning 400 years, classical and modern Chinese music, and the choral, folk-inspired works of Bartok and Shostakovich. The intimate theatre seats 457. For more information call 362-8719.

Symphony Space (864-5400) on Broadway and 95th, a former skating rink and cinema turned performing arts center, also delves into the eclectic. Notable former performers and untiring supporters of Symphony Space include Itzak Perlman, Pinchas Zuckerman on violin, Billy Taylor on jazz piano, and Estelle Parjay in various roles. (Box office open Tues.-Sun. noon-7pm; telephone orders Tues.-Sun. noon-6pm.) **The Colden Center for the Performing Arts** at Queens College in Flushing, Queens, has a beautiful theatre and a year-round program of international quality concerts, opera, and dance—usually at world-class ticket prices. For program information call 793-8080. (Subway: #7 to Main St., Flushing, and then the Q17 or Q25-34 bus to the corner of Kissena Blvd. and the LIE.) Fans of old-fashioned Americana may prefer the **Yankee Tunesmiths Ancient Fife and Drum Corps.** (Call 845-3133 for information.) **The Ukrainian Bandura Ensemble of New York,** 84-82 164th St. (658-7449) in Jamaica, Queens, keeps its own tradition alive.

Music in Churches

New York's churches wed the pristine with the upbeat in their capacity as music halls. Though the true godfathers of gospel keep the faith farther uptown, the Midtown sacred jazz scene belongs to **Saint Peter's.** On the first Sunday of every month, St. Peter's hosts a gala jazz mass. On the other Sundays, at 5pm, jazz vespers are intoned, followed at 7pm by a full-fledged jazz concert. ($5 donation for the concert.) In addition, the hippest ministry in town brings you art openings and exhibits, theatre, lectures, and more. (See Theatre and Midtown Sights.) John Garcia Geyel, Pastor to the Jazz Community, oversees all tuneful good deeds. St. Peter's scats at 619 Lexington Ave. at 52nd St. (435-2200.)

The **Cathedral of St. John the Divine,** Amsterdam and 112th, presents an impressive array of concerts, art exhibitions, lectures, theatre, and dance events. Call the box office for information at 662-2133. Farther uptown, between 120th and 122nd St. on Riverside Drive (864-2929), the **Theatre at Riverside Church** (capacity 275) hosts theatre, music, dance, and video performances. **St. Michael's Church** on Amsterdam Ave. and 11th St. (663-0555) offers similar fare. On a smaller scale, **St. Paul's Chapel,** built in 1776 and located on Broadway between Church and Fulton St. is Manhattan's only surviving pre-Revolutionary War church. George Washington came here to pray after his inauguration. The exquisite interior, lit by Waterford crystal chandeliers, provides the perfect setting for free concerts of classical and church music. (Concerts Mon. and Thurs. at 12:10pm, and Tues. at 12:45pm.) Call 602-0747 for information.

Movies

Hollywood makes the movies, but New York popularizes them. Most movies open in New York weeks before they're distributed across the country, and the response of Manhattan audiences and critics can shape a film's success or failure nationwide. Just grab a copy of any newspaper for an overview of what's playing. Magazines such as *New York* and *The New Yorker* provide plot summaries and evaluations in their listings.

A number of museums show artsy flicks downstairs. Check out the **Metropolitan Museum of Art,** Fifth Ave. at 82nd St. (570-3939), which shows free films in the summertime (with museum admission) on Fridays and Saturday at 7pm, usually fairly standard silver screen and foreign classics (box office opens at 5pm on the day of the performance; limit 4 tickets per person). The **Museum of Modern Art: Roy and Nivta Titus Theatres,** 11 W. 53rd St. (708-9490), serves up an unbeatable diet of three great films per day (free with museum admission). Or try **Adam Clayton**

Powell, Jr., State Office Building, at 163 W. 125th St. (873-5040) off Seventh Ave. for contemporary and classic cinema created by and about African Americans as well as work done by black filmmakers from South America, Africa, and the Caribbean. (Admission $5, seniors and students with ID $3. Lectures by contemporary filmmakers $5.)

   The 68th Street Playhouse, on Third Ave. (734-0302) specializes in first-run foreign films. For cinematic exposure to Chinese culture, go to the **Sun Sing Theater,** 75 E. Broadway (619-0493). The **Thalia Soho,** 16 Vandam St. (675-0498), features classic foreign and U.S. revivals, as do **Theater 80 St. Mark's,** 80 St. Mark's Place (254-7400) and **Biograph Cinema,** 225 W. 57th St. (582-4582), between Seventh and Broadway. For an inspiring movie-going experience, try the **Ziegfeld Theater,** 141 W. 54th St. (765-7600). One of the last grand movie houses that hasn't been sliced up into a "multiplex," the Ziegfeld offers standard box-office attractions.

   If you have a taste for hot political film festivals, try the 92nd St. **"Y,"** 1395 Lexington Ave. (427-6000). The **8th St. Playhouse** (674-6515), between MacDougal St. and Sixth Ave., features music films by day and cult classics by night. Its midnight series includes the *Rocky Horror Picture Show* on Friday and Saturday, a campy classic—expect your fellow moviegoers to put on the best show ($6).

   The American Museum of the Moving Image, 35th Ave. at 36th St., Astoria, Queens (718-784-4520) has three theatres for the screening of their pet film series. They also show videos, silent films, comedy films from the golden era, and retrospectives of great actors and directors. Movies are free with a paid admission to the museum. (Admission $5, seniors and students $2.50.)

   Anthology Film Archives, 32-34 Second Ave. at E. 2nd St. (505-5181), a forum for independent filmmaking, focuses on the contemporary, the off-beat, and the avant-garde chosen from U.S. as well as foreign production. The resident cinema guru has created the Archives' most enduring series—"The American Narrative"—featuring 300 great American films. (Admission $5, students with ID $4.)

   The Brooklyn Museum, 200 E. Parkway, Brooklyn (718-638-5000), shows U.S. and foreign films in conjunction with their exhibitions. Showings include documentaries, art films, and children's programs. (Free with museum admission.)

   Charas Teatro La Terrazza, 360 E. 10th St. (982-0627), a Lower East Side collective, profiles the diverse artistic expressions of ethnic groups in New York City. Charas screens movies, hosts dance festivals, and sponsors performances by Latino and Caribbean music ensembles. The film series usually runs from June to October.

   The Collective for Living Cinema, 41 White St. (925-2111), combines two cinematic specialties—Hollywood legends and new productions by the local avant-garde. The collective also runs exhibits, workshops, and seminars related to modern cinema. Call ahead to see what they've got up their collective sleeve.

   Followers of Eastern European cinema should contact the **Ethnic Folk Arts Center,** 66 W. 12th St. (691-9510) for details on their popular annual series of notable Czech, Hungarian, Soviet, and Polish films. Francophiles can satisfy their craving for Godard by inquiring at the **French Institute/Alliance Française** about current film offerings. The institute is located at Florence Gould Hall, 55 E. 59th St., but its films are screened at Tinker Auditorium, 22 E. 60th St. Each year, **The Japan Society** mounts five prodigious retrospectives of the greatest Japanese achievements in film. The screenings take place on Fridays at 6:30pm and the film schedule can be obtained by visiting the society at 333 E. 47th St. or by calling 752-0824.

   Untiring adherents of the avant-garde should contact the **Millenium Film Workshop,** 66 E. 4th St. (673-0090). This group presents 75 programs of primarily experimental 16mm films from September through June. If you're visiting in May, you might want to check out New York University's student film retrospective. NYU shows over 200 student works at screenings that run from 1pm to 1am. The price is right: $5, less with student ID. For information, inquire at the Loeb Student Center, 566 LaGuardia Place, or call 998-1795.

If you've grown disgusted with the cinematic offerings of the bourgeois capitalist superstructure, you may wish to learn of the subversive activities at **Revolution Books,** 13 E. 16th St. (691-3345). On auspicious nights, films, videos, and lectures are presented in the crowded bookstore. The schedule varies unpredictably but dedicated revolutionaries have been known to make do; plus, the price ($2) will please the proletarian purse.

For a real deal, check out the library. All New York Public Libraries show free films ranging from documentaries to classics to last year's blockbusters. Screening times may be a bit erratic, but you can't beat the price.

Eclectic and cosmopolitan fare fills the menu at the **Public Theatre,** 425 Lafayette St. (598-7171). **Angelika Film Center,** 18 W. Houston St. (995-2000), boasts six theatres showing new Hollywood hits as well as off-beat and foreign films. **Loews 19th Street East 6,** Broadway at 19th St. (260-8000), shows all of the blockbusters all of the time. The **Carnegie Screening Room,** Seventh Ave. between 56th and 57th (757-2131), is a subsidiary of Carnegie Hall, and hence presents no Schwarzenegger, but lots of well-read cinema at the same location as the **Carnegie Hall Cinema** (265-2520). **Lincoln Plaza 1, 2, and 3,** Broadway at 63rd St. (757-2280), specializes in contemporary foreign cinema. At the **Children's Sculpture Garden,** 112th St. and Amsterdam, on Wednesdays in the summertime, you can see silent films shown with live organ accompaniment. (Call 662-2133 for the schedule.)

TV

Yes, TV. Trade an insult with David Letterman or ask a sensitive question of Phil Donahue's guests. Several TV shows film in the Big Apple before a live audience. To join the starstruck throng, call the guest relations offices at the networks about ticket availability. (NBC 664-4444; ABC 887-7777; CBS 975-4321.) Tickets for seats are often in great demand, but are distributed by the networks without charge. Plan ahead.

Radio

Classic Rock	WNEW 102.7, WXRK 92.3
Top 40	WRKS 98.7, WHTZ 100.3
Country	103.5
News	WCBS 880AM, WINS 1010AM
Public (Talk and Music)	WBAI 99.5
Rap	shows Fri.-Sat. night; Red Alert on 98.7 10pm-midnight, Chuck Chillout on 107.5 10pm-2am
Sports	WFAN 60AM

Bars and Clubs

A wilderness of human flesh;
Crazed with avarice, lust and rum,
New York, thy name's Delirium.
    —*Byron R. Newton, Owed to New York, 1906*

It's your fault if you're bored in New York. Bars and clubs kick hard nightly all over the city. If you're low on funds, fill up during Happy Hour at a nondescript bar or pick up a couple of 40-oz. Buds from a deli before you hit the scene. Any club you get into will hit you with a mean cover and then try to push $5 mixed drinks on you. You may end up buying a few, but it'll cost you less if you stick in one place for a long time and order pitchers. In the volatile nightlife scene, bars and clubs rise and fall like successive empires, and new institutions are built upon the ruins of old, decayed ones. Clubs have distinctive hours of operation, best described as fluid. Owners themselves often don't know what their club will be like from week to week. They do know that they'll be open late, or rather, early. Show up someplace at 10pm and you'll probably be the first on the dance floor. Crowds don't arrive at many spots until 11pm or midnight, and by 1am things get going. The lights often go out between 4 and 6am. Those still charged with adrenalin at dawn will have to seek out an "After Hours." They flourish all over the city. Ask a knowledgeable bartender or a cool New Yorker where to find one; printing names would lead to their demise. In fact, the city's hippest club, **The Deep** doesn't have a single location—it surreptitiously hops around from bar to bar. You may find yourself waiting outside a club for a long time. If you don't have the "look," expect to wait on line indefinitely. Wearing black or being a single female should up your odds of getting through. On the positive side, there's always another place to try, no matter what the hour. Cover charges vary during the week—Fridays and Saturdays cost the most (up to $20 per person). Weekends also bring flocks of out-of-towners. For lower covers and entertaining crowds, try "clubbing" early in the week, particularly on Wednesdays. You can often find complimentary or reduced fare passes to clubs at the New York Convention and Visitors Bureau or at Village music stores stacked by the register.

Although *New York* magazine, the *Village Voice,* and *After Dark* list who's playing, showtimes, and sometimes cover charges, you should always call ahead to check. The most extensive listings can be found in *The Music Exchange* and *Good Times,* two pop-music newspapers, available at most stores on **Music Row** on 48th St. between Sixth and Seventh. For students, the New York University/Greenwich Village area (especially the East Village) makes a good starting point. Those with a little more cash can try First or Second Ave. in the 60s and 70s, an area sprinkled with chic, sleek clubs. A preponderance of gay bars and discos can be found in the West Village along Greenwich Ave. and farther west.

Good listings of gay and lesbian happenings appear in the *Village Voice,* as well as in the *Gay Guide,* a free publication distributed at alternative bookstores and bars, or the *New York Native,* a somewhat racy gay newspaper sold at most newsstands. In general, men far outnumber women at gay clubs. Much lesbian socialization is underground.

It can be difficult (and futile) to distinguish alternative nightlife from downtown nightlife in general: the hippest clubs have one or two "gay nights" a week, and same-sex couples can go "clubbing" in most with-it places. Club schedules change; be sure to call ahead to make sure that you know what (and who) you'll find when you arrive.

Dance Clubs

> *New York's like a disco, but without the music.*
> —Elaine Stritch

Palace de Beauté, 860 Broadway (228-8009), between 17th and 18th St. A new club, full of unrealized potential. Excellent DJs, including Jellybean, attract an uptown moussewielding and downtown leather-clad crowd. Open Tues.-Sat. 10pm-4am. Cover $15.

M.K., 204 Fifth Ave. (779-1340) at 27th St. Subway: Broadway BMT to 28th St. Once trendy, now slipping, but still worth a gander. Four floors, each with own decor, lure glitterati with snob appeal; designed to imitate an old "gentleman's club." Open daily 7:30pm for dinner, 11pm-2am for dancing. Cover Sun.-Thurs. $5, Fri.-Sat. $15.

Building, 51 W. 26th St. (576-1890). A hip-hop crowd pulses in a sci-fi setting. The dancing sizzles as D.J. Kid Capri from the Bronx asks, "How many people gonna get sex tonight?" The floor roars. Open Thurs.-Sat. 10pm-4am. Cover $5-10.

Nell's, 246 W. 14th St. (675-1567), between Seventh and Eighth. Subway: Seventh Ave. IRT to 14th St. Dingy neighborhood belies the sumptuous opulence of the huge Victorian-style sitting room inside. Overstuffed chairs, chandeliers, and bejeweled Beautiful People upstairs. Angular dance floor downstairs. Posing Paramusians in tow. Nell's is not a gay club, nor does it have a designated gay night, but it is a popular gay spot. So long as you look like you have just stepped out of a Polo ad no one cares what you do. Open daily 10pm-4am. Cover Sun.-Thurs. $5, Fri.-Sat. $10.

Tramps, 45 W. 21st St. (727-7788). Screaming violins and clattering washboards pack the sweaty dance floor. Louisiana Zydeco rocks nightly with help from blues, reggae, and rock bands. Call for schedule and cover.

Spo-Dee-o-Dee, 565 W. 23rd St. (206-1990), at Eleventh Ave. At the long antique bar, you can listen to live music or gaze at the most beauteous of the Beauteous People. Two sets, blues and rock, with dancing in between. Open daily 6pm-4am. Cover $10, plus 2-drink minimum.

Mars, 30 Tenth Ave. (691-6262), on West End Drive, way over on the West Side, practically on the Hudson River. Formerly the notorious "Danceteria." Housed in a one-time meat packing factory with roof access. Each floor has a different theme; a sight to behold. Thurs. often rap night. Sun. gay night. Open Thurs.-Sun. 10pm-4am. Cover Fri.-Sat. $15, Thurs. and Sun. $10.

Cave Canem, 24 First Ave. (529-9665), between 1st and 2nd St. Restaurant with dance floor in an old Roman bath. Trendy classic. Open Tues.-Sun. 6pm-4am. Cover $5 on weekends.

The Pyramid, 101 Ave. A (420-1590), between 6th and 7th. Subway: Lexington IRT to Astor Place. No sign over the door, just a big lighted pyramid. Transvestite punk and 60s lighting. Those seeking "unusual" will fit right in. Avant-garde performances nightly. Thurs. is "Girl Bar" for lesbians; two nights a week especially for gay men. Transvestite go-go dancers on the bar (yes, on the bar), Sun. night gay cabaret. Open daily 4pm-4am. Cover Sun.-Thurs. $5 after 10:30pm, Fri.-Sat. $10.

Red Zone, 440 W. 54th St. (582-2222). A new club with a decent crowd of acidhouse fans. Open Wed.-Sat. 10pm-4am. Cover $10-15.

CBGB & OMFUG 315 Bowery (982-4052), at Bleecker St. Subway: Lexington IRT to Bleecker. They say the initials stand for "country, bluegrass, blues, and other music for uplifting gourmandizers," but almost since its inception in 1976, this club has been the home of American punk. It now features foreign bands and pop, along with hardcore. Mon. is audition night. Hard-core matinee Sun. at 3pm admits ages 16 and over. Open daily 9pm-4am. Cover $5-10.

Bentley's, 25 E. 40th St. (684-2540), between Park and Madison. Predominantly black crowd dancing to incredible rhythms at impossible speed. Even the yuppies have a good time. Thurs. (6pm-2am) is Reggae-Soca-Calypso night. Fri. 9-11pm free, $10 after 11pm. Sat. 10:30pm-4am $5-10.

Uncle Charlie's, 56 Greenwich Ave. (255-8787), between Seventh Ave. South and Charles St. The biggest and best-known gay club in the city—schools of West Village guppies and people in bright colors. B&T (bridge and tunnel) gays make the commute. Fun. No cover charge.

Au Bar, 41 E. 58th St. (308-9455), between Park and Madison. Au dear. Uptown, upstated, woodpaneled slickster hangout. Very English private school, chatting about Tom Stearns in the library. Open daily 9pm-4am. Cover $10-15.

The Cubbyhole, 438 Hudson St. (243-9079). Not exactly a clean, well-lighted place, but one of the few established women's spaces in the city. Bar, jukebox, beautiful people. When asked on Letterman what clubs they went to in New York, Madonna and Sandra Bernhardt mentioned this one.

Mission, 531 E. 5th St. (473-9096), between Ave. A and B. DePeche Mode and Cure fans, complete with hairspray and ticket stubs from New Jersey, fill this tiny club. They promise to let you in for free if you mention you saw them in *Let's Go*. Open Thurs.-Sat. 10pm-4am.

Palladium, 126 E. 14th St. (473-7171). Subway: Lexington IRT to Union Sq. Once the #1 in chic, Palladium's preëminence has faded, but it still draws crowds. Palladium functions on several levels, all embellished by the works of NYC artists and psychedelic bathrooms. Open Thurs.-Sat. 10pm-4am. Cover $20 (reduced admission passes pop up everywhere).

Quick, 6 Hubert St. (925-2442) off Hudson, 5 blocks south of Canal. Designed by Broadcast Arts, the same animators responsible for Pee Wee Herman's playhouse. In its previous incarnation, this club was called "Area," and used to be the arch-rival and evil double of Palladium. Present gimmicks include large ceramic pigs and small porcine go-go dancers. Thursday's gay night has a $10 cover—the entertainment features a drag queen lip-syncher and hip house music. No A/C: gets too hot for comfort in summer. Open Wed.-Sun. 10pm-4am. Cover Thurs. "Gay night" $5-10, Fri.-Sat. $15.

Tracks, 531 W. 19th St. (627-2333), west of Tenth and east of Hudson. "Tracks" actually exists only on Tuesday nights—when the worldbeat club "Kilimanjaro" turns black and gay. One of the best gay clubs in the city, regardless of your color: excellent music, sprawling dance floors, and an unpretentious crowd. There is also a higher representation of lesbians here that at many other gay clubs. Madonna's number one single "Vogue" was based on a dance that got started here: "voguing" involves stringing together a series of dramatic poses to the beat of the music. Cover $5.

Wetland Preserve, 161 Hudson St. (966-4225). Organic wine and healthy snacks to keep you empty; bohemians lacking barbers dance to happening rock. Open daily 10pm-4am. Cover $5-10.

The Bar, Second Ave. and 4th St. (no phone). The ultimate in generic. Gay, mixed crowd. Pop and disco. No cover.

Spike, 120 Eleventh Ave. (243-9688). Young men go way west for a trip back in time to discover what the 70s gay scene was like. As the name indicates, there's no shortage of leathermen here.

Duchess II, 70 Grove St. (242-1408). A lesbian bar for women of all ethnic backgrounds.

Tunnel Bar, 7th St. and First Ave. (no phone). Cowboyish decor and East Village gay crowd, plus a generous sampling of clones. Porn videos 2 nights per week, as well as regular movies. No cover.

Cuando Cultural Center, 9 Second Ave. (603-9056), just off Houston. Now housing the Carwash, this nomadic nightclub hops around. Major DJs spin new tunes, including the fiercest rap on the streets. Call to see if it has moved or is no longer operating. Tight security. Cover $5-10. No alcohol.

Jazz Clubs

Augie's, 2751 Broadway (864-9834). Jazz all week until 3am. The saxophonist sits on your lap and the bass rests on your table. Quality musicians and a cool crowd. Open daily 8pm-3am. No cover.

Angry Squire, 216 Seventh Ave. (242-9066), between 22nd and 23rd. Jazz every night with a local crowd and mellow tunes. Simple tables with wine casks hanging above the bar. Open daily 5pm-3am. No cover.

Blue Note, 131 W. 3rd St (475-8592). A jazz classic.

Pat's in Chelsea, 110-112 W. 23rd St. (242-9596), off Sixth Ave. The tinfoil in the window cringes from the mediocre jazz. Ritzy bar with a more mature crowd. Open daily 6pm-4am.

Bradley's, 70 University Place (473-9700), at 11th St. Subway: Lexington IRT to Union Sq. Nightly piano and bass duos that cut through the smoke. Usually crowded. Drink minimum $5 at tables; no minimum at the bar. Music daily 9:45pm-4am.

Dan Lynch, 221 Second Ave. (667-0911) at 14th St. Subway: Lexington IRT to Union Sq. Dark smoky room with Casablanca fan, long bar, and "all blues, all the time." Swinging, friendly, deadhead crowd drowns the dance floor. Pool table in back. Open daily 8pm-4am; blues and jazz start at 10pm. Jam session Sat.-Sun. 4:30-9pm. Cover Fri.-Sat. $5.

Sweetwater's, 170 Amsterdam Ave. (873-4100) at 68th St. Subway: Broadway IRT to 66th St. Cool jazz blended with uptown chic. Shows Mon.-Fri. at 9 and 11pm, Sat.-Sun. at 9pm and midnight; also downstairs at 6pm. Open Mon.-Fri. noon-4am, Sat.-Sun. 4pm-4am. Cover $10 plus 2-drink minimum downstairs; $10 cover plus $10 dinner minimum upstairs.

Michael's Pub, 211 E. 55th St. (758-2272) off Third Ave. Subway: Lexington IRT to 59th or 51st St. Woody Allen played his clarinet here instead of picking up his 3 Academy Awards for *Annie Hall.* He still sneaks in some Mon. nights. Sets Mon. at 9 and 11pm, Tues.-Sat. at 9:30 and 11:30pm. Open Mon.-Fri. noon-1am. Cover $15-25. 2-drink minimum at the tables; no minimum at the bar.

J's, 2581 Broadway (666-3600), between 47th and 48th St., 2nd fl. A classic jazz bar. Top-notch music, dim lighting over red brick walls, intimacy without claustrophobia. Owner Judy Barnett, a jazz singer herself, concentrates on discovering new talents. After the set, the musicians schmooze at the bar. Open Mon.-Thurs. 5pm-12:30am, sets from 8:30pm; Fri. 5pm-1am, sets from 9pm; Sat. 7pm-1am, sets from 9pm; Sun 7pm-1am, sets from 10pm. No cover; $5 minimum at bar; $10 at tables.

Birdland, 2745 Broadway (749-2228) at 105th St. A supper club serving reasonably good food and top jazz. The place feels Upper-West-nouveau but the music is smoked-out-splendid-52nd St. Blue Note Records even makes recordings here. Sun. jazz brunch. Open 4pm-4am, Sun. noon-4pm and 5pm-4am. Sun.-Thurs. $7 music charge plus $5 minimum, at the bar $5 minimum; Fri.-Sat. at the tables $10 music charge plus $10 minimum at the tables, at the bar $5 music charge plus $5 minimum. Appetizers $5-7, entrees $12-16, pasta $11-13, sandwiches $8-10. Mon.-Sat.

Apollo Theater, 253 W. 125th St. (749-5838). Subway: Broadway IRT to 125th St. Use caution in the neighborhood. This historic Harlem landmark has heard the likes of Duke Ellington, Count Basie, Ella Fitzgerald, Lionel Hampton, Billie Holliday, and Sarah Vaughan. In his zoot-suit days, Malcolm X shined shoes here. Now undergoing a revival. Show tickets $5-30. Arrive at least ½ hr. early for cheap tickets. Amateur night starts Wed. at 7:30pm. Call the theatre to check what's playing.

Other Bars

Automatic Slims, 733 Washington St. (645-8660). Simple bar in the West Village with the best selection of blues and screamin' soul, complemented by the guitars and pensive faces of South-side stars. Open daily 5pm-4am.

Dan Minlano's, 49 E. Houston (no phone). The celebrity crowd drifts here on the weekends, and Guinness Stout flows on tap. Sit at the long oak bar and check out the photo of Marciano about to knockout Louis. Open daily 6pm-3am.

Peculiar Pub, 145 Bleecker St. (353-1327). Beer from 43 different countries. Collect and trade flavors. Open Sun.-Thurs. 4pm-2am, Fri. 4pm-4am, Sat. 2pm-4am.

King Tut's Wah Wah Hut, 112 Ave. A (254-7772), in the East Village. Heavy metal biker crowd plays ecstatic pool. Antique couches melt into surreal psychedelic walls, platinum hair, and wrinkled tattoes. Open daily until 4am.

Downtown Beirut, 158 First Ave. (260-4248). Hardcore crowd flooded with Eastern European youth listening to the best jukebox in town, with over 15 Clash songs listed. Happy Hour ($2.25 draft) noon-8pm. Open daily noon-4am.

Downtown Beirut II, 157 Houston St. (614-9040). Also full of the young and the hardcore, but live music only on weekends, and only the second best jukebox in town. Open daily noon-4am.

Lucky Strike, 59 Grand St. (943-0479), off W. Broadway. SoHo prices attract droves of the ultra-magna-beautiful, scantily clad in black. $3.50 Budweisers with similarly overpriced food in the back makes this more of a sight than a watering hole. Open daily noon-4am.

Coffee Shop Bar, 29 Union Sq. West (243-7969), facing Union Sq. Park. Venetian blinds guard the long bar and the vogue thirtysomething crowd. Demurely hip. Open daily until 4am.

Pool Bar, 643 Broadway (no phone), at Bleecker St. A flight of stairs leads down to a dance floor and pool table. Beautiful bartenders serve expensive drinks while psychedelic funk attempts to get the place grooving. Open Mon.-Thurs. 6pm-4am, Fri.-Sat. 6pm-3am. Cover Thurs.-Sat. $2-3.

Westend, 2911 Broadway (622-8830) at 113 St. Columbia University and prep school hangout once frequented by Kerouac, Burroughs, and Rohrbaugh. Huge sitting areas, including outdoors, give way to the small dance room with bands in the back (cover $7). Cheap pitchers with a great beer selection. Open daily noon-4am.

Marlin, 2844 Broadway (no phone), between 109th and 110th. A watering hole with inexpensive drinks and a well-rounded crowd. Open daily until 4am.

Teddy's, N. 9th St. and Berry St. (384-9787), in Greenpoint, Brooklyn. Subway: G to Nassau St. The new artiste crowd starts drinking here, and only you can find out where they end up. True adventures often born in this bar. Open daily until 4am. Jazz on Wed. nights.

Island Club, 285 W. Broad St. (226-4598) at Canal St. Dreads celebrating to the Irie tunes of Jah in a blanket of smoke. Live it up—righteous! Open Wed.-Sat. 10pm-4am.

Eclectic Music

Ballroom, 253 W. 28th St. (244-3005) at 8th Ave. A slinky cabaret on the edge of Chelsea, near the Flower and Fleece Market. Borderline art deco decor with a funky seasonally vegetative Tapas Bar. Eclectic offerings range from Long Island Retro to Village Avant-Garde. Often dance, comedy, or performance art tactics enrich the music. Open in Summer, Tues.-Sat. 4:30pm-1am, Sun. from noon. Showtime Tues.-Sat. 9am, Sun. 3pm. Admission $15 plus two-drink minimum.

Bottom Line, 15 W. 4th St. (228-7880). At Mercer St. in Greenwich Village. Subway: #1, 2, 3, or 9 to Christopher St. or A, C, E to W. 4th St. A sombre, loftlike space, where rainbows weave on the walls, jet against black. If you can't find a seat, you can sit at the comfy bar, (you don't have to order a drink) surrounded by old show photos. A mixed bar of music and entertainment—from jazz to kitsch to country to theatre to good old time rock and roll. Tickets $13.50-15. Double proof of age (21 and over) required, but some all age performances. Shows Sun.-Thurs. at 8 and 11pm, Fri.-Sat. at 8:30 and 11:30pm.

Cat Club, 76 E. 13th St. (505-0090). Heavy metal headbanging and wheezing guitars usually prevail, but Sunday night belongs to a gang of Lindy Hop enthusiasts called the New York Swing Dance Society. Watch an older couple glide leisurely across the floor like a harbor cruiseship while menace youth twirl. Big band and swing dance tracks, brassy razzle-dazzle. Music 8pm-1am.

Continental Divide, 25 Third Ave. (529-6924), at St. Marks Pl. Subway: #6 to Astor Place. Punks, posers, artists, literati and the occasional skinhead. Terribly East Village. Interior decoration evokes turbulent prehistoric punk; dinosaurs, pterodactyls, cavemen, thesauri all partying in a stone-age tableaux. Decent nouveau-Mexi grub served. Shows Fri. midnight, Sat. 11pm, and Sun.-Thurs. 10pm. No cover.

Eagle Tavern, 355 W. 14th St. at Ninth Ave. Subway: A, C, E to 14 St. A true Irish pub in the heart of the meat-packing district. Barside blarney and poignant folk music spoken. Live music nightly (mostly free) with some special appearances by more celebrated talents ($6). Native strings outfits saw it up on Saturday nights. Shows start at 9pm.

Greene Street, 101 Greene St. (925-2415). This restaurant-bar recalls the setting for *The Sting* or *The Untouchables:* splendid guilded decor on the verge of being riddled by bullets. Twilit, leafy, and cavernous, with a piano stationed somewhere far below. Jazz is their forte, with an accent on piano music. No cover charge. Open 5:30pm-midnight. Dinner starts at 6pm, sets at 7pm; 2-drink minimum on weekends at the bar.

Indigo Blues, 221 W. 46th St. (221-0033), between Broadway and Eighth. Located in the basement of the Hotel Edison. Jazz and Blues. Fare served up nightly in a high modernist glass and brick den. Former and recent heavyweights have included Milt Jackson, Freddie Hubbard, Betty Carter, and Stanley Jordan. Music starts after 9pm. Cover $10-20 depending on the attraction, plus a variable minimum if you sit at a table (no ingestive minimum at the bar).

Lone Star Roadhouse, 240 W. 52nd St. (295-2950). Subway: #1,2,3,9 to 50th St. A friendly Tex-Mex cantina where the good old boys and Southern square dancing gals mix it up with Macy's cowboys and posers with silver spurs. Authentic entertainment covers no-frills rock,

R&B, country, funk, and zydeco. Red-checkered table cloths, roadside kitsch, and long-neck Buds. Music nightly; cover $8-22.

Kilimanjaro, 531 W. 19th St. (627-2333), between Tenth and Eleventh. African music reigns supreme here, though forays into Calypso, reggae and world have been known to occur. Open Sun., Tues.-Thurs. 8:30pm-3am, Fri.-Sat. 8:30pm-5am. Cover $10-20.

Knitting Factory, 47 E. Houston St. (219-3055), near Mulberry St. Subway: 6 to Spring St. or B, D, F, Q to Broadway-Lafayette St. Free-thinking musicians anticipate the Apocalypse with a wide range of piercing edge performances. Everything about the factory says cult and anarchy. Several shows nightly, performers are changed as regularly as underwear, and a general state of sonic intoxication is high and flying. The earlier you come, the cheaper the beer will be. Cover $10-15.

Red Blazer Too, 349 W. 46th St. (262-3112) between Eighth and Ninth. Subway: A,C,E to 50th St. Dance cheek to cheek in the stardust of fab golden oldies. Tuesdays constitute a musical romp through 20s and 30s, Wednesday Big Bands take the stage, Fri.-Sat. is blistery Dixieland, and Thursdays were made for swing. Jazz Age crowd. Music Sun. at 6pm, Mon.-Thurs. 8:30pm-12:30am, Fri.-Sat. 9pm-1am.

Sounds of Brazil (S.O.B.), 204 Varick St. (243-4940), at the corner of Seventh and Houston in the Village. Subway: #1,2,3,9 to Houston. This luncheonette turned dance club presents bopping musicians playing sounds of Brazil, Africa, Latin America, and the Caribbean in a setting inflicted with tropicana. When they say world beat here, they mean it. Open for dining Tues.-Thurs. 7pm-2:30am, Fri.-Sat. 7pm-4am. Music from 9pm Tues.-Thurs., Fri.-Sat. from 10pm. Cover Mon.-Thurs. $12-18, Fri. $17. Sat. $18.

Village Gate, 160 Bleecker St. (475-5120), near Thompson St. Subway: #6 to Bleecker. They'll give you a beat and extricate your funny bone. Every Monday Salsa meets Jazz downstairs in the big room 9pm-2am, same on the Terrace Tues.-Sun. from 10pm. Jazz regulars play Monday and Tuesday nights. Sat.-Sun. 2-6pm open mike for college jazz prodigies; Sat.-Sun. 6-10pm professional jazz cats take over the beat. Open daily 6pm-2am. Salsa meets Jazz $15-20; original plays $32.50. Comedy upstairs $8, jazz on the Terrace free with a $6.50 drink minimum.

Village Vanguard, 178 Seventh Ave. (255-4037), south of 11th St. Subway: #1,2,3,9 to 14th St. A windowless canvern shaped like a wedge, as old and venerable as jazz itself. The walls are thick with memories of Lenny Bruce, Leadbelly, Miles Davis, and Sonny Rollins. The place has the lived-in look; the music lives. Sets at 10 and 11:30, Fri.-Sat. also at 1am. Every Mon. The Mel Lewis Jazz Orchestra unleashes their torrential big band sound on the sentimental journeymen. Cover $12 plus $7.50 drink minimum on weekdays, $15 plus.

Wetlands, 161 Hudson Street (966-4225). A giant Summer of Love mural in the back room sets the tone, a Volkswagen bus curio shop swims in tie dyes, and mood memorabilia harken to the No Nukes years in this 2-story whole earth spectacular. Downstairs you can chill out in a flowerchildren's love patch. Mondays and Fridays Wetlands brings you reggae, Tuesdays it's as close as you get to Grateful Dead, Wednesdays things get mixed up. Thursdays blues and rock arrive, Saturday nights pyschodelic mania kicks in and Sundays things are back to the mellow groove with folk. Shows start nightly after 9:30. This eco night club does some canvassing on the side, sponsoring benefits in the cause of a healthier earth. Opens Sun.-Thurs. 5pm, Fri.-Sat. 9pm. Cover $5-15 (no drink minimum).

Zanzibar and Grill, 550 Third Ave. (779-0606) at 36th St. Saloon in the shade. Ceiling fans turn slowly and a 25¢ feed to the jukebox earns you a Xavier Cugat or a Perez Prado tune. Catch the waiter in a good mood and he will croon "It's Suppertime" (naturally to the tune of Gershwin's "Summertime") as he serves you fried chicken. Open 6pm-3 or 4am. Two shows nightly at 9:30 and 11:30pm. Cover $5-6 on weekdays, $10-15 on weekends.

O'Lunney's, 12 W. 44th St. (840-6688), between Fifth and Sixth. A steak and burgers restaurant that serves up live country and western as a digressive. Occasional folk music thrown into the stew. Open Sun.-Fri. 11am-2am, Sat. 6pm-2am. Music Sun.-Thurs. 7-11:30pm, Fri.-Sat. 7pm-2am. No cover.

Comedy Clubs

The Original Improvisation, 358 W. 44th St. (765-8268), between Eighth and Ninth. A quarter century of comedy—acts from Saturday Night Live, Johnny Carson, David Letterman. Richard Pryor and Robin Williams got started here. Shows Sun.-Fri. at 9pm, Sat. at 8 and 10:30pm. Cover Mon.-Thurs. $8, plus $8 drink or food min.; Fri.-Sat. $12, plus $9 min.

Chicago City Limits 351 E. 74th St. (772-8707). Improv theatre as suggested by the audience and sketch humor à la *Saturday Night Live.* Shows Wed.-Thurs. at 8:30pm, Fri.-Sat. at 8 and 10:30pm. Cover Wed.-Thurs. $12.50, Fri.-Sat. $15.

Comedy Cellar, 117 MacDougal St. (254-3630), between W. 3rd St. and Bleecker St. Subterranean annex of the artsy Olive Tree café. Intimate, atmospheric. Shows Sun.-Thurs. 9pm-2am, Fri. 9 and 11:30pm, Sat. at 8pm, 10pm, and midnight. Cover Sun.-Thurs. $5, plus 2-drink minimum; Fri.-Sat. $10, plus $7 drink minimum. Make reservations for the weekend.

Stand Up NY, 236 W. 78th St. (595-0850) at Broadway. Comics from Carson, Letterman, HBO, Showtime, MTV. Handsomely appointed fun, often with a political edge. Surprise drop-ins by Steven Wright. Shows Sun.-Thurs. at 9pm, Fri. at 8:30 and 11:30pm, Sat. at 8pm, 10:15pm, and 12:30am. Cover Sun.-Thurs. $7, Fri.-Sat. $12. 2-drink min.

Caroline's at the Seaport, 89 South St. (233-4900). Caroline's has quickly become the top spot for comedy in New York, with a youngish, upscale crowd and big names from TV and the comedy circuit. Restaurant upstairs, café outdoors. Shows Tues.-Thurs. and Sun. 7-11pm; cover $12.50 plus 2-drink min. Shows Fri.-Sat. 7pm-1am; cover $15 plus 2-drink min.

Mostly Magic, 55 Carmine St. (924-1472), between Sixth and Seventh. Night club/restaurant with comedy/magic. Shows Tues.-Thurs. at 9pm, cover $10, food or drink min. $5, Fri.-Sat. 9 and 11pm, cover $15, food or drink min. $5.

Catch a Rising Star, 1487 First Ave. (794-1906), near 77th St. Local and West Coast comics slay a youthful crowd. Shows Mon.-Thurs. at 9pm, Fri. at 8:30 and 11pm, Sat. at 7:30pm, 10pm and 12:30am. Cover Sun.-Thurs. $8, Fri.-Sat. $12; 2-drink min. Make reservations after 5pm on previous day.

The Boston Comedy Club, 82 W. 3rd St. (477-1000), between Thompson and Sullivan. Comedy with a funny accent. Shows Sun.-Thurs. at 9pm, Fri. at 9:30 and 11:30pm, Sat. at 10pm and midnight. Cover Sun.-Thurs. $5, Fri.-Sat. $10; 2-drink min.

Shopping

At the Whitney Museum, you can buy a $60 canvas sack imprinted with a bold, constructivist message that reads "I Shop Therefore I Am." Whether Descartes or your mother does your shopping, the image is what sells in this City of Images, when you buy anything from an "I love Brooklyn" sweatshirt on the street to a Polo-emblazoned pair of socks from Ralph Lauren's believe-me-or-not *palazzo* on Madison.

Buyable things beckon on every New York street corner. And impromptu vendors left lemonade stands by the wayside long ago. Peddlers sell earrings, stockings, elixirs, and gimmicks that are best labeled "etc."; department stores sell designer gold brooches and Calvin Klein underwear. Shopping in the city doesn't have to bankrupt you—it's all a question of knowing where to hunt for what. On the streets, don't hesitate to bargain, especially for electronic goods. Always test a product before you buy it. New and used book bargains can be found on Broadway between 93rd and 98th. Streetwise bookinistes also sell assorted old records and several-month-old magazines.

In Soho, enormous **Canal Jean,** the original home of the surplus clinic, at 504 Broadway (226-1130), brims with neon ties, baggy pants, and silk smoking jackets. Poke around the bargain bins out front. (Open Sun.-Thurs. 10am-8pm, Fri.-Sat. 10am-9pm.) On weekends, check out the flea market at the western end of Canal for honest-to-goodness antiques along with the usual funk junk. Back up Broadway, in Greenwich Village, the **Antique Boutique,** 712 Broadway near Astor Place (460-8830), sells both stunning vintage clothing and interesting new designs. (10% discount for students with ID. Open Mon.-Sat. 10:30am-midnight, Sun. noon-8pm.) At the jazzy **Unique Clothing Warehouse,** 718-726 Broadway (674-1767), chic creative clothing and fun footwear come cheap. (Open Sun.-Thurs. 10am-9pm, Fri.-Sat. 10am-midnight.)

Some **Greenwich Village** boutiques seem to have been art galleries in their past lives. Leather hunters should try the shoe stores along 8th St. between Fifth and Sixth, the saddlebag shops on W. 4th St., and the handmade sandal stores off Bleecker St. For mainstream fashion with a funky flair, check out **Reminiscence,** 74 Fifth Ave. near 13th St. (243-2292; open Mon.-Sat. 11:30am-8pm, Sun. 1-6pm). Most anyone wearing Reminiscence pants will be mistaken for a real New Yorker. Across town, those with the stamina to burrow through mountains of clothes can find some amazing bargains at **Gabay's,** 225 First Ave. (254-3180) between 13th and 14th, which sells seconds from major New York department stores (open Mon.-Fri. 9am-5:30pm, Sat. 9am to 5pm, Sun. 10am-4pm). Bargain electronic gadgets populate **Forty-Seventh Street Photo,** 115 W. 45th. Knowledgeable staff oversees the frenzied atmosphere. (Open Mon.-Thurs. 9am-6pm, Fri. 9am-2pm, Sun. 9am-5pm.) Buy highfalutin designer clothes second-hand at **Encore,** Madison at 82nd St. (879-2850; open Mon.-Wed. and Fri.-Sat. 10:30am-6pm, Thurs. 10:30am-7pm, Sun. 12:30-6pm), or at **Michael's,** on Madison between 79th and 80th (737-7273; open in summer Mon.-Fri. 9:30am-6pm; otherwise Mon.-Sat.).

Department Stores and Malls

At the **SoHo Emporium,** 375 Broadway (966-7895), between Broome and Spring St., some 40 independent boutiques vie tooth and claw with each other for your patronage. Everything goes on sale here, from furs and jewelry to crafts and crystal. A fortune teller on hand can assist you with your most urgent shopping needs. (Open Tues.-Sun. noon-8pm.) And mall shopping on an unfathomable scale transpires daily at the 60 shops and restaurants in the concourse of the **World Trade Center** at West and Liberty St. (466-4170).

Some business moguls acquire their threads at **Barney's New York** (945-1600), a 10,000-square-foot coliseum situated at 2 World Financial Center on a riverbank overlooking the Hudson. Barney's features collections of sportswear, formal wear, shoes, and oh-so-fine shirts from Truzzi. (Open Mon.-Wed. and Fri. 10am-7pm, Thurs. 10am-9pm, Sat. 10am-6pm, Sun. noon-6pm.) Another outlet sells at Seventh Ave. (929-9000) and 17th St. Although they may sound like nicknames for subatomic particles, Merns and Syms are the hardest working nephew-uncle tag team in the world of discount wear. **Syms,** 45 Park Plaza, has cornered the middle-of the road market (791-1199; open Tues.-Wed. 8am-6:30pm). In the shadow of Syms, at 2 Vesey St., **Merns** (227-5471) features much the same repertoire that made his uncle famous at much the same going rate (30 to 50% of the nationally advertised price tags). Pay next to nothing for conservative styles in tweed, corduroy, or cotton; some assembly may be required. (Open Mon.-Fri. 9:30am-6:15pm, Sat. 9:30am-5:45pm.)

Abraham & Strauss, the inventor of the vertical shopping mall, ascends to commodity heaven with eight levels of fashion, toys, electronics, and hard-to-find items. **A&S Plaza** (Sixth Ave. and 33rd St.) also features the "Taste of the Town" international food court, an entire floor of noshing and funk. (Plaza open Mon. and Thurs.-Fri. 9:45am-8:30pm, Tues. 9:45am-6:45pm, Sat. 10am-6:45pm, Sun. 10am-6pm.)

No purchasing pilgrimage would be complete without a visit to the world's largest department store, **Macy's,** 151 W. 34th St. (695-4400), between Broadway and Seventh. The colossus sells 500,000 different items. (see Sights above). You can eat breakfast, lunch, and dinner at Macy's, get a facial and a haircut, mail a letter, have your jewelry appraised, purchase theater tickets, and convert foreign bills into Uncle Sam's green leaves. Of course, you can also shop. (open Mon. and Thurs.-Fri. 9:45am-8:30pm, Tues.-Wed. 9:45am-6:45pm, Sat. 10am-6:45pm, Sun. 10am-6pm.)

Courtly **Lord and Taylor,** 424 Fifth Ave. (341-3344), between 38th and 39th St., has made a specialty of stocking clothes by American designers, but its furniture department transcends the trendy with such *couture* classics as Henredon sofas, Chinese porcelain lamps, and reproductions of Louis XV tables. Scores of New Yorkers come to be shod at the legendary shoe department, and to be treated in Lord's manner: caring service, free coffee in the early morning, and unsurpassable Christmas displays. The first in history to use the picture window as a stage for anything other than merchandise, the store began this custom in 1905, during an unusually balmy December that had failed to summon the appropriate pre-

Christmas meteorological garnish. Lord and Taylor filled its windows with mock storms and blizzards, reviving the Christmas spirit for the gloomy citizens. (Open Mon. and Thurs. 10am-8:30pm, Tues.-Wed. and Fri.-Sat. 10am-6:45pm, Sun. noon-6pm.)

For the fashion-conscious, shopping at **Saks Fifth Avenue,** 611 Fifth Ave. (753-4000), between 49th and 50th St., molds character. This institution has aged well and continues to combine good taste with smooth courtesy. Sales make the whole affair vaguely affordable. (Open Mon.-Wed. and Fri.-Sat. 10am-6pm, Thurs. 10am-8pm.) As the Trump empire starts to crumble, to the victorious crowing of righteous peoples everywhere, you may want to catch a glimpse of one of the tycoon's last major ostentations before it is bought by raiders and converted into condos. The **Trump Tower** gleams with gaud, marble, and gold opalescence. Inside, a fountain of plenty climbs the walls of a six-story atrium of upscale boutiques and restaurants. Capitalism is alive and well here, though slightly feverish. (Open Mon.-Sat. 10am-6pm.)

Bloomingdale's, 1000 Third Ave. (705-2000) at 59th St., affectionately known as Bloomie's, is a wild shopping adventure in the spirit of a safari. With show business pizazz, the store's buyers have scoured the markets of China, India, Israel, and the Philippines and returned with funky ideas for rugs, clothes, and furniture. The store also stocks Western classics by Yves Saint Laurent, Ralph Lauren, and Calvin Klein. The festive atmosphere borders on the chaotic, as a thousand simulcasting televisions coo about products, salses commandos squirt perfumes fumigator style, and rakish music plays over the scent of Giorgio. See the young and the spoiled congregate here on Sundays. Don't miss Petrossian, the czar of caviar whose entire store pays homage to the fishy luxury. (Open Mon. and Thurs. 10am-9:30pm, Tues.-Wed. and Fri.-Sat. 10am-6:30pm, Sun. noon-6pm.) Sit in luxury's lap at legendary **Bergdorf-Goodman,** 754 Fifth Ave. (753-7300), between 57th and 58th. (Open Mon.-Sat. 9:30am-5:30pm.)

If the name doesn't set you rolling, the smorgasbord of odd merchandise will. Come ogle at **Hammacher Schlemmer,** 147 E. 57th St. (421-9000), between Third and Lex, a gadget fancier's fantasy land. Marvel at such exotica as a self-stirring French saucepan, a computerized fortune teller, and the Whiz Bang Popcorn Wagon. Bear in mind that Hammacher's zeal for automated convenience has provided the world with the steam iron, electric razor, and pressure cooker. (Open Mon.-Sat. 10am-8pm, Sun. noon-5pm.) Pay down-to-earth prices for clothes and accessories at **Alexander's,** 731 Lexington Ave. (593-0880) at 59th St., the Robin Hood of New York's rich and gloating department stores.

Specialty Stores

> *New York, indeed, is the heaven of every man with*
> *something useless and expensive to sell.*
> —*H.L. Mencken*

The Annex Antiques and Flea Market, Sixth Ave. at 25th St. (243-5343). New Yorkers in the know do their "antiquing" here. 200-odd dealers offer 17th- and 18th-century linens and porcelains, military paraphernalia and lace, vintage garments, snuff boxes, oriental rugs, rare books, antique toys, dolls, and clocks. From the depths of a suburban garage to the velvet cushions of an estate jewelry collection, worthy trifles assemble here for your viewing pleasure. Open Sat.-Sun. 9am-5pm. Admission $1.

Chevas, 1466 Second Ave. (535-7501) at 77th Street. Behind dramatically hung draperies, Chevas paints and designs clothes, cuts hair, decorates interiors, and sells fun bric-a-brac. Open Mon.-Sat. 9am-9pm, Sun. noon-7pm.

Jan Feenstra Creative Boutique, 219 E. 89th St. (427-4795), between Second and Third. Feenstra, an impressionable and impressionistic, exotic and quixotic, zany and witty artist, tells you stories while running this boutique. A closet-sized dollhouse with art nouveau lamps, hatpins, and crystal balls. Open Tues.-Fri. noon-8pm, Sat. 10am-6pm, Sun. 1-7pm.

Godiva Chocolatier, Inc., 560 Lexington Ave. (980-9810). The controlled substance has been molded to reproduce all forms of nature and all manner of corporate whims. Whether shaped like golfballs, tennis rackets, or cubist sculpture, the chocolate tastes divine. Even if you don't buy it, come take a calorie-free look at the best-pressed chocolate in the world. Open Mon.-Thurs. 10am-6pm, Fri. 10am-7:15pm, Sun. noon-6pm.

The Last Wound-Up, 889 Broadway (529-4197). If you can wind it, yo'll find it here. Egg-laying chickens, ambulatory elephants, bouncing genitals, and rolling eyeballs. Wind-up basketball, baseball, and football, and a crazy King Kong making his way up the Empire State penny bank. Demure turn-of-the-century music boxes and disk music boxes grind their way through oldie tunes. Open daily 10am-7pm.

The Soldier Shop, 1222 Madison Ave. (535-6788). If you dream in battle formations, you've met your match. If not, salute boredom. The humble tin soldier brings in a lot of business here. Painted little infantrymen of all times and empires march, fire, bang drums and play the fife throughout the store. Wall-to-wall bookshelves stocked with military memoirs, battle and campaign accounts, and histories of conquest. Weapons and military regalia complete the martial ensemble. Mon.-Fri. 10am-5:30pm, Sat. until 4:30pm.

Dollhouse Antics, 1343 Madison Ave. (876-2288) at 94th St. First-class doll real estate plus most mundanities miniaturized: coffee sets, Scrabble boards, toilets, napkins and tables covered by artfully stitched baby tablecloths. Come to start a collection or just to feel like Gulliver. Mon.-Fri. 11am-5:30pm, Sat. 11am-5pm; July-Aug. closed Sat. and Mon.; in Dec., also open Sun.

Mouse'N Around Too, Sixth Ave. and 33rd St., 7th floor (947-3954), at the A&S Plaza. Favorite latter-day cartoon greats march off the screen and onto every imaginable merchandizable surface. Mickey imitates Dan Quayle on the clocks, Bugs Bunny docs on shirtfronts and telephones, and Betty Boop does her Marilyn impressions on beach towels. The biggest collection of cartoon watches outside the Disney research labs. Open Tues.-Wed. and Sat. 10am-6:45pm, Mon. and Thurs.-Fri. 10am-8:30pm, Sun. 10am-6pm.

Steuben, 717 Fifth Ave. (752-1441), at 56th St. Less a store than a museum, Steuben sells engraved glass pieces and glass and crystal representations of flora and fauna. The State Department does its gift-shopping here for heads of state, confident that world peacekeeping will be best kept by a present of a crystal elephant or dolphin. Remaining glass beasts go to the houses of hoi polloi. Open Mon.-Sat. 10am-6pm.

Tiffany & Co, 727 Fifth Ave. (755-8000), between 56th and 57th. So revered for its high-quality jewelry that many of its original wares sit in permanent exhibits of museums. You pay for endurance—this stuff doesn't break. Gaze at creations by Elsa Peretti and that precocious pop-culture progeny, Paloma Picasso. Check out the windows, especially at Christmas time.

Tender Buttons, 143 E. 62nd St. (758-7004), between Third and Lexington. A t.easure-trove of billions of buttons, fashioned from materials ranging from lucite to taqua nut to abalone to silver. If you carelessly lost the button on your favorite Renaissance doublet, you will find a replacement here. Budding zoologists can purchase the entire animal kingdom conveniently approximated on chameoleonic buttons. Open Mon.-Fri. 11am-6pm, Sat. 11am-5pm.

Rita Ford Music Boxes, 19 E. 65th St. (535-6717), between Madison and Fifth. Wind them up and hear them go. Dappled stallions surge up and down as tiny lanterns glow. Open Mon.-Sat. 9am-5pm.

The Erotic Baker, 582 Amsterdam Ave. (362-7557), between 88th and 89th. Pre-made and custom-ordered (24 hr. in advance) wholesome baked goods, shaped to approximate nature's designs. Some PG-13 baking too. Open Mon.-Thurs. 11am-7pm, Fri.-Sat. 11am-8pm.

Handloom Batik, 214 Mulberry St. (925-9542), between Spring and Prince St. Reams of color-me-Matisse batik fabrics stacked like layers of pastry. Wooden statuettes of cats, frogs, and fish pose, Indonesian icons hang from the ceiling. Open Wed.-Sat. 11am-7pm; in winter also Sun. 1-6pm.

Clothing

Alice Underground, 380 Columbus Ave. (724-6682) at 78th St. Also at 481 Broadway (431-9067). Nothing curiouser than an unannotated purring cat named Alice recall's the store's namesake. Small men's selection, but some wonderful cummerbunds, bow ties, and silk dinner jackets will outfit you in no time as Bond in *Casino Royale.* Women have choices galore, from chic to funk to Victorian. Open daily 10am-8pm on Columbus, 10am-7pm on Broadway.

Naf Naf, 1188 Madison Ave. (289-6333). Fun, sassy, and irreverent French sports and casual wear. For the oversized comfy look. Open Mon.-Sat. 10am-6pm, Sun. noon-5pm.

Bookstores

Whether your taste runs to European fine art or Third World revolution, whether you seek a Serbo-Croatian dictionary or a first-edition copy of Freud's *On the Interpretation of Dreams,* Manhattan is the right island for you. Barnes and Noble, Doubleday, and Waldenbooks have a number of hard-to-miss-or-avoid stores throughout the city. These chains sell current best-sellers for good prices, but offer homogenized selections in a bland commercial atmosphere. If New York has made you feel lost, navigate your course to the **Hagstrom Map and Travel Center,** 57 W. 43rd St. (398-1222), where you can get your bearings with travel books, maps, globes, and nautical charts. (Open Mon.-Fri. 9am-5:30pm.) The **Complete Traveller Bookstore,** 199 Madison Ave. (685-9007), carries the widest selection of guidebooks on the eastern seaboard (open Mon.-Fri. 9am-7pm, Sat. 10am-6pm, Sun. noon-5pm), while the **Traveller's Bookstore,** 22 W. 52nd St. (664-0995), specializes in books about England and travel-related novels (open Mon.-Fri. 9am-6pm, Sat. 11am-5pm). Good radicals shop at **Revolution Books,** at 13 E. 16th St. (691-3345), most inappropriately off Fifth, for international tracts on everything from Marxism to Maoism (open Mon.-Sat. 10am-7pm), while good ratiocinationists while hours away at **Murder Ink,** 271 W. 87th St. (362-8905; open daily 11am-7pm, Thurs. until 10pm) and the **Mysterious Bookshop,** 129 W. 56th St. (765-0900; open Mon.-Sat. 11am-7pm). If books could kill, these would have committed multiple homicide. Those who love life as lived by others will adore the **Biography Bookshop,** 400 Bleecker St. (807-8655; open Tues.-Fri. 1-9pm, Sat. noon-10pm, Sun. noon-6pm). For coffeetable tomes, try **Hacker Art Books, Inc.,** 45 W. 57th St. (688-7600), a multilingual den of texts on fine and applied art (open Mon.-Fri. 9am-6pm), or **Wittenborn Art Books,** 1018 Madison Ave. (288-1558), a romp through Western art from the Middle Ages on (open Mon.-Sat. 10am-5pm). **Oan Oceanie—Afrique Noire Books,** 9 E. 38th St. (779-0486), carries books on tribal art. Every ethnic text around has managed to get through immigration and position itself on the shelf of a New York bookstore (open Mon.-Fri. noon-6pm). The **Liberation Bookstore,** 421 Lenox Ave. (281-4615), specializes in African American history and literature. (Open Tues.-Fri. 11am-7pm, Sat. 11:30am-6:30pm.) **Levine Jewish Books and Judaica,** 5 W. 30th St. (695-6888), has been selling religious supplies and books since 1890. (Open Mon.-Wed. 9am-5pm, Thurs. 9am-7pm, Fri. 9am-2pm, Sun. 10am-5pm.) **Paragon Book Gallery,** 2130 Broadway (496-2378), carries books on China, Japan, and India. (Open Mon.-Fri. 10am-6pm.) **Zen Oriental,** 521 Fifth Ave., has Japanese books. (697-0840; open Mon.-Sat. 10am-7pm.) Specialty bookstores also cater to sexual orientation. **A Different Light Bookstore,** 548 Hudson St. (989-4850), is the city's best-known gay bookstore. (Open Sun.-Thurs. 11am-9pm, Fri. and Sat. 11am-11pm.) The **Oscar Wilde Memorial Bookstore,** 15 Christopher St. (255-8097), stocks primarily gay men's books. (Open Sun.-Fri. noon-7:30pm, Sat. 11am-8pm.) **Judith's Room,** 681 Washington Place (727-7330) specializes in books of lesbian interest. (Open Mon.-Thurs. noon-8pm, Fri.-Sat. noon-10pm, Sun. noon-7pm.)

Non-English speakers will be relieved to find **French and European Publications, Inc.,** 115 Fifth Ave. (673-7400; also at 610 Fifth Ave., 581-8810), where they can purchase dictionaries from Tagalog to Yoruba or visit a French and a Spanish bookstore. (Open Mon.-Sat. 10am-6pm.) Albert Einstein and Thomas Mann both shopped at **Mary Rosenberg,** 17 W. 60th St. (307-7733), one of the country's largest German and French bookstores. (Open Mon.-Fri. 9am-5:30pm, Sat. 9am-3:30pm.)

If you'd rather be reading dialogue, pick up a script or a libretto at **Applause Theater and Cinema Books,** 100 W. 67th St. (496-7511), with over 4000 titles (open Mon.-Sat. 10am-6pm, Sun. noon-6pm), or at **Drama Bookshop,** 723 Seventh Ave. (944-0595; open Mon.-Fri. 9:30am-7pm, Wed. 9:30am-8pm, Sat. 10:30am-5:30pm, Sun. noon-5pm). **Richard Stoddard Performing Arts,** 18 E. 16th St. (645-9576), specializes in out-of-print books. Go gawk at over 4000 Playbills. (Open Mon., Tues., Thurs.-Sat. 11am-6pm.) Comic book addicts can browse at **Funny Business Comics,** 666 Amsterdam Ave. (799-9477; open daily noon-5pm) or **Manhattan Comics,** 228 W. 23rd St. (243-9349; open Mon.-Wed. 10am-6:15pm, Thurs. 10am-6:30pm, Fri. 10am-10pm, Sat. 10am-8pm, Sun. 11am-5pm.) Comic connoisseurs should dash to **Forbidden Planet,** 821 Broadway (473-1576), for out of print, limited editions from 1930 to the present.

Books of Wonder, 464 Hudson St. (645-8006) or 132 7th Ave. (989-3270), maintains a carefully selected stock of excellent children's books. (Open Mon.-Sat. 11am-7pm, Sun. noon-6pm.) Shelves of Dr. Seuss span **Eeyore's Books for Children,** at 2212 Broadway (362-0634) and 25 E. 83rd St. (988-3404). (Open Mon.-Sat. 10am-6pm, Sun. noon-5pm.) If the lion leads you to think you're at the public library, you're almost not wrong: **The Corner Bookstore,** 1313 Madison Ave. (831-3554), is a tiny treasure house all its own, with a delectable selection of books for all ages (open 10am-8pm).

Rare Books

Pageant Print and Book Shop, 109 East 9th St. (674-5296), also promises hours of pleasurable browsing among its wide selection of fine books and prints. (Open Mon.-Thurs. 10am-6:30pm, Fri. 10am-8pm, Sat. 11am-7:30pm.)

Argosy Bookstore, 116 East 59th St. (753-4455) hoards inspiringly out-of-print rare and used books, alongside a glut of modern first editions, autographed editions, and medical books. (Open Mon.-Fri. 9am-5:30pm.)

J.N. Bartfield Books, 30 W. 57th St. (245-8890) Leatherbound sets grace the shelves; open Mon.-Fri, 10am-5pm).

General Interest

Strand, 828 Broadway at 12th St (473-1452). New York's biggest and most-loved used book store. A must-see. Eight miles of shelf space holding nearly 2 million books. Staffers will search out obscure titles at your bidding. Ask to see a catalog, or better yet, get lost in the shelves on your own. The best. Open Mon.-Fri. 9:30am-9:30pm, Sat. 9:30am-6:30pm, Sun. 11am-6pm.

Gotham Book Mart, 41 W. 47th St. (719-4448). Legendary, venerable bookstore selling new and used volumes. Largest selection of contemporary poetry in the city, huge stock of drama, art, and literary journals. Upstairs an art gallery hosts changing exhibitions. Open Mon.-Fri. 9:30am-6:30pm, Sat. 9:30am-6pm.

Shakespeare & Company, 2259 Broadway (580-7800) at 81st St. Overwhelming selection of new books, dazzling variety of periodicals, unbearable mass of travel books, 2-story high shelves. Refined, yet enormous. Open Sun.-Thurs. 10am-11pm, Fri. and Sat. 10am-midnight.

Barnes and Noble, 105 Fifth Ave. (807-0099) at 18th St. Three million volumes in one location. The most exciting link in the otherwise sterile national chain that has revolutionized bookselling. Especially extensive selections in the areas of medicine, engineering, business, computers, and design. Sale annex across the street has four floors of bargain bestsellers and "books for a buck." Open Mon.-Fri. 9:30am-7:45pm, Sat. 9:30am-6:15pm, Sun. 11am-5:45pm.

Endicott Book Sellers, 450 Columbus Ave. (787-6300), between 81st and 82nd. Carpeted and wood-paneled. Lounge on the couch in the back room as you browse and skim. Mostly modern literature. Open Sun.-Mon. noon-8pm, Tues.-Sat. 10am-9pm.

Gryphon, 2246 Broadway (362-0706) between 80th and 81st. Small and homey, with used books and records. Excellent annex with wider selection and lower prices at 246 W. 80th St., just 1 block down off Broadway, on the 4th floor. Particularly strong in history. Open daily 10am-midnight.

Rizzoli, 31 W. 57th St. (759-2424) between Fifth and Sixth. On Central Park South. Beautiful, with many old prints sold at discounts. Open Mon.-Sat. 9am-8pm, Sun. noon-8pm.

Three Lives and Co., 154 W. 10th St. (741-2069) at Waverly. Pure mellow—Persian rugs, shaded lamps, modern literature. Open Mon.-Sat. 11am-9pm, Sun. 1-7pm.

Books & Company, 939 Madison Ave. (737-1450) between 74th and 75th. Delightful selection in a classy setting. Particularly strong in 20th-century literary criticism and philosophy. Open Mon.-Sat. 10am-6pm, Sun. noon-5pm.

Madison Ave. Bookshop, 833 Madison Ave. (535-6130) between 69th and 70th. Many books by live authors. Open daily 10am-6pm.

Spring St. Books, 169 Spring St. (219-3033) near W. Broadway. Casual; lots of periodicals. Open Mon.-Fri. 10am-11pm, Sat. 10am-1am, Sun. 11am-9pm.

Coliseum Books, 1771 Broadway (757-8381) at 57th St. A big bookdom with a little of everything. Open Mon. 8am-10pm, Tues.-Thurs. 8am-11pm, Fri. 8am-11:30pm, Sat. 10am-11:30pm, Sun. noon-8pm.

Barnard Bookforum, 2955 Broadway (749-5535) at 116th St. Barnard College's bookseller, with extensive offerings, especially in history. Open Mon.-Fri. 10am-10pm, Fri.-Sat. 11am-7pm.

St. Mark's Bookshop, 12 St. Mark's Place (260-7853). Small. Good selection in religion and philosophy, art periodicals. Open Mon.-Fri. 11am-10:40pm, Fri.-Sat. 11am-11:40pm.

Doubleday Bookshop, 724 Fifth Ave. (397-0550) between 56th and 57th. Flagship store of chain, one of the largest bookstores in the country. Lots of hardcovers, special order books. Limited selection of baseball lore. Open Mon.-Sat. 9am-midnight, Sun. noon-5pm.

Record Stores

The largest record store in New York is **Tower Records,** 1961 Broadway at 66th St. (799-2500), and 692 Broadway at 4th St. (505-1500; open daily 9am-midnight); near the latter branch are superb used record dealers who also sell bootlegs and imports, such as **Bleecker Bob's Golden Oldies,** 118 W. 3rd St. (475-9677; open Sun.-Thurs. noon-1am, Fri.-Sat. noon-3am) and **Venus Records,** 13 St. Mark's Place (598-4459; open Mon.-Fri. noon-8pm, Sat.-Sun. noon-midnight).

Rocks in Your Head, 157 Prince St. offers alternative music along the lines of Sonic Youth (open Sun.-Thurs. 1pm-8pm, Fri. and Sat. 1pm-1am).

Downtown Records (705 6th Ave., 924-5791. Open Mon.-Sat. 10am-8pm, Sun. noon-6pm) concentrates on rap and urban contemporary.

Music Masters, 25 W. 43rd St. (840-1958), between Fifth and Sixth. A solid selection of classical recordings, with emphasis on LPs and CDs, as well as their own recordings, converted from antiquated 78s to crisp-sounding 33s. Nostalgia and Broadway enthusiasts will enjoy the semi-dark, almost dusty atmosphere and the wide selection. Don't be surprised if Stephen Sondheim or Leonard Bernstein wanders in. Open Mon.-Fri. 10am-5:30pm, Sat. 10am-2:30pm.

24-hr. Pharmacies

Kaufman Pharmacy 557 Lexington (755-2266) at 50th St. Prescriptions accepted as well as credit cards.

Love Discount, 2030 Broadway (877-4141) at 69th St. No prescriptions but credit cards accepted.

Manhattan Love, 2181 Broadway (595-7711) at 77th St. No prescriptions, credit cards accepted.

Sports

> *I . . . propose that those in charge of the . . . Olympic*
> *Games invite New York to participate as a separate*
> *entity . . . The New York Decathlon would consist of*

*four events instead of the usual ten, since everyone in
New York is very busy . . . The four events would be
Press Agentry, Dry Cleaning and Laundering, Party-
going, and Dog-owning.*

—*Fran Lebowitz*

While most cities would be content to field a major league team in each big-time
sport, New York opts for the Noah approach: there are two baseball teams, two
hockey teams, and two football teams (although the Giants are now quartered
across the river in New Jersey). In addition to local teams' regularly scheduled season games, New York hosts a number of celebrated world-class events like the New
York Marathon and the United States Tennis Association Open. The city papers
overflow with information on the upcoming events. Amateur and recreational ath-
letes do their thing here too. The City of New York Parks and Recreation Department maintains playgrounds and parks for everything from archery and croquet
to rodeo and shuffleboard.

The legendary but mortal **New York Yankees** play ball at Yankee Stadium in
the Bronx (293-6000). Tickets range from $2.25 for bleacher seats to $12 for lower
and love box seats. The regular season runs from late March until the end of September. On Family Days at Yankee Stadium, the deserving family can get half-priced
seating for every one of its members. Call for information, or pick up the mini-
brochure at the Visitor's Bureau.

The **New York Mets,** the pinstriped heroes of the Pepsi Generation, go to bat
at Shea Stadium in Queens (718-507-8499; tickets $1-12). On promotion dates,
sponsors give away baseball cards, wallets, helmets, banners, and other memorabilia. Family days incite frenzies too. Long live Strawman.

The **New York Giants** have recently moved their lair to East Rutherford, NJ
(201-935-8222) where they can be found battling each autumn. Meanwhile the **Jets**
try to tame the Dolphins and the Colts at Shea. The **Knicks** and the **Rangers** share
the court/rink at Madison Square Garden (563-8300) where they shoot and score
from late fall to late spring. The *Islanders* hang their skates at the Nassau Coliseum
(516-794-9300) on Long Island.

Tennis enthusiasts can choose between the prestigious **United States Open,** for
which it is nearly impossible to obtain tickets in a legal manner, and the not-so-
slammin' yet respectable **Tournament of Champions** which features the same name-
brand players but less hype and more tickets. The U.S. Open takes place in late
August and early September at the United States Tennis Association's (USTA) Tennis Center in Flushing Meadows Park in Queens (718-271-5100). The Tournament
of Champions, squeezed in between August 21 and 26, serves as a warm-up for the
Open. Dial the Forest Hills courts 718-268-5100. The **Virginia Slims Championship**
comes to Madison Square Garden in mid-November.

Forsake the rat race for some equine excitement. **Horse racing** fans can watch
the stallions go by at **Belmont Race Track** on every day but Tuesday, and may even
catch a grand slam event. Call 718-641-4700.

On the third Sunday in October, two million spectators turn out to cheer 16,000
runners in the **New York City Marathon.** The race begins on Verrazano Bridge
and comes to a close as the quick and the dead arrive at Central Park's Tavern on
the Green.

Swimming

Beaches

Coney Island Beach and Boardwalk (2½ mi.), on Atlantic Ocean. From W. 37th St. to Corbin
Place, in Brooklyn (718-946-1350).

Manhattan Beach (¼ mi.), on Atlantic Ocean. Oriental Blvd., from Ocean Ave. to Mackenzie
St. in Brooklyn (718-946-1373).

Orchard Beach and Promenade (1¼ mi.), on Long Island Sound in Pelham Bay Park, Bronx (885-2275).

Rockaway Beach and Boardwalk (7½ mi.), on Atlantic Ocean. From Beach 1st St., Far Rockaway, to Beach 149th St., Neponsit, Queens (718-318-4000).

Staten Island: South Beach, Midland Beach, and Franklin D. Roosevelt Boardwalk (2½ mi.), on Lower New York Bay. From Fort Wadsworth to Miller Field, New Dorp. Take bus #51 from the ferry terminal.

Wolfe's Pond Park Beach (¼ mi.), on Raritan Bay and Prince Bay, from Holton to Cornelia Ave. (718-984-8266). Take the bus going to Main St. and get off at Cornelia. Follow signs for Wolfe's Pond. A hike.

Indoor Pools

Manhattan: Asser Levy, E. 23rd St. and Ave. A. Carmine Street, Seventh Ave. South and Clarkson St. (397-3107). East 54th Street, 342 E. 54th St. (397-3154). John Rozier Hansborough, Jr., 35 W. 134th St. (397-3134). West 59th Street, 533 W. 59th St. (397-3159).

Brooklyn: Brownsville, Linden Blvd. and Christopher Ave. Metropolitan, Bedford and Metropolitan Ave. (718-965-6576). St. John's, Prospect Place, between Troy and Schenectady Ave. (718-965-6574).

Queens: Roy Wilkins, 119th St. and Merrick Blvd. (718-276-4630).

The Bronx: St. Mary's, St. Ann's Ave. and E. 145th (822-4681).

Outdoor Pools (open June-Sept.)

Manhattan: Highbridge, Amsterdam Ave. and W. 173rd St. (397-3173). Jackie Robinson, Bradhurst Ave. and W. 146th St. (397-3146). Sheltering Arms, Amsterdam Ave. and W. 129th St. (397-3126).

Brooklyn: Betsy Head, Hopkinson and Dumont Ave. (718-965-6581). Kosciuszko, Marcy and DeKalb Ave. (718-965-6585). Red Hook, Bay and Henry St. (718-965-6579).

Queens: Astoria, 19th St. and 23rd Drive (718-626-8620). Fisher, 99th St. and 32nd Ave. (718-520-5375).

The Bronx: Claremont, E. 170th St. and Clay Ave. (822-4217). Crotona, E. 173th St. and Fulton Ave. (822-4440). Mullaly, E. 165th St. and River Ave. (822-4343).

Daytrips

This city drives me crazy, or, if you prefer, crazier; and I have no peace of mind or rest of body till I get out of it.

—*Lafcadio Hearn, 1889*

Long Island

Long Island is easy to stereotype, but difficult to comprehend. For some, the Island evokes images of sprawling suburbia, dotted with malls and office buildings; others see it as the privileged playground of Manhattan millionaires; for still others it is a summer refuge of white sand and open spaces. Fewer see the pockets of poverty on Long Island, or its commercial and cultural centers. Yet each of these visions is accurate in its own way, and perhaps in conjuction they create an understanding of what the Island—home of Billy Joel, J.P. Morgan, and Jackson Pollock—is all about.

While in theory, "Long Island" includes the entire 120-mile-long fish-shaped land mass, in practice the term excludes the westernmost sections, Brooklyn and Queens.

The residents of these two boroughs, at the head of the "fish," will readily remind you that they are officially part of the City. This leaves Nassau and Suffolk counties to comprise the real Long Island. East of the Queens-Nassau line, people read *Newsday*, not the *Times* or the *Daily News:* they back the Islanders, not the Rangers, during ice hockey season, and they revel in their position as neighbor to, rather than part of, the great metropolis.

Until the 20th century, Long Island was sparsely populated, a typical Northeastern melange of farms and villages on land considered especially good for potato farming. Its docks and ports fed a strong maritime industry. The north and south forks of the tail of the fish, in Suffolk County, still maintain this rural flavor. Some towns "out on the island" might well be in New England, with their white clapboard churches and village squares.

But it was inevitable that such serenity so close to the City would be discovered. The first New York millionaires built their country houses on the rocky north shore, creating the exclusive "Gold Coast" recorded in its 1920s heyday by F. Scott Fitzgerald's *Great Gatsby.* The 1950s were a turning point for the Island; as New York City expanded, cars became more affordable, and returning soldiers sought dream houses for their baby-boom families. The new Long Island neighborhoods provided an escape from the city and a wholesome, safe atmosphere in which to raise children. There emerged a tidy mass of "development" neighborhoods, lined with street after street of identical houses framed by manicured shrubbery, each with a grassy yard for the kids and a garage for the new car. The 10,000 units of identical Levit box houses, finished in 1951, established "Levittown" as the first housing development in the world built using mass production techniques; some workers did nothing but install doorknobs, while others only painted front stoops. The completed residences were put on the market at a total cost of $7990 (a $90 down payment and monthly payments of $58).

The 50s also saw the creation of Long Island's transportation system, the essential link to New York City for hordes of commuters. The Island's main artery, the Long Island Expressway (LIE, officially called State Highway 495) grew to 73 exits, stretching 85 mi. from Manhattan to Riverhead. This expansion, along with the creation of the rest of the Island's "parkway" system, was supervised by Robert Moses, a legendary state planning official. Moses' vision of the Island as a car driver's paradise had no place for public transportation. Eventually the Long Island Railroad (LIRR) was expanded to complement his highway system. Today the Island's population has outgrown all its forms of transportation, and traffic tends to jam during rush hour on the expressway.

The construction of a transportation network has made even the outlying parts of the Island accessible. The cluster of communities on the South Fork known as the Hamptons attracts a weekend crowd from New York with its pristine beaches and pastoral seclusion. Each Hampton has its own sands, styles, and stereotypes. Look in Southampton for old money, Westhampton for new money, and East Hampton for artistes. Don't look for Northampton—there isn't one. Bridgehampton, appropriately, lies between Southampton and East Hampton.

Contrary to conventional tourist wisdom, year-round residents do exist and thrive in off-season. Nevertheless, there will always be New Yorkers who merely "summer" on the Island. Today, the summer season brings an entire subcommunity of wealthy Manhattanites and modern-day Gatsbys to the Island.

Practical Information

Visitor Information: Long Island Tourism and Convention Commission (794-4222), Eisenhower Park, Hempstead Turnpike, East Meadow. Privately run.

Airports: John F. Kennedy Airport (see New York City listing). LaGuardia Airport (see New York City listing). Long Island MacArthur Airport, Ronkonkoma, Suffolk. For general information call 467-3210, for airline telephone numbers 467-6161. A small local airport, providing primarily charter and private flights LIE Exit 573. Suffolk's other small airports are the Brookhaven Airport (281-5100) and the East Hampton Airport (537-0560).

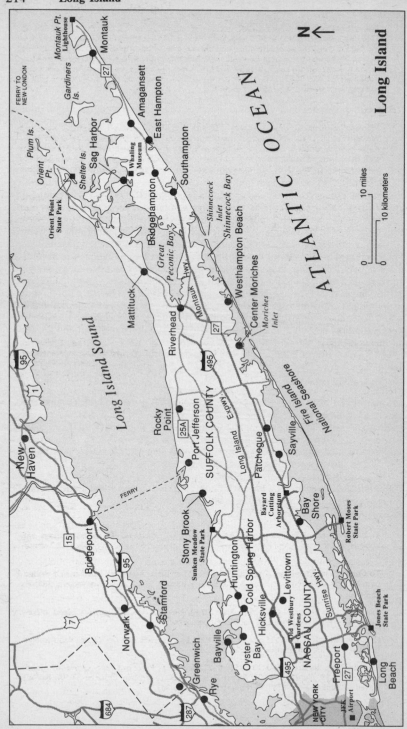

N

Long Island

ATLANTIC OCEAN

Montauk Pt. Lighthouse
Montauk
27
Gardiners Is.
Amagansett
East Hampton
Sag Harbor
Whaling Museum
Bridgehampton
Southampton
Shelter Is.
Orient Pt.
Plum Is.
Orient Point State Park
FERRY TO NEW LONDON
Shinnecock Inlet
Shinnecock Bay
Westhampton Beach
Great Peconic Bay
Mattituck
Riverhead
Montauk Hwy.
27
Center Moriches
Moriches Inlet
495
Long Island Sound
Rocky Point
25A
Port Jefferson
SUFFOLK COUNTY
Patchogue
Sayville
Fire Island National Seashore
New Haven
95
1
Stony Brook
Sunken Meadow State Park
Bayard Cutting Arboretum
Bay Shore
Robert Moses State Park
Bridgeport
15
Huntington
Cold Spring Harbor
95
1
Stamford
Levittown
Old Westbury Gardens
Sunrise Hwy.
Jones Beach State Park
7
Norwalk
Bayville
Oyster Bay
Hicksville
NASSAU COUNTY
Greenwich
Rye
Freeport
Long Beach
684
287
495
27
NEW YORK CITY
JFK Airport
Long Island Expwy.

10 miles
10 kilometers

Trains: Long Island Railroad (LIRR), train information 822-5477, tour information 718-990-7948, lost articles 718-990-8384. The Island's main public transportation facility has four central lines. Fares vary according to destination and time of day ("peak" or "off-peak"). Peak fares (5:30-9am on trains from Long Island to Manhattan and 4:30-8pm on trains from Manhattan to Long Island) range from $4.25-14. Off-peak fares, charged at all other times, range from $3-9.50. The LIRR also offers educational and recreational tour programs as well as escorted sightseeing tours from May-Nov.

Buses

Metropolitan Suburban Bus Authority (MBSA): daytime bus service in Queens, Nassau, and Western Suffolk (542-0100). Bus information 222-1000. Service runs along most major highways, but the routes are complex and irregular—make sure you confirm your destination with the driver. Some buses run every 15 min., others every hr. In Nassau, the fare is $1.15, but crossing over into Queens costs an additional 15¢, and transfers cost 10¢. Disabled people and senior citizens pay half-fare.

Suffolk Transit: (360-5700, open Mon.-Fri. 8:30am-4:30pm). Fare policy same as Nassau. The S-92 bus loops back and forth between the tips of the north and south forks, with 9 runs daily, most of them between East Hampton and Orient Point. Call to confirm stops and schedules. The route also connects with the LIRR at Riverhead, where the forks meet. No service Sunday.

Greyhound: 66 W. Columbia St. (483-3230), in Hempstead, and 90 Broadhollow Rd. (427-6897), in Melville.

Hampton Jitney Inc.: on Long Island 283-4600, in Manhattan 212-936-0440. 15-25 upscale buses daily from Manhattan to the South Fork and back. One-way fares $10-22. Catch buses on 41st St. between Lexington and Third Ave. They go directly to Westhampton, but then stop at almost all villages and towns on the South Fork, up to Montauk. Call their classy operators for detailed schedule and fare information.

Sunrise Express: 800-527-7709, in Suffolk 477-1200. Their "NY Express" runs 4 times per day from Manhattan to the North Fork ($15, $28 round-trip). Catch buses on the corner of 44th St. and Third Ave. They go directly to Riverhead, but then stop at almost all villages on the South Fork up to Greenport. Reservations required. Bicycles and pets allowed. Call for schedule information.

Long Island Airports Limousine Service: Nassau 933-2020, Suffolk 234-8400. Buses and vans available 24 hr.

Ferries

To Shelter Island: from North and South Fork about every 15 min. from 5:40am (5:15am on Mon.) to 1am.

North Fork: Greenport Ferry, 749-0139. North Ferry Rd., on the dock. For passenger and driver $5, $5.50 round-trip. 50¢ each additional passenger, 50¢ for a walk-on (without a car).

South Fork: North Haven Ferry, 749-1200. South Ferry Rd., on the dock. Same fares as Greenport Ferry.

To Block Island: Viking Lines, 668-5709. P.O. Box 730, Montauk. Call for reservations. $28 same day round-trip, $15 one way; ages 5-12 $15 round-trip, $10 one way; bicycles $2 round-trip.

To Connecticut: Steamboat Co., 473-0286. 102 West Broadway, Port Jefferson. To Bridgeport. $24-$28 car and driver; $8 each additional passenger; $30 unlimited passengers, children ½-price.

Fisher's Island Ferry: 203-443-6851. State Street, New London, CT. Fisher's Island to New London. $26 car and driver; $8 each additional passenger.

Cross-Sound Ferry: 323-2525 or 323-2743. P.O. Box 33, New London. Orient Point to New London. Call for information and reservations.

Sayville Ferry Service: 589-0810 or 589-0822. Sayville to Pines or Cherry Grove ($9 round-trip, seniors $8, children $4.50), Barret Beach ($6.50 round-trip, children $3.50), Sailor's Haven or Sunken Forest ($7.50 round-trip, children $4).

Taxis: Ollie's Airport Service, in Nassau. North Shore 829-8647, South Shore 937-0505. Open 24 hr. Vans, limousines, and cars. **All-Suffolk Transport,** 800-848-4885, 467-3388, or 563-0808. Bus, taxi, and limousine service.

Car Rental: Avis Rent-a-Car, nationwide reservations 800-331-1212. In Nassau, 357 Old Country Rd., Westbury (222-3255). In Suffolk, 20 East Jericho Turnpike, Huntington Station (271-9300). **Hertz Rent-a-Car,** worldwide reservations 800-654-3131. In Nassau, 225 Northern Blvd., Great Neck (482-5880). In Suffolk, Long Island MacArthur Airport (737-9200).

Bike Rental: Country Time Cycles, Main Rd. (298-8700), in Mattituck. 10-speeds $20 first day, $10 each additional day; $50 per week. Credit card required. **Piccozzi's Service Station,** Rte. 114 (749-0045), in Shelter Island Heights. A 10-min. walk from the north ferry. 3-speeds $12 for 4 hr., $16 for 8 hr.; 12-speeds $14 for 4 hr., $18 for 8 hr. $70 per week for either. Cash deposit or credit card required.

Help Line: Rape Hotline, 222-2293.

Area Code: 516.

Accommodations

Finding a place to stay on the Island can be a daunting prospect for the budget traveler. Daytrippers in Nassau will probably be better off heading back to the city to crash for the night. Most of the decent hotels in Nassau exact indecent rates ($100-150 per night). Likewise, the majority of the smaller motels do not cater to tourists but to business travelers and romantic couples (quite a few advertise special rates for "short stays"). Suffolk County provides a wider variety of accommodations, many of them more attuned to the demands of the tourist market. In general, however, places close during the off season and fill up quickly during the summer. Still, with some planning, you can find a good Island deal.

Nassau

Hicksville Motor Lodge, Duffy Ave. (433-3900), in Hicksville. LIE Exit 40S. A decent motel in what used to be a Howard Johnson's. Doubles $74.

Days Inn, 828 South Oyster Bay Rd. (433-1900), in Hicksville. LIE Exit 43. Part of a chain. Many business types, supplied by nearby Grumman defense plant. Doubles $75.

Gateway Inn, 1780 Sunrise Hwy. (378-7100), in Merrick. LIE Exit 38S (Meadowbrook Pkwy.). Comfortable 60- room inn on the South Shore, convenient to Jones Beach. Doubles $75.

Suffolk

Montauket, Tudhill Rd. (668-5992). Follow the Montauk Hwy. to Montauk, at the traffic circle take Edgemere, which becomes Flamingo, and make a left onto Fleming and then another left. Open mid-March to late Nov. The Island's best bargain. Almost always full on weekends. Doubles $30.

Pines Motor Lodge, corner of Rte. 109 and 3rd St. (957-3330), in Lindenhurst. LIE to Southern State Pkwy. East, Exit 33. Doubles $60.

Vineyard Motor Inn, Rte. 25 (722-4024), in Jamesport on the North Fork. At end of LIE, take Rte. 58 and then Rte. 25. Doubles $65, off-season $55.

Mattituck Bed and Breakfast, 795 Pike St. (298-8785), in Mattituck near the beach. Victorian manor house with wrap-around porch and flower gardens. Doubles $70-85.

Ranger Guest House/Anchor's Rest, 74 Old Riverhead Rd. (728-8955), in Hampton Bays. LIE Exit 70, then Sunrise Highway Exit 65N. Private residence with 3 rooms on the second floor and a shared bathroom. Guests receive a house key. Breakfast included on weekends. During the week $45, weekend package $100.

132 North Main Guest House, East Hampton (324-2246 or 324-9771), 1 mi. from the beach. LIE Exit 70, then Sunrise Hwy., which becomes Montauk Hwy. Main house, cottages, and cabana on 2 acres of grounds. Summer weekend rate for doubles $90-140, during the week $60-110.

Easterner Resort, 639 Montauk Hwy. (283-9292), in Southampton. Sunrise Hwy. Exit 66. 1- and 2-bedroom cottages, tennis court, new pool. Summer weekend package $150, during the week $70. Off-season: weekend $85, during the week $60.

Oceanside Beach Resort, Montauk Hwy. (668-9825), in Montauk. Refrigerators in each room, kitchen areas, pool. Close to town and beach. Doubles $41-79.

Shelter Island

Azalea House, 1 Thomas Ave. (749-4252). A new B&B at the center of the island. Doubles $65, off-season $50.

The Belle Crest House, 163 North Ferry Rd. (749-2041), in Shelter Island Heights. Country inn with lovely garden. Rooms infested with American antiques. Open March-Dec. Singles or doubles from $45.

Referral Services

Bed and Breakfast of Long Island, P.O. Box 392, Old Westbury, NY 11568 (334-6231). Covers the entire Island. Port Jefferson $48, Sayville near Fire Island $70, Southold contemporary on the beach $75, Southold colonial $80, Hamptons $75-85.

Twin Forks Reservation, P.O. Box 657, Hampton Bays, NY 11946 (728-5285). B&B in Suffolk county. All homes are inspected and approved. Doubles: South Fork $80, North Fork $75.

A Reasonable Alternative, Inc., 117 Spring St., Port Jefferson, NY 11777 (928-4034). Rooms in private homes all along the shores of Nassau and Suffolk. Doubles $75-80.

Camping

Camping makes financial sense if you plan to spend any amount of time on the Island, without spending too much money. On the down side, there are only a few months when the weather blows fair enough for comfort, and even then, the humidity can be quite draining. On a more practical note, you will find the Island's campsites tangled in a mystifying web of local, state, and federal regulations. Most Island camping facilities are restricted to local residents; you can camp on most of the Island only if you already live there. But at least a few places will welcome visitors to these shores.

Battle Row (293-7120), in Bethpage, Nassau. The only county-run facility not restricted to residents. Eight tent sites and 50 trailer sites available on a first come, first serve basis. Electricity, restrooms, showers, grills, and a playground. Tent sites for Nassau residents $5, others $7; with hookup $8, $12. Open April-Nov.

Heckscher Park (800-456-2267 or 669-1000), in East Islip, Suffolk. A state-run facility. Make reservations by calling the toll-free state number. 69 tent and trailer sites. Restrooms, showers, food, grills, fishing, horseback riding, and a beach. Open May-Sept.

Hither Hills (668-2554 or 669-1000), in Montauk. Carl G. Fisher, creator of Miami Beach, bought 10,000 acres here in 1926, but the Depression forestalled his development plans and he sold the lands to the state. 165 tent and trailer sites. Restrooms, showers, food, grills, fishing, tennis, and a beach. Reservations required. Open April-Nov., but no frills Oct.-Nov.

Fire Island National Seashore (597-6633), in Watch Hill. Adjacent to the only area in New York State formally designated by the Federal government as "wilderness." It's nice to know the people in Washington are earning their pay. Restrooms, showers, food. Reservations necessary (call Fri. 9-11am). 4-night max. stay.

South Haven Park (286-1040), in Brookhaven. LIE Exit 68. Campground, rowboats, stable. Suffolk residents $8, others $18. Open Memorial Day to the close of the autumn duck-hunting season.

Wildwood Park (800-456-2267), at Wading River. Location of Mackay Radio Station, source of Voice of America and one of the largest stations in the country (not open to the public). Former estate of Charles and John Arbuckle, multimillionaire coffee dealers who first packaged coffee rather than selling it in bulk. 322 tent and trailer sites, restrooms, showers, food, fishing, and a beach. Tent sites $10, trailer sites $16. Reservations advisable.

McCann Trailer Park (477-1748), in Greenport. Privately run. 150 tent and trailer sites. Laundry rooms, restrooms, showers, grills, food, beach, pool, hay-rides, and a game room. Tent sites $10, trailer sites $16. Reservations required. Open May-Oct.

Food

Long Island food has a split personality, promising both native food (Islanders love to eat out) and tourist food. Tourist food, found mostly in the fashionable resorts out east, is wonderful if you have already made your first million, but otherwise not worth discussing. Restaurants catering to Islanders, on the other hand, populate Nassau and most of Suffolk, doing very well for themselves without droves of rich Manhattan patrons. Many of these Island favorites specialize in ethnic fare—Chinese, Italian, Greek—brought here via the New York melting pot. But if you're interested in trying some more indigenous food, check out the bountiful farm stands of the East End and the infallible seafood restaurants of Suffolk.

Nassau

An amazing variety of reasonably priced restaurants, from Turkish to Viennese, add spice to Nassau, pleasing those whose wallets have been numbed by the extravagance of New York. You are practically always assured of a good meal at one of the Chinese eateries found at virtually every shopping center in Nassau: some good *moo shi* vegetables or beef and broccoli should send you on your way with a full stomach for about $5. Naturally, every shopping-center Chinese restaurant has its Italian equivalent, often next door. A bad pizza is hard to find, and Long Island lasagna merits a bite.

Last but not least is the glorious and inimitable Long Island diner, not to be confused with any less classy diner-traditions. Originally decommissioned dining cars parked on streetsides to provide short-order cooking, diners have evolved on Long Island (largely under Greek management) into often luxurious and always economical all-purpose, any-hour pitstops. Whether you are rolling out of bed for an early start or returning from the late show, you should be able to find something savory on the massive menu which a curt waiter lugs to your table and tosses in front of you. A Greek salad costs around $6 and feeds at least two anchovy-starved travelers. If you order a complete dinner (about $10) you'll probably end up with some leftovers for Rover.

Homer's Oriental Restaurant, 126 Spruce St., Cedarhurst (374-6111). Part of Homer's epic Chinese restaurant empire. The hot and sour soup takes its name very seriously. Try one of the house specials. Order carefully and dinner can cost as little as $8 per person. Open daily 5-9:30pm. Southern State Pkwy. to Rockaway Blvd., which becomes Rockaway Tpke., make a right just past the railroad tracks, a left onto Central Ave., and then a left at the fourth traffic light.

Christiano's, 19 Ira Rd., Syosset (921-9892). Legend has it that this unassuming eatery inspired local youth Billy Joel to write his hit "Italian Restaurant." Order a bottle of white, a bottle of red, or perhaps a bottle of rosé instead. Excellent food and prices (most entrees around $6) and a stellar eggplant parmagiana. Open Mon.-Thurs. 11:30am-1am, Fri. 11:30am-2am, Sat. 1pm-2am, Sun. 1pm-1am. LIE to Exit 42N (South Oyster Bay Rd.), go north, cross the Jericho Tpke., continue on Jackson Ave. for 1 mi., and hang a right onto Ira Rd. The sequel, **Christiano's II** (933-7272), pastaletizes in Plainview at 361 South Oyster Bay Rd. Open Mon.-Thurs. 11am-midnight, Fri.-Sat. 11am-1am, Sun. noon-midnight.

Pizza Delight, 1048 Old Country Rd., Plainview (931-3910). Pizza for the ultra-sophisticated. Try the "white pizza," which has olive oil, mozzarella, and ricotta—but no tomato sauce. One pie ($14) serves 3 or 4. The broccoli rolls deserve praise. Open Mon.-Thurs. 10am-10pm, Fri. 10am-11pm, Sat. 11am-10pm, Sun. noon-10pm. LIE to Exit 41S, on Rte. 107 go through Hicksville, make a left onto Old Country Rd. and go ¼ mi. past the Seaford-Oyster Bay Expwy.

All Seasons Restaurant, 300 W. Jericho Tpke., Huntington Station (351-5820). Don't be deceived by the pastel and glass late 80s exterior, or by the live trees and floor-to-ceiling tiles: this is a diner, albeit with a twist. Vivaldi would be proud—each of the four dining rooms is decorated in the theme of a different season. Spring is lovely during the day, and winter is always nice; autumn echoes a bit too much for comfort. Complete dinners around $10.

Open Mon.-Thurs. 6:30pm-midnight, Fri.-Sun. 6:30pm-2am. LIE to Exit 40N and follow the Jericho Tpke. to Huntington Station.

Empire Diner, 42 Jerusalem Ave., Hicksville (433-3350). Excellent dinner fare. Humbler than its name suggests. If you're lucky you'll get a waiter with a Cockney accent. Open daily 6am-1am. LIE to Exit 41S (Route 107), go through Hicksville and take the left fork to Jerusalem Ave.; the diner is on the right.

Homer's International, 7940 W. Jericho Tpke., Woodbury (364-3030). One of a kind. Besides a regular menu of Asian and Continental cuisine, Homer's features an avant-garde "all you can eat" international food bar ($11), where you can satisfy that craving for calimari with dumplings or sesame chicken with mussels. You can also select fresh vegetables and meats, prepared in the sauce of your dreams. Open Sun.-Thurs. 5-10pm, Fri. 5-11pm, Sat. 5-11:30pm. LIE to Exit 40N, Jericho Tpke. through Jericho and Syosset.

Genuwine's, 4112 Hempstead Tpke., Bethpage (735-0708). Great for brunch ($6-11). After you buy your first drink for $3 you can receive unlimited refills. Open Sun.-Mon. 4-10pm, Tues.-Thurs. 5-11pm, Fri. 4pm-midnight, Sat. 5pm-1am. LIE to Exit 44, Seaford-Oyster Bay Expwy. to Exit 7.

Fuddruckers, 725 Merrick Ave., Westbury (832-8323). Carefully engineered to produce the best all-around hamburger experience a human can have. Look through the glass walls to see freshly ground beef being prepared in the kitchen or watch the mini bun-bakery while you wait for your order. Then garnish that burger at the gourmet fixings bar. 1/3-lb. burger $4, ½-lb. burger $4.55. Open Sun.-Thurs. 11am-10pm, Fri. 11am-11pm, Sat. 11am-midnight. LIE to Exit 40S (Jericho Tpke.), go south and turn left onto Post Lane, which after 4 mi. will become Merrick Ave.

Suffolk

For a truly wholesome food experience, visit one of **Lewin Farms'** two separate pickin' patches. At the one on Sound Ave. in Wading River (929-4327), you can pick your own apples, nectarines, and peaches at 39¢ per lb. (Open May-Dec. Wed.-Mon. 8am-6pm. LIE to Exit 68N, go north to Rte. 25A and east to Sound Ave.—it's the first farm on Sound Ave.) At the other (727-3346), 123 Sound Ave. in Calverton, you can pick strawberries, raspberries, plums, pears, peaches, nectarines, beans, onions, peas, squash, and tomatoes, as well as pumpkins (from late Sept.-late Oct. $5 for as much as you can carry). But you can't pick your frined's pumpkins. (Open June-Nov. daily 8am-6pm. LIE to Exit 71N, drive on Edwards Ave. to Sound Ave.; the farm is ¼ mi. down on the left.)

Seasons Restaurant, 3845 Veteran's Memorial Hwy., Ronkonkoma (585-9500). A bright restaurant with a traditional and light menu. Fish and chips $7, great quiche of the day $5. Open Mon.-Fri. 5:30-10pm, Sat.-Sun. 5:30-11pm. LIE to Exit 57S onto Veterans' Memorial Hwy.

Driver's Seat, 62 Jobs Lane, Southampton (283-6606). A well-known Hamptons meeting place. Eat indoors or outdoors or at the bar. Entrees, including jumbo burgers, quiche, and local seafood, run $5-16. Open daily 11:30am-4pm. Rte. 27E to Southampton town center.

Carl's Mariners Inn, Bayview Ave., Northport (261-8111). Tired of sawdust restaurants with oyster shells? Come to Carl's for superior seafood served informally at pier-side. The popular bar enhances the experience. Sup on lobster at dusk and see the scuttling sailboats in the fading light through the large dining room windows. Lemon sole $12. Open daily 11am-10pm. LIE to Exit 41N, drive north on Rte. 106 to Rte. 25A, turn right and motor to Northport.

Lobster Roll Restaurant (267-3740), Montauk Hwy., Amagansett. Lyrical seafood shack surrounded by dunes and seagulls. Dinner $10. LIE to Exit 70, Rte. 3S to Sunrise Hwy., which becomes Montauk Hwy.; the restaurant lies about 3 mi. out of town center, on the right.

Meeting House Inn (722-4220), Meeting House Creek Rd., Aquebogue. Seafood and steaks alongside Meeting House Creek. Sing along with Rose, who tickles the ivories on Friday and Saturday evenings. Reservations suggested. Dinners around $12. Open Mon.-Thurs. 11:30am-10pm, Fri.-Sat. 11:30am-11pm, Sun. 11:30am-3pm. LIE to Exit 73, Rte. 25E to Aquebogue, cross Rte. 105 and make a right onto Edgar, cross the railroad tracks and bear left onto Meeting House Creek Rd.

The Ground Round, intersection of Rte 111 and Rte. 347, Smithtown Bypass, Hauppage (265-5102). Clowns, cartoons, balloons, popcorn, peanuts, and an enormous TV for sports, all in a faux-Wild West setting. Lots of fried stuff; a basic hamburger goes for $6. Happy Hour 3-7pm. Open daily 11am-2am. LIE Exit 57N to Smithtown.

Ponderosa Steakhouse. Cormer Middle City Rd., Rte. 83, Selden (732-7044). Casual steak and chicken and an all-you-can-eat salad buffet with over 80 items. Sirloin steak and salad bar $11. Open Mon.-Thurs. 11:30am-9pm, Fri.-Sat. 11:30am-10pm, Sun. 11:30am-8:30pm.

The Dining Car, 1890 Rte. 25A, East Setauket (751-1890). Sit in the dining car used by President Hoover, in 1 of 2 cabooses, or in the main dining room. Lunches from $9-15. Chicken Kiev dinner $12. Live jazz Fridays and Saturdays and occasional piano music and dancing during the week. Open daily 11:30am-11pm; bar open until 2am. LIE to Exit 62 onto Nichols Rd. and follow the signs to Stonybrook, make a right at Rte. 25A, and another right at the trains.

56th Fighter Group, Republic Airport, Rte. 110, Farmingdale (694-8280). English farmhouse in the midst of a World War II encampment, complete with bunkers, sandbags, low-flying planes, and Glenn Miller. It must be seen to be believed. Lunches from $5; dinners from $10. Open daily 11am-midnight. LIE to Exit 49S onto Rte. 110 and follow signs to the airport.

Sights

Nassau

Nassau's points of interest are often overlooked by tourists and residents alike, in favor of the glamor and glitz of New York City's attractions. But general ignorance of Nassau can be bliss for tourists seeking the solace of undiscovered sights.

The Blue Ribbon of the Atlantic is an 8-ft.-tall onyx, gold, and silver trophy awarded to the nation that holds the speed record for North Atlantic travel. This title has been held by the U.S. and the trophy kept in the **United States Merchant Marine Museum** (773-5000 or 466-9696) in King's Park since 1952. The museum stows away in a beautiful Gold Coast mansion overlooking the Long Island Sound, just over the Throgs Neck Bridge. Take LIE to Exit 33N, then Lakeville Rd., which becomes Middleneck Rd., and turn left on Steamboat Rd.

If you need space, you are likely to find it at one of the several other lavish Gold Coast properties, now open to the public, where you can vegetate in some of this country's most extravagant gardens. Among the largest is the **Planting Fields Arboretum,** site of insurance magnate William Robertson Coe's Oyster Bay home, Coe Hall (922-0479 or 922-9206). Constructed from 1918 to 1921 in the Tudor Revival style, the residence has rows upon rows of mind-boggling windows. Only eight decorated rooms are open to the public; unless you are an enthusiast for interiors, you may be better off using your imagination and admiring the building from the outside. (House open Mon.-Fri. 1-3:30pm. Admission $2, seniors and children $1.) Take LIE to 41N, go north on U.S. 106 to Rte. 25A and follow the signs. The massive Arboretum consists of 409 acres of some of the most valuable real estate in the New York area. Two huge greenhouses, covering 1½ acres, contain the largest camellia collection in the northeast. The flowers burst into bloom during the unlikely months of January, February, and March, just when most city denizens begin to forget what flora look like. Other quirky highlights include a "synoptic garden" of plants obsessively arranged according to their Latin names, from A to Z—every letter is represented. The **Fall Flower Show,** held in mid-October, attracts huge crowds every year. Christmas time brings the annual **Winter Festival,** while summertime brings artists like Wynton Marsalis, who give outdoor concerts here. But don't arrive expecting massive stimulation. The place is understated, ideal for the private contemplation of some extraordinary beauty. (Grounds open daily 9am-5pm. Admission $3 per car.)

The **Sands Point Preserve,** on Middleneck Rd. in Port Washington, is notable primarily for its astounding architecture. This densely forested 216-acre property originally housed railroad heir Howard Gould. He built his Hempstead House here in 1910, after the model of a Tudor period English castle. He also built some of Long Island's most lavish stables; called **Castlegould,** they are modeled after Ireland's turreted Kilkenny Castle. Daniel Guggenheim purchased the estate in 1917, and in 1923 his son Harry built **Falaise** on the cliffs overlooking the Long Island

Sound. A Norman-style manor house, Falaise includes medieval and Renaissance architectural elements in its design. Together these buildings form one of the most remarkable surveys of European architecture this side of the Atlantic.

Castlegould now hosts the visitors' reception center, and one wing of the building serves as the "Americana Storage/Study Collection." Here you may wander around shelves of china and silver in an atmosphere that combines elements of a museum with elements of an attic. One-hour escorted tours of Hempstead House are offered Monday through Wednesday ($2); advance reservations are encouraged. (Open May to mid-Nov. Sat.-Wed. 10am-5pm. Admission $1, July 4-Labor Day $2.) Take LIE to Exit 36N (Searingtown Rd., which becomes Port Washington Blvd. and then Middleneck Rd.).

The **Polish American Museum,** at 116 Bellevue Ave. in Port Washington (883-6542), maintains hundreds of volumes, along with church artifacts and army items. (Open daily 10am-4pm. Free.) The museum stands 2 blocks from the Port Washington LIRR stop. By car, take LIE to Exit 36N (Searington Rd.), go north about 5 mi., and make a left onto Main St., which connects with Bellevue Ave.

At **Old Westbury Gardens,** on Old Westbury Rd. (333-0048), yet another extravagant estate, nature overwhelms architecture. You can feel the setting take over as you enter the wrought iron gates and drive down the gravel road lined with towering evergreens. The elegant house, built by John Phipps in 1906 and modeled after 19th-century English country manors, stands in the shadow of its surroundings. Although these grounds may not sprawl as the Planting Fields do, they abound with more things floral and with a more coherent sense of organization. The two lakes are ornamented by sculptures, gazebos, and water lilies, and a vast rose garden adjoins a number of theme gardens (such as the "grey garden," which contains only plants in shades of silver and deep purple). Plan on spending an afternoon here, armed with a book or a talkative friend. Take LIE E. to Exit 39S (Glen Cove Rd.), make a right onto Old Westbury Rd., and continue another ¼ mi.

Botany freaks should also visit **Clark Gardens** and the **Bailey Arboretum.** Clark Gardens, at 193 I.U. Willets Rd. in Albertson (621-7568), set on much smaller grounds, has over 20 specialty displays and three ponds, as well as five honey-producing beehives. (Open Mon.-Fri. 8am-4:30pm, Sat.-Sun. 10am-4:30pm. Admission $2, seniors and children $1.) Take LIE to Exit 37S, go south 1 mi. on Willis Ave. and then left onto I.U. Willets Rd. for about ¼ mi. The Bailey Arboretum (676-4497) blossoms on Bayville Rd. in luxurious Locust Valley. Here you can find some of the largest trees on the Island, a miniature castle carved by a German master craftsman, and one garden with handicapped access. (Open May-Oct. Tues.-Sun. 9am-4pm. Admission $1.) Take LIE to Exit 41N (U.S. 107N), go right on U.S. 25A, then left onto Wolver Hollow Rd. and follow the signs.

Of course, if you happen to be touring these gardens, you have an excuse to drive around the ritzy North Shore. Take a few turns off the major roads to drive past some breathtaking (and some breathtakingly vulgar) homes of the rich and anonymous. Make sure your gas tank is full; it's easy to lose track of time as you argue with your car-mates over the comparative merits of Tudor Revival and Contemporary.

Those tired of manicured gardens and delicately pruned trees can find nature in a more untamed condition at one of the preserves scattered throughout the county. The **Garvies Point Museum and Preserve** (671-0300), one of the best of its kingdom, encompasses a small museum (with exhibits on regional geology, archeology, and anthropology) and 60 acres of woods, thickets, fields, and ponds. In their natural state, especially around sunset in autumn, they bear monumental post-British beauty. (Museum open May-Oct. daily 9am-4:45pm. Admission 25¢. Preserve open year-round Mon.-Fri. 8am-dusk, Sat.-Sun. 9am-dusk. Free.) Take LIE to Exit 39N, follow Glen Cove Rd. north for 5 mi., take the left fork (Rte. 107) to its end, and turn right. Go left on Cottage Rd. and follow the signs. The museum hosts a popular annual **Indian Feast** the weekend before Thanksgiving.

The **Tackapousha Museum and Preserve** (785-2802), on Washington Ave. in Seaford, has managed to convince some of its animals that day is night and night is day, offering viewers an opportunity to become familiar with what goes on in the natural world while most creatures are sound asleep. (Museum open daily 10am-4:45pm. Admission 25¢. Preserve open daily dawn-dusk.) LIE to Exit 44S, follow the Seaford-Oyster Bay Expwy. to its end, go east on U.S. 27A (Merrick Rd.), and left on Washington Ave. The **Theodore Roosevelt Sanctuary and Museum** (922-3200) pays special homage to the President's accomplishments as a naturalist. Here the National Audubon Society administers a center for the rehabilitation of injured birds. (Grounds open daily 9am-5pm. Museum open daily 1-4:30pm.)

Believe it or not, Nassau even has some activities focusing on people, not just on shrubs. Quite a few places in the county keep a sense of local history alive. Don't miss Nassau's top cultural attraction, **Old Bethpage Village Restoration** (420-5280), on Round Swamp Rd. in Old Bethpage. In this "history preserve," bits and pieces of Long Island's 19th-century heritage have been gathered in one timeless spot and reassembled in the form of a typical pre-Civil War village. As you enter the general store or the blacksmith's shop, employees clad in period costume will explain their occupation. The hatter is especially informative. A series of special events takes place every weekend afternoon; sheep shearing is an absolute blast. Overall, the village succeeds remarkably well in recreating the 1850s, and because it is county-run, Bethpage manages to avoid being obnoxiously commercial. Of course, Americana's charm can wane, especially in summer when this place packs solid with tourists. Winter visitors beware: the village caters to a multitude of school groups when the temperature drops. Columbus Day weekend brings the **Long Island Fair,** a popular old-fashioned festival. Take LIE to Exit 48, then hang a right onto Round Swamp Rd. and a left onto the winding driveway.

You can relive history on a more modest scale at two attractions near each other in Oyster Bay, a small and sleepy town on the North Shore. Take LIE to Exit 41N and go north past U.S. 25A on U.S. 106, which becomes first Pine Hollow Rd. and then 6th St. You can get to **Sagamore Hill,** perhaps the most important residence in Nassau County, by turning right off 6th St. in the town center and then following the signs to Cove Neck Rd. An official National Historical Site, Sagamore Hill was the summer residence of Theodore Roosevelt during his presidential term. Roosevelt met here with envoys from Japan and Russia during the summer of 1905 to set in motion negotiations that would lead to the Treaty of Portsmouth, which ended the Russo-Japanese War. Despite a few recent robberies, the house remains jam-packed with "Teddy" memorabilia, and its Victorian clutter evokes a powerful sense of Roosevelt's era; the collection of antlers speaks for his sporting interests. (Open Wed.-Sun. 9:30am-5pm. Admission $1, seniors and children free.)

While you're in Oyster Bay, check out **Raynham Hall** (922-6808), 20 West Main St., a left turn off 6th St. in the town center. A study in architectural epoque-clashing incongruity, this house has a colonial salt-box façade in front, and a rear preserved in an overlaid Victorian style. Inside you can find colonial rooms and Victorian rooms side by side and see how home life evolved during the 18th and 19th centuries.

Since the days of Melville, U.S. culture has given a suitably prominent place to that most prominent mammal, the whale. To indulge a cetacean obsession or merely to brush up on what you have been missing, nothing compares to the **Cold Spring Harbor Whaling Museum** (367-3418), on Main St. in Cold Spring Harbor. The museum, built in honor of a small whaling fleet that sailed from Cold Spring Harbor in the mid-19th century, features a 30-ft.-long fully rigged vessel, one of only six remaining whaleboats of its kind in the world. Also extraordinary here is the collection of scrimshaw, detailed whalebone carvings done to pass the long hours at sea. (Open Labor Day-Memorial Day Tues.-Sun. 11am-5pm. Admission $2, seniors $1.50, children $1. Handicapped access.)

But harpoons and creaky old houses do not tell nearly all of Nassau's history. The **African-American Museum,** at 110 North Franklin St. in Hempstead (485-0470), currently hosting traveling exhibitions, will soon provide expanded exhibition space for its permanent collection on the history of African Americans on Long Island. Future shows scheduled include "Climbing Jacob's Ladder," a presentation about the African American church, and "From Fields to Factories," about the migration to the North. (Open Tues.-Sat. 9am-4:45pm, Sun. 1-4:45pm. Free.) Take LIE to Exit 39S and go south to the town center on Hempstead Ave., which becomes Fulton Ave.; turn left onto Franklin St. and go four lights down.

And while Long Island remains unrivalled in the field of Long Island history, its traditional fine arts museums must go head to head with those in Manhattan. Art museums on the Island tend to be small and modest, offering a nice change from cavernous and comprehensive New York galleries. The cutting-edge "computer imaging facility" at the **Fine Arts Museum of Long Island,** 295 Fulton Ave. in Hempstead (481-5700), requires no apologies. Here five computers feature the interactive graphic design of contemporary computer artists. The art is mesmerizing; you may find yourself spending long hours staring at a computer screen. (Open Wed.-Sat. 10am-4:30pm, Sun. noon-4:30pm. Free.) Take LIE to Exit 39S onto Hempstead Ave., which turns into Fulton Ave. Also, the nearby **Hofstra Museum** (560-5672), on the campus of Hofstra University, has one of the Island's major collections, with galleries of ethnology and Modern American and European art as well as a 42-piece sculpture garden. The museum is famous for its innovative exhibitions, and recently hosted a popular Henry Moore retrospective. (Open Tues.-Fri. 10am-5pm; off-season Tues. 10am-9pm, Wed.-Fri. 10am-5pm, Sat.-Sun. 1-5pm. Free.) Take LIE to Exit 38S and Meadowbrook Pkwy., go west on Hempstead Tpke. for four traffic lights, turn left onto the campus and follow the signs.The **Heckscher Art Museum** (351-3250), Rte. 25A and Prime Ave. in Huntington, houses European and U.S. paintings and sculptures dating from the 16th century to the present. (Open Tues.-Fri. 10am-5pm, Sat.-Sun. 1-5pm. Suggested donation $1, seniors and children 50¢.) Take LIE to Exit 49N, go north on Rte. 110, and make a right onto 25A followed by a left onto Prime Ave.

Jones Beach State Park (784-1600) contains one of the most famous beaches in the world. Its vast facilities stretch over 2413 acres of ideal beachfront on the South Shore in Wantaugh, practically in Queens. The parking facilities at Jones Beach accommodate some 23,000 cars. On account of its convenient location, though, only 40 mi. away from the concrete heart of Manhattan, even this lot may not be large enough: on sizzling summer weekends the beach seems carpeted with brightly colored blankets and umbrellas. Along the 1½-mi. boardwalk you can find deck games, roller-skating, miniature golf, basketball, and nightly dancing. The **Marine Theater** inside the park hosts rock concerts (see Nassau Entertainment). There are eight different bathing areas on either the rough Atlantic Ocean or the calmer Zachs Bay, plus a number of beaches restricted to residents of certain towns in Nassau County. During the summer you can take the LIRR to Freeport or Wantaugh, where you can get a bus to the beach. Call 212-739-4200 or 212-526-0900 for information. **Recreation Lines, Inc.** (718-788-8000) provides bus service straight from mid-Manhattan. If you are driving, take LIE east to the Northern State Pkwy., go east to the Meadowbrook (or Wantaugh) Pkwy. and then south to Jones Beach.

Suffolk

For a comparatively rural and undeveloped place, Suffolk County is chock-full of first-rate and offbeat attractions. Many of Suffolk's colonial roots have been successfully preserved; the county boasts some of the finest colonial house-museums in the country. The shores are lined with salty old towns full of shady streets and brimful of atmosphere—refreshing retreats from the din of New York.

A few caveats are in order, though. Suffolk transforms during the summer, when the water warms up, the sun shines, the hotels double their rates, and it seems as if half of New York is tagging along as you stroll down the streets. Be especially wary of sun-filled weekends, because thousands of other people will have the same bright idea as you. Ordinarily most places in Suffolk are about two or three hours away from Manhattan by car, bus, or LIRR. But the easy ride gets hard on Friday afternoons and even harder on Sunday evenings, when flocks of urban dwellers clog the roads.

Visit Suffolk County off-season or mid-week in order to bypass this traffic hassle; you may save a great deal of money in the bargain. The drawback to this plan is that many of the county's most interesting sites are open only on the weekend. You can also break up your trip by stopping at one of numerous roadside farm stands, where you can often pick your own produce (see Suffolk Shopping). Better yet, pull over and take a tour of one of Long Island's vineyards and wineries, many of which offer free tours and tastings (see Wine Country).

After shopping at the **Walt Whitman Mall,** the nearby **Walt Whitman's Birth-place** will seem a more appropriate memorial to the great American poet whose 1855 *Leaves of Grass* established a democratic free-verse style that revolutionized poetry. The small, weathered farmhouse at 246 Old Walt Whitman Rd., Huntington Station, was built in 1816 by Walt Whitman, Sr., the Bard of Long Island's dad. You can find a several-hundred-volume library of Whitmanalia here amid simple rusted and worn furnishings. (Open Wed.-Fri. 1-4pm, Sat.-Sun. 10am-4pm. Free.) Take LIE to Exit 49N, drive 1¾ mi. on Rte. 110 and turn left onto Old Walt Whitman Rd. The **Vanderbilt Museum** (262-7888), on Little Neck Rd. in Centerport, preserves some American extravagance to contrast with Whitman's American simplicity. Built by William Kissam Vanderbilt II (1818-1944), great grandson of the famed "Commodore" Cornelius Vanderbilt, the 43-acre North Shore estate enjoys a great view of Northport Harbor and the Long Island Sound. (House open May-Oct. Tues.-Sat. 10am-4pm, Sun. noon-5pm.) Also on the grounds is the **Vanderbilt Planetarium** (262-7888), one of the largest and best-equipped in the country. The magnificent nearly four-ton projector can simulate the night sky from any place on earth at any season of the year, all the way back to the dawn of humankind. On clear evenings, when public shows are scheduled, an observatory with a 16-in. reflecting telescope also opens to the public.

Sagtikos Manor (665-0093), on Rte. 27A in Bay Shore, built on 10 acres of land in 1692, remains the finest example of colonial architecture on the Island. The hub of Long Island's pre-revolutionary aristocracy, the 42-room mansion housed the commander of British forces during the revolution and hosted George Washington during his presidency. Built by the Van Cortlandt family, it soon passed into the hands of the Thompsons, who lived there until the 20th century. Its current owner, Robert Gardiner, descends from another family of early Suffolk settlers. The only part of the building open to the public includes an exhibit of the 18th-century postal system used by revolutionary leaders as well as the old kitchen with its original paint made of lime, buttermilk, and blueberries. (Open July-Aug. Wed.-Thurs., Sun. 1-4pm; June and Sept. Sun. 1-4pm. Admission $1.75.) Take the Southern State Pkwy. to Exit 40 (the Robert Moses Causeway) and drive 1½ mi. The house is on the left, after Manor Lane.

The **William Floyd Estate** (399-3020), at 245 Park Dr. in Mastic Beach, yet another magnificent and historic site, is the furnished home of a signer of the Declaration of Independence—William Floyd—and eight of his descendants. Floyds lived here from 1724 to 1975. The 25-room furnished mansion is set on 613 acres of South Shore property facing Fire Island. Here, instead of being restored, hidden, or closed off, the modernized sections of the house have been preserved and adjoin the older sections, documenting the evolution of family life in an ancestral home. There are guided tours of the house, but don't miss the self-guided tours of the grounds and the family cemetery. (Open July-Aug. Fri.-Sun. 10am-4pm; June Sat.-Sun. 10am-4pm. Groups by reservation only. Free.) Take LIE to Exit 68S, then the William Floyd Pkwy. for 7 mi. Make a left onto Havenwood Drive, which becomes Neighborhood Drive, and a left onto Park Drive.

Your scientific interests may be sparked by the **Brookhaven National Lab Exhibit Center,** located on the William Floyd Pkwy. in Brookhaven (282-2345). Dan's were. See old fashioned reactors, huge magnets, and an experiment show with lots of impressive explosions. (Open July-Aug. Sun. 10am-3pm, or by appointment weekdays. Free.) Take LIE to Exit 68N onto William Floyd Pkwy.; the lab experiments about 1½ mi. down.

At the **Mattituck Historical Society Museum** on Rte. 25 in Mattituck, an 19th-century homestead has been maintained as a lived-in home—complete with a unique collection of clothes, children's toys, rope beds, musical instruments, and kitchen artifacts. (Open July-Aug. Sat.-Sun. 2-4pm. Free. Write P.O. Box 766, Mattituck, NY 11952 for a calendar of events that include Victorian teas, a flea market, antique shows, and doll shows. The **Corwith House** (537-1088) in Bridgehampton, on the corner of Montauk Hwy. and Corwith Ave., was built by the Corwith family in the late 1700s. This Greek Revival structure exhibits a multitude of period objects; the rooms are set up to show the way they might have looked during different eras. Next door stands the **George W. Strong Blacksmith and Wheelwright Shop,** with a working forge and many blacksmith's tools. The shop was moved here from its original site in Wainscott, a few towns to the east. (Both open June-Labor Day Mon. and Thurs.-Sat. 10am-4pm.)The **Guild Hall Museum,** at 158 Main St. in East Hampton, ensures that even the most sophisticated New Yorkers escaping to the Hamptons do not have to suffer art withdrawal. The collection specializes in the many well-known artists of the eastern Island region from the late 19th century to the present. Guild Hall hosts changing exhibitions, films, lectures, concerts, plays, art classes, and special events.

Wine Country

If the West Coast seems too far to travel for fine wine, try the North Fork, where 12 wineries and 40 vineyards produce the best Chardonnay, Cabernet Sauvignon, Merlot, Pinot Noir, and Riesling in New York State. Local climate and soil conditions rival those of Napa Valley. Two Long Island wines were even chosen to be served at President Bush's inauguration. Quite a few of the Island wineries offer free tours and tastings, which add up to big fun. To get to the wine district LIE to its end (Exit 73), then Rte. 58, which becomes Rte. 25 (Main Rd.). North of and parallel to Rte. 25 is Rte. 48 (North Rd. or Middle Rd.), which also has a number of wineries. Road signs announce tours and tastings.

Palmer Winery, 108 Sound Ave. (722-4080), in Riverhead. Take a self-guided tour of the most advanced equipment on the island and see a tasting room with an interior assembled from two 18th-century English pubs.

Pindar, a 200-acre vineyard, produces the widest variety of wines on the Island. Open daily 11am-6pm.

Mattituck Hills Winery, Bergen and Sound Ave. (298-5964), in Mattituck.

Bridgehampton Winery (537-3155), on Sag Harbor Tpke. in Bridgehampton. Guided tours June-Sept. daily 11am-6pm. The winery holds special summer events including the effervescent Chardonnay Festival.

Sag Harbor

Out on the South Fork's north shore nestles Sag Harbor, one of the best-kept secrets of Long Island. Founded in 1707, this port used to be more important than New York Harbor: in 1789, Washington signed the document creating Ports of Entry to the United States, and of the two named, "Sagg Harbour" appeared before New York. At its peak, this darling village was the fourth largest of the world's whaling ports. It boasts the second-largest collection of colonial buildings in the U.S., as well as cemeteries lined with the gravestones of Revolutionary soldiers and sailors. James Fenimore Cooper began his first novel, *Precaution,* while staying in a Sag Harbor hotel in 1824.

Today it is hard to imagine bustling activity on the quiet, tree-lined streets of salt-box cottages and Greek Revival mansions. In town, you should see the **Sag Harbor Whaling Museum** (725-0770), in the former home of Benjamin Hunting, a 19th-century whale ship owner. After you enter the museum—through the jaw-bones of a whale—take special note of the antique washing machine, locally made in 1864, and the excellent scrimshaw collection.

The **Whalers' Presbyterian Church,** built in 1844 in the Egyptian Revival style, displays a hodgepodge of Greek, Chinese, and Turkish architectural elements. Its old burying ground was used as a fort when the British occupied the town during the Revolution. Imagine this building with the 187-ft.-tall steeple that crowned it until the hurricane of 1938. Sag Harbor is also home to **Temple Adas Israel,** the oldest synagogue on Long Island. Constructed in 1898 on a plot of land costing $350, it served the early Jewish immigrants who arrived when Joseph Fahys started a watchcase factory here. The building combines traditional European construction with strong colonial motifs. Note the Gothic-style stained glass windows and the carvings done by local craftsmen.

Montauk

At the easternmost tip of the South Fork, Montauk is one of the most popular destinations on Long Island. The place generates natural exhilaration: as you look out at the Atlantic Ocean and realize that you can go no farther, that you have reached the end, that there is nothing but water between you and Portugal. The image of Montauk's famous lighthouse is what comes to mind for many people when they think of Long Island. But be warned that Long Island sights don't get any farther away than this: the trip from Manhattan can take up to four hours. On the bright side, though, once you get past the Hamptons, life gets substantially less congested. Take LIE to Exit 70 (Manorville), then go south to Sunrise Hwy. (Rte. 27) which becomes Montauk Hwy., and drive east. You will know you have arrived when the highway ends and the water lies before you.

Montauk offers numerous accommodations and activities, but the **Montauk Point Lighthouse and Museum** (668-2544) is the centerpiece of a trip here. Like the marker that greets a mountain climber who has reached a summit, the lighthouse marks the end of the island for the weary driver. Virginia Woolf would be proud. This lighthouse is exactly as it should be: set on the rocky edge of the water, its sloping white sides are adorned bluntly by a single wide band of brown. Its bulky, solid form rises with a utilitarian elegance from amid a cluster of smaller, weaker buildings. The builders knew exactly what they were doing back in 1796, when the 86-ft. structure went up by special order of President George Washington. Back then, the lighthouse was 297 ft. away from the shoreline.

On a clear day, you should climb the 138 spiralling steps to the top, where you can look out over the seascape, across the Long Island Sound to Rhode Island and Connecticut. The best seasons for viewing are the spring and fall, when the sea has scarcely a stain on it; the thick summer air can haze over the view. Even on a foggy day you may want to climb up anyway, to see if you can spot the so-called "Will o' the Wisp," a clipper ship (sometimes sighted on hazy days) under full sail with a lantern hanging from its mast. Experts claim that the ship is a mirage resulting from the presence of phosphorus in the atmosphere, but what do they know anyway. (The schedule of hours is complex: open April 30-June 19 Sat.-Sun. 11am-4pm; June 20-Sept. 18 daily 11am-6pm; Sept. 19-Oct. 10 Fri.-Mon. 11am-5pm; Oct. 11-Dec. 5 Sat.-Sun. 11am-4pm. Admission $2, children $1.)

Fishing and whale-watching are among Montauk's other pleasures. **Lazybones'** half-day fishing "party boat," which is more party than boat, makes two trips daily, from 7am to noon and from 1 to 5pm, leaving from Tuma's Dock next to Grossman's. Call Captain Mike at 668-5671 for information. The **Okeanos Whale Watch Cruise** is one of the best in the business though a tad expensive. The cruises are run by the non-profit Okeanos Research Foundation, which helps finance its studies of whales by taking tourists out on its 90-ft. ship, accompanied by a biologist and research team of whale experts. You may see fin, minke, and humpback whales. Adults pay $25 for the opportunity, children $15.

The Island's Islands: Fire and Shelter

Fire Island, one of the more extraordinary natural sites off of Long Island's shores, is actually a 32-mi.-long barrier island protecting the South Shore from the roaring waters of the Atlantic. The state has designated most of Fire Island as a state park or federal "wilderness area," legally protected from development, but 17 summer communities have designated the rest of it as their resort area and have forged their own niche there. Fire Island's unique landscape will make you forget there ever was such a city as New York. Cars are allowed only on the easternmost and westernmost tips of the island: there are no streets, only "walks." Fire Island was a hip spot for a lot of counterculture during the 60s, and today maintains a laid-back atmosphere; two of Fire Island's many resorts, Cherry Grove and the Pines, continue to have predominantly gay communities.

The **Fire Island National Seashore** is the main draw here, and in summer it offers fishing, clamming, and guided nature walks. The facilities at **Sailor's Haven** include a marina, a nature trail, and a famous beach. Similar facilities at **Watch Hill** include a 20-unit campground, where reservations are required. Smith Point West has a small visitor information center and a nature trail with disabled access (289-4810). Here you can spot horseshoe crabs, whitetail deer, and monarch butterflies, which flit across the country every year to winter in Baja California.

The **Sunken Forest,** so-called because of its location down behind the dunes, is another of the Island's natural wonders. Located directly west of Sailor's Haven, its soils support an unusual combination of gnarled holly, sassafras, and poison ivy. From the summit of the dunes, the forest looks like a well-tended lawn: the trees are laced together in a practically unbroken mass.

Ferries shuttle between the South Shore and the park from May through November. From Bay Shore, they sail to Fair Harbor, Ocean Beach, Dunewood, Saltaire, and Kismet. From Sayville (589-8980), ferries leave for Sailor's Haven, Cherry Grove, and Fire Island Pines. From Patchogue, ferries go to Davis Park and Watch Hill. LIRR stations lie within a short distance of the three ferry terminals, making access from New York City relatively simple. (See Practical Information.)

Shelter Island is one of the more unique spots on Long Island, or rather, near Long Island; it swims in the protected body of water in between the North and South Forks. Accessible by ferry (see Practical Information) or by private boat, this island of about 12 square mi. offers wonderful beaches and a sense of safety from the intrusions of the outside world. That doesn't mean you'll have to rough it here, because the island has virtually everything that you might need, including a coalyard, four insurance agencies, and a real estate attorney.

Entertainment and Nightlife

While the Island's entertainment options do not compare with those of the city, with a little planning, you can still do quite a few things. Many Long Islanders looking for a night on the town will hop on the LIRR and head for Manhattan, leaving local entertainment spots uncrowded. But there is no reason to sit at home twiddling your thumbs after the sun sets over the Long Island Sound.

Nassau

Movie screens abound here. Recent years have seen the subdivision of existing theatres and the construction of new ones; on the island the single-screen theatre is an endangered species. The **Glen Cove Odeon** (671-6668) has seven screens, and **Port Washington Movies** (944-6200) has 10. The Long Island newspaper *Newsday* lists all the local theatres and their showings. A ticket usually costs around $5, a good $2 cheaper than in Manhattan.

The **New Community Cinema** in Huntington (423-7653), just over the Nassau border, is an open secret among local residents and one of the only places on Long Island where you can safely call your movie a "film." It provides a great alternative to the huge and more commercial theatres, with its screenings of offbeat documentaries and foreign art films.

After the movie, your options are more limited; Nassau has never been known as a late-night paradise. You may just want to relax to some live jazz at **Sonny's Place,** 3603 Merrick Rd., Seaford (826-0973). Sonny extracts an $8 cover charge here on Friday and Saturday nights and enforces a two-drink minimum. During the week the music plays on, without the cover or minimum. For dancing, try **Gatsby's,** a fashionable spot on a stretch past the green light at 1067 Old Country Rd. in Westbury (997-3685). On weekends you can forgo the $5 cover charge by eating dinner here. A good burger costs $5.75. They have a DJ on Thursday and a live band on weekend nights.

Nassau's comedy clubs feature unknown but rising talents as well as established New York names. **Chuckles,** at 159 Jericho Tpke. in Mineola (746-2709), has a $5-12 cover and a two-drink minimum, with shows Wednesday through Sunday. You are more likely to hear belly laughs than chuckles at **Governor's Comedy Shop,** 90A Division Ave., Levittown (731-3358). Jokesters attempt to slay the crowd Tuesday through Saturday. (Cover $7-15 and 2-drink minimum.)

Nassau also performs for the more refined. **The Great Neck Symphony** (466-5155) gives regular concerts throughout the county, and the **Long Island Philharmonic** (239-2222), a highly respected orchestra, performs at the Tilles Center for the Performing Arts. Located on the C.W. Post Campus of Long Island University, on Northern Blvd. in Greenvale (299-2600), the **Tilles Center** has recently been renovated, and you can enjoy a concert under its strikingly sloping white ceiling. **The Arena Players Repertory Theatre,** 296 Rte. 109 in East Farmingdale (293-0674) and the **Broadhollow Theater** at 229 Rte. 110, Farmingdale (752-1400), have full calendars of productions. Performances can be uneven, especially by New York standards, and the choice of shows tends toward the commercial. Still, as the theatres have gained a more solid footing they have shown signs of branching out, and are worth a look, especially when a favorite goes up. Local universities also have active theatres: the **Olmstead** at Adelphi University in Garden City (741-2313) and the **John Cranford Adams Playhouse** at Hofstra University, on Fulton Ave. in Hempstead (560-6644).

National rock concert tours stop during the summer at the **Jones Beach Marine Theater,** Jones Beach State Park, Wantaugh (785-1600). Joining the bandmembers for a dance is impossible here unless you have a rowboat; the stage is separated from the bleachers by a wide stretch of water. In a production of "Showboat," the actors made their entrances and exits by motorboat. Now the theatre hosts concerts exclusively. The **Westbury Music Fair,** on Brush Hollow Rd. in Westbury (334-0800), has a tremendous theatre in the round, and usually hosts traditional big names on tour: if Wayne Newton happens to be on the road, you will catch him here.

Suffolk

The most exciting nighttime entertainment in Suffolk (if you don't count just breathing the night air and listening to the crickets) can be found on the grounds of the parks and museums, which perpetually produce piano recitals and host harpsichord concerts. This outdoor musical life, as with most things in Suffolk, becomes much more active in the summer. Performance dates and times are also hard to monitor. It's best to call around and get the schedules from the parks (see Suffolk Sights). Be aware that some of these parks restrict admission to local residents, and a few charge exorbitant fees to keep tourists out. Get the scoop before setting out.

So maybe music by dead Europeans is not your style. You can instead choose to strut over to one of the most chic dance clubs on Long Island, **Paris New York,** at 1017 East Jericho Tpke. in Huntington (351-1315 or 351-8837). Here you can listen to DJ Slaze, famed for his remix of Depeche Mode's hit "Master and Servant," as he plays leading-edge industrial-house-gothic music for a loyal crowd of local college students. You are sure to be entertained if you enjoy wearing black or watching people who do. Farther out on the Island, **CPI** (the Canoe Place Inn), located on the East Montauk Hwy. in Hampton Bays (728-4121), caters to a more mature crowd. You must be 21 or over and wearing proper attire to enter, but once in you can stop at the piano lounge, listen to live patio jazz, or move on the massive dance floor.

Serious theatre thrives at the **Theater Three,** 412 Main St., Port Jefferson (928-9100). The **John Drew Theatre** at Guild Hall, 158 Main St. in East Hampton (324-4050), is somewhat more upscale.

For stand-up comedy in Suffolk, look to: **Boomer's,** 1509 Main St., Port Jefferson (473-9226), with shows from Thursday to Saturday nights and an $8-15 cover; **Joker's Wild,** 503 Lake Ave., St. James (584-9565) with a cover of $5; and **Thomas McGuire's Comedy,** 1627 Smithtown Ave., Bohemia (467-5413), with a $9 cover and shows Friday and Saturday nights.

Shopping

Residents shop out of their cars in Nassau, while tourists shop their hearts out in Suffolk. Nassau has miles of malls; Suffolk specializes in the quaint.

Nassau

Shopping as recreation is essentially a suburban science, but in Nassau's malls (pronounced MAWLS), the unofficial centers of the county's commercial and social life, it has been refined to an art form. Here at last the residents of the Island's dozens of distinct communities leave their cars behind and come face to face, often for long periods of time, as they wait for teenage clerks to make change daintily while trying not to break their four-inch nails. The **Roosevelt Field Mall** (742-8000), the largest in the northeast, was built on the site of the airfield Charles Lindbergh flew from in his historic crossing of the Atlantic. A plaque and a pavilion in front of the entrance to Macy's mark the exact spot. The mall has 185 shops and department stores. Nearby, at the **Roosevelt Raceway Flea Market,** thousands of indoor and outdoor merchants convene every Sunday. This is the definitive flea market, and those with the patience to wade through yards of airbrushed T-shirts and mountains of plastic sailor's hats will certainly find something desperately necessary at half the regular price.

The famous **Miracle Mile,** on Northern Blvd. in classy Manhasset, caters to a different crowd. Practically all the fashionable Fifth Avenue stores have annexes lining this stretch of highway, from Gucci to Brooks Brothers, from Lord and Taylor to Ralph Lauren. Of course, in a distinctive Long Island twist, not a soul actually window-shops on foot. The large parking lots behind these stores fill with Jaguars, Mercedes, and BMWs, and shoppers hop in and out of their vehicles to shuttle from lot to lot. The whole affair is quite a sight; browsing and gawking are absolutely free.

Suffolk

> Crowds of men and women attired in the usual costumes, how curious you are to me . . . And you that shall cross from shore to shore years hence are more to me, and more in my meditations, than you might suppose.
> —Walt Whitman, "Crossing Brooklyn Ferry"

Although Whitman tried to "project the history of the future," he probably did not predict that one day Suffolk folk would choose their usual costumes in a mass of shopping centers including the atrium-like **Walt Whitman Mall,** on Rte. 110 in Huntington (271-1741). There is no greater honor on Long Island than having a mall named after you, where thousands of fans can go endlessly shopping. The slightly bigger **Smith Haven Mall** (724-1433) contains 150 shops and four large department stores.

The hallmark of Suffolk shopping, though, is undoubtedly the multitude of antique stores of the isn't-that-cute variety. If you like this kind of thing, this is the place for you. If you don't, beware. These stores can be habit-forming; before you know it you'll be collecting salt and pepper shakers and hoarding duck-shaped soaps. Some notable stores: Jacobean Valdimar, 5 Main St., Cold Spring Harbor (692-7775); The Skylight, Main St., Amagansett (267-6565); East End Antiques,

68 Park Place, East Hampton (324-9262); Winckel Antiques, Main St., Eastport (325-9518).

Atlantic City

They did not pass go. They did not collect $200. They started at the finish line and raked in the cash. The riches-to-rags-to-riches tale of Atlantic City began half a century ago when it reigned as the monarch of resort towns. Vanderbilts and Girards graced the boardwalk of the town that inspired the Depression-era board game for would-be high rollers, *Monopoly*. Fans of the game will be thrilled to see the real-life Boardwalk and Park Place that they've squabbled over for years. But their opulence has faded. With the rise of competition from Florida resorts, the community chest began to close. Atlantic City landed on the luxury tax of the game board, suffering decades of decline, unemployment, and virtual abandonment.

But in 1976, state voters gave Atlantic City a reprieve by legalizing gambling, making the game a reality. Casinos sprang up on the Boardwalk, while the owners ignored the boarded-up streets below. Those who enter the casinos soon forget the dirt and dank outside, especially since the owners make sure you never have to leave. Each velvet-soaked temple of tacktitude has a dozen restaurants, entertainment, and even skyways connecting to other casinos. The chance to win big bucks draws everyone to Atlantic City, from high-rolling millionaires to senior citizens clutching their one last chance. One-quarter of the U.S. population lives within 300 mi. of Atlantic City, and fortune-seeking pilgrims flock to its shore to toss the dice.

Practical Information

Emergency: 911.

Visitor Information: Public Relations Visitors Bureau, 2308 Pacific Ave. (348-7044), conveniently located near Mississippi Ave. Open Mon.-Fri. 9am-4:30pm. Just next door you can leaflet to your heart's content at the home of the Miss America pageant, the **Atlantic City Convention and Visitors Bureau,** 2310 Pacific Ave. (348-7100 or 800-262-7395). Open Mon.-Fri. 9am-5pm.

Bader Field Airport: 345-6402. Serves Newark only. Buses run between Bader Field and the Boardwalk.

Pamona Airport: 800-428-4322 (Serves Washington, Philadelphia and New York.)

Amtrak: (800-872-7245) at Kirkman Blvd. off Michigan Ave. Follow Kirkman to its end, bear right, and follow the signs. To: New York City (1 per day, 2½ hr., $28); Philadelphia (5 per day, 1½ hr., $14); Washington, DC (1 per day, 3½ hr., $38). More connections to DC and NYC through Philly. Open Sun.-Thurs. 6am-10pm, Fri.-Sat. 6am-12:20am.

Buses: Greyhound/Trailways, 345-5403 or 344-4449. Buses every hr. to New York (2½ hr., $19) and Philadelphia (1¼ hr., $9). **New Jersey Transit,** 800-582-5946. Runs 6am-10pm. Hourly service to New York City ($21.50) and Philadelphia ($10), with connections to Ocean City ($1.50), Cape May ($3.50), and Hammonton ($3.25). Also runs along Atlantic Ave. (base fare $1). Both lines operate from **Atlantic City Municipal Bus Terminal,** Arkansas and Arctic Ave. Open 24 hr.

Pharmacy: Parkway, 2838 Atlantic Ave. (345-5105), 1 block from TropWorld. Delivers locally and to the casinos.

Hospital: Atlantic City Medical Center (344-4081), at the intersection of Michigan and Pacific Ave.

Bookstore: Atlantic City News and Book Store (344-9444), at the intersection of Pacific and Illinois Ave. Most comprehensive collection of gambling strategy literature east of Las Vegas. Buy with your head, not over it.

Help Line: Rape and Abuse Hotline, 646-6767.

Post Office: Martin Luther King and Pacific Ave. (345-4212). Open Mon.-Fri. 8:30am-5pm, Sat. 10am-noon. **ZIP code:** 08401.

Area Code: 609.

Atlantic City lies just past midway down New Jersey's coast, accessible by the **Garden State Parkway.** It is accessible by train from Philadelphia and New York. Hitching is not recommended.

Gamblers' specials make bus travel a cheap, efficient way to get to Atlantic City. Many casinos will give the bearer of a bus ticket receipt $10 in cash and sometimes a free meal. Look for deals in the Yellow Pages under "Bus Charters" in New Jersey, New York, Pennsylvania, Delaware, and Washington, DC. Also check the Arts and Entertainment section of the *New York Times*.

Greyhound/Trailways has same-day round-trip specials to Atlantic City.

Getting around Atlantic City is easy on foot. The casinos pack tightly together on the Boardwalk along the beach. When your winnings become too heavy to carry, you can hail a **Rolling Chair,** quite common along the Boardwalk. Though a bit of an investment ($1 per block for 2 people, 5-block min.), Atlantic City locals or erudite foreign exchange students chat with you while they push. The less exotic and less expensive **yellow tram** runs continuously for $1. On the streets, catch a **jitney** ($1), running 24 hr. up and down Pacific Ave., or a NJ Transit Bus ($1) covering Atlantic Ave.

Accommodations and Camping

Large, red-carpeted beachfront hotels have replaced four green houses, bumping smaller operators out of the game. Expect to pay a hundred bucks for a single. Smaller hotels along **Pacific Avenue,** a block from the Boardwalk, have rooms for less than $60, and rooms in Ocean City's guest houses are reasonably priced, though facilities there can be dismal. Reserve ahead, especially on weekends. Many hotels lower their rates during the middle of the week. Winter is also slow in Atlantic City, when water temperature, gambling fervor, and hotel rates all drop significantly. Campsites closest to the action cost the most; the majority close September through April. Reserve a site if you plan to visit in July or August.

Irish Pub and Inn, 164 St. James Place (344-9063), near the Boardwalk, directly north of Sands Casino. Clean, cheap Celtic rooms with shared bath right next to the action. Antique furniture, old-world courtesy, and a Gaelic terrace set a well-bred bed-and-breakfast mood. Singles $20-30. Doubles $45. Key deposit $5. Open Feb.-Nov. Downstairs pub serves good Irish food 24 hr.

Hotel Casino, 28 S. Georgia Ave. (344-0747), just off Pacific Ave. Small run-down rooms off a narrow hallway. Singles $35-40. Doubles $45. Key deposit $10. Open May-Oct.

Birch Grove Park Campground, Mill Rd., in Northfield (641-3778). 300 acres. Attractive and secluded but still near the casinos. Sites $15 for 2 people, with hookup $17.

Pleasantville Campground, 408 N. Mill Rd. 70 sites. Sites $24 for 4 people with full hookup.

Food

After cashing in your chips, you can visit a cheap **casino buffet.** Most casinos offer all-you-can-eat lunch or dinner deals for $10-12; sometimes you can catch a special for around $5. Trump charges $11 for lunch and $13 for dinner. The town provides higher quality meals in a less noxious atmosphere. For a complete rundown of local dining, pick up a copy of *TV Atlantic Magazine, At the Shore,* or *Whoot,* all free, from a hotel lobby, restaurant, or local store.

Pacific Avenue is awash in steak, sub and pizza shops. Since 1946, the **White House Sub Shop,** Mississippi and Arctic Ave., has served world-famous subs and sandwiches. Celebrity supporters include Bill Cosby, Johnny Mathis, and Frank Sinatra, rumored to have subs flown to him while he's on tour ($5-7.50, half-subs $2.50-4). (Open Mon.-Sat. 10am-midnight, Sun. 11am-midnight.) For renowned Italian food including the best pizza in town, hit **Tony's Baltimore Grille,** 2800 Atlantic Ave. at Iowa Ave. (Open daily 11am-3am. Bar open 24 hr.) Though you may be turned off by the crowds, you can get great slices of pizza from one of the many

Three Brothers from Italy joints on the Boardwalk. The **Inn of the Irish Pub** at 164 St. James Place (34-9063), serves modestly priced, hearty dishes like deep-fried crab cakes ($4.25), honey-dipped chicken ($4.25), and Dublin beef stew ($5). This hardy, oaky haven has a century's worth of Joycian élan and Irish memorabilia draped on the walls. (Open 24 hr.) For an oceanside dessert, try custard ice-cream or saltwater taffy.

Entertainment

Casinos

You have to see the casinos to believe them. Inside, thousands of square feet of flashing lights and plush carpet surround the milling crowds; few notice the one-way ceiling mirrors concealing big-brother gambling monitors. Figures in formal wear embody Atlantic City's more glamorous past, but T-shirt-and-jeans gamblers now outnumber their flashy cohorts. The seductive rattle of chips and clicking of slot machines never stops. Outside the gambling matrix, cafés and lounges teem with calculating con men, bargain-blazing seniors, and midwestern R.V. travelers in matching "We Love Oklahoma" shirts. Glittery crooners entertain all day. Fun and excitement for the whole Nielsen family.

All casinos line Boardwalk, within a dice toss of each other. Even if you wanted to, you couldn't miss the newest beast on the block, the **Taj Mahal** (449-5150), an absurdist Disney-like meditation on a fairy-tale palace, courtesy of Donald Trump. Here, limestone elephants greet you at the entrance, and the sight of dayglow onion domes wreathed in flickering Christmas lights confirms that you have arrived at the supreme house of kitsch. The Taj Mahal commodifies a complex so expensive that missed payments threw Trump's billion-dollar empire into turmoil. Trump has two other casinos, each displaying his name in huge lights—the **Trump Castle** (441-2000) and **Trump Plaza** (441-6000). Other show-and-strut-heavies include **Bally's Park Place** (340-2000), and **Resorts International** (344-6000). Caesar's Boardwalk Regency (348-4411), Harrah's Marina Hotel (441-5000), and the Atlantis (344-4000), are hot clubs. Rounding out the list are the **Clairidge**, Indiana Ave. and the Boardwalk (340-3400), and **Showboat**, States Ave, and the Boardwalk (343-4000). The **Sands**, Indiana Ave. and the Boardwalk (441-4000) and **TropWorld Casino**, Iowa Ave. and the Boardwalk (340-4000) have extensive facilities that include golf and tennis. You may be amused by the two "moving sidewalks" that carry customers from the Boardwalk to the only two casinos without a Boardwalk entrance. Not surprisingly, these sidewalks move in only one direction.

Open nearly all the time (Mon.-Fri. 10am-4am, Sat.-Sun. 10am-6am), casinos douse you with alcohol as long as you're gambling (you must be 21 to get in) and many lack windows and clocks, preventing you from noticing the hours slip away. To curb almost inevitable losses, stick to the cheaper games: blackjack, slot machines, and the low bets in roulette and craps. A book like John Scarne's *New Complete Guide to Gambling* will help you plan an intelligent strategy, but keep your eyes on your watch or you'll have spent five hours and five digits before you know what hit you.

High-priced casino entertainment, featuring magicians, comedians, songstresses, and musicals, can sometimes be found at a discount. Call casinos to find out or consult *Whoot*, the weekly free "entertainment and casino newspaper." Atlantic City and adjacent shore towns maintain an active nighttime schedule, and many clubs host solid rock and jazz outfits: consult *Whoot* or *Atlantic*.

Beaches and Boardwalk

You can bet the ocean is just a few spaces away. Atlantic City squats on the northern end of long, narrow **Absecon Island,** which has 7 mi. of beaches—some pure white, some lumpy gray. The **Atlantic City Beach** is free, and often crowded. Adjacent **Ventnor City's** sands are nicer. The legendary **Boardwalk** of Atlantic City has been given over to the purveyors of the quick fix, packed with junk-food stands, arcades, souvenir shops, and carnival amusements. Take a walk, jog, or bike in Ventnor City, where the Boardwalk's development tapers off.

Princeton

The town of Princeton slumbers peacefully off Rte. 1, 50 miles southwest of New York City and 11 miles north of Trenton. This disarming town has a charming university to match. **Princeton University** has turned out presidents (James Madison and Woodrow Wilson), tycoons (J.P. Morgan), writers (F. Scott Fitzgerald), and movie stars (Jimmy Stewart and Brooke Shields). But no avatars.

Practical Information

Emergency: 911.

Visitor Information: Princeton University Communication/Publication Office, Stanhope Hall (258-3600). Campus maps and current information, including the *Princeton Weekly Bulletin,* with a calendar of events. Open Mon.-Fri. 8:30am-4:30pm. **Orange Key Guide Service,** 73 Nassau St. (258-3603), in the back entrance of MacLean House. Free 1-hr. campus tours, pamphlets, and maps. Tours Mon.-Sat. at 10am, 11am, 1:30pm, and 3:30pm, Sun. at 1:30 and 3:30pm. Office open Mon.-Sat. 9am-5pm, Sun. 1-5pm. **Princeton University Telephone Information,** 258-3000. Open daily 8am-11pm.

Trains: Amtrak, 800-872-7245. Connects Princeton Junction, 3 mi. south of Princeton on Rte. 571, to New York City (7 per day, 1 hr., $21) and Philadelphia (7 per day, 1 hr., $17). Stops at Princeton only in the early morning and evening. Station open Mon.-Fri. 6am-8:30pm, Sat.-Sun. 7:15am-8:30pm. **New Jersey Transit** (201-460-8444; in NJ 800-772-2222) runs 6am-midnight serving Princeton Junction. To New York City (1 hr., $9.25). Prices include a 5-min. ride on the "dinky," an itsy-bitsy train connecting the town and campus to the outlying station. Dinky stops at University Place across from the McCarter Theater.

Buses: New Jersey Transit, 800-772-2222. Runs 6am-midnight. Buses stop at Princeton University and Palmer Sq. Take bus #606 to Trenton (every ½ hr., $1.90 exact change). **Suburban Transit** has 3 Princeton locations: Nassau Pharmacy, 80 Nassau St. (921-7400); Cox's Store, 182 Nassau St.; and the Amoco Station in Princeton Shopping Center. To New York (every ½ hr., $7, $13 round-trip).

Taxi: Associated Taxi Stand, 924-1222. Open daily 6am-midnight.

Post Office: Palmer Sq. behind Tiger Park (921-9563). Open Mon.-Fri. 8am-4:30pm, Sat. 8:30am-noon. **ZIP code:** 08542.

Area Code: 609.

Located in the green heart of the "Garden State," Princeton lies within commuting distance of both New York City and Philadelphia. Driving from New York City, take the Holland or Lincoln Tunnel to the New Jersey Turnpike and take exit 9 at New Brunswick and go 17 mi. south on Rte. 1. From Philadelphia, take I-95 north to Rte. 206 and on to **Nassau Street,** Princeton's main strip, with shops clustered on one side and the university set back on the other. **Palmer Square,** the center of Princeton's business district, sits right off of Nassau between Witherspoon and Chambers St.

Accommodations, Food, and Entertainment

The town itself has no cheap accommodations. Budget motels clutter Rte. 1 and the environs of giant Quaker Bridge Mall, 4 mi. south of Princeton, served by local bus (see Practical Information above). The **Sleep-E-Hollow Motel,** 3000 U.S. 1, Lawrenceville (609-896-0900), rides 5 mi. south of Princeton, offering beds in Tine-E, well-worn rooms. (Singles $28.50. Doubles $32.50.) For more than one person, the nearby **McIntosh Inn,** U.S. 1 and Quaker Bridge Mall (609-896-3700), is reasonable. Clean, large, and user-friendly rooms fall not far from the tree. (Singles $42. Doubles $49. Extra cot $3.)

Most of Princeton's reasonably priced restaurants line Nassau and Witherspoon St., which intersects Nassau just across from the main gates of the university. Loud and crowded **P.J.'s Pancake House,** 154 Nassau St., has old wooden tables etched with student graffiti. The clamor gives way to a quieter breakfast crowd. Good food, but most meals cost $5-7. (Open Mon.-Thurs. 7:30am-10pm, Fri. 7:30am-midnight, Sat. 8am-midnight, Sun. 8am-10pm.) A popular student hangout and bar, **The Annex,** 128½ Nassau St., seems darker and often less noisy than P.J.'s, serving Italian entrees ($5-7), as well as omelettes and sandwiches ($2-3.50). (Open Mon.-Sat. 11am-1am.) You can gorge yourself on average Mexican food at **Marita's Cantina,** 134 Nassau St., in a $6 all-you-can-eat lunch buffet (Mon.-Fri. 11:30am-2pm). Live bands play Thursdays. (Open daily 11:30am-11pm; bar until about 1:15am.) **Thomas Sweet Ice Cream,** at Palmer Sq. across from the Nassau Inn, provides the perfect end to any meal. Have them blend a topping into their homemade ice cream ($2-3). (Open Sun.-Thurs. 11am-11pm, Fri.-Sat. 11am-midnight.)

On May 17, 1955, Princeton students held one of the first pro-rock 'n' roll demonstrations in the U.S., blaring Bill Haley and the Comets' "Rock Around the Clock" until 1am when the Dean woke up and told them to turn it off. For some of that distilled male Ivy League tradition, down a drink in **The Tap Room,** in the basement of the Nassau Inn on Palmer Sq. (921-7500). A Princeton tradition since 1937, the pub has aging but freshly polished wood booths. Lovey Williams plays guitar Tuesday and Thursday nights until 10:30pm. (Open Mon.-Thurs. 11:30am-midnight, Fri.-Sat. 11:30am-1am.) Check Princeton's *Weekly Bulletin* for the scoop on films, concerts, and special events. Students and professional actors perform at the **McCarter Theater** (452-5200), on campus in the Kresge Auditorium. (Box office open Mon.-Sat. noon-5pm.)

Sights

The 2500-acre landscaped campus of Gothic Princeton University seems to stretch on forever, virtually uninterrupted by streets of any kind. The **Orange Key** (see Practical Information above) provides free tours geared toward prospective students intent on hearing the myths of the nation's fourth oldest school (founded in 1746). Those who become part of the school's graduating class can place a commemorative plaque and a patch of ivy on the outer wall of **Nassau Hall.** Completed in 1756, it stood as the colonies' largest stone edifice and Princeton's original university building; it also served as the capitol building of the original U.S. colonies for several strange months in the summer of 1783. The two magnificent bronze tigers represent the school's mascot. **Whig** and **Clio Hall,** named and modeled after a Greek temple, are home to the oldest college literary and debating club in the U.S. **Prospect Gardens,** a huge bed of flowers in the shape of Princeton's shield, grow particularly beautiful in the summertime.

The sculptures scattered throughout the campus come from the $11 million **Putnam Collection.** The profile of one modern piece behind Nassau Hall bears a striking and comical resemblance to former President Richard M. Nixon. Picasso's *Head of a Woman* stands in front of the **University Art Museum** (452-3762). Tours of the outdoor sculptures (works by Calder, Moore, Picasso, and Smith) or of the museum's permanent indoor collection can be arranged through the university. (Museum open Tues.-Sat. 10am-4pm, Sun. 1-5pm. Free.)

New Haven

You know you're in the right place when you see a T-shirt that reads "Harvard's a disease—Yale's the cure." But the hype surrounding the centuries-old Ivy League rivalry obscures the fact that Yale was founded in 1738 by a group of clergymen who defected from decadent Harvard to create a commercial city with the scriptures as its fundamental law. Today a few idealists still inhabit this simultaneous university town and depressed city. Academic types and a working class population live somewhat uneasily side by side—bumper stickers proclaiming "Tax Yale, Not Us" embellish a number of street signs downtown. New Haven has a reputation as something of a battleground, and Yalies tend to stick to areas on or near campus, further widening the rift between town and gown.

New Haven is laid out in nine squares. The central one, **The Green,** lies between **Yale University** and City Hall, and grants a pleasant escape from the hassles of city life nonetheless. A small but thriving business district borders the green, consisting mostly of bookstores, boutiques, cheap sandwich places, and other services catering to students and professors. Downtown New Haven, and particularly the Yale campus, is littered with distinctive buildings. The omnipresence of American Collegiate Gothic in spires, towers, and ivy-covered buildings lends the campus a unity of design—and a haunted-house feel—that its Cambridge cousin lacks.

Yale Information Center, Phelps Gateway, 344 College St. (432-2300), facing the Green, gives tours and distributes free campus maps. Pick up a 50¢ walking guide and *The Yale,* a guide to undergraduate life ($2). (Open daily 10am-3:30pm. Free 1-hr. tours Mon.-Fri. at 10:30am and 2pm, Sat.-Sun. at 1:30pm.)

James Gambel Rodgers, a firm believer in the sanctity of printed material, designed **Sterling Memorial Library,** 120 High St. (432-2798). The building looks so much like a monastery that even the telephone booths come shaped like confessionals. Rodgers spared no expense to make Yale's library look "authentic," even decapitating the figurines on the library's exterior to replicate those at Oxford, which, due to decay, often fall to the ground and shatter. (Open summer Mon.-Wed. and Fri. 8:30am-5pm, Thurs. 8:30am-10pm, Sat. 10am-5pm; academic year Mon.-Fri. 8:30am-midnight, Sat. 10am-5pm, Sun. 2-10pm.) The massive and windowless **Beinecke Rare Book and Manuscript Library,** 121 Wall St. (432-2977), should not be confused with secret societies on campus that protect their members' identities with veils of brick and stone. Instead this intriguing modern structure has been paneled with Vermont marble cut thin enough to be translucent; supposedly its volumes (including one Gutenberg Bible and an extensive collection of William Carlos Williams' writings) could survive even nuclear war. (Open Mon.-Fri. 8:30am-5pm, Sat. 10am-5pm.)

Along New Haven's own Wall St., between High and Yale St., the neo-Gothic sculptured gargoyles on the **Law School** building are actually cops and robbers.

Most of New Haven's museums populate the Yale campus. The **Yale University Art Gallery,** 1111 Chapel St. (432-0600), opened in 1832, claims to be the oldest university art museum in the Western Hemisphere. It has noteworthy collections of John Trumbull paintings and Italian Renaissance works. (Open summer Tues.-Sat. 10am-5pm, Sun. 2-5pm; academic year Tues.-Wed. and Fri.-Sat. 10am-5pm, Thurs. 10am-8pm, Sun. 2-5pm. Free.) The **Yale Center for British Art,** 1080 Chapel St. (432-4594), sponsors some pretty wacky exhibits—last year they displayed a collection of snuff boxes. Sniff it out. (Open Tues.-Sat. 10am-5pm, Sun. 2-5pm. Free.) The **Peabody Museum of Natural History,** 170 Whitney Ave. (436-0850; 432-5099 for recorded message), houses Rudolph F. Zallinger's Pulitzer Prize-winning mural, which portrays the North American continent as it appeared 70 to 350 million years ago. Other exhibits range from Central American cultural artifacts to a dinosaur hall displaying the skeleton of Mr. Brontosaurus. (Open Mon.-Sat. 10am-5pm, Sun. noon-5pm. Admission $2, seniors $1.50, ages 5-15 $1.)

New Haven's reasonably priced food caters to the student population. Ever since Frank Pepe tossed the first American pizza here some years back, locals have revered the time-honored Italian fare. Wooster Street contains two of the best shops in the country: **Pepe's** at 157 Wooster (865-5762; open Wed.-Mon. 4-11pm) and **Sally's** at 237 Wooster (624-5271; open daily 5-11pm). New Havenites take their pizza seriously; fans bicker about who outbakes who, but, as food critic Linda Rottenberg as pointed out, both joints make great pies. Pepe's white pizza, a study in dough and clam sauce, receives summa grades. Arrive early at either place to avoid the lines.

Atticus Café, 1082 Chapel St. A charming bookstore/café with friendly if harried service. Try their soups served with swell half-loaves of bread ($3-4). Open Mon.-Fri. 8am-midnight, Sat. 9am-midnight, Sun. 9am-9pm.

Naples Pizza, 90 Wall St. A Yale tradition, updated with a video jukebox. Try a pizza with broccoli, pineapple, or white clams ($7.25) with a pitcher of beer ($5). Open June-Aug. Mon.-Wed. 7-9pm, Thurs.-Fri. 7-11pm; Sept.-May Sun.-Thurs. 7pm-1am, Fri.-Sat. 7pm-2am.

Daily Caffè, 376 Elm St. Started by a Yale graduate; quickly becoming the haunt of the university's coffee and cigarette set. Soups, salads, and Sartre under $3, with an impressive selection of *caffès.*

Claire's, 1000 Chapel St. (562-3888). A homey restaurant that touts its gourmet vegetarian menu. The real draw is Claire's rich cake ($2.25 per slice). Open daily 8am-10pm.

Ashley's Ice Cream, 278 York St. (865-3661). Creamy ice cream and a myriad of sinful dessert options like Reverse Chocolate Chip and Chocolate Banana ice cream ($1.50-2.75). Open Sun.-Thurs. noon-midnight, Fri.-Sat. noon-1am.

Yankee Doodle Coffee Shop, 258 Elm St. (865-1074). A tiny, diner-like place, squeezed into a 12-ft.-wide slice just across the street from the Yale Boola-Boola Shop. $1.40 gets you eggs, toast, and coffee. Open Mon.-Sat. 6:30am-2:30pm.

Louis Lunch, 263 Crown St. (562-5507). The wife-and-husband team serves the best flame-broiled burger on the East Coast for $2. The fresh ground beef patty arrives on white toast without condiments. They say "Have it our way or no way at all." They also claim the menu has not changed in 40 years. Open Mon.-Fri. 9-11am and 11:30am-4pm.

New Haven offers plenty of late-night entertainment. Check **Toad's Place,** 300 York St. (777-7431) to see if one of your favorite bands is coming to town. While you get tickets, grab a draft beer ($1) at the bar. (Box office open daily 11am-6pm; tickets available at bar after 8pm. Bar open Sun.-Thurs. 8pm-1am, Fri.-Sat. 8pm-2am.) **Partner's,** 365 Crown St. (624-5510), is a favorite gay hangout. (Open Sun.-Thurs. 4pm-1am, Fri.-Sat. 4pm-2am.) The **Anchor Bar,** 272 College St. (865-1512), just off the Green, serves a slew of imported beers; a local paper recognized its jukebox as the best in the region. (Open Mon.-Thurs. 11am-1am, Fri.-Sat. 10am-2am.)

Once a famous testing ground for Broadway-bound plays, New Haven's thespian community carries on today, but to a much lesser extent. The **Schubert Theater,** 247 College St. (562-5666; out of state 800-228-6623), a large part of the town's on-stage tradition, still produces plays. (Box office open Mon.-Fri. 11am-5pm, Sat. noon-3pm.) Across the street, **The Palace,** 246 College St. (624-8497), host concerts and revues. Not to be outdone, New Haven's **Long Wharf Theater** (787-4282) received a special Tony Award for achievement in Regional Theater in 1978. (Tickets $21-26, student rush $5. Season June-late Sept.)

Yale itself accounts for an impressive bulk of the theater activity in the city. The **Yale Repertory Theater** (432-1234) has produced such illustrious alums as Meryl Streep, Glenn Close, James Earl Jones, and William Hurt, and continues to produce excellent shows. (Open Sept.-May. Student tickets half-price.) The **University Theater,** 22 York St., stages undergraduate plays throughout the academic year and during graduation. Tickets shouldn't set you back more than $8. In summer, the Green becomes the site of free **New Haven Symphony** concerts (865-0831), the **New Haven Jazz Festival** (787-8228), and other free musical series. The Department of Cultural Affairs, 770 Chapel St. (787-8956), can answer questions about concerts on the Green.

On the banks of the Housatonic River south of New Haven, the smaller town of **Stratford,** a miniature version of its counterpart in England (see *Let's Go: London*), is home to the **American Shakespeare Theater,** 1850 Elm St. (375-5000), exit 32 off I-95. (Tickets $19-29.) During the summer Shakespeare Festival, some of the country's most able actors and directors stage the Bard's plays while strolling minstrels, musicians, and artists grace the grounds.

Inexpensive accommodations are extremely hard to find in New Haven. The hunt grows especially difficult around Yale Parents weekend (mid-Oct.) and graduation (early June). **Hotel Duncan,** 1151 Chapel St. (787-1273), has decent singles for $40 and doubles for $55, both with bath. Plan ahead; prices are higher without reservations. The **Nutmeg Bed & Breakfast,** 222 Girard Ave., Hartford 06105 (236-6698), reserves doubles in New Haven B&Bs at $35-45. (Open Mon.-Fri. 9am-5:30pm.) The nearest parks for camping are **Cattletown** (264-5678; sites $7), 40 minutes away, and **Hammonasset Beach** (245-2755; sites $8.50), 20 minutes away.

To obtain free bus and street maps, and information about current events in town, stop in at the **New Haven Visitors and Convention Bureau,** 900 Chapel St. (787-8822), on the Green. (Open Mon.-Fri. 9am-5pm.) To get to New Haven, consider **Amtrak,** Union Station, Union Ave. (777-4002 or 800-872-7245). The station is newly renovated, but the area is unsafe at night. To or from Yale, take city bus A ("Orange St."), J, or U ("Waterbury"), or walk 6 blocks northeast to the Green. Trains chug to Boston ($29-34), Washington, DC ($66), and New York ($21). **Metro-North Commuter Railroad,** Union Station (497-2089 or 800-638-7646), runs trains to New York's Grand Central Station for half of Amtrak's fare ($8-10.75). (Ticket counter open daily 6am-10:30pm.) New Haven's **Greyhound** station at 45 George St. (772-2470), resides in a rough area. Take a cab or don't walk there alone. The 'hound has frequent service to: New York ($11), Boston ($26.50), Providence ($23), Cape Cod/Hyannis ($32), and New London ($9). (Ticket office open daily 7:30am-8:15pm.) **Peter Pan Bus Lines,** Union Station (467-8777), offers buses to Boston ($29).

Connecticut Transit serves New Haven and the surrounding area from 470 James St. (624-0151). Most buses depart from the Green. (Open Mon.-Fri. 9am-4:30pm. Information booth at 200 Orange St. open Mon.-Fri. 9am-5pm.) **Thrifty Rent-a-Car,** 37 Union St. (562-3191 or 800-367-2277), offers economy cars starting at $40 per day ($30 on the weekend), with 125 free mi. (Open Mon.-Fri. 8am-6pm, Sat. 8am-2pm, Sun. 10am-2pm.) You must be 25 with a major credit card. **Carolyn's Checker Cab** (468-2678) can take you from downtown to the airport in Newark for $8-9.

New Haven (unlike Yale) is a cinch to get into. The city lies at the intersection of I-95 (110 mi. from Providence) and I-91 (40 mi. from Hartford). At night, don't wander too freely out of the immediate downtown area and the campus, as surrounding sections are notably less safe. The Yale area is well patrolled by campus police. The downtown area is also patrolled by police on the lookout for illegally parked cars. Around 4pm on weekdays tow trucks roll out in full force; be sure to read parking signs carefully.

New Haven's **area code** is 203.

Appendices

Free New York

While New York is one of the most expensive places in the world to live, it shouldn't cost an arm and a leg to see. For free, you can get a glimpse of Little Old New York at the McGraw-Hill Building or take a tour of the Public Library, the New York Stock Exchange, or the Commodities Exchange Center at the World Trade Center. Some museums—the Met, MoMA, the Whitney, the International Center of Photography, the Cooper-Hewitt, the Guggenheim, the Jewish Museum, and the American Craft Museum—have weekly "Free" times or relaxed voluntary donation policies, most of them on Tuesday evenings. You can gawk at smaller galleries without spending a penny, and some museums will let you in for free on every day of the week—The Alternative Museum, The American Museum of Immigration, Hall of Fame for Great Americans, The Forbes Magazine Galleries, the AT&T Infoquest Center, China House, IBM Gallery of Science and Art, the gallery at the Central Park Arsenal, the Nicholas Roerich Museum, the Whitney branch at 2 Federal Reserve Plaza, the Schomburg Center for Research in Black Culture, the Garibaldi-Meuci Museum on Staten Island, the Staten Island Children's Museum, and Bible House. The Bronx Zoo charges no admission Tuesday through Thursday;

the Staten Island Zoo stays free all week. Shakespeare shows for free in Central Park if you can wake up early enough to obtain a ticket. Music schools don't charge for their concerts; try Juilliard, the Greenwich Music School, and the Bloomingdale House of Music. You can take free tours of Grand Central Station, the Lincoln Center Library, and Central Park; you can pay your respects at Grant's Tomb or at the U.N. General Assembly at no charge, or drop in on colonial dwellings like the Dyckman House or Hamilton Grange. You can listen to a prestigious free lecture series at the Cooper Union school, or to free poetry at the 92nd Street Y.

Frustrated hoofers can attain inner peace at **Macy's Tap-O-Mania.** The world's largest assembly of tap dancers click their heels on 34th St. between Broadway and Seventh (560-4495). It takes a musicologist's musicologist to tell if the entertainment entrepreneurs at CitiCorp are competing or cooperating with the ministers next door at St. Peter's. Scholarly disputes notwithstanding, the **Market at CitiCorp Center** (559-2330) brings out big bands at lunchtime (noon-1pm or 1-2pm) to entertain the 9-to-5 crowd. The menu for summer 1990 included jazz, light classical, fusion, chamber music, big bands, African Sankofa, and a fashion show. CitiCorp incorporates the corner of 53rd St. and Lexington Ave.

The **Mark Goodson Theater,** 2 Columbus Circle (751-0600), provides cost-free midday art and music.Meanwhile other corporate magnates mount their musical agenda. **Rockefeller Center** puts on Tuesday and Thursday concerts (at 12:30pm) June through July at the Exxon Park, at 49th and Sixth. On Wednesdays also at 12:30pm, the Rockefeller series moves to McGraw Hill Park at 48th and Sixth. For schedule information call 698-8901. **The World Financial Center** strives to live up to its "Classic Cool;" its plaza hosts an impressive summer bash from June to September. Entertainment includes art exhibits, chamber music, contemporary dance, and jazz greats like Dave Brubeck. The Duke Ellington Orchestra, the Artie Shaw Orchestra, and Buster Poindexter have all played here in the past. Serious classical music wafts alongside strains of classic rock-and-roll: the Shostakovich String Quartet shared the bill with Flash Cadillac, the beat boys from *American Graffiti.* Admission is free to almost all of the events. Call 945-0505 for more information.

The **World Trade Center** (466-4170) also maintains a full summer entertainment schedule at its Austin J. Tobin Plaza, July 4 through August 31. Start off the week with Catskill Mountain Monday, Caribbean Tuesday, and Jazz Wednesday.

The **South St. Seaport Museum** (699-9424) presents its "Parliament Sound Series" June 28 through August 16 on Thursdays at 6:30pm. The museum also sponsors the Summer Outdoor Concerts, held July 14 through August 11 on Saturdays at 8pm. Both series take place at Pier 16. The **Summer Garden Series** brings classical music to the Museum of Modern Art's delightful sculpture garden at 14 W. 54th St. (July-Aug. Fri.-Sat. at 7:30pm; call 708-9850).

The **Washington Square Music Festival** (431-1088) includes a chamber music society that makes a concerted effort in July and a big band jazz series that swings in August. All performances take place at 8pm in Washington Square.

Come summertime, troopers willing to brave the heat enjoy concerts, dances, comedy, theater, and film at absolutely no charge. The *Summer in New York* brochure, available free at the Visitors Bureau and at other info booths around the city (see Practical Information), presents a comprehensive catalog of gratis summertime events. You can get information on free New York Parks activities at the Central Park **Arsenal** (360-8111).

In August, **Lincoln Center** comes to the great outdoors for a series of music, dance, and theater productions held in Damrosch Park and at all the plazas, day and evening. Call the 24-hr. hotline at 877-2011 for more information. **The Lower Manhattan Cultural Council** targets downtown sites for music and dance performances and for staged readings of classics and lesser perks. Call 269-0320 for details. **American Landmark Festivals** include a series of free summertime concerts: 12:30pm Wednesdays at Federal Hall, 1pm Thursdays at Green Auditorium, 2pm Saturdays at Roosevelt Birthplace, and 2pm Sundays at Hamilton Grange. Additional Sunday afternoon recitals pass the time at the Dairy in Central Park. Every Sunday in August, the **Bronx Arts Ensemble** performs at Fordham University.

Shows start at 4pm. The Bronx sponsors a music festival that runs from July to August, with free concerts on weeknights and weekend days in Bronx parks. Call 590-3980 for information.

The **Brooklyn Summer Series** fills the bill with a wide-ranging schedule of performances, holding concerts in Brooklyn parks, playgrounds, and even shopping malls. **Celebrate Brooklyn,** a May 22 through September 2 multimedia extravaganza, features jazz, rock, worldbeat, blues, and big brass as well as dance, ballet, and theater at the Prospect Park Bandshell in Brooklyn. Performances begin at 8pm. (Suggested contribution $1; Subway: F to Seventh Ave. Or take the B-69 or B-75 bus to Prospect Park West and 9th St. For program information call 718-768-0699.) **Brooklyn Botanical Garden** (718-622-4433) hosts Pappless Shakespearean drama and storytelling evenings as well as jazz and chamber music.

The borough of **Queens** organizes its own "Arts in the Park Festival" at Forest Park Seufert Bandshell (718-291-1100), located at Forest Park Drive and Woodhaven Blvd. Concerts take place July through August (July 7, 13, 14, 21, 28; Aug. 4, 11, 18, 25) at 7:30pm. The Council also promotes a series of concerts for children (July 12, 14, 26; Aug. 2, 9, 16, 23), which take the stage at 10:30am. Free entertainment abounds in this borough. The Queens Council on the Arts publishes two bimonthly calendars of events, the *Queens Leisure Guide* and the *Cultural Guide to Queens.* If you can't find these in hotels or public libraries, or if you want more detailed information, call their state-of-the-art Culture Hotline (291-1100) which can tell you about any free concerts or cultural events in Queens.

24-hour New York

> *New York's a small place when it comes to the part*
> *of it that wakes up just as the rest is going to bed.*
> —*P.G. Wodehouse*

For nocturnal New Yorkers, some restaurants keep humming all night. **Pizza Joint Too,** 70 W. 71st St. (799-4444), where John and Charlie while away the hours, only closes from 5-6am. On the Upper East Side, few eateries keep on cooking after midnight. If you're stranded there after hours, try the **Skyline Restaurant,** 1055 Lexington Ave., a diner that could have been painted by Edward Hopper., where the regular crowd, notably Andrew, orders greasy french fries until 2am. The following places never close:

Around the Clock, 8 Stuyvesant St. (598-0402).
Astor Riviera, 452 Lafayette St. (677-4461).
Bagel Buffet, Sixth Ave. at 8th St. (477-0448).
Empire Diner, 210 Tenth Ave. at 22nd St. (243-2736).
Fulton Seafood Deli, 52 Fulton St. (393-1137).
Happy Deli, 181 Broadway (587-1105), between John and Cortlandt St.
H&H East, 1551 Second Ave. (734-7441), between 80th and 81st.
Kiev, 117 Second Ave. (674-4046).
Sarge's, 548 Third Ave. (679-0442).
Veselka, 144 Second Ave. (228-9682).
Lindy's, 825 Seventh Ave. (582-9530); open 24 hr. Fri.-Sat.

Opening Times of Major Sights

American Museum of Natural History	Sun.-Tues. and Thurs. 10am-5:45pm, Wed. and Fri.-Sat. 10am-9pm
Museum of Broadcasting	Tues. noon-8pm, Wed.-Sat. noon-5pm
Bronx Zoo	Mon.-Sat. 10am-5pm, Sun. 10am-5:30pm
Cathedral of St. John the Divine	daily 7am-5pm
Central Park Arsenal	Mon.-Fri. 9:30am-4:30pm
Central Park Children's Zoo	daily 10am-4:30pm

Cloisters	March-Oct. daily 8:30am-5:15pm; Nov.-Feb. Tues.-Sun. 9:30am-4:45pm
Cooper-Hewitt Museum	Tues. 10am-9pm, Wed.-Sat. 10am-5pm, Sun. noon-5pm
Empire State Building observatory	daily 9:30am-midnight
F.A.O. Schwarz	Mon.-Sat. 10am-6pm, Thurs. 10am-8pm, Sun. noon-6pm
Forbes Magazine Galleries	Tues.-Sat. 10am-4pm
Frick Collection	Tues.-Sat. 10am-6pm, Sun. 1-6pm
Grant's Tomb	Wed.-Sun. 9am-4:30pm.
Guggenheim Museum	Tues. 11am-7:45pm, Wed.-Sun. 11am-4:45pm
Hamilton Grange	Wed.-Sun. 9am-4:30pm
International Center of Photography	Tues. noon-8pm, Wed.-Fri. noon-5pm, Sat.-Sun. 11am-6pm
Isamu Noguchi Museum	April-Nov. Wed. and Sat. 11am-6pm
Jewish Museum	Sun. 11am-6pm, Mon. and Wed.-Thurs. noon-5pm, Tues. noon-8pm
Macy's	Mon. and Thurs.-Fri. 9:45am-8:30pm, Tues.-Wed. 9:45am-6:45pm, Sat. 10am-6:45pm, Sun. 10am-6pm.
Metropolitan Museum	Sun. and Tues.-Thurs. 9:30am-5:15pm; Fri.-Sat. 9:30am-8:45pm.
Museum of Modern Art	Fri.-Tues. 11am-6pm, Thurs. 11am-9pm
National Academy of Design	Tues. noon-8pm, Wed.-Sun. noon-5pm
New York Aquarium	daily 10am-4:45pm, holidays and summer weekends 10am-5:45pm
New York Stock Exchange	Mon.-Fri. 9:20am-4pm
Pierpont Morgan Library	Tues.-Sat. 10:30am-5pm, Sun. 1-5pm
Riverside Church	Mon.-Sat. 11am-3pm, Sun. 12:30-4pm
South Street Seaport ticket booth	daily 10am-5pm, until 6pm on summer weekends
Statue of Liberty	daily 9am-5:15pm
United Nations	daily 9am-6pm
Whitney Museum	Tues. 1-8pm, Wed.-Sat. 11am-5pm, Sun. noon-6pm
World Trade Center observatory	daily 9:30am-11:30pm
Zabar's	Mon.-Fri. 8am-7:30pm, Sat. 8am-midnight, Sun. 9am-6pm.

By Appointment Only

The following sights require that you book in advance.

Black Fashion Museum	155-7 W. 126th St. Call 662-1320 for a weekday tour.
Conference House	Hyland Blvd., Tottenville, Staten Island. Guided tours by appointment Wed.-Sun. 1-4pm.
Fulton Fish Market	South Street Seaport. Tours given on the first and third Thurs. of the month. Call to reserve; 669-9416.
Gondola rides	in Central Park. Call 517-3623.
Gracie Mansion	in Carl Schurz park. Call 570-4751. Tours on Wed. only.
"Macy's by Appointment" service	a department of the department store at Herald Square. Call 560-4181.
Seventh Regiment Armory	Park Ave., between 66th and 67th St. Call 744-8180.
Kaufman-Astoria Studio	in Queens. Call 784-4520.
Living Museum	in Queens Village. Call 464-7525.
University Club	1 W. 54th St. Call 247-2100.

Major Annual Events

January	Chinese New Year (sometimes early Feb.), Chinatown; Martin Luther King, Jr. Memorial Day Parade, Fifth Avenue; National Boat Show, New York Coliseum; Volvo Grand Prix Master Tennis, Madison Square Garden; Ice Capades, Madison Square Garden; Winter Antique Show, 7th Regiment Armory
February	Washington's Birthday Parade (Feb. 21), Fifth Avenue; Black History Week, American Museum of National History; Start Your Own Business Show, New York Coliseum; Westminster Kennel Club Dog Show, Madison Square Garden; Queens Purim Parade
March	Ringling Bros. and Barnum & Bailey Circus, Madison Square Garden, kicked off by Parade of Circus Animals from Twelfth

Ave. and 34th St. at 10am the day before the first performance; St. Patrick's Day Parade, Fifth Avenue (March 17); Greek National Day Parade, Fifth Avenue; Virginia Slims Championships (Women's Tennis), Madison Square Garden; Annual Spring Flower Show, Macy's; Pascha (Greek Easter), Astoria—sometimes falls in April or May instead, according to the Greek Orthodox calendar; Easter Lilies Display, Rockefeller Center

April Easter Day Parade, Fifth Avenue, informal Easter parade near St. Patrick's Cathedral; Japanese Cherry Blossom Festival, Brooklyn Botanic Garden;Great Easter Egg Event, Bronx Zoo; International Art Exposition, New York Coliseum

May Armed Forces Day Parade, Fifth Avenue; Israel Parade, Fifth Avenue; Ukrainian Festival, East 7th St.; Ninth Avenue International Food Festival (37th-57th St.); SoHo Festival, Prince St.; Washington Square Outdoor Art Show, Greenwich Village; Park Avenue Festival, 14th and 32nd St.; Park Avenue Antiques Show, Seventh Regiment Armory; Spring Flower Show, World Trade Center; Brooklyn Heights Promenade Art Show, Esplanade (Remsen-Clark St.); Norwegian Independence Day Parade, Bay Ridge, Brooklyn (67th-90th St.); Memorial Day Weekend: Czechoslovak Festival, Bohemian Hall, Astoria; Asian Pacific-American Festival, Queens Botanical Garden; Bronx Day, Van Cortlandt Park

June Kool Jazz Festival; Newport Jazz Festival; Puerto Rican Day Parade, Fifth Avenue; Museum Mile Celebration, Fifth Ave. (82nd-105th St.); Metropolitan Opera performances in parks; Weekend Summergarden concerts at MoMA's sculpture garden; New York Women's Jazz Festival and Guggenheim Concerts, Damrosch Park, Lincoln Center; 52nd Street Festival; Summer Pier Concerts, Fri. and Sat., South Street Seaport; Indian Festival, Central Park; Jewish Festival (usually 2nd Sun.), E. Broadway (Rutgers-Grand St.); Gay Pride March from Columbus Circle (June 28); Rose Shows, New York Botanical Garden, Bronx and Queens Botanical Garden, Flushing; Festival of St. Anthony of Padua, Sullivan St., SoHo; Lexington Avenue Street Fair (23rd-34th St.); Shakespeare Day, Brooklyn Botanical Garden; Feast of San Paulinus, Williamsburg (N. 8th-Havermeyer St.), Brooklyn; Queens Day, Flushing Meadow Park; Queens Ethnic Music Festival, Bohemian Hall

July Macy's Firework Display (July 4) from Hudson River barges (79th-125th St.); Mostly Mozart Music Festival, Avery Fisher Hall, Lincoln Center; Japanese Oban Festival, Riverside Park; Harbor Festival (end of June-July 4), Battery Park; Our Lady of Pompeii Feast, Carmine St. near Bleecker St., Greenwich Village; American Crafts Festival, Lincoln Center Plaza; Irish Festival, 116th St. in Rockaway; Summer Festival, Sailors Snug Harbor Cultural Center, Staten Island.

August Greenwich Village Jazz Festival; New York Folk Festival; New York Philharmonic concerts in parks; Lincoln Center Out-of-Doors Festival; Harlem Week; Fiesta Folklorica, Central Park; New York Ecuadorian Parade, 37th Ave., Jackson Heights

September Labor Day Parade, Fifth Avenue; New York Film Festival, Lincoln Center; Festival of San Gennaro, Mulberry St. (Houston St.-Washington Sq. Park), Little Italy; Steuben Day Parade (German-American), Fifth Avenue; U.S. Open Tennis Championships, USTA National Tennis Center, Flushing Meadow; Washington Square Outdoor Art Show; New York is Book Country, Fifth Avenue (47th-57th St.); Columbus Avenue Festival (66th-79th St.); Tama Country Fair, Third Avenue (14th-34th St.); Annual Fifth Avenue Mile Race (82nd-62nd St.); Governor's Cup Race, New York Bay; Atlantic Antic, Brooklyn; New York Grand Prix, Meadow Lake, Flushing Park; Richmond County Fair, Richmondtown Restoration, Staten Island

October Columbus Day Parade (Oct. 12), Fifth Avenue; Halloween Parade (Oct. 31), Greenwich Village; Mayor's Cup Schooner

	Race, South Street Seaport; Pulaski Day Parade, Fifth Avenue; Hispanic American Parade, Fifth Avenue; New York City Marathon (from Verrazano Bridge to Tavern on the Green); Autumn in the Atrium Flower Show, CitiCorp Center
November	Veteran's Day Parade (Nov. 11), Fifth Avenue; Macy's Thanksgiving Day Parade, Broadway (Huge balloon floats assembled the previous evening at 79th and Central Park West); National Horse Show, Madison Square Garden
December	Christmas Tree lighting, Rockefeller Center; Christmas Tree and Baroque Creche, Metropolitan Museum; Chanuka candle lighting at City Hall; Christmas caroling, Fifth and Park Ave.; Brass choirs, Rockefeller Center; Christmas in Richmond Town, Richmond Town Restoration, Staten Island; Korean Harvest and Folklore Festival, Flushing Meadows-Corona Park; Yuletide Festival, Wave Hill, Bronx; New Year's Eve, Times Square—at midnight, a big apple drops from Times Tower, ushering in the new year.

INDEX